The Polish Revolution

TIMOTHY GARTON ASH

The Polish Revolution: Solidarity

Third Edition

Yale University Press New Haven and London

This third edition published in the United States by Yale University Press in 2002.

First published in Great Britain by Jonathan Cape Ltd 1983.
Second edition published by Granta Books 1991.
Third edition published in Great Britain by Penguin Books 1999.

Printed in the United States of America

Library of Congress Control Number: 2002104102

ISBN 978-0-300-09568-5 (pbk. : alk. paper)

A catalogue record for this book is available from the British Library.

10 9 8 7 6 5 4

For D.

Ogromne wojska, bitne generały,
Policje—tajne, widne i dwu-płciowe—
Przeciwko komuż tak się pojednały?—
Przeciwko kilku myślom . . . co nie nowe! . . .

Colossal armies, valiant generals,
Police—secret, open, and of sexes two—
Against whom have they joined together?
Against a few ideas . . . nothing new!

Cyprian Norwid (1821–83)

Contents

Acknowledgments

My thanks are due, firstly, to the *Spectator*, *The Times* and *Der Spiegel* for generously supporting my journeys to Poland and my writing about it. Without the Information Centre for Polish Affairs, the Research Department of Radio Free Europe and the Archive of *Der Spiegel*, the research for this book might have lasted until the next Polish upheaval. The Librarians of St Antony's College, the Bodleian and the Social Studies Centre, Oxford, and the Polish Library, and the Polish Librarian at the British Library also gave me invaluable assistance.

For generous help, and stimulating discussion on the subject of this book, I would like to thank Neal Ascherson, Brian Beedham, Christopher Bobiński, Christopher Booker, Mark Brayne, Abraham Brumberg, Jan Chodakowski, Richard Davy, Judy Dempsey, John Fox, Mark Frankland, Michael Giedroyć, Maciej Jachimczyk, Leszek Kołakowski, Andrzej Łodyński, Steven Lukes, Oliver MacDonald, Jerzy Milewski, Edwina Moreton, Bohdan Nahaylo, Zdzisław and Halina Najder, Jacek Rostowski, Jacques Rupnik, George Schöpflin, Aleksander Smolar, Bolesław Sulik, Alexander Tomsky and Magda Wójcik. Anders Åslund, Wojciech Karpiński, Tony Kemp-Welch, George Kolankiewicz, Tadeusz Kowalik, Zbigniew Pełczyński, Gienek Smolar, Kazik Stepan and Michael Taylor have, in addition, read various parts of an earlier draft, and greatly improved it by their comments. Errors are all my own. Xandra Hardie and Jane Hill have edited with infinite patience. I shall always be grateful to Graham C. Greene for his encouragement and advice over many years. James Fenton originally suggested I write a short book about Poland. He has provoked a long one. I cannot begin to thank all those in Poland who made this book possible. Some of their names will be found in the index. My greatest debt, however, is concealed in the dedication.

For the third edition, I owe a great debt of gratitude to Tim Snyder, who prepared extensive materials for the revision, new Postscript and Bibliography, based on a thorough and critical survey of work published since 1983. Both his impeccable research and his characteristically incisive comments have made a major contribution to the resulting text.

I am most grateful to the organisers of the Jachranka Conference described at the beginning of the Postscript, especially to Christian Ostermann and James Hershberg of the Cold War International History Project, Malcomm Byrne of the National Security Archive and Andrzej Paczkowski of the Institute for Political Studies in Warsaw. I also thank Mark Kramer of Harvard University for sending me earlier versions of his important work on Soviet-Polish relations in 1980-81.

Many thanks, also, to Zbigniew Brzeziński, Stuart Proffitt, Thomas W. Simons, Aleksander Smolar and Tim Snyder for their very helpful comments on part or all of the Postscript.

Preface

'Purpose of journey to Poland?' asked the visa form.

Having explained that I was a historian from Oxford, researching into the German resistance to Hitler in Berlin, and now wishing to acquaint myself with the Polish resistance, I wrote: 'Polish resistance'. The visa clerk grinned as he stamped the form.

So it was that on Monday 18 August, the fifth day of the Gdańsk shipyard strike which gave birth to Solidarity, I flew from Berlin to Warsaw with a visa marked 'Purpose of journey . . . Polish resistance'.

I spent that night at Paderewski's 'Hotel Bristol', an establishment of such crumbling grandeur and sublime seediness that it seemed to have been built for Graham Greene. My room had three illuminated call-buttons: porter, waitress, shoeboy. I pressed them each in turn. Nobody came. A scraggy cat stalked through the french windows in the dining-room. There were cockroaches in the bath.

Early the next morning I flew to Gdańsk, together with one exceptionally tall journalist from Brazil and one exceptionally small journalist from Vienna. My *Herr Kollege* from Vienna was dressed in an immaculate white suit and carried a beautiful leather suitcase as well as a typewriter—all slightly too large for him. At Gdańsk airport we commandeered the only taxi.

'Stotch-Knee-Yah!' *Herr Kollege* now surprisingly remarked to the taxi-driver, who, immediately understanding the word *stocznia*, meaning 'shipyard', roared with laughter and through a red light.

We soon reached the scene which the world was to see on its television screens: the blue-grey shipyard gates festooned with flowers and photographs of the Pope, a cheerful crowd before them, loudspeakers blaring out patriotic hymns, farmers bringing baskets of food. Shouldering our way through the crowd, we were greeted at the gate by a young worker, naked to the waist but carefully identified as a picket by a red-and-white armband. After examining our passports he heaved open the gate and proudly led us down the short works' drive, through two lines of shipyard workers in dusty blue overalls. 'Brazylia! Austria! Anglia!' they shouted. 'Hooray! Hooray! Hooray!' I shall never forget the look on those lined, smiling faces. It was a look of simple enthusiasm and gratitude: as if we had personally brought the diplomatic support of England, Austria and Brazil, as the farmers brought bread.

Two hours later I met my *Herr Kollege* leaving the yard. *'Ruhe Siegesreden—Karnivalstimmung!'* ('calm—victory speeches—carnival atmosphere') he confided, telegraphically, as he stepped briskly past. Clearly for him the experience was already over, wrapped up in these neat compound nouns and tucked away in his beautiful leather suitcase, ready for the front page. Tomorrow would bring another piece.

I did not leave the shipyard with my boon companion. And I have not yet 'wrapped up' the experience.

In Part I of this book I have tried to write a coherent narrative of that most paradoxical of European revolutions which began in the Lenin Shipyard. I set out to give sufficient information and analysis for the main developments of the period from August 1980 until the military takeover in December 1981 to be comprehensible to a reader whose knowledge of them may be confined to what the daily news media have conveyed. For reasons of space, my introductory essay on the causes of the Polish revolution is more compressed than I could have wished, but I have indicated in the notes the excellent accounts which are now available in English on this subject.

Naturally, my narrative concentrates heavily on the precipitate growth of the Solidarity movement, and the relationship of its national leadership with the communist regime. On the crucial questions about that relationship (e.g. did Solidarity 'go too far'? When was the coup prepared?) I have cited the evidence at some length, since there has been so much partial quotation, mis- (and some dis-) information in Poland and the West. There is an enormous amount still to be discovered and written, about, for example, the impact of Solidarity on different sorts and kinds of people, the other independent organisations spawned by Solidarity, the internal development of Solidarity in different areas, about the Church and about the communist Party (to describe its cliques and camarillas, its obscure networks of patronage and mutual obligation, requires the technique, skill and dedication of a Lewis Namier). I have tried to make a convincing outline map, not a comprehensive Ordnance Survey.

At the same time I have drawn extensively on my personal experience to illustrate and illuminate this narrative. I hope that readers who were not in Poland at this time will allow themselves to become just a little drunk on the air of the Rzeszów Commune or the Lenin Shipyard, before moving on to sober hindsight.

In Part II I have drawn together the threads of the narrative, to discuss what Solidarity changed in Poland, and in what sense these sixteen months can be described as a revolution. In conclusion, I examine some common western reactions to Solidarity, western government policies towards Poland, and a few of the lessons which the Polish experience may hold for us in the West.

Traversing this live volcano of contemporary history, I have endeavoured to combine the crafts of historian and journalist. I would not have attempted this foolhardy exercise if it had been probable that, as in Britain or America, the inside story told by official records would come to light in the foreseeable future. But since the release of those records (insofar as they exist) is as probable as the restoration of the monarchy in Warsaw or Moscow, the most important objection to the enterprise of writing contemporary history—crippling incompleteness of sources—is partly met. The available sources on the revolutionary side are already remarkably rich, since freedom of information was one of the points in which Solidarity most emphatically contrasted with the communist regime. However, I trust my account will be further enriched, and modified, by the testimonies of more participants.

Throughout I have been conscious of Walter Raleigh's warning 'that who-so-euer in writing a modern Historie, shall follow truth too neare the heeles, it may happily strike out his teeth'. Not the least depressing feature of the worldwide discussion of Solidarity has been the propensity of all parties to indulge in splenetic attacks on the others' *motives*, rather than reasoned criticism of their arguments. All criticism of the latter kind will be the more welcome.

T.G.A. Oxford, April 1983

Preface to the Third Edition

Sixteen years ago, when this book was first published, I wrote that the release of the records of the communist authorities was as probable as the restoration of the monarchy in Warsaw or Moscow. Well, the monarchy has not been restored in either place (although in the mid-1990s there was a brief campaign by British Poles for the Duke of Kent to become the King of Poland), but communism and the Soviet Union have ended and many of those records have indeed become available. We also have more sources on the Solidarity side, and can see the events of 1980–1 in a longer perspective.

To take account of all this would mean to write a new book. That, in turn, would destroy the value of the old one, which lies in a personal description and analysis of what it looked, sounded, smelled and felt like at the time. My 'what it felt like at the time' is seen mainly from the viewpoint of someone close to, and obviously sympathetic with, Solidarity, but it includes our nervous guesswork about things now better known, such as the intentions of Leonid Brezhnev and his colleagues in the Soviet Politburo.

I have therefore left the main text as it was, correcting only a few errors of fact. Where there is speculation about the high politics of the Warsaw Pact, it will be clear to the reader that this has been superseded by new evidence, which is discussed at length in a new Postscript.

In the Postscript, I address three main areas. First, what do we now know about the hidden drama of the Polish and Soviet leaderships' response to Solidarity? In particular: were the Soviets prepared to invade and did General Jaruzelski therefore, as he passionately claims, chose the 'lesser evil' in declaring martial law on 13 December 1981? Second, there is the subject of the relations between workers and intellectuals in Solidarity. In the 1990s, this has been the main focus of scholarly controversy about the history of Solidarity, and the debate started from a critique of the interpretation given (or allegedly given) in this book. Finally, I look briefly at what happened to Solidarity after 1981, and what is left of Solidarity (with both a large and a small s) in the free, democratic, capitalist Poland of 1999.

For this edition, I have also updated the Chronology and added a new Bibliography.

T.G.A. OXFORD/STANFORD, AUGUST 1999

THE POLISH REVOLUTION: SOLIDARITY

Introduction:

Why Poland? Why Workers? Why 1980?

The Poles rebel against a mild oppressor, because they can; against a harsh one, because they must.

Saying from the 1860s

CRISIS (from Greek): a serious breakdown in the process of economic growth in capitalism. Crisis is a phenomenon solely connected with the capitalist economies and does not occur in other socio-economic systems . . .

From the official *Encyklopedia Powszechna*, Warsaw

When I first came to Poland I kept hearing a very strange word. 'Yowta', my new acquaintances sighed, 'yowta!', and conversation ebbed into melancholy silence. Did 'yowta' mean fate, I wondered, was it an expression like 'that's life'?

'Yalta' (Polish pronunciation 'yowta') is where the story of Solidarity begins. 'Yalta' for the Poles means that, after their army had been the first to resist Hitler, after Britain had gone to war in defence of Poland's independence and Polish servicemen had fought courageously in defence of Britain, after some six million of their compatriots (one in every five citizens of the pre-war Polish Republic) had died in the war—after all this, their country was delivered up by their western allies, Britain and America, into the famously tender care of 'Uncle Joe' Stalin.

While it can be argued that Churchill and Roosevelt had no alternative, since when the Big Three met at Yalta in the Crimea in February 1945 the Red Army already occupied the territory of the former Polish Republic, and while in the final communiqué of that meeting Stalin solemnly promised 'the holding of free and unfettered elections as soon as possible on the basis of universal suffrage and secret ballot',[1] such a deliverance was an equivocal blessing, for anyone. But to understand why it was in Poland that the first workers' revolution against a 'Workers' State' erupted in

August 1980, you must understand why the prospect of Soviet 'liberation' was so particularly appalling to the great majority of Poles in 1945.

To understand this you must return to the beginning of Poland's recorded history with the baptism of King Mieszko I in the Latin rite in the year 966. Poland thus became the easternmost bulwark of Latin Christendom. The kingdom grew and prospered until, uniting with the Grand Duchy of Lithuania, its vast territories extended over most of what is now the western Soviet Union. Polish armies occupied Moscow. In the sixteenth century this Polish-Lithuanian Commonwealth developed a unique political system. Supreme power lay with parliamentary gatherings of the nobility, who sought perfect liberty for themselves, and perfect equality among themselves. Such was their respect for the rights of the individual noble, that in time the extraordinary institution of *Liberum Veto* gave every single member of parliament (*sejm*) the right to veto any Bill. One vote against sufficed. It was unanimity or nothing! Such was their mistrust of central authority that they converted the monarchy into an elective office. The kings whom they elected in tumultuous mass assemblies on a great meadow outside Warsaw were often reduced to despair or even flight. 'Poland stands by unrule' (*'Nierządem Polska stoi'*) the unruly nobles proclaimed as their motto, refusing to vote their monarchs the necessary funds for a professional army. On an island like Britain, or on the other side of the Atlantic, this Noble Democracy might just have lasted. But Poland lay on the open plains between two hungry autocracies, Russia and Prussia.

Despite last-minute efforts to reform and strengthen the kingdom, culminating in the famous liberal Constitution of 3 May 1791, Poland was simply carved up by her neighbours, Russia, Prussia and Austria, in the 'Partitions' of 1772, 1793 and 1795. Poland disappeared from the map of Europe as an independent state for the next one hundred and twenty-three years. But it refused to disappear as a nation.

Though in the 'Golden Century' of Noble Democracy Poland had been known as the 'paradise of heretics', a haven of religious tolerance and diversity, the Poles' fervent patriotism was now expressed through an ever closer identification of the nation with the Roman Catholic Church, against the creeds of their oppressors,

German Protestantism and Russian Orthodoxy. Again and again, in 1794, and 1830–1, and 1863–4, and 1905, they expressed their longing for freedom through heroic insurrections, which were crushed with habitual brutality by Tsarist Russia. While the masses prayed to 'Mary, Queen of Poland', a great part of the 'intelligentsia' (what would have been called in nineteenth-century England the 'educated classes', but a more coherent social group, with a special aristocratic ethos and sense of patriotic duty) kept alive the values of 'Polishness' and burnished the myths of the glorious Polish past. In exile, Romantic poets like Adam Mickiewicz developed a Messianic allegory in which Poland, the 'Christ among nations', suffered, was crucified, but would rise again for Europe's redemption. The Church, the insurrectionary tradition, the cultural work of the intelligentsia and romantic Messianism forged what can best be described as the Polish national conscience.

This whistle-stop tour* through ten centuries of history must serve to establish three points which are as important as they are basic: the Poles are an old European people with an unquenchable thirst for freedom; freedom in Polish means, in the first place, national independence; the Polish national identity is historically defined in opposition to Russia.

In the nineteenth century this opposition might be described as the clash of Polish democracy with Russian despotism, Polish individualism with Russian collectivism, Polish Catholicism with Russian Orthodoxy. The revolutionary replacement of one kind of Russian orthodoxy with another in 1917 might have been expected to appease the conflict. But the relationship between the new Polish and Russian states which emerged from the ashes of the First World War began with another war: the Polish-Soviet war of 1920. It ended in another world war, after Stalin had joined Hitler in the fourth and most terrible Partition of Poland, under the terms of the Secret Protocol to the Nazi-Soviet Non-Aggression Pact.

The Poles remember 17 September 1939, when Soviet troops invaded eastern Poland, just as vividly as 1 September. More than one million Poles (roughly one-tenth of the population of Soviet-

*For a grand tour the reader should turn to Norman Davies's magnificent *God's Playground. A History of Poland* (Clarendon Press, Oxford, 1981).

occupied Poland) were deported eastward by the Soviet authorities—fewer than half of them returned, carrying children who would not forget Siberia. One such child was Andrzej Gwiazda, later to become a leader of Solidarity. His tender feelings towards the Soviet Union may be imagined. It is now established beyond any reasonable doubt that thousands of Polish officers were murdered on Stalin's orders at Katyń in 1940. The Warsaw Uprising, launched by the underground Home Army (AK) in 1944 as a last desperate attempt to keep control of Poland's liberation in non-communist Polish hands, was crushed with unsurpassed brutality by the Germans, while the Red Army held back just a few miles away on the left bank of the Vistula, and Stalin for weeks refused to allow American aircraft carrying supplies to refuel on Soviet airfields.

And so to 'Yalta'.

In 1945 the majority of Poles, like the majority in other European countries after the catalysis of total war, did not wish simply to return to the pre-war *status quo*. Unlike many young Poles today, for whom 'like before the war!' is the highest possible praise, many of them had bitter memories of the Second Republic, with its rural poverty and ill-treatment of the Jewish and Ukrainian minorities. The peasantry, who still comprised roughly half the working population, cried out for a fairer distribution of land, and all the parties of the pre-war Left were committed to giving it to them. In a free election in a free Poland there would almost certainly have been a strong vote for the Peasant Party and for the reformist programme of the Polish Socialist Party (PPS), as there was in Britain for the Labour Party.

But there was no society in eastern Europe *less* prepared voluntarily to accept *Soviet* socialism, imposed by Russian bayonets. Soviet socialism did not start from scratch in Poland; it started with a huge political and moral debit. Stalin himself said that introducing communism to Poland was like putting a saddle on a cow; the Poles thought it was like putting a yoke on a stallion. This fundamental, historic opposition and incompatibility is the most basic cause of the Polish revolt against 'Yalta' and Soviet socialism in 1980. For thirty-five years Poland's communist rulers tried either to break the stallion to the yoke or to mould the saddle to the cow. It was always probable that they would fail.

The Power and the Society

'Yalta', then, means the way in which Stalin broke the promises he made at Yalta, as he was bound to if he wished to impose Soviet socialism on Poland. For in a genuinely 'free and unfettered election' the puppet communist party, formed in Russia in 1942 (since the pre-war Polish communist party had been dissolved and its leaders murdered on Stalin's orders) did not stand a chance. The advance of the Soviet liberators was therefore closely followed by a second army of NKVD men, arresting and deporting leaders of the non-communist resistance to Hitler. As early as 8 March 1945 Winston Churchill wrote despairingly to Roosevelt about

> ... the liquidations and deportations ... and all the rest of the game of setting up a totalitarian regime ... if we do not get things right now [he went on] it will soon be seen by the world that you and I by putting our signatures to the Crimea settlement have underwritten a fraudulent prospectus.[2]

In the 'election' finally held in January 1947 a million voters were summarily disenfranchised, thousands of Peasant Party meml s and 142 candidates were simply arrested, the vote count was rigged.[3]

I have no space to spell out the full catalogue of force and fraud by which Soviet domination was imposed on Poland, or the suffering of the civil war which accompanied it. It is sometimes suggested that the Sovietisation of Poland only began in earnest with the American declaration of Cold War in late 1946. The reverse is nearer to the truth: the Cold War was, in part, a western response to the Sovietisation of Poland which began when the first NKVD man set foot on Polish soil.[4] It is, however, true that Poland's first post-war communist leader, Władysław Gomułka, recognised the tactical need to mould the saddle to the cow—that is, to take a slower 'Polish road' to Soviet socialism—if the new regime was ever to win some genuine legitimacy in this stubborn and hostile nation. He did not, for example, envisage the immediate forced collectivisation of agriculture. Only after he was replaced by a Stalinist stooge, Bolesław Bierut, was this tactical restraint abandoned. Then the collectivisation of agriculture was announced, the Polish Socialist Party (PPS) was dunned into a most unequal merger with the communist Polish Workers' Party to form the Polish United Workers' Party (PZPR—hereafter simply 'the Party'), and, in the period of full-blooded Stalinism, from c. 1949 to 1954, they tried to break the stallion to the yoke.

At the end of this period the Leninist-Stalinist political system had been installed in Poland which, in essentials, was still in place in 1980. The nature of this system has been well characterised by the former East German dissident Rudolf Bahro as a 'politbureaucratic dictatorship'.[5] Supreme power is normally concentrated (barring direct intervention by the Soviet Union) in the Party's Politburo, a body with ten to twenty members, chaired by the Party leader (formally, Party First Secretary). Historically, as in the Soviet Union, the personality of the Party leader has marked the 'eras' in a fashion typical of a dictatorship. The Politburo's decisions are transmitted to society through two linked pyramids of political bureaucracy, the Party and the state administration, the latter being in practice subordinate.[6]

The security of the regime depends at all times on the potential coercive power of the security and armed forces (with the ultimate threat of the Red Army, two divisions of which are permanently stationed on Polish soil). The *relative* importance of Party, security services and military in preserving communist rule in Poland varies with circumstances: when the Party lacks even grudging popular *acceptance* the direct coercive power of the security and armed forces becomes correspondingly more important. Though theoretically integrated into the Party-state, the security and military apparatuses have their own direct links with the Soviet Union, often at the highest levels, and play a significant role in the internal factional struggles of the Party.[7] Historically, they have not been mere 'executors' of the current Party leader's 'line'. The basic structure of the politbureaucratic dictatorship is thus simple, totalitarian and monolithic; but its day-to-day politics are fraught with internal tensions and contradictions, which become most acute in periods of political crisis like 1980–2.

The Party controls not only the appointment of its own full-time officials, known collectively as the *apparat*, but also all the most important appointments in almost every walk of life: central and local government officials, managers in industry and commerce, publishers, newspaper editors, senior army officers, judges, trades union leaders, university rectors, headmasters, leaders of youth and women's organisations, bankers, fire brigade commanders... For this purpose, the Party's Central, regional and local committees maintain lists of positions, and of people judged fit to fill them. The Soviet term for these lists, *nomenklatura*, has come to be applied by extension to the class of people holding such positions. In 1972 the *nomenklatura* was expanded to increase the Party's central control, so that by 1980 there were probably some 200,000 to 300,000 *nomenklatura* jobs.

The *nomenklatura* can accurately be described as a client ruling class. Its members enjoy power, status and privileges (in varying degrees) by virtue simply of belonging to it. They may not individually own the means of production, but they do collectively control them. In the 1970s they were popularly known as 'the owners of People's Poland'. By contrast with other class systems, economic and political power are concentrated permanently in the same hands. Neither is this a purely functional elite. The children of the *nomenklatura* enjoy automatic advantages, so long as they remain loyal to the system. In the 1970s these advantages were comparable with hereditary privilege in the West: if you were the son of a senior apparatchik you had a much higher standard of living, better education and career chances than your contemporary, the son of a worker.[8] If one includes families, perhaps 1½ million people depend directly on the continuance of Party monopolies for their jobs, powers or privileges.

In Poland, the ruling class has a characteristic face. Recruited from workers' and peasants' sons, for ideological reasons and because they were most likely to be loyal to the new system, these young men trooped hopefully into power. If the initial revolutionary *élan*, the 'new frontier' spirit, soon evaporated in a swamp of inefficiency and lies, the poor peasant's son (remembering the misery of a rural childhood in pre-war Poland) had none the less taken an undreamed-of step up the social ladder and acquired a vested interest in the system. Further advancement, moreover, depended on a consistent 'negative selection' since the qualities of unquestioning obedience and loyalty to the Party were rewarded, while individual initiative, innovation and spontaneity were generally discouraged. In the 1950s and 1960s the faces which stared out of the solemn black-and-white portrait photos in *Trybuna Ludu* ('The People's Tribune', the Polish *Pravda*) might still be those of bony, puritan old communists like Gomułka, or the ascetic features of Jewish intellectuals; in the 1970s they were supplanted by the broad, slab features and fatty jowls of the peasant sons. At fifty the ruling class had the face it deserved.

This regime can accurately be described as 'totalitarian' in the sense that it *aspires* to total control over every aspect of its citizens' lives, to break every social bond outside its aegis, to destroy 'civil society'. Wherever two or three are gathered together, there the Party-state desires to be. Ideally, this control will extend even to the subject nation's collective memory, to history, for 'he who controls the past controls the future'. Yet every national case in eastern Europe was different, and nowhere did the reality fall farther short of the totalitarian ideal than in Poland.

Here the sprawling political bureaucracy never became a really swift, effective executor of central orders; on the contrary, it developed a matchless expertise in obstructing or twisting changes ordered from above. The Polish Party was never purged by a Stalinist terror as brutal as in Hungary or Czechoslovakia. 'Some sort of filter mitigates extremes in Poland',[9] Czesław Miłosz (the exiled Polish poet awarded the Nobel Prize in 1980) comments—but the filter was surely strengthened in this case by the communists' awareness that they were an embattled minority attempting to rule a hostile people, and simply could not afford to deplete their own ranks. Outside the ranks of the Party, Stalinism was both too severe and too mild. It was too severe for the Party to win the voluntary co-operation of several groups whose co-operation it just might have won by more conciliatory methods: thousands of former members of the Home Army (AK), their education and skills of great potential value, were harassed, sacked, imprisoned and judicially murdered.[10] It was too mild to break the back of 'civil society', as was done, for example, in Hungary in three years of terror after the Russian invasion in 1956.

Even in the worst years of Stalinism, Polish communism was distinguished by half-measures, partially executed. Specifically, the Polish communists failed to collectivise private agriculture and to subjugate the Church. (Perhaps they would have needed another Russian invasion to do so.) Little more than 9 per cent of agricultural land was collectivised by 1956, and during the 'Polish October' of that year four-fifths of the collective farms were spontaneously dissolved by their members.[11] The Primate, Cardinal Stefan Wyszyński, returned in triumph to Warsaw from three years' 'internment' in a remote monastery. The Church rose still more in popular esteem for being yet again persecuted by an alien power.

The fact that Wyszyński's Church succeeded in keeping the allegiance of most of the peasant families who flocked to find work in the new socialist industrial centres is of capital importance for an understanding of Solidarity. This stubborn allegiance of the young working class, at once pious and patriotic, was unique in eastern Europe. So was the manner in which the Church and non-communist intellectuals kept alive the Poles' autonomous collective memory—the national conscience—against the Party's determined efforts to destroy it.

In 1956 the Poles had succeeded in preserving two vital bastions of pluralism, the Church and private agriculture, and an exceptional degree of independence in intellectual and cultural life. Here there were still the social bases for self-determination.[12] In 1980 a simple terminology was widely adopted by Solidarity members to describe the essential conflict in Poland since 1945: it was, they said, a struggle between 'the society' (*społeczeństwo*) and 'the power' (*władza*). Yet the mass adoption of this terminology by workers in 1980 is itself a crucial historical development. It would be wrong for the historian to join them in projecting the constellation of 1980—the confrontation between a self-aware, united 'society' and a weak, divided 'power', the utter alienation of the working class from the Party-state which ruled in its name—back into the year 1945 or 1956.

Workers in a 'Workers' State'

True, 1956 was the first date which Solidarity chapels embroidered on their banners, because it was the first year in which Polish workers stood up for their rights against the communist regime, at the cost of their lives. On 28 June 1956 workers of the Stalin engineering works in Poznań (better known, before and since, as the Cegielski works) came out on the streets to protest at their worsening economic position. Makeshift placards held aloft by the swelling crowd demanded 'Bread and Freedom'. Polish Internal

Security forces put down the rising in two days of street fighting, during which at least fifty-three people were killed and hundreds injured. Poznań gave birth to a potent myth linking two ideas of freedom, the workers' freedom from want and the nation's freedom from foreign domination; a myth all the more potent because any reference to the Poznań events was soon censored out of the official media. Officially, the events became non-events, the dead unpersons.

However, in 1956 the workers' protest was still mainly channelled through the *soi-disant* workers' Party. In this, Poland in 1956 was like Czechoslovakia in 1968 rather than Poland in 1980. The nearest thing 1956 had to a Lech Wałęsa, a young Warsaw car-worker called Leszek Goździk, was actually secretary of the Party group in his factory. The man who re-emerged as Party leader in the dramatic days of the 'Polish October', Władysław Gomułka, was the first and last Polish communist to be, briefly, a national hero. He was a national hero in October 1956 above all because people thought he was defying the Russians. In Warsaw, the workers waited in their factories, preparing to defend this new and supposedly reformist Polish communist leadership, against the Red Army if necessary.[13]

It would be wearisome to detail the slow process of disillusionment which followed this heady dawn. Suffice it to say that Khrushchev's acceptance of Gomułka proved to be not the beginning of a new period of democratisation in and through the Party, of rational economic reform, cultural liberalisation and increased respect for human and civil rights, but rather the beginning of the end of that happy ferment of 'renewal' which effervesced across Poland in the autumn of 1956.

For the workers, two elements of this gradual restabilisation of the politbureaucratic dictatorship were especially painful. First, the 'workers' councils' which had emerged spontaneously in many factories in 1956 were 'merged' by a law of 1958 into theoretically independent 'Conferences of Workers' Self-Government' (KSR). In practice this put them back under Party control. Instead of being genuinely independent bodies expressing the grievances of the workers they became (to use Lenin's metaphor for trades unions in the communist system) just another 'transmission belt' for conveying the Party's wishes (e.g. increased production) to the workers.

Secondly, for political reasons the pioneering proposals made by many Polish economists for reforming the bureaucratic command economy were largely ignored. (Whereas they were largely implemented in Hungary—Polish economists have long been prophets without power in their own country.) Over the next fourteen years, repeated attempts at decentralisation and the introduction of some market mechanisms were repeatedly frustrated by a combination of bureaucratic inertia, vested interests, limited imagination in the Gomułka leadership and perhaps also a desire to show that at least in economics Poland could stick to a Soviet model. Having failed to destroy the private sector in agriculture, the regime consistently neglected it, thus eating away at the roots of economic growth. Meanwhile, the characteristic concentration on a few heavy industrial branches meant that the workers rarely saw the products of their labour in the form of consumer goods. The annual increase in real wages in the 1960s was, according to the distinguished Polish economist Włodzimierz Brus, 'not even statistically significant'.[14] By the end of the decade industrial safety and social facilities for the workers had been badly neglected, while a newly married couple had to wait on average seven years before being assigned a flat of their own.

One of the few remaining popular benefits of this irrational, lopsided political economy was the regime's guarantee of low staple food prices, some of which had been frozen for a decade. Though shortages of meat and dairy products were acute by 1970 (mainly due to the cumulative neglect of private agriculture) when the working-class housewife did obtain her joint in the state-owned butcher's (as opposed to on the burgeoning black market) it was very cheap. But the economic distortions caused by this price freeze became so acute that the Gomułka leadership decided they would have to increase staple food prices, by up to 36 per cent. They chose to do this, without warning, on 13 December 1970, just a fortnight before Christmas—which shows how far they had lost touch with the mood of the people.[15]

The result was an earthquake of working-class protest which toppled Gomułka and shook the regime. In Gdańsk thousands of shipyard workers marched on the Party's regional headquarters, demanding that the price rises be withdrawn. Within a few days the government was faced with strikes and protests across much of the country. Several big Warsaw factories were occupied. This time the bloodshed came in the Baltic ports, where armed police and professional Polish soldiers once again shot and killed Polish workers. Gomułka had ordered them to crush what he now called 'counter-revolution', though even the Soviet Politburo did not endorse this interpretation.

December 1970 is the single most important date in the prehistory of Solidarity. In December 1970 the giant which the socialist regime had itself created, the new working class, first flexed its muscles, seized the men who claimed to rule in its interest by the scruff of their necks, and shook them. At least three vital lines of causality run from here to August 1980.

The first could be seen most clearly in an industrial enterprise of which the world would hear more. The Lenin Shipyard in Gdańsk was already one of Poland's shop-window socialist enterprises—the kind of place they took visiting heads of state to see. The workforce, more than 15,000 strong, was a mixture of raw young peasant sons and older men, many 'resettled' from the pre-war eastern provinces which had been incorporated into the Soviet Union as a result of 'Yalta'. December 1970 fused them for the first time into a cohesive community with a common purpose. The shooting of their comrades in front of the shipyard gates on Wednesday 16 December transgressed that especially sacred unwritten commandment of the Polish religion of freedom, 'Pole shall not kill Pole'. The more the authorities attempted to suppress the memory of the December dead in subsequent years, the more fiercely the people of the coast remembered. Forced underground, the myth of the martyrs grew in the fertile subsoil of the national conscience. To the shipyard workers, with their strange mixture of patriotic peasant piety and workers' self-respect bred by socialism, the Poles murdered by Poles, workers murdered by a 'Workers' State', became the symbol for all their accumulated grievances. To one shipyard worker in particular, a private farmer's son and member of the strike committee in 1970, the duty to honour the martyrs' memory became a driving force, almost an obsession. His name was Lech Wałęsa. In his subsequent career, myth and history, subjective and objective causes, become inextricable.[16]

Secondly, the workers deliberately organised themselves outside the aegis of the Party, and formulated proto-political demands. This was particularly notable in the tough north-eastern port of Szczecin where the shipyard workers successfully adopted the pre-war technique of the occupation-strike. In January 1971, protests having resumed after the Christmas break, more than thirty Szczecin factories set up a network of strike committees which effectively controlled the everyday life of the city. Their demands included not only the withdrawal of the price rises, but also the recognition of the strike committees as authentic, permanent representatives of the work force (like the 'workers' councils' of 1956), and, in the longer term, new, free, independent trades unions—prefiguring August 1980.

In 1971, however, the outcome was rather different. On the evening of 24 January the new Party leader, Edward Gierek, unexpectedly appeared at the gates of the occupied Warski Shipyard in Szczecin. There followed an unprecedented nine-hour-long confrontation in which Gierek adopted a tone of frankness and humility ('When it was proposed that I take over the leadership of the Party, at first I thought I would refuse . . . I am only a worker like you . . .').[17] Somehow it worked. After deluging him in complaints about the official trades unions, the lies of the official media and the inefficiency of the ruling class, the workers finally shouted, in words which were to become first famous and later infamous: *'Pomożemy! Pomożemy!'* ('We will help you!') and went back to work. The next day saw a similar marathon confrontation in the Lenin Shipyard and another personal triumph for Gierek. Unlike in 1956, the workers' protest had not initially been channelled through the Party, but many of the strike leaders were Party members and the strikers finally agreed to give the Party another chance.

It is difficult to overstate the extent to which the whole of Gierek's political strategy in the next decade was dictated by the workers' revolt in 1970–1, and the extent to which Solidarity was shaped by the workers' bitter recollection of its outcome. In his speeches Lech Wałęsa would often recall how he himself had shouted *'Pomożemy!'* . . . 'And what did Gierek do with our help?' he would ask.

Gierek's 'Great Leap'

What Gierek did is already the subject of excellent learned articles, satires and sermons on human folly.[18] Briefly, he seems to have started from the correct premise that communist ideology would not furnish the means of political legitimation for the Polish Party in the 1970s. In fact he knew the workers did not believe the ideological guff of propaganda any more than he did. They wanted some jam today, not the promise of paradise tomorrow. He tried to play the national card, for example by rebuilding the royal castle in Warsaw, but such gestures had a very limited effect. In any contest for patriotic legitimacy the Party was bound to lose hands down against the Church, indeed against almost anyone except Moscow. He tried to woo the Church and intelligentsia into more active 'patriotic' co-operation by offering greater tolerance in intellectual, cultural and religious life.

But his trump cards were economic. Basically he proposed to win the support of the majority of the population by bringing them a steadily rising material standard of living, visible in the shops as consumer goods, on top of the traditional socialist advantages of full employment, social security and stable prices. As political boss of industrial Silesia he had become expert at the game of distributing goods and privileges so as to satisfy different factions in the apparatus, and, more important, to 'divide and rule' between different sections of society. The miners, for example, had been especially well paid and well supplied with meat to keep them passive. These Tammany Hall politics Gierek now intended to apply on a national scale. The great leap forward, the Polish *Wirtschaftswunder* (economic miracle), would start with a spurt of industrial development using technology and plant imported from the West and initially paid for by the West. Exports from these new plants to the West would then earn the hard currency to pay back the loans.

Gierek's broad strategy was neither unique nor wholly absurd.* Both János Kádár in Hungary and Erich Honecker in East Germany

*Several western writers have followed the Polish sociologist Jadwiga Staniszkis in labelling the Polish political system under Gierek 'corporatist'. This label does not seem to me useful (1) because the differences between this and any western 'corporatist' system are greater than the similarities, and (2) because the similarities to the political system before 1970 are greater than the differences. A change in strategy by the new Party leadership, which left the basic structure of the politbureaucratic dictatorship unchanged, hardly justifies a new label for the whole system.

developed models of 'consumer socialism'. Both used western loans to finance the necessary imports, and the *per capita* hard currency debt of both Hungary and East Germany was larger than Poland's as late as 1979.[19] Both ran into difficulties in the worsening world economic climate of the late 1970s. Honecker initiated a tactical *rapprochement* with the (Protestant) Church; Kádár set an example of tactical intellectual tolerance. Both tried to play the national card.

What was unique about Gierek's 'great leap forward' was its scale, the breathtaking incompetence with which it was executed, and the society with which he had to deal. The Five-Year Plan for 1971–5, finally adopted in June 1972, concentrated heavily on a few industries—steel, shipbuilding, petro-chemicals—for which the export prospects were poor even before the oil crisis. Although few communist regimes have been less ideological, the over-ambitious Plan goals, the obsession with heavy industry and the incredible, vainglorious 'Propaganda of Success' bear the unmistakable marks of the experience which many of the new Politburo had shared in the Stalinist Union of Polish Youth (ZMP). Gierek's monument is the gigantic, unfinished 'Huta Katowice' steelworks, a huge economic white elephant for which the only rationale is political: it lies in the heart of his former Silesian fief, providing jobs for the boys; a specially-built broad-gauge railway runs from its gates straight to the Soviet Union.

The implementation of the Plan, moreover, was so uncontrolled that gross investment in fixed assets rose by a staggering 69.5 per cent instead of the planned 38.5 per cent; real wages by 36 per cent instead of 17 per cent (official figures).[20] The Gierek team persuaded themselves that rapidly rising real wages would correspondingly increase productivity, as well as performing the vital political service of keeping the workers quiet. In practice their strategy raised expectations rather than productivity. At the same time there were no major structural reforms, which might have ensured that western imports were used effectively. Greater autonomy was rightly given to the managers of larger companies, now reorganised into groups known by their Polish initials as WOGs. The short-term effect of this half-hearted reform was, however, to further overheat the economy, as rival managers used their new freedom to invest more borrowed money, pay out more wages, and, more often than not, to enrich themselves on the side.

Any coherent plan for the rapid modernisation of Poland would have begun with the modernisation of private agriculture, which, despite all its handicaps, was consistently more efficient than the socialised sector. Increased food supplies from the private sector to the state-run shops could have helped to secure the regime's minimal legitimacy with the urban working class, while agricultural exports could have paid for some of the imported western technology. As one Polish writer pithily observes, '... Ham and beef are wanted by all, but Polish machine tools and cars will not be bought by anyone who is quite sane.'[21]

At the beginning of the Gierek era a little of this economic common sense does seem to have penetrated to the top, but it was soon defeated by the unholy alliance of bureaucracy and ideology. To the ideology of Soviet socialism private agriculture was, of course, anathema. The bureaucrats therefore had cast-iron arguments with which to defend their vested interests. There was a formidable industrial lobby inside the Party, and none for private agriculture. In fact, the late 1970s saw a further, rapid 'socialisation' of agriculture: the proportion of arable land privately farmed fell from 86 per cent in 1970 to 75 per cent in 1980, with a corresponding, predictable decline in production. At the same time both domestically-produced and, increasingly, imported meat was pumped into the shops to feed the consumer boom. According to official figures the average *per capita* consumption of meat rocketed from 53 kg in 1970 to 70 kg in 1975. As a direct result of these policies, Poland, which had been a major food exporter in the 1950s, ran up a staggering $4.5 billion deficit in food and agricultural trade with the West in the period 1970–80.[22] The system of fixed, heavily subsidised staple-food prices reached new heights of surreality when bread became cheaper than animal fodder. Private farmers, rationally enough, began feeding their animals bread...

Though most of the economic follies of the Gierek 'great leap' were a direct result of the failures of the system and the leadership, the price freeze was caused by social pressure. In this regard, the Polish workers had won themselves a virtual power of veto in 1970–1. After Szczecin and Gdańsk had gone back to work the textile workers of Łódź—Poland's Manchester—came out on strike. This time it was the new Prime Minister, Jaroszewicz, who asked 'Will you help us?', and the furious crowd of badly paid, undernourished women answered: 'No!' Next day the 13 December price rises were finally withdrawn. So in 1976 basic food prices were still mostly pegged to the 1967 level, while the regime continued to shower money on to the workers.

In June 1976, without prior warning or consultation with the workers, the government once again tried to remedy this yawning imbalance between demand and supply by introducing food price rises of, on average, 60 per cent (69 per cent on meat). Workers across the country went on strike; the Baltic shipyards were once again occupied, the strikers set about electing a committee, drawing up lists of demands . . . From the Ursus tractor factory near Warsaw several thousand workers marched to the transcontinental railway lines and stopped the Paris-Moscow express. In Radom, south-west of Warsaw, workers reverted to the more primitive forms of protest which had been seen in Poznań exactly twenty years before. A large crowd marched to the Party headquarters and, receiving no satisfaction, set fire to it. That evening a visibly shaken Prime Minister Jaroszewicz announced the withdrawal of the price rises 'for further consideration': there had, he said, been useful 'consultations' with the workers.[23] Meanwhile, police and security thugs moved in to take a savage revenge on the workers of Radom and Ursus, forcing them to run the gauntlet through two lines of truncheon-wielding police, who called this, with delicate irony, the 'path of health'. Harsh sentences were handed down by civil courts; thousands of workers were sacked. But it was the regime which had capitulated.

A Great Convergence

In their last four years, from summer 1976 to summer 1980, Gierek and his crew were like the pilots of an airliner which has gone into a nosedive. Starting with the so-called 'economic manoeuvre' of late 1976, they tried every trick they knew, but the machine would not respond to the controls. The dive became steeper and steeper; the engines burned out; the pointer on the hard currency debt dial whizzed up into the red, from the $10 billion mark in 1976 to around $17 billion in 1979. In this uncomfortable position a remarkable thing happened in the body of the aircraft. Hesitantly at first, hindered by the stewards, then with growing confidence, the passengers began to get together, to organise themselves, to sign petitions to the crew and demand a change of course...

The single most important initiative grew directly out of the Radom and Ursus trials. Learning that many of the accused workers had no resources with which to defend themselves a diverse group of intellectuals clubbed together to help. In September 1976 they founded the Workers' Defence Committee, which would become known throughout the world by its Polish initials KOR. Other intellectual initiatives had preceded KOR: most importantly a wave of protests against proposed changes to the Constitution in 1975 formally enshrining the leading role of the Party in the state and Poland's 'unshakeable fraternal bonds' with the Soviet Union. Many others were to follow KOR.[24] But its foundation was a turning-point.

In its original form it was the first bridge thrown over the fatal gulf between workers and intellectuals, which had been so painfully apparent in December 1970, when most intellectuals remained silent during the workers' protest (many still smarting under the memory of the workers' indifference during the students' protest in March 1968, its brutal suppression and the subsequent official anti-Semitic—'anti-Zionist'—campaign and cultural pogrom). Without this bridge Solidarity would have developed, if at all, very differently.

In its original composition, KOR threw bridges over some deep divides within the critical intelligentsia: it included former communists and members of the pre-war Polish Socialist Party (PPS), for example, the venerable economist Edward Lipiński; former protégés of the Stalinist regime, like the novelist Jerzy Andrzejewski, and former prisoners of Stalin, like Antoni Pajdak; a veteran of Piłsudski's First World War 'Legions' and students whose first battles had been fought with the communist police in March 1968.[25]

KOR was an icebreaker. In its wake, more and more intellectuals dared to participate in some kind of opposition activity. Within three years, Poland developed a whole opposition counter-culture without parallel in the Soviet bloc. There were two excellent uncensored literary magazines and upwards of ten uncensored journals of opinion. The largest of the underground publishers, Nowa, produced some hundred works, including a Polish translation of Orwell's *Animal Farm* and a pocket-sized handbook giving instructions for dealing with the secret police. A 'New Wave' of young poets from the Polish 'class of '68' punctured the mendacious bubbles of official propaganda with sharp, electrifying political poems. People paid high prices for these forbidden fruits; they devoured them in a night and then passed them on to their friends, so the circle of readers was far larger than the few thousand copies which were somehow run off on the hidden duplicators. A growing number of scholars took part in the 'Flying University' (TKN), founded in January 1978, which held unofficial seminars in private flats on all those areas of Polish history and life which were officially taboo.

I cannot do justice in a few sentences to the richness and excitement of this unique opposition counter-culture;[26] and I must perforce confine myself to those parts of it which are directly relevant to the pre-history of Solidarity. Yet one is bound to ask why all this opposition activity was tolerated by the Gierek regime. There can be little doubt about the technical feasibility of repression. At a meeting in 1978 a colonel of the security service was asked why the police did not destroy the underground publishers. 'We know all the addresses, we could destroy everything in one night,' he sighed, 'but *the high-ups won't allow us to*' (my italics).[27] The 'high-ups', notably Gierek himself, seem to have thought that this flowering of intellectual opposition would not amount to a serious political threat, while tolerance might win them a broader measure of co-operation from the intelligentsia. Perhaps this reflected their low regard for ideas in general. But two other factors contributed to this major miscalculation.

The first was détente. Although the Polish opposition did not on the whole support détente, in the late 1970s détente supported the Polish opposition. In early 1977 the most active younger members of KOR were arrested, and materials collected for a trial. Then, in July 1977, they were all quite unexpectedly amnestied. Thereafter KOR activists would be abused, harassed, sacked from their jobs, many times detained for questioning and held for the forty-eight hours allowed by law before charges had to be preferred—but they would not be held for a longer period until August 1980 (and even then the fiction of successive forty-eight hour detentions was carefully preserved). By 1977 Gierek was already in desperate financial straits, while the 'Helsinki process' was in full swing and the

Carter administration made the most explicit 'linkage' between the economic and human rights components of détente. That year both Chancellor Schmidt and President Carter visited Warsaw. At a press conference Carter loudly praised the Polish record on human rights and religious tolerance, in the next breath announcing a further $200 million of US credits.[28] 'Linkage' could hardly be more explicit than that. If the KOR activists had still been imprisoned, it is doubtful if the credits would have flowed so freely.*

The second factor is the Church. It was by no means self-evident that the Polish Catholic Church would spring to the defence of intellectuals who still described themselves as democratic socialists (although there was no ideological uniformity in KOR, and one founder-member was a priest). Before the Second World War the socialist and Catholic milieux in Poland had been bitterly antagonistic: they were 'Two Nations'. The story of how this gulf came to be bridged in the three decades after 1945 is a complex and fascinating one, which can be only crudely summarised here.[29] It was a convergence from both sides. Within the Church, a brilliant group of philosophers and writers concentrated around the Kraków weekly *Tygodnik Powszechny* (including Karol Wojtyła, the future Pope John Paul II), the Warsaw monthly *Więź* ('Link', its editor, Tadeusz Mazowiecki, subsequently one of Lech Wałęsa's closest advisers) and the Clubs of the Catholic Intelligentsia (KIK) gradually formulated a new Catholic social philosophy, fitted generally to the demands of the twentieth century. This merged with the political strategy which the Church hierarchy under Wyszyński developed specifically to combat the demands of a totalitarian regime.

By 1968, Poland's two Cardinals, Karol Wojtyła in Kraków and the Primate, Stefan Wyszyński, in Warsaw, were already spelling out the list of God-given human and civil rights which the state must respect: the right to a life of dignity; the right to freedom; the right to participate in public life, and so on. This marked a significant change even from the Polish Millennium celebrations of two years before (the thousandth anniversary of the baptism of Mieszko I), when the Church had talked more about its own historic rights than about the universal rights of the individual and

*For more on the connection between détente and Solidarity see below, pp. 33 ff.

society. When Gierek set out to woo the Church, it responded with increased demands, which included not only, for example, permission to build more churches and seminaries, but, centrally, more respect for the human rights of *all* Poles, believers and non-believers. In a sermon delivered in September 1976 the Primate declared: 'It is the clergy's duty to defend the workers' interests against hasty and ill-considered government measures ... it was painful that workers should have to struggle for their rights against a workers' government.'[30]

Such language from the pulpit had a direct influence on workers. It also furnished a common vocabulary for socialist intellectuals. The *rapprochement* with the Church from the Left took place at several levels. For Leszek Kołakowski it was a stage in a profound philosophical quest which led him from militant atheism in the Stalinist period to the provisional conclusion that the best substitute for Christianity is probably Christianity. For the young historian Adam Michnik it followed rather from the historical discovery that the Church had been the single most important defender of human and civil rights against totalitarian encroachments in Poland since 'Yalta' (a message spelt out in his influential book *The Church, the Left, Dialogue*, published in Paris in 1977). For KOR's most dynamic political activist, Jacek Kuroń, it was initially more a calculation of political tactics.

The operative facts are that the non-communist Polish Left now abandoned the outdated stereotype of the bigoted, nationalist, 'reactionary', anti-Semitic Church (which lived on as a terrible phantom in the mind of the western Left); that Catholic and non-Catholic intellectuals found more and more common ground in the defence of common values, common sense and basic rights against the late Gierek regime; and that the Church of Wyszyński and Wojtyła cast its protective mantle around increasingly outspoken opposition.*

*One anecdote gives the flavour of the time. When an unofficial lecture organised by Kraków students on 'Orwell's *1984* and Poland today' was broken up by police, the organiser went in some distress to his parish priest. A few days later there was a meeting in church, with an address, subject ... 'Orwell's *1984* and Poland today'. This meeting was not disrupted. Among his many firsts, Pope John Paul II, then Archbishop of Kraków, must be the first divine to have ordered *1984* to be read in churches.

This opposition cannot be described by the western or pre-war Polish categories of 'Left' and 'Right'. Although elements of pre-war traditions (Socialist, Peasant, 'National Democratic') resurfaced, these differences were blurred by changed circumstances and deliberately suppressed in the common struggle against the communist authorities. None the less, three tendencies can be identified, whose *differences* would be important for the history of Solidarity.

The first might be described as 'fundamentalist national opposition' and tended to concentrate on the traditional ideal of national independence in conscious defiance of the existing political reality ('Yalta', with no prospect of military liberation while the Soviet Union remained a nuclear superpower). From this time-honoured starting-point of romantic idealism the clandestine Polish League for Independence (PPN) produced a number of lucid studies, looking forward, for example, to Poland's place in a peacefully reunited Europe alongside a reunited Germany. Working openly, the Movement for the Defence of Human and Civil Rights (ROPCiO) linked these long-term goals to the short-term demand for respect of the Helsinki Agreements. Finally, the small Confederation for an Independent Poland (KPN), founded symbolically on 1 September 1979, came closest in words to the unconditional, insurrectionary defiance of the nineteenth century. Their professed aim was a Polish Third Republic freed from 'Soviet domination' and 'the dictatorship of the Polish United Workers' Party'.[31]

At the other end of the spectrum there was what has been called the 'loyal opposition', which accepted both Poland's position within the Soviet bloc and the basic principles of the communist system. Representative of this tendency was the 'Experience and the Future' (DiP) group, which produced two devastating analyses of Poland's social and economic collapse by 1980. DiP contained many Party and non-Party members of the Warsaw 'Establishment'. Its proposed remedies were mostly structural reforms and policy changes, arrived at by negotiation and compromise *within the Party, initiated by the Party*, and controlled from *above*. It thus carried on the Marxist 'revisionist' hopes of 1956—the hopes that the system could be internally 'revised' to make it democratic and efficient—and indeed the leading figures of the 'loyal opposition' came from the 'class of '56'.

For the third tendency, by contrast, Marxist 'revisionism' had died its final death under the batons of the Warsaw police in March 1968, and under the tracks of the Soviet tanks in Prague in August. It was an illusion to think that a ruling communist party could ever generate and sustain a real democratisation of the system from above—in fact, as Kołakowski wrote from involuntary exile, 'democratic communism' was like 'fried snowballs'. At the same time they recognised that Poland could not achieve 'freedom'—i.e. full sovereign national independence—in the foreseeable future. Of course no one could be certain where the limits of Soviet tolerance would be at any particular time; but the example of Hungary in 1956 and Czechoslovakia in 1968 seemed to preclude any attempt at independent control of defence, foreign and security policy, a radical transformation of the Party, or a frontal challenge to its 'leading role'.

The 'class of '68' none the less thought they discerned a new way forward within these invisible limits. While 'bureaucratic despotic socialism' would not be transformed from above, Kołakowski argued in a seminal essay 'On Hope and Hopelessness',[32] its internal contradictions made it susceptible to *pressure from below*. To exert this pressure the Poles should organise themselves outside the structures of the Party-state. These 'self-organised' social groups and movements would then gradually expand the areas of negative liberty and self-determination open to the citizen. In the end the structures of the Party-state might become little more than stage sets, the facades of a Potemkin village for the eyes of the new Tsars in Moscow, while behind them Polish society would be re-formed in an increasingly open, democratic and pluralist way. The economic success and political stability of this relatively autonomous 'civil society' would reassure Soviet leaders, whose control of Poland's foreign and defence policy would not be challenged. This strategy was elaborated in a series of essays by KOR members like Jacek Kuroń and Adam Michnik, who christened it 'the New Evolutionism'. Significantly, in September 1977 KOR rebaptised itself 'Committee for Social Self-Defence—"KOR"' (KSS—'KOR'),* thus expressing the larger aspiration. In the

*For brevity, and in accordance with popular usage, I shall refer to it throughout simply as KOR.

terminology which now became current, they sought the gradual emancipation of 'the society' from 'the power'.

There is a direct connection between this third opposition strategy and the birth of Solidarity. Kuroń's slogan 'Don't burn down Party committees, found your own!' could hang as a motto over all the workers' protests of 1980. Although KOR encouraged sundry civic initiatives in all walks of life, the most important were without doubt the private farmers' Self-Defence Committees and the workers' Committees for Free Trades Unions. In September 1977 a group of KOR collaborators founded an unofficial paper, *Robotnik* (The Worker),* which was aimed specifically at a working-class readership. On its smudged, small-printed sheets the lessons of past workers' protests (1956, 1970) were drawn in language workers could understand. The first unofficial free union cell was formed on the initiative of *Robotnik*, by a former Radom worker called Leopold Gierek (no relation) in November 1977.[33]

Then, on the eve of May Day 1978, a 'Founding Committee of Free Trades Unions on the Coast' announced its existence in Gdańsk. Among its earliest members were the people who would launch and lead the Lenin Shipyard strike in August 1980: Andrzej Gwiazda, a bearded and intense engineer, Bogdan Lis, a 25-year-old worker (and Party member), Alina Pieńkowska, a 24-year-old nurse, Bogdan Borusewicz, a KOR member, and Lech Wałęsa, a fly character who had been fired from the Lenin Shipyard in 1976 after an outspoken speech at a meeting of the official unions. (The reform of those unions promised by Gierek in 1970–71 had, predictably, come to nothing.) Soon they were producing their own small edition of *Robotnik* (called *Robotnik Wybrzeża*—The Worker on the Coast), which they distributed at factory gates and outside churches after Mass, dodging the secret police.[34]

In September 1979 this extraordinary underground paper devoted a whole issue to a 'Charter of Workers' Rights', prefiguring many of the demands which were to be made in summer 1980: for better wages, shorter working hours, improved safety precautions, promotion by merit, abolition of police privileges, and, above all, for new, independent trades unions:

*The original *Robotnik* had been founded by Józef Piłsudski before the First World War.

> Only the independent trades unions, which have the backing of the workers whom they represent, have a chance of challenging the authorities; only they can represent a power the authorities will have to take into account and with whom they will have to deal on equal terms.[35]

The Charter was signed by sixty-five activists—workers, technicians engineers, intellectuals. All, on the principle of openness adopted by much of the opposition, gave their full addresses, and the minority who were fortunate enough to have telephones gave their telephone numbers as well. An appendix cited the relevant clauses of the International Labour Organisation's Convention and the International Covenant of Economic, Social and Cultural Rights, both ratified by the Polish government, to prove the legality of their demands.

It is naturally difficult to separate the workers' own autonomous political learning process from the direct influence of KOR. But certainly these tiny free union cells, *Robotnik's* translation of KOR's general strategy into specific tactics (how to organise an occupation strike, what to demand) and the nationwide opposition network played a major role in helping discontented workers to generalise their grievances, formulate remedies, and co-ordinate their activities. In this sense one could argue that before August 1980 KOR worked very much as Lenin recommended (in *What is to be Done?*) the conspiratorial communist party should work, raising the political consciousness of the proletariat in key industrial centres. With two crucial differences: KOR's goal was evolution not revolution; and KOR's whole ethos was based on the refusal of the Lie. Unlike the 'loyal opposition' they would not use any part of the 'doublespeak' which is as vital as guns to the survival of a communist regime. In this respect following Sakharov and Solzhenitsyn they proposed to speak and write as if they lived in a free country.

By 1979, then, there was already the embryo of that tacit alliance of workers, intelligentsia and Church, unprecedented in Polish history, unique in the Soviet bloc, unseen in the West, which was to grow into Solidarity. The quality of this convergence is beautifully illustrated by the life-story which one young worker told me, sitting in a Warsaw café one rainy afternoon in the autumn of 1980. Born in 1954, at the end of the Stalinist period, he was the thirteenth son of a peasant farmer and the first member of his family born in hospital. When he was three, his father had sold their small private farm and moved to the growing industrial town of Ursus, near Warsaw. At seventeen he left technical school, getting a job in the tractor factory and attending evening classes. With his muscular physique and clean-cut, rugged features he looked like one of those Socialist Heroes of Labour who used to leer out of the placards on the factory walls, the Stakhanovites who had laid a record number of bricks in one shift or performed some other superhuman feat of socialist productivity. With his background he should have been a pillar of the 'Workers' State'.

But he wasn't. For a start, he was a Catholic. Then he was appalled by the brutality and injustice of police reprisals in Ursus after the June 1976 protests, by working conditions in the factory, by the inequality of wage distribution, by the corruption and inefficiency of the management (*nomenklatura*, of course). In his own workshop the noise level was 95 decibels (he told me); a girlfriend at the Warsaw 'Róża Luksemburg' factory was invalided out due to mercury poisoning—aged twenty-nine. What was to be done? Well, in his housing estate, as all over Poland, the local padre comes round at Christmas time to sprinkle holy water and chalk the initials of the three kings—Kacper, Melchior, Baltazar—and the date of the new year on the doorposts of the faithful. From the tenor of this padre's sermons it appeared he might be in contact with the opposition. So as the priest sprinkled holy water and chalked 'KMB-1977' the young parishioner confessed that he was interested in KOR, and asked if the reverend father could show him something from the unofficial press. At once, the reverend father produced a sheaf of samizdat papers, among them *Robotnik*—and so began a political education which continued through direct contacts with opposition activists from Warsaw.

Three years later this young worker was, at age twenty-six, the chairman of the whole Warsaw region of Solidarity. His name was Zbigniew Bujak.

Bujak's story, with its wonderful complicity of ancient and modern, KMB and KOR, the three kings and the social self-defence committee, the Church and the opposition, is a parable of post-war Poland. Where else could it have happened?

Of course Bujak was exceptional. In 1979 the number of workers actively engaged in organised opposition could still be measured in hundreds. But the *potential* support in his generation and class was enormous. Poland was by now an exceptionally youthful country: nearly one-third of the industrial working class was under twenty-five.[36] From the uncensored works of the opposition (notably DiP's devastating 'Report on the State of the Republic'), from the researches of Polish sociologists, and, above all, from what they themselves said in the forums provided by Solidarity, we can construct a group portrait of this generation.[37]

At home, they had imbibed the memories and myths of national resistance (the 'national conscience') with their mothers' milk; but unlike their parents they had no personal experience of terror, Hitlerite or Stalinist. They had never lived in fear. Unlike their parents, they could not expect dramatic social advancement. The first generation of peasant sons sat tight in their offices. The young generation, although better educated than those in authority over them, could mostly reckon with a lifetime on the same factory floor. Their material expectations had, however, been dramatically raised by Gierek's great leap. In their early teens they had experienced a dizzy increase in their standard of living; after the puritan stagnation of the late Gomułka years, the shops had been suddenly filled with food, jeans, transistor radios and cassette-players from the West; new buildings had shot up around them; they had been told they might reasonably expect to move into a new flat in a few years—and even, if they were very lucky, to acquire a car. Moreover, they had been able—for the first time ever—to take a holiday in the West. The little Polski Fiat, piled high with provisions and children, became a familiar sight in Vienna and West Berlin. They had seen with their own eyes the noxious evil of the capitalist West—and they rather liked it.

Now these raised expectations were being disappointed. Everywhere they looked they saw standards falling. As the economy broke down, the shortages became ever more frequent and infuriating: this week there was no shaving-cream, next week the shelves were spilling over with shaving-cream but there were no razor-blades; this week there was meat but no cooking-oil, next week cooking-oil but no meat. The queues lengthened. As in Gomułka's last years, working conditions in the factories and mines actually deteriorated: according to official statistics there were more deaths per thousand workers in 1979 than in 1970. People might laugh at a shortage of shaving-cream, but a shortage of leather gloves for shipyard workers handling icy metal was no laughing matter. Medical care deteriorated as the hard currency allocation for imported drugs was slashed. Alcoholism became a national disease. By 1980 one million Poles were classified as alcoholics: 40 per cent of all alcohol consumed was reportedly drunk at the place of work.

Moreover, it was characteristic of the Gierek boom that the gains were unevenly distributed. Relatively speaking, the rich got richer and the poor got poorer. According to the DiP report, by 1979 there was a wage differential of 1: 20. Increasingly, the dollar became a second currency (partly used on the black market, partly in official shops where a whole range of otherwise unavailable goods could be bought for hard currency), and this produced a new divide between 'haves' and 'have nots': those who had access to dollars and those who didn't. Meanwhile, many members of the communist ruling class appropriated state funds to build themselves luxurious villas: corruption on an unprecedented scale spread from the top down. (Arguably it was a *principle* of Gierek's handling of the *apparat* and *nomenklatura*.) While the socialist model steel-town of Nowa Huta (near Kraków) still had just one hospital with a maximum of 1,000 beds for a population of more than 200,000, well-appointed new sanatoriums were built for the ruling class.

All these symptoms of growing inequality offended deeply against the egalitarianism which this generation of workers and students had imbibed with their socialist education at school. The propaganda which continued vaingloriously to proclaim 'you've never had it so good!', when any fool could see they had had it better, was simply an insult to their intelligence. What is more, there was absolutely no secular institution through which they felt they could express their discontent. All the unreal 'representative' structures of the state, all those intermediate organisations through which a totalitarian regime attempts to control, mobilise and (if it is wise) consult its citizens—the Party, the youth movement, the official trades unions—these were subjects of indifference or contempt. Their attachment and fierce loyalty went first to the family, second, to a close circle of friends, and, third, to what Wałęsa would describe as 'the family which is called Poland'—the nation.

This was the generation which would flock to the Solidarity standards and give the mass movement its youthful dynamism. Solidarity filled that yawning gap between the family and the nation; Solidarity was the first secular organisation which had ever spoken for them; it was their movement, their generation's bid for political participation.

And a 'Miracle'

In October 1978 there occurred a shocking external intervention in the internal affairs of People's Poland. Cardinal Karol Wojtyła, Archbishop of Kraków, was elected Pope. The nation celebrated this 'miracle', spontaneously, in churches and on the streets. The regime was dismayed, though Gierek's Politburo put a brave face on things, and welcomed the elevation of a 'son of the Polish nation'. In June 1979, after some diplomatic wrangling, the Pope returned to his native land for the most fantastic pilgrimage in the history of contemporary Europe. As he progressed across the country, addressing hundreds of thousands in Warsaw's Victory Square, in Gniezno, the cradle of Polish Catholicism, before the shrine of the Black Madonna at Częstochowa, inside Auschwitz, and then, climactically, a vast congregation on the meadows of his beloved Kraków, he expounded his personal vision under the blazing sun.[38]

In a beautiful, sonorous Polish, so unlike the calcified official language of communist Poland, he spoke of the 'fruitful synthesis' between love of country and love of Christ. At Auschwitz he gave his compatriots a further lesson in the meaning of patriotism, recalling, with reverence, the wartime sacrifice of the Jews and Russians, two peoples whom few Poles had learned to love. He spoke of the 'inalienable rights of man, the inalienable rights of dignity'. He spoke of the special mission of the Slav Pope to reassert the spiritual unity of Christian Europe, east and west, across all political frontiers. Invoking the romantic Messianism of Adam Mickiewicz, he spoke of the special lesson which Christian Poland had to teach the world, and the special responsibility which this laid on the present generation of Poles. 'The future of Poland', he declared from the pulpit of his old cathedral, 'will depend on how many people are mature enough to be nonconformists.'[39]

This language, this vision, came like a revelation to countless young Poles. In Victory Square the crown interrupted his sermon with a rhythmic chant, 'We want God, we want God, we want God in the family circle, we want God in books, in schools, we want God in government orders, we want God, we want God . . .'[40]

'People are preaching with me,' the Pope said: and indeed his preaching built magnificently on the ground plan of the young generation's common but unarticulated values. 'Yes,' they said, as they wandered homeward through the flower-strewn streets, 'now I see—that *is* what I believe.'

As important as this triumphant articulation of shared values was the popular experience of—there is no better word for it—solidarity. The police disappeared from the streets; perfect order was kept by volunteer ushers wearing the papal insignia. Despite the great heat and crush the vast crowds never once became violent. The drunks disappeared too: a voluntary ban on alcohol was generally observed. On the *Blonia*, which is to Kraków what Port Meadow is to Oxford, nearly two million people stood together, applauded together, sung their old hymns together, listened silently together. That intense unity of thought and feeling which previously had been confined to small circles of friends—the intimate solidarity of private life in eastern Europe—was now multiplied by millions. For nine days the state virtually ceased to exist, except as a censor doctoring the television coverage. Everyone saw that Poland is not a communist country—just a communist state.

John Paul II left thousands of human beings with a new self-respect and renewed faith, a nation with a rekindled pride, and a society with a new consciousness of its own essential unity. From this time forward the Manichean dichotomy between 'society' and 'power' became more than an intellectual construct. KOR's use of the word 'society' had been more prescriptive than descriptive; it combined the Enlightenment postulate of a 'natural identity of interests' within 'civil society' and the Romantic postulate of the natural unity of the nation, to indicate what *should* be rather than what was. In reality the 'objective' economic interests of different groups within Polish society were, of course, different and often conflicting. In the past, conflicts within Polish society had been exploited by the Russians to fragment the Polish insurrections (for example, by setting peasants against landlords in 1863–4). They had been exploited, quite skilfully, by Edward Gierek in his strategy of economic 'divide and rule'. But in a situation where the whole economy was breaking down this ceased to be possible. The Pope's visit probably marks the point at which the subjective reality of social/national unity overtook the 'objective' reality of social division. To take our terms from Aquinas rather than Marx: in that nine-day-long outpouring of love and joy the unity of Polish society was transformed from the Potential to the Actual.

There is no doubt the communist 'power' was heading for a crisis anyway: the nosedive was going to end in a crash, another attempt to increase food prices was almost certainly going to produce another explosion of working-class protest. But the form the explosion took in 1980—the quiet dignity of the workers, their peaceful self-restraint, the rhetoric of moral regeneration, the ban on alcohol, the breadth of spontaneous social support—this follows from the mass experience of that fantastic pilgrimage in June 1979. It is hard to conceive of Solidarity without the Polish Pope.

In December 1979 the Committee of Free Trades Unions on the Coast arranged an unofficial ceremony before the gates of the Lenin Shipyard to mark the anniversary of the 1970 shootings, as they had done the previous year. (They were helped by student activists from the opposition Young Poland Movement, RMP, thus symbolically healing the rift between students and workers which had been so apparent in Gdańsk in 1968 and 1970.) Although most of the Free Trades Union activists were placed under preventive arrest, and despite a massive police presence, more than 5,000 people gathered at the appointed time. After the national anthem and the laying of wreaths, a student spoke on behalf of the arrested unionists:

> The history of the Polish People's Republic does not consist only of Party conferences and 5-year Plans . . . We have to remember the Stalin terror, the June events in Poznań, the students' March, December on the coast, June in Radom and Ursus. That is the history of our nation . . . Today, having learned from our experiences, we know how to struggle with calm, obstinacy and solidarity.[41]

In Poland, history—the real, people's history of People's Poland is remembered by months. Such is the cumulative arithmetic of the collective memory that one can almost express the causes of Solidarity as an equation of months: 'August' (1980) = 'June' (1956) + 'March' (1968) + 'December' (1970) + 'June' (1976).

After a minute's silence, a short, square-shouldered man with drooping moustaches erupted on the scene. Lech Wałęsa had secretly made his way to the gate, evading arrest. Introducing himself as a strike leader from 1970, but also as one who had cried *'Pomożemy!'* to Edward Gierek, he said that not one of the strikers' demands had been fulfilled, least of all the demand for a monument to the December martyrs. In vain had they put their trust in the Party. Now they knew that 'Only an organised and independent society can make itself heard. Therefore I appeal to you to organise yourselves in independent groups for self-defence. Help each other. Get in touch with the existing groups . . .' If this was the central strategy of KOR, his last admonition was pure Wałęsa. Everyone should come back next year, same place, same time, he said, and each *carrying a stone*. If the authorities refused to build a monument, they would build it themselves![42]

Meanwhile the Party was preparing for its Congress, due in February 1980, and inside the Party, too, a chorus of criticism rose from below. Workers in factory Party cells roundly denounced the privileges of the Party elite, the continued deterioration of supplies and the absurd 'Propaganda of Success'. Like the 'loyal opposition', local Party organisations now clamoured for the *Party* to take the initiative of reform. But Gierek responded in characteristic fashion. On the one hand he wooed the Congress with a show of 'frankness' about the economic difficulties, and with vague promises of more 'socialist democracy' and a return to 'Leninist norms'. On the other, he offered a scapegoat in Piotr Jaroszewicz, the highly unpopular Prime Minister; it was the government, not the Politburo, which was responsible for the economic 'mistakes', he implausibly suggested. With this cosmetic change he saved his own position for a few months longer, but many local Party activists and revisionists were profoundly disappointed. Some of them, too, now began to wonder if the way out of the crisis really led through the Party.

Like other revolutions, the Polish revolution of 1980–81 was not caused simply by growing economic 'immiseration' and exploitation. The Gierek era is a perfect illustration of Tocqueville's famous observation that revolutions tend to happen not when things have been getting worse but when things have been getting better. The Gierek regime raised the material expectations of the population, and especially of the younger generation, to a level which it could only disappoint. The curve of rising expectations, sharply disappointed, is a classic precondition for revolution. Its half-hearted tolerance of the opposition encouraged the growing conviction that people could change things by organising themselves outside and against the totalitarian Party-state. This opposition saw a remarkable convergence of widely differing intellectual traditions and interest groups, of workers, intellectuals and the Church, in the defence of common, basic rights—a convergence which was the conscious labour of outstanding individuals. Helped by the intellectual opposition, small groups of workers learned, from their own experience of protest in 1956, 1970 and 1976, to become (in Lenin's word) the 'vanguard' of the revolution. Tradition, G. K. Chesterton once remarked, is the democracy of the dead, and perhaps only in Ireland is this democracy as vital as in Poland. It is impossible to place an exact value on the transformation of consciousness wrought by the Polish Pope.

The economic crisis was thus a necessary, but by no means a sufficient, cause of the revolution. The decisive causes are to be found in the realm of consciousness rather than of being. By 1980 this unique society, at once sick and self-confident, frustrated but united, faced a weak and divided power elite which no longer had the means to win voluntary popular support yet had not the will to command obedience by physical coercion. Although the individual components are novel—the alignment of the Church, the agitation of workers against a 'Workers' State'—the basic shift of political self-confidence and will from the rulers to a section of the ruled is familiar from the pre-history of earlier revolutions.

The precipitant cause of the revolution is, however, to be found in the realm of political economy. 1979 had seen the first actual (officially admitted) decline in National Income in the history of People's Poland. As western creditors at last became chary, the new

Prime Minister, Edward Babiuch, announced a hair-raising plan to eliminate Poland's trade deficit ($1.3–1.5 billion) by the end of the year. This would involve an estimated 25 per cent increase in exports, while supplies to the domestic market would have to be cut by 15 per cent in the last quarter of 1980.[43] Some increase in food prices was now unavoidable. Having learnt a little from the blunders of 1970 and 1976, the Politburo decided to introduce the price rises in a covert way, by transferring better cuts of meat to the so-called 'commercial butchers', where prices were already much higher; and to break the news quietly at the beginning of July, when people should be absorbed in preparing for their summer holidays.

This sleight-of-hand did not save them. Workers in the Ursus tractor factory and the great 'Huta Warszawa' steelworks immediately laid down their tools, and only resumed work after management had conceded wage increases of more than 10 per cent. It soon became clear that the authorities had prepared a strategy of swift concession to all purely economic, local demands, supplemented if need be by container-loads of meat rushed to troubled areas. On 11 July managers of major plants were apparently flown to Warsaw and given corresponding instructions. The workers, divided, might yet be defeated.

In the event, the effect of this strategy was the reverse of that intended: it actually fanned the flames of industrial unrest across the country, since workers elsewhere quickly learned of their comrades' victories, and concluded that a strike was a surefire way for them, too, to win a compensatory wage increase. What confounded the government was the speed with which information about the strikes spread around the country, despite the complete silence of all the government-controlled mass media (the Party daily, *Trybuna Ludu*, first mentioned 'work stoppages' on 4 August). It is hardly an exaggeration to say that most of this information came from one telephone in one small Warsaw flat, where Jacek Kuroń, assisted by a student of English from the Kraków Student Solidarity group, kept a round-the-clock strike watch. From here, and from a score of other telephones, the latest news was assembled and passed on to KOR contacts all over Poland, to western correspondents, and to western radio stations (Radio Free Europe in Munich, the BBC in London) which broadcast it back to the country, in Polish, within hours. Millions of workers were thus informed. The disproportion between the resources of the opposition information-gatherers and the resources of the state was staggering. If Gierek had decided at the beginning of July to detain a few tens of activists, to cut a few hundred telephone lines, and to control the international exchanges, the history of that summer might have been very different.

Instead, the strategy of appeasement was pursued despite an ominous escalation of the strikers' demands. In mid-July the 10,000 strong work force of the FSC truck factory in Lublin, south-east of Warsaw, proclaimed a peaceful occupation-strike, not merely for higher wages, but for a list of thirty-five points which included the abolition of 'commercial butchers', the reduction of police and army privileges (e.g. higher family allowances and pensions) and a free press. No sooner had they been bought off with money, meat and promises, than the Lublin railwaymen came out, blocking the vital railway lines to the Soviet Union, along which, it was widely believed, Polish foodstuffs had rolled to fill the Moscow shops in time for the Olympics. The Lublin Party paper referred darkly to 'anxiety among our friends' (a code-word, of course, for Poland's Soviet bloc allies). The railwaymen's demands included work-free Saturdays and trades unions 'that would not take orders from above'. This time the strike was settled only after a Deputy Prime Minister, Mieczysław Jagielski, had come in person to make peace with money.[44]

While strikes continued to break out like bushfires, in Warsaw, in Łódź, in Wrocław—one hundred and fifty in all by 8 August—Edward Gierek, in a last, characteristic gesture of supreme indifference, flew off for a three-week holiday in the Crimea, still apparently confident that his lieutenants could silence the workers by a judicious use of his own patent mixture: money, meat and promises. But on Thursday 14 August the nationwide protest was joined by a voice which he could not ignore. It spoke, as it had to his predecessor, from Gdańsk.

PART I: REVOLUTION

Inside the Lenin Shipyard: Workers, August 1980

The ruling party has been brought before a tribunal of the class from which it allegedly derives its pedigree and in whose name it pretends to govern.

Statement by the Polish League for Independence (PPN), 21 AUGUST 1980

What I remember most vividly from the Lenin Shipyard is not the leaders, Lech Wałęsa or Andrzej Gwiazda, but the figure of one ordinary striker. He was in his mid-twenties, lithe, with short cropped hair and piercing eyes. There was something about him which reminded me irresistibly of the young Home Army soldier played by Zbigniew Cybulski in Wajda's great film *Ashes and Diamonds*. Perhaps it was the bravado with which he liked to clamber up on the shipyard gates. (You can see him in some of the photos from the strike.) Perhaps it was the girl he brought in to share the excitement. Anyway, I nicknamed him Cybulski. With hindsight, I can see the rightness of this memory: for it was young men like Cybulski who would come into their own in Solidarity, and give the moment its extraordinary youthful energy and fearlessness.

Then I remember a quite different figure: a shy elderly clerk in the dispatch department of the docks, who told me he had learned his English in the 1930s from a governess called Miss Crisp. I remember him because he was obviously afraid of what the police and army might do. He was afraid, and none the less he had come to volunteer his services as an interpreter.

Above all I remember a sense of being carried along on some mighty river, which led, majestically and inevitably, to the estuary of the Gdańsk Agreement, and thence to the sea of Solidarity. This memory only shows how deceptive memory can be. For there was nothing inevitable about the outcome of the August strikes. The progress of the Lenin Shipyard occupation (like the authorities' response) was the result of countless arguments, individual decisions, chance and moments of sheer confusion. As Lech Wałęsa later explained, with cheerful exaggeration, 'the strike kept collapsing every five minutes.'

In fact when Bogdan Borusewicz had organized a meeting of 'Free Trades Unions on the Coast' activists with Jacek Kuroń in Warsaw earlier in the month, they had been pessimistic about the chances of a strike taking off at all in the Lenin yard. In July they had tried and failed to organise a strike against the price rises. But by early August there was the example of successful strikes elsewhere, and the special case of Anna Walentynowicz. 'Pani Ania' ('Mrs Ania'), as the shipyard workers all affectionately called her, was a stout, ruddy lady in her early fifties who had worked for thirty years in the Lenin. She was probably the most popular member of the Free Unions group. On 9 August she was sacked—the latest in a series of reprisals which began, typically, with her collecting candle stubs from a nearby graveyard to make new candles for the anniversary of December 1970. (The police accused her of stealing!)[1] A demand for her reinstatement was bound to win support. So the Free Unions group decided to try again.

Before dawn on Thursday 14 August three young workers, briefed by Borusewicz, smuggled posters prepared by the Young Poland people past the noses of half-awake security guards. By half-past five they had gathered small groups around their posters, which demanded the reinstatement of Anna Walentynowicz and a thousand złoty compensatory pay rise. By six, when the first shift had clocked in, they set off from the locker-rooms on a long march through the vast yard, bearing aloft makeshift banners and shouting to their mates to join them. Men put aside their blowtorches and clambered down from the sheer sides of half-finished ships. Soon they numbered more than a hundred, but they were still utterly dwarfed by the huge cranes which straddle the yards like giant grasshoppers.[2]

When they reached the main gate—Gate No. 2—part of the crowd wanted to carry on through the gate and out on to the streets, as they had in 1970. 'You know what happened in front of this gate in 1970!' the young leaders cried, and just managed to halt the surge forward by proposing a minute's silence in memory of the December martyrs, and then singing the national anthem. Next they set about forming a strike committee. They were interrupted, however, by the Director of the whole shipyard, Klemens Gniech, a vigorous and not unpopular man, whose presence and authority shook them. When he clambered up on an excavator and promised negotiations, on condition the strikers first went back to work, the crowd began to waver.

At this crucial moment a small, square-shouldered man with a large moustache scrambled up on the excavator behind Gniech. He tapped the Director on the shoulder. 'Remember me?' he said, 'I worked here for ten years, and I still feel I'm a shipyard worker. I have the confidence of the workers here. It's four years since I lost my job . . .'[3] The feisty little electrician was still a popular figure around the yards—many remembered his speech the previous December (see above, p. 34)—and the crowd roared its approval when he declared an occupation-strike. Wałęsa had arranged with Borusewicz and the others to come into the yard about six o'clock. It is not clear why he failed to do so: by his own account it proved impossible to smuggle him in earlier.[4] In the event his arrival at the main gate, after clambering over the twelve-foot-high perimeter wall, possibly saved the strike from collapse.

Under his leadership a strike committee was soon formed, with delegates from most departments of the yard. At the strikers' insistence, the Director's car was dispatched for Pani Ania, and she was brought back in a gleaming, chauffeur-driven limousine, to resounding applause. Negotiations then got under way in the yard's 'Health and Safety' centre, where Wałęsa faced the Director across one of the long tables in the low, neon-lit assembly hall, between a model schooner (of the kind usually seen in yacht clubs) at one end and a statue of Lenin at the other. On the table was a microphone connected to the works radio, so that all negotiations would be broadcast across the yard . . . the strikers insisted on this democratic principle.

By now they had five main demands: the reinstatement of Anna Walentynowicz *and* Lech Wałęsa; a two thousand złoty pay rise; family allowances on a par with those of the police (believed to be much higher); security from reprisals for all the strikers; and, most remarkable of all, a monument to the victims of December 1970. On this last point the workers would not be moved. Gniech explained that the area in front of the main gate was designated for a new works hospital, a new supermarket, and a parking lot . . . the strikers preferred a monument. The management offered a commemorative plaque in the yard's so-called 'Tradition Room' . . . the strikers demanded a monument. One of them exploded:

'We are haggling here over the dead heroes like beggars under a lamp post. You're talking about planning problems . . . people have been waiting for a monument to fifteen thousand Polish soldiers murdered by the Soviet government in Katyń thirty years . . . I beg your pardon, forty years ago. How much longer . . .'[5]

Another seized the microphone and appealed directly to the workers outside: did *they* want the monument?

A huge, sustained cheer rolled in through the windows. Gniech retreated for consultations.

In the late afternoon he returned with news that permission for the monument had been given, in principle, by the 'highest authorities' (another indication that a top-level 'flexible response' had been prepared to counter the expected workers' protests).

If the authorities thought this bold concession would defuse the strike they were soon proved very wrong. For Wałęsa it was an incredible victory, and with a new self-confidence he shouted into the microphone that the strike would go on until all the demands were met—and while they were about it, they had better talk about new trades unions too . . . Instead of going home, appeased, several thousand strikers settled down for the first of many nights they would spend inside the yard (some had already brought in a spare pair of overalls). Pickets were posted on all the gates, and guards at regular intervals around the perimeter wall.

Next day, Friday 15 August, the 'Tri-City'—the Baltic conurbation of Gdańsk, Gdynia and Sopot—became uncannily quiet, as the public-transport workers came out in sympathy. So did the 'Paris Commune' shipyard in Gdynia, with its bitter memories of December 1970 (the strike leader here was a *twenty-year-old* worker sacked from the Lenin yard). Yet the strike committee in the Lenin was nervous and divided. Gniech played a clever hand, after the fashion of the Gierek era, offering differential pay rises. Wałęsa clung to the principle of solidarity (which had been thrashed out in the Free Trades Unions group's secret discussions): 'We all want the same increase,' he said, 'it's two thousand [złotys] for everybody or nothing!'[6] He reiterated the other demands. But the strike committee was swollen by a number of older workers, who were prepared to settle for money.

And, despite all Wałęsa's eloquence, that is what they did. At lunchtime on Saturday 16 August a majority of the expanded strike committee voted to accept the management's offer of a zł. 1,500 rise. Gniech hurried off to announce over the works radio that all employees must leave the yard by six o'clock in the evening.

Wałęsa was meanwhile confronted by furious delegates from other striking factories who, as in Szczecin in January 1971, had converged on the largest shipyard. 'If you abandon us, we'll be lost,' shouted Henryka Krzywonos, the manly figure of a woman who led the bus and tram drivers, 'buses can't face tanks!'[7] Alina Pienkowska, the courageous, pinch-faced nurse from the Free Trades Unions group, and Ewa Ossowska, a 'Young Poland' (RMP) activist, tried to stem the flow of workers out of the gates, but their voices were drowned by the works radio. Some women in the crowd outside the gate spat and jeered at the departing strikers. Wałęsa listened to the protests, smelt the anger and swiftly changed his mind.

If they wanted it, the strike would continue, he said, and now as a *solidarity* strike . . .

For an anxious hour he drove slowly around the yard on an electric trolley, flanked by the statuesque figure of Anna Walentynowicz and the girlish Ewa Ossowska, like some improbable carnival float symbolising The Struggle of the Workers Supported by Virtue and Youth, shouting through a megaphone to make himself heard above the Director's voice over the works radio. Despite his eloquence, there were probably as few as one thousand workers left inside the gates by six o'clock. But the authorities still did not send in the security forces (which were nowhere to be seen in the town centre) and so the strike survived.

This was another turning-point. With hindsight, it looks an almost necessary catharsis, which purged the strike leadership of the timid and those interested mainly in their pay-packets. (With hindsight, Wałęsa would claim he saw this at the time.)[8] In their place came delegates from, initially, some twenty factories in the

Gdańsk area, and more opposition activists from the Young Poland Movement (bringing their guitars) and the fundamentalist ROPCiO (see above, p. 24). In the next twenty-four hours they did two things which lifted the strike into a new dimension.

First, they formed an 'Interfactory Strike Committee' (MKS), comprising two representatives from each striking enterprise, who took their places at one end of the large 'Health and Safety' hall. That evening a typed and duplicated communiqué was handed out from the gates. As the result of an agreement between the work forces of the striking enterprises, it declared, an Interfactory Strike Committee had been formed with its 'seat' in the Gdańsk shipyard. Its purpose was to co-ordinate all the actions and demands of the striking enterprises. A common list of demands would be worked out, and the strike continued until they were met. 'The Interfactory Strike Committee', it went on, with calm self-confidence, 'is empowered to conduct talks with the central authorities.' (N.B. central, not local!) 'After the ending of the strike the Interfactory Strike Committee will not dissolve itself and will control the realisation of the demands as well as organising Free Trades Unions.' Signed by the Interfactory Strike Committee, printed by the 'Free Printers of the Gdynia Shipyard'![9]

If this first communiqué of the MKS was testimony to the cumulative learning process of the opposition in Poland, and the quality of the new strike leaders, (consider the conditions in which it was drafted: the confusion, exhaustion and anxiety), the list of 16 Demands which they produced at the end of a long, sleepless night would be a milestone in the history of the Soviet world. The people directly responsible for this historic breakthrough were the Free Trades Unions activists—Andrzej Gwiazda, his wife Joanna, ('We call her Joan of Arc,' said Cybulski, when he pointed her out to me), Bogdan Lis, Bogdan Borusewicz of KOR—whose ideas were already well formulated; but their proposals were debated, modified and improved by all the delegates, who hastened to add their own particular grievances. By Sunday evening the list had reached its final form, with 21 Demands.

They begin:

(1) Acceptance of Free Trades Unions, independent of the Party and employers in accordance with Convention 87 of the

International Labour Organisation (ILO) concerning trades union freedoms, ratified by the Polish People's Republic (PRL).

(2) Guarantee of the right to strike, and the security of strikers and persons who help them.

(3) Respect for the freedom of speech, print and publication guaranteed by the Constitution of the PRL, and therefore no repression of independent publications and access to the mass media for representatives of all denominations.

(4) a. Restoration of former rights to—
people dismissed from work after the strikes of 1970 and 1976;
students expelled from universities for their convictions
b. Release of all political prisoners (including Edmund Zadrożynski, Jan Kozłowski and Marek Kozłowski)
c. Prohibition of reprisals for beliefs.

(5) Publication in the mass media of the formation of the Interfactory Strike Committee and its demands.

(6) Initiation of real steps to extricate the country from the crisis situation by
a. providing full public information on the socio-economic situation
b. giving all social groups and strata the possibility of participating in discussions on a reform programme.[10]

The drafting hand of the opposition activists is very evident here: in the top priority given to independent trades unions; in the breadth of interests represented—workers, students, prisoners of conscience, believers of *all* denominations; in the scrupulous references to the Constitution and international covenants ratified by the government (cf. the 'Charter of Workers' Rights' in *Robotnik*, above, pp. 26–7); and in the identification of social participation, rather than any revisions *within* the Party-state apparatus, as the key to fundamental reform.

Only after these six general demands does the list move on to the specific, sectional material interests of the Tri-City strikers: payment for the strike period at holiday rates from the funds of the Central Council of Trades Unions (CRZZ); a 2,000 złoty wage rise 'as compensation for the price rises'. Yet even the economic and social points reflect the common grievances of most of the Polish people, indeed of most of the peoples living under Soviet regimes anywhere: food shortages, pricing and distribution inequalities (points 10 to 12), the preferment given to Party members irrespective of their abilities (i.e. *nomenklatura*) and the privileges enjoyed by the Party and security apparatuses (point 13), inadequate pensions (14 and 15), poor medical care (16), insufficient crêche and nursery places for working mothers (17), inadequate maternity leave (18), insufferably long waiting-lists for housing (19), having to work on Saturdays (21). This was far more than a charter of demands for the workers of the Tri-City; it was, at the least, a charter for all Poland.

Comprehensive as the list seems, it is none the less important to note the demands which it did not contain. During the feverish debate on that Saturday night, Tadeusz Szczudłowski, a ROPCiO fundamentalist fresh from serving a three-month prison sentence for organising an unauthorised demonstration on the anniversary of the 3 May 1791 Constitution, proposed to demand the total abolition of censorship. 'You know what happened when they abolished censorship in Czechoslovakia in 1968?' Borusewicz drily asked, and put a line through the proposal. A demand for free elections was similarly rejected—this, too, they were certain the Soviet leadership would not swallow. They did not need anyone to lecture them about the 'geopolitical reality'.

Szczudłowski, however, came up with another proposal which everyone approved. Why not, he said, make a wooden cross to the memory of the December dead and have the local priest dedicate it when he came to say Mass on Sunday morning? The cross was soon put together by a couple of ship's carpenters, but the priest, Father Henryk Jankowski, was reluctant to celebrate Mass on state property, when the strike had been officially ended. Finally, the Bishop of Gdańsk gave his personal blessing to the proposal, after calling up the Gdańsk Party First Secretary, Tadeusz Fiszbach.

So at nine o'clock on the morning of Sunday 17 August, Father Jankowski celebrated Mass at a makeshift altar on a platform inside Gate No. 2. The blue-grey gates were adorned with flowers and a large, framed colour photograph of the Pope. A clear summer sky did service as a *baldachino*. Loudspeakers sent the strikers' prayers booming across the silent town. After Mass, Jankowski blessed the crude wooden cross, which was subsequently set in the waste ground to the left of the gate, in front of some rusty railings. Later, a sheet of paper, decorated with a ribbon in the national colours and a small image of the Madonna, was pinned to the cross. It bore some lines from Byron's 'Giaour', well-known in Poland through the translation by Adam Mickiewicz:

For Freedom's battle once begun,
Bequeath'd by bleeding sire to son,
Though baffled oft is ever won.

But the unknown striker who made this dedication omitted the word 'bleeding'. In this place, of all places, there should be no more bloodshed . . .[11] Where else but in communist Poland would a strike be launched with Holy Mass and lines from Byron?

Moved and strengthened by these ceremonies, hundreds of workers passed back through the gates to rejoin their comrades, so that numbers were soon well over the two thousand mark again. Early on Monday morning, Gniech made one last attempt to regain control, using the works radio (which he controlled from his office) to inform the first shift streaming into the yard shortly before 6 a.m. that the strike had been settled on Saturday, that he, the Director, was in charge of the yard, and that normal working should be resumed.[12] Wałęsa punctured that bubble after two hours of disarray, and the first shift went to work—in the strike. Gniech stayed in his office for the rest of the occupation, like a Captain stranded on the bridge while his ship sailed into battle under the command of the crew.

By the morning of Tuesday 19 August, when I arrived in Gdańsk, the occupied yard was settling into a kind of daily round. A column of commercial vehicles waited amidst the crowd before the gate, each one representing a striking enterprise which had resolved to join the Interfactory Strike Committee (MKS). The new delegates' names were taken by the pickets and then announced over the loudspeakers with elaborate formality—'Pan Tadeusz Kowalski of the Mopot Furniture Factory, Pan Ryszard Kochanowski and Pani Anka Smolar of the Gdynia Metal Bearing Combine'—as the battered vans passed between the two lines of applauding strikers down the short works drive. It had all the pageantry of a court ball: each new arrival was announced with the flourish that might have been accorded by a tail-coated footman to a Count Potocki or a Prince Radziwiłł.

Housewives, students and private farmers from the surrounding countryside brought baskets and bags of food, as gifts. These were carefully checked by the pickets for alcohol, since one of the first resolutions of the MKS on Sunday morning had been to ban all alcohol from the yard. (On Monday the municipal authorities of Gdańsk and Gdynia suspended the sale of alcohol in those two cities, following a formal request from the Strike Committee!) All the food was carried, or trundled on carts (so ample were the gifts), to a well-organised 'strike kitchen', where a cheerful team of women piled up a mountain of ham and cheese rolls. Strikers talked to their wives and children through the rusty railings to the left of the gate.

Inside the gate you walked past the grim-looking works hospital and across a patch of grass to reach the large Health and Safety hall. Patients from the hospital strolled around in dressing-gowns, enjoying the early-morning sun. Older shipyard workers, in blue overalls, cloth caps and metal-tipped boots, reclined under the dusty fir-trees, while the 'Young Poland' people strummed folk songs on their guitars. A little later, the loudspeakers would blare out 'We all live in a yellow submarine'. As my dapper Viennese colleague telegraphically remarked, there was a carnival atmosphere.

By now, the three tables running the length of the assembly hall were three-quarters filled with delegates co-opted on to the Interfactory Strike Committee, each pair with a folded paper sign giving the name of their enterprise (at the end of the day, more than 250 enterprises had joined).[13] At the far end, on a low platform, sat the 'Presidium'—the 'board', as it were, of the larger MKS—with some fifteen members. Here was the bowed, ascetic figure of Andrzej Gwiazda and his wife Joanna; here was the 27–year-old Bogdan Lis, a manual worker from the same factory as Gwiazda, slim, black-bearded, intense; here were the statuesque figures of Henryka Krzywonos and Anna Walentynowicz—the Mother Courage of the yard; and here were worker-delegates from the most important factories in the Tri-City, 'elected' by a show of hands on to the Presidium. Here they sat, beneath the Polish flag and the cross. To their left, the statue of the man after whom the yard was named, Lenin, his base a convenient shelf for empty tea mugs.

The tables were littered with duplicated strike announcements (run off by the 'Free Printers of the Shipyard'), copies of *Robotnik* and the Young Poland paper, *Bratniak* (title of the pre-war university student corps), doodle sheets, bottles of mineral water, ashtrays, half-eaten rolls. Amidst the delegates stood a young, bearded man, whose appearance reminded me of the young Marx. In fact, he was the Catholic editor of *Bratniak*. 'Ah, so you're the editor of that,' I heard a worker address him, 'I've been meaning to ask you, when you wrote . . .' It was a reception of which the young Marx could only dream.

At the back of the hall, beside the model schooner, a bank of electronic equipment: the amplifiers and relays which had supplanted the works radio, and a small forest of private cassette recorders. These products of the Gierek boom played an important role in the organisation. Almost every day the delegates returned to their workplaces (where the strike was generally a much less exuberant affair) to report to their mates with a cassette-recording of the day's high spots. In many factories this recording was actually broadcast over the works radio. In the Lenin, I noticed a small group amusing themselves by listening to a tape of Gierek's meeting with the shipyard workers in this very hall in 1971. They would not be fooled so easily this time round!

The hours and days of waiting passed in an orgy of discussion. Workers clustered in small, excited groups from which you caught the words 'democracy!', 'equality!', 'freedom!' and 'shit!'. I remembered being told by someone who witnessed the fall of Saigon how the Viet Cong automatically assumed the heroic postures seen in Soviet films when they rode into town on their tanks to liberate the capital. It was like that here. The workers looked for all the world like extras in an Eisenstein film. The level of the debates varied. I remember one particularly passionate argument about whether a number of chickens should be fattened up for a few days or slaughtered at once. But the strike leaders used the long hours to ram home, again and again, the priorities: *independent* unions, the right to strike, on these two points hung all the rest . . .

The day was given shape by the Mass which was celebrated regularly now at five o'clock in the afternoon, just inside the gate, with the strikers as choir and the crowd outside as congregation.

Then Wałęsa climbed up on a truck, to emerge above the Pope and the flowers at the gate, for his regular evening chat with the supporters. On the ground he could appear a slightly comical figure, always seeming to move slightly too fast and too jerkily, like Charlie Chaplin in an early film run through a modern projector. This faint incongruity was accentuated by the presence of his faithful bodyguard, Henryk Mażul, a bulky, impressive figure with a deeply lined face, thirty years a shipyard worker, and before that a Home Army resistance fighter, who rolled along beside him wherever he went, taking one stride for Wałęsa's three. (They called Mażul, affectionately, 'the gorilla'.) It struck me then that this Chaplinesque quality was one of the keys to Wałęsa's popularity. He was one of them, the personification of the 'little man', a truly representative individual, and he spoke their language, not the Newspeak of the apparatchiks. Every day, in his 'vespers', he recounted in words of one syllable the progress of their struggle with 'the power' (*władza*).

'The power' had not been idle. On Monday afternoon the Gdańsk Provincial Party Committee had held an emergency meeting, attended by Stanisław Kania, the Politburo member responsible for internal security matters. The Gdańsk Party Secretary, Tadeusz Fiszbach, by reputation a pragmatic and relatively clear-sighted man, emphasised the authentic working-class character of the protests and apparently urged a 'political' rather than a police or military solution. The C-in-C of the navy, Admiral Janczyszyn, declared that the armed forces would not do anything which might shake their link with society. (In plain words: his sailors could not be relied on to shoot their brothers in the shipyard.) Kania seems to have come away with his own assessment confirmed: on balance, so far, against the use of force.[14]

That evening Gierek spoke to the nation on television, solemn and bespectacled beneath the white eagle. His tone was avuncular. He expressed his sympathy with people tired of shortages, admitted 'errors' in the execution of economic policy, threatened a little—the political system could not be changed, 'enemies of socialism' would be confounded—promised a little—reform of the existing trades unions (CRZZ)—exhorted the strikers to go back to work for the good of the nation. The old mixture; but this time the strikers were quite unmoved. 'That does not concern us,' Wałęsa said simply, 'we have our 21 Demands, we'll talk to a government team... We are waiting for the authorities [*władza*] to come to us.'[15]

In fact a government commission under a Deputy Prime Minister, Tadeusz Pyka, was engaged in a last attempt to 'divide and rule' in the Tri-City. They let it be known that they would negotiate generous settlements with individual workforces who would, as the local radio expressed it, 'distance themselves' from organisations like KOR and the Young Poland Movement.[16] The Lenin yard woke up on Wednesday morning to the alarming news that delegates from seventeen factories, including their powerful neighbours, the Northern and Repair Shipyards, had held separate talks with the Pyka commission the previous evening. Wałęsa dashed off to address the workers of the Repair yard over the boundary fence, but for once he had no audience. Only late that evening did the seventeen return to the MKS. The Pyka negotiations broke down partly because of some petty chicanery on the government side (altering agreements during typing),. partly because Pyka was not empowered to concede enough on the spot, but mainly because the rapid growth of the MKS (more than 300 enterprises by Wednesday evening) and the pressure of public opinion made it impossible for the delegates of the seventeen to settle without being ostracised as blacklegs. It was another victory for solidarity, which finally established the authority of the MKS as the sole, sovereign negotiating body for all the strikers of the Tri-City. (Delegates from the errant Northern and Repair yards were hastily elected on to the Presidium.) Pyka retreated to Warsaw, to be replaced on Thursday 21 August by a more skilful negotiator, Mieczysław Jagielski, the Deputy Prime Minister who had settled the Lublin strike in July.

That day saw a revealing incident in the Lenin hall. At one point in the debates a nervous-looking man in his mid-thirties walked up to the podium and begged attention for a 'historic announcement'. Challenged by the Chairman he identified himself as Ireneusz Leśniak, deputy head of the personnel department. Then he read a ten-minute-long prepared statement, clogged with pathos, concluding in a plangent appeal to Edward Gierek 'who is for us like the Pope' to come to the shipyard as he had in 1971, 'you, Edward Gierek, who alone we trust, because you are to us like a father.' Astonishingly, the delegates crowned this peroration with resounding applause.

Then Anna Walentynowicz, 'Pani Ania', took the microphone: 'I know Mr Leśniak,' she said, 'I know him because he has persecuted me for years—it was he who sacked me two weeks ago...' Suddenly the hall was on its feet, delegates who a moment before had applauded so vigorously now crowded around the white-faced Leśniak on the podium, fists raised, threatening to lynch him. Wałęsa seized the microphone, shouted for calm, and then personally escorted Leśniak through the now silent crowd to the gate.[17]

The incident revealed something disturbing and something fine about the large assembly (more than 600 people) which the MKS had now become. That they could applaud such a speech at all indicated how unclear many delegates still were about their strategy and goals. Yet it was fine to see the restraint and dignity with which, after Wałęsa's intervention, *the provocateur* was complimented out of the yard. One cannot adequately describe the workers' conduct in the Lenin Shipyard (and subsequently in Solidarity) without mentioning the word 'dignity'. Dignity was a value which they both preached and practised, under the gaze of the Pope whose visit had been such a lesson in dignity. It was curious to compare this quiet dignity of simple men with the frantic jostling of the western photographers who now thronged into the yard, their camera snouts almost knocking the wafer out of Wałęsa's hand as he knelt to take communion in the open air.

On Friday 22 August Jagielski finally agreed to open negotiations with the MKS. This marked the beginning of the third and most complex phase of the strike. After the initial three days of confused, fragile occupation-strike, ending in the near-collapse of Saturday afternoon, after a week of solidarity-strike, growing steadily in numbers, organisation and confidence, they had now reached the goal of actual negotiations with the central authorities—who had come to them, as they demanded. Their hand was strengthened by two further developments.

First, their example had been followed by workers in the other industrial strongholds. The Warski Shipyard in Szczecin, with its memories of 1971, had soon become the centre of another Interfactory Strike Committee. (An unsolicited pay rise of 10 per cent, precipitately announced on the first Saturday of the Gdańsk strike, had encouraged rather than pre-empted this action.) Here, 36 Demands were displayed on a large billboard at the gate: a mixture of material and local grievances, points recalled from 1971, and points taken from the reports of the Gdańsk demands broadcast by the Polish Services of Radio Free Europe and the BBC.[18] On Tuesday a third MKS had been formed in the important northern industrial city of Elbląg, representing some 10,000 strikers, and they had sent a delegate to say they would follow the lead of Gdańsk. The Politburo was thus faced with two highly organised regional general strikes, as well as a rash of individual strikes—in Warsaw, in Ursus, in Nowa Huta near Kraków, in Bydgoszcz, in Toruń . . .

Secondly, the Gdańsk leadership had been strengthened by direct support from the intelligentsia. On Thursday a local writer, Lech Bądkowski, and an academic from the Gdańsk Polytechnic had been elected onto the Presidium. (I recall Bądkowski reciting a long, long poem—'about the sea', Cybulski told me—to a rapturous reception in the hall.) Two KOR activists, Konrad Bieliński, who worked for the unofficial publishers Nowa, and a courageous lady lawyer called Ewa Milewicz, had arrived with a car-load of uncensored literature. Bieliński turned his samizdat experience to producing a Strike Information Bulletin, and chose the title *Solidarność* (Solidarity). It was the obvious choice, for as Wałęsa and Gwiazda never tired of repeating, solidarity was the key to success. The first number appeared on Saturday 23 August, in a print-run of about 20,000. Other KOR activists, however, were now placed under 'preventive arrest' in Warsaw.

On Wednesday, the MKS learned from Radio Free Europe about an 'Appeal' addressed both to the authorities and to the striking workers by sixty-four distinguished intellectuals. It urged a solution without bloodshed and 'the freedom of trades union association without outside interference . . . The place of all the progressive intelligentsia in this fight', it declared, 'is on the side of the workers.'[19] On Friday evening two signatoris of the Appeal, Tadeusz Mazowiecki, editor of the liberal Catholic weekly *Więź* (Link) and Bronisław Geremek, an outstanding medievalist, drove to Gdańsk to present it to the strikers. Their arrival on the eve of the first major negotiations could not have been more opportune. We are only workers, Wałęsa told them, these government negotiators are educated men, we need someone to help us . . . and together they sketched out the idea of a 'Commission of Experts' to advise the strike committee and check the small print of any agreement. In the fresh, confident atmosphere on Saturday morning (the hall was alive with people sweeping, dusting, straightening chairs in readiness for the official visitors) the MKS readily agreed to this proposal.

It was an important decision. That morning I had breakfast in Warsaw with the historian Bohdan Cywiński, a bearded, Tolstoyan figure, who developed a striking comparison with the 1905 revolution in Russian Poland. That, too, he explained, was preceded by years of intellectual ferment. Then as now the 'flying university' had brought together various intersecting circles of the intelligentsia. But when the time came, in 1905, the intellectuals were amazed by the scale of the workers' demands, and swept away by their actions. Next day Cywiński was himself swept away—by aeroplane to Gdańsk, to join the Commission of Experts advising the strikers. Rarely can a historian have been proved so soon and so gratifyingly right by history.

The role of these 'experts' was to be controversial. 'Experts' was a misnomer. Few of them had any special expertise in trades union matters. Geremek was the author of an original book on marginal life in early medieval Paris, Cywiński a historian of ideas. Andrzej Wielowieyski was Mazowiecki's colleague at the Warsaw Club of the Catholic Intelligentsia, also a generalist. An independent economist, Waldemar Kuczyński, the economic historian Tadeusz Kowalik, and an attractive but excitable lady sociologist from the 'class of '68', Jadwiga Staniszkis, completed the team under Mazowiecki's chairmanship. They were thus advisers rather than experts, bringing lucid, trained minds to bear on unfamiliar problems, like the ideal British civil servant.

Yet their brief was complex. On the one hand, they were there to advise the strikers and prevent them being tricked (again). On the other hand, they were there to secure a solution without bloodshed, which meant casting the workers' demands in a language which the regime could accept. They were there to sell a deal to the government; but also to make a deal which the government could sell to Moscow. This imminent ambiguity of their position is illustrated by an extraordinary anecdote from their journey to Gdańsk on Sunday morning. They were not allowed to fly with the early plane to Gdańsk. A few hours later, however, they were accompanied to the next flight by a colonel of the secret police (SB), who told them: 'Gentlemen, we hope you will help the Polish People's Republic in this difficult moment . . .'[20]

For the sake of clarity and immediacy I shall describe the events of this last phase of the strike in diary form.

Day Ten: Saturday 23 August

At two o'clock in the afternoon the Provincial Governor* arrives for preliminary talks. Jerzy Kołodziejski, a slim, sensitive-looking man, is led in through the ranks of blue-overalled strikers. They give him a mixed reception: some polite applause but also shouted abuse. Wałęsa treats him with demonstrative courtesy. A small working-party, with the shipyard Director present as an observer, soon agrees that the main negotiations should begin at 8 p.m.[21]

At eight o'clock Jagielski and his team arrive in a coach. As it nudges its way through the crowd before the gate, people drum furiously on the sides and windows. Then the Deputy Prime Minister, pale and tight-lipped, runs the gauntlet of two thousand hostile eyes. On the platform in the main hall he shakes hands punctiliously with all the Presidium, before walking back between the long tables and across a small lobby into the room which will be used for the talks. Here, the two sides will have to sit in low lounge chairs, facing each other across formica tables. The whole wall between this room and the lobby is made of glass, and throughout the proceedings a succession of strikers, supporters and photographers will peer and leer and let off their flashbulbs through the glass wall, like a never-ending crowd of schoolchildren at an aquarium. Worse still, for the government team, every word they say will be relayed by loudspeakers across the yard, and taped by hundreds of cassette-recorders.

*i.e. the *wojewoda* (voivod), senior state official in the *województwo* (voivodship), Poland's basic administrative region. Since a major reform in 1975 there have been 49 *województwa* (voivodships). This is the regional unit for both the Party and the state apparatuses. There are thus 49 voivodship Party First Secretaries and 49 voivods. I use the English term Province for a *województwo* and Provincial Governor for a *wojewoda*.

It will be a play with many parts, and no fewer than three choruses: the delegates in the hall, the workers in the yard and the women before the gate. The reactions of each of the choruses will transmit themselves back to the glass room, sometimes as a murmur of applause, sometimes as silence, pressuring the main actors within. Wałęsa alone will prove a master at playing to all three audiences.

Jagielski has a sharp, ascetic face, thinning hair neatly brushed back, and the diplomat's habit of toying with an unlit cigarette. To his right sits the square-jawed Gdańsk Party First Secretary, Tadeusz Fiszbach, and the schoolmasterly figure of the Provincial Governor. To his left one man stands out by virtue of his grossness. Fat-faced, pot-bellied, grunting as he sinks into the low chair, Zbigniew Zieliński, one of the bosses of Poland's heavy industry, and now a powerful Secretary of the Central Committee, looks like a caricature of a corrupt communist functionary. Directly opposite him sits Andrzej Gwiazda, founding father of the 'Free Trades Unions on the Coast', with the bearded, emaciated face of an El Greco saint, and memories of a lifelong struggle which began in Siberia. These two faces tell the story of two worlds, and two moralities, which now confront each other across the table.

This evening's talks are particularly revealing because the government side has not yet adjusted to this novel equality. Through the western newsmen who cram the lobby, the world is therefore given a glimpse of the way in which a politbureaucratic dictatorship habitually treats its subjects: a very chastened dictatorship, it is true, and uncommonly bold subjects, but old habits still set the tone. Jagielski begins by speaking to the workers as to children. Enunciating slowly and deliberately into the microphone he takes the demands point by point. On point 1 he offers only a new Trades Union Bill and reforms of the old unions. On point 4 he declares: 'On the basis of information given me before my departure, there are no political prisoners in Poland ...' An audible groan from the chorus in the hall—'I received this statement from the Minister of Justice.' Wałęsa leans forward to the microphone: 'Prime Minister, these three cases are known to us and to the public. We know what kind of trials they were ... We attended these trials. I can say straight out because I'm a worker and don't mince words, that they were fixed.' Thunderous applause from the chorus.

A dispute then erupts about telephone links with the rest of the country, which the strikers demand must be restored as a precondition for continuing the talks. Zbigniew Zieliński heaves himself out of his chair, with the air of a man who can settle this little question for once and for all. 'Last night a hurricane passed through Warsaw,' he explains, 'destroying buildings in large areas of the city. I was in Warsaw at the time... You can see whole streets—for instance the avenue from the airport—where huge trees, huge limes, beautiful limes are completely destroyed. The central telephone exchange was completely demolished!' Alina Pieńkowska quietly points out that telephone links were cut last Friday, a week before there was any mention of a storm. Jagielski looks embarrassed at the clumsiness of Zieliński's lies. The delegates in the hall laugh, but there is an edge of bitterness to their laughter. How well they know his sort! Who among them has not faced some provincial Zieliński refusing some commonsense request with the same sort of barefaced lie.

As one striker puts it, in the doggerel verse with which they while away the hours of waiting:

Już od lat są te metody
Zna je stary, zna je młody
Dużo słów, a sensu brak
*Ogłupienia wierny znak.**[22]

Zieliński later emphatically denies that Party officials enjoy any privileges.

Jagielski, however, begins a long exposition of the economic disaster which would follow if the strikers' economic and social demands were to be met. An across-the-board zł. 2,000 pay rise would, he claims, increase the amount which the government has to pay out in wages by 25 per cent. On the subject of the health service he unexpectedly launches into a personal digression about his own suffering under the German occupation: how his father and two brothers were murdered, how his mother went mad after inhuman torture, how he himself was beaten and tortured for a year by the Gestapo... It is a bid to establish

*For years now we've had these methods/Know them of old, know them of new/Many words, but no sense/Surest sign of idiocy.

his credentials as a Polish patriot, but the hall does not respond to the pathos.

By half-past ten it is clear that little substantive progress will be made in this first session. Jagielski indicates that more movement may be possible after tomorrow's plenary meeting of the Party's Central Committee. A short joint communiqué says simply that the two sides have met and presented their positions.

The delegates in the hall are undismayed. Before settling down for the night on a bed of chairs, one stocky packer calmly tells me, in his pidgin English, 'I think tomorrow we change government . . .'

Day Eleven: Sunday 24 August

And the government is changed . . . At the Fourth Plenum of the Central Committee Edward Babiuch, the Prime Minister appointed in February, is offered up, like his predecessor, as a scapegoat. His replacement is called Józef Pińkowski, a name most people hear for the first time. The old trades union boss, Szydlak, the much-hated propaganda chief, Jerzy Łukaszewicz, and one other full Politburo member lose their seats, together with two candidate members—all of them Gierek's men. In their place, the most prominent of Gierek's critics, Stefan Olszowski, is hauled back from banishment as Ambassador in East Berlin (where he had been conspicuous by his absence), while his right-hand man, Tadeusz Grabski, is promoted to Deputy Prime Minister. Gierek apologises publicly to 'those comrades who earlier noticed the accumulation of various irregularities [!], who tried to do something about them, and to whom we did not listen.'[23] He survives as Party leader in name (although according to the Party monthly, *Nowe Drogi*, of October–November, a group under the chairmanship of Stanisław Kania had taken overall control already on 16 August).[24]

Many of the strikers watch the end of the Plenum on television. When the Party men on the screen rise to sing 'The Internationale' the delegates stand up, as if at an inaudible command, to answer them with the national anthem. 'Arise, ye prisoners of want', pipes the box, 'Poland is not yet lost', thunders the hall, and the television is hidden behind a forest of hands raised in the V for Victory sign.

Day Twelve: Monday 25 August

A day of frustrated waiting. In private the Presidium of the MKS meets with the Commission of Experts. Mazowiecki asks if the MKS might be prepared to accept what he calls 'variant B', a fall-back negotiating position settling for major democratisation of the existing trades unions. One after the other, the worker-delegates reject this idea. Unlike some of the delegates in the hall, who applauded Leśniak as if they might once again cry '*Pomożemy!*', the strike leaders know exactly what they want. 'We are even prepared to give up the zł. 2,000 pay rise,' Wałęsa's fellow-electrician Florian Wiśniewski says later, 'but on the question of free trades unions we shall not be moved.'

Later, a war of nerves about the telephone links. In the early evening what they call (adapting communist terminology) a Plenum (i.e. a full session) of the MKS resolves that talks should be resumed with the government commission only when Gdańsk is reconnected with the rest of the country. A few hours later, the Provincial Governor comes back to the yard with news that the lines to Warsaw and Szczecin are working again. He makes no comment on the 'hurricane'.

Day Thirteen: Tuesday 26 August

Shortly before eleven o'clock the Jagielski team are brought in quietly through Gate No. 1, where there is no angry crowd to frighten them. In this second round of talks, Gwiazda, Lis, Wiśniewski and Wałęsa all pound away at the imperative of free trades unions, not only for the Tri-City but for all Poland. Jagielski redoubles his professions of goodwill, but continues to stonewall on the central issue. The frustration of the MKS delegates in the hall is well captured in a sarcastic feuilleton written by Ewa Milewicz of KOR for tomorrow's *Solidarność* (the Strike Information Bulletin). The dialogue they hear through the loudspeakers, writes Milewicz, is 'in fact nothing but a double monologue'. 'The more the Deputy Prime Minister protests his sincerity, the more sincere becomes our laughter in the hall.'[25]

What the delegates do not hear through the loudspeakers is the private discussions of the working-group which is set up at the end of the day's public talks, in mid-afternoon. Here the dialogue is real. Lis, Gwiazda and a warehouseman called Kobyliński, together with three of their advisers, Mazowiecki, Kowalik and Staniszkis, face the Provincial Governor, the Minister and Deputy Minister of Engineering, and Professors Rajkiewicz, Jackowiak, and Pajestka (ex-Chairman of the state Planning Commission, dismissed a few months ago for criticising Gierek's economic policy). This meeting is marked, according to the subsequent account by Jadwiga Staniszkis, by 'a peculiar half-relaxed atmosphere and gentle, ironic tones'. The government team proves ready to discuss, in a strictly hypothetical way, what should be done if independent unions are to be created. Staniszkis reports that the government side 'suggested between the lines that they preferred to be forced from below' rather than run the risk of being criticised as Dubček had been criticised in 1968 for 'encouraging from above . . .'[26]

The hall, meanwhile, is mightily encouraged by the news that a fourth Interfactory Strike Committee has been formed in Wrocław, the capital of Lower Silesia. If the miners and the industrial centre of Gierek's old fief, Upper Silesia, come out in solidarity, the regime will have the strongest industrial muscle of Poland against it.

This evening's television news brings carefully selected extracts from a sermon delivered by the Primate at the shrine of the Black Madonna at Jasna Góra (Częstochowa). From these extracts it appears, to the strikers' dismay, that the aged Cardinal Wyszyński is taking the government's side, warning that prolonged strikes could harm the nation. At Gate No. 3 someone adds a short text to the image of the Black Madonna. It reads: 'The Madonna is on strike.' This is a significant pointer to the workers' attitude to the church. The Poles have a remarkable ability to hear what they want to hear from their Church leaders, and disregard the rest. Thus young Poles love and venerate the Pope, but lustfully ignore his teachings on sexual morality. The workers respect the Primate, but cheerfully ignore his warnings against the strike.

Day Fourteen: Wednesday 27 August

The miners are out! The good news comes from Wałbrzych, a major mining centre in Lower Silesia, together with promises of solidarity strikes from other mines if the authorities have not met the 21

Demands by 1 September. The fortieth anniversary of the outbreak of the Second World War—when the Germans opened fire on the Westerplatte, not a mile from here—now looms as a deadline for something like a nationwide general strike.* The Gdańsk MKS alone represents some 500 enterprises today: there is not enough room for all the delegates in the hall, not to mention all the journalists, opposition activists, students and hangers-on.

Behind closed doors, however, the working-group is wrestling over the precise form of words to be used in any (hypothetical) agreement on the first point. The government advisers, grimmer than at the first meeting two days ago, demand a formula by which the new unions will explicitly acknowledge the 'leading role of the Party'—that key ideological formula now written into the Constitution. With this formula, the authorities may hope to persuade their Soviet bloc neighbours, and, most important, Moscow, that these new unions will still be ultimately subordinated to the Party, which is still 'ultimately' the only true representative of the Polish working class . . . Mazowiecki and Kowalik—the former a Catholic, the latter a socialist, but both formed by the political experience of 1956—immediately accept the necessity of this compromise, although they propose the formula 'the leading role of the Party in the state', to emphasise that the Party will not have a leading role inside the unions themselves. Jadwiga Staniszkis, of a younger generation, objects to any such compromise, and declines to join the smaller group deputed to draft it.

Staniszkis also objects to the fact that the proposed compromise, although accepted in principle by the strikers' leaders (the Presidium), is not put to the vote in a full Plenum of the Interfactory Strike Committee. Mazowiecki persuades Wałęsa against this course of action, since an announcement in the hall would be tantamount to an announcement in the world press—and that might prejudice negotiations! In the hall itself, meanwhile, there is already some discontent about the secrecy of the working-group's proceedings. Wałęsa defends this secrecy as a 'tactical manoeuvre'.[28]

*It was officially estimated that *c.* 750,000 workers in some 750 enterprises took part in the August strikes. This is certainly an underestimate.[27]

I notice how skilfully Wałęsa manages this unruly assembly. Whenever the arguments become furious and voices from the floor are raised in anger he summons up the ghosts of General Dąbrowski's Polish legions, whose splendid marching-song is now the national anthem.

'Poland is not yet lost so long as we live . . .' he intones, and all controversy is stilled as everyone rises to their feet, 'March, march Dąbrowski, From Italian soil to Poland . . .' and the roof nearly lifts off, all dissension swept away in this never-failing catharsis, 'Under thy command, We rejoin the nation . . .' and is it of Wałęsa or Dąbrowski that they sing?* It is pure Polish magic. You know the magician has turned it on deliberately, almost cynically. Yet as he sings he is transformed: no longer is he the feisty little electrician in ill-fitting trousers, the sharp talker with many human weaknesses; no longer does his authority derive merely from his patter and repartee; now he stands up straight, head thrown back, arms to his sides, strangely rigid and pink in the face, like a wooden figure by one of the naïve sculptors from the Land of Dobrzyn where he was born.

Day Fifteen: Thursday 28 August

11 a.m. Jagielski returns for the third round of public negotiations. Bądkowski leads off for the strikers on the third point: censorship. The strikers emphasise that their objective is the legal restriction of censorship, not its abolition. At present there is no law at all on censorship, only the arbitrary exercise of power by censors following secret instructions (on the authority of an open-ended decree from 1946). Gwiazda advocates 'instituting a right of appeal against censorship decisions and making a clear public statement of what is, and what is not, permitted. Then it would be known what we may say and what we may not, and we could discuss it.' I like the qualifying 'and we could discuss it'—indicating that the notions of 'may' and 'may not' are strictly relative, not to be dictated by the authorities. Encouragingly, Jagielski opines that in principle he

*After the imposition of martial law people did in fact sing a new version of the national anthem, with Wałęsa's name in the place of Dąbrowski's.

agrees with the strikers on this point—the detailed wording of the agreement can be left to the working-group.

On the fourth point, concerning political prisoners and freedom of conscience, Gwiazda declares, 'This is a matter of the utmost importance. It will determine whether our country can be described as a police state or a democracy. We live in a land where national unity is imposed by the police truncheon . . .' Applause from the hall. 'Finally, we would like to know what guarantees there are, what solid guarantees, that such things will not occur again. On paper our laws are splendid, but the practice is far removed from them.' More applause.

On the question of freedom of worship, Jagielski emphasises the scale of churchgoing in Poland, and, he says, 'Party members also attend . . . Even those in senior positions' (thus do Poland's communist rulers seek legitimacy). Later, Jagielski recalls the Primate's homily and urges the strikers to meditate upon it. But the Presidium has received a formal statement from the Press Bureau of the Episcopate, declaring that the homily was cut and broadcast without permission for propaganda purposes. Uproar in the hall. Wałęsa proposes a break to clear this up, but before the break Jagielski plaintively complains about the ubiquitous western newsmen (at one time there were reported to be fifty television crews in the yard). 'I have never negotiated Polish affairs in front of foreign correspondents,' he says. 'Who are these people . . . are they Polish?' He suggests the western correspondents be expelled, but the Presidium unanimously reject this: the world must be informed of their struggle.

Jagielski, however, does not return after the interval. He has flown to Warsaw.

Solidarność no. 8 appears on the tables with the headline: 'PRIMATE OF POLAND CENSORED!' That Wyszyński was censored is certain. However, his long and somewhat rambling homily—most of it about family life and other unpolitical affairs—had undoubtedly a cautionary tone. This could not be said of the communiqué which the Main Council of the Episcopate issued on the evening of Wyszyński's ill-fated address, and which the editors of *Solidarność* are just preparing to print. With compelling clarity this spells out the 'inalienable rights of the nation': the right to freedom of worship, the right to a decent existence for every family, the right to truth, to bread, to know the complete history of the country, to private property in agriculture, to labour in dignity, to a fair day's wage for a fair day's work, and, finally, to 'autonomous representation'. And then it quotes the Second Vatican Council: 'Among the fundamental rights of the human being is the right of workers to free association in unions which genuinely represent them . . .'[29] The Episcopate's support for the strikers' central demand could hardly be more explicit than that.

It seems to me that this astonishing litany of human rights is a key document. If you ask, 'What is the ideology of the majority of the strikers?' then a large part of the answer can be found in the consistent propagation by the Polish Catholic Church, since the late 1960s (see above, pp. 22 ff.), of the idea that every human being is endowed with certain fundamental, inalienable rights. Now of course the etymology of human rights is mainly secular, stemming from the Enlightenment. Yet the strange fact is that most Poles received these ideas not from the heirs of the Enlightenment but from their Church and their Pope. To be sure, the ideals of socialism which they were taught at school play a significant part in the thinking of young workers like Cybulski: but millions of young people throughout eastern Europe receive a very similar education, and they do not speak the language of freedom and dignity which is spoken here. A litany of human rights!

Day Sixteen: Friday 29 August

'Do you think the Russians will invade?' How tired they are of being asked that question by foreign journalists! They have lived with the threat of Russian invasion for so many years, as mountain peoples live with the threat of avalanche, and here are these garish tourists with their cameras and microphones, thrilling at the prospect of tragedy. Like good mountaineers they have taken precautions. They have not gone on to the streets. They have excised all demands which their own and their neighbours' experience suggest will be unacceptable to Moscow. And only yesterday *Solidarność* no. 8 declared categorically:

> Our demands are intended neither to threaten the foundations of the socialist regime in our country nor its

> position in international relations, and we would not support anyone who wanted to exploit the present circumstances to that end; on the contrary, we would oppose them.[30]

True, this was not an official statement of the MKS, but it is distributed in an edition of some 60,000 copies—and the strikers identify themselves with it.

None the less, today there is a visible undercurrent of anxiety in the yard. Jagielski and his team have not returned—what is happening in Warsaw? Waiting is made easier by the ritual daily round, but it is still just that: waiting. Older delegates remember 1970—the tanks before the gate, the gas, the killing.

As we later learned, the strikers' anxiety was justified. In a heated Politburo meeting, at least one member, Władysław Kruczek, suggested that they should consider declaring a 'state of emergency'. However, the member in charge of internal security, Stanisław Kania, rejected this out of hand. The Defence Minister, General Wojciech Jaruzelski, pointed out that the constitution made no provision for a 'state of emergency,' only for a 'state of war,' and said that under present conditions martial law could not be implemented. At the end of the day, Jagielski and the chief negotiator for Szczecin, Barcikowski, were instructed to negotiate peaceful settlements as fast as possible. For the moment there would be no repetition of 1970. This time, perhaps, Polish workers would not have to die so that one Party leader could be replaced by another.

Day Seventeen: Saturday 30 August

'PROLETARIANS OF ALL FACTORIES—UNITE!'—a large banner is strung above the main gate.

About half-past ten Jagielski finally arrives, by the main gate this time, and cheerfully shakes hands all round. In the glass room Gwiazda reads out the working-group's draft agreement on points 1 and 2, passing rather quickly over the controversial passage about the new unions 'recognising that the PZPR plays the leading role in the state, and not disturbing the established system of international alliances...' Jagielski, with a certain flourish, announces his acceptance of the first point. A roar of applause from the hall:

they have won, after all, they have done the 'impossible'. But Jagielski immediately goes on to draw attention precisely to that controversial passage, observing 'with satisfaction' that the Interfactory Strike Committee was 'unambiguous' on the 'ideological and political profile of these trades unions . . .'

The second point promises not only the 'right to strike' but also the personal security of the strikers and 'persons helping them'. 'Mr Chairman,' the voice of Jagielski comes crisply through the loudspeakers, 'I should like to know before the final signing . . . are the words "persons helping them" necessary at all? Think about it gentlemen . . .' But his voice is drowned by a surge of indignation. Everyone knows that this innocuous phrase covers the opposition activists, more of whom have been arrested in Warsaw in the last few days, and here is Jagielski trying to wheedle his way out of his commitment.

'We accept, we accept . . .' Jagielski cries above the babble. He wants to get this over with. In Szczecin Barcikowski arrived at eight o'clock this morning, and they have almost completed their agreement. After the ceremonial initialling of the first two points, Jagielski suggests that everyone go back to work tomorrow. They can then reach agreement on the other nineteen points at their leisure! No game. He then declares that he must fly to Warsaw for the Fifth Plenum of the Central Committee, to obtain its agreement to the points signed, but will be back at 19.00 hours. 'I'm a farmer,' he jokes, 'and I know from experience that Saturday is a lucky day.' 'Our Lady's Day,' shouts someone from the floor. 'Yes, Our Lady's Day . . . my parents used to start the harvest on a Saturday . . .' Hoots of approval.

Wałęsa smiles and agrees. Then he glances around, senses the discontent and makes one of his lightning reassessments: no, he says, no, we need more time, we want to do this properly, we'll be back at work on Monday. A last admonition from Wałęsa to 'stop the arrests of those KOR people' and the Deputy Prime Minister is on his way.

Jubilation. Wałęsa carried shoulder high to the main gate. '*Sto lat, sto lat* . . .' they sing, 'Let him live for a hundred years . . .', the Polish equivalent of 'For he's a jolly good fellow'. Wałęsa clambering up on an excavator, as he did at the very beginning more than a fortnight ago. A short speech drowned in applause: 'Mr

Deputy Prime Minister has left for Warsaw... to do his—er—business there... we told him: "If you don't come back our next demand will be, 'we want the Prime Minister'!"' It's not true, of course, but they love it. Then everyone dashing about, talking at the tops of their voices, signing each others' leaflets as souvenirs. Someone has somehow managed to produce T-shirts with the word SOLIDARNOŚĆ across the front, in that bright red logo of jumbly letters which will soon be known around the world.

On the Presidium table in the main hall there now stands a model of the planned monument. About one metre high, it shows four* towering silver crosses, symbolising the workers' protests of 1956, 1970, 1976 and 1980, joined to form a square. Each cross bears an anchor, which in Poland symbolises not only the sea but also struggle and redemption—it was the badge of the Home Army during the war. I am told that the designer, an engineer in the shipyards, has been sketching such a monument for years, but all his previous sketches have shown low and brooding constructions. This soaring vertical design, conceived in the last few days, captures the new atmosphere of hope.

Yet as the day wears on, the yard succumbs to increasingly bitter controversy—today of all days. A girl from one of the fundamentalist national opposition groups bursts into the advisers' room, wildly accusing them of betraying the working class. In the hall, delegates start wondering about that political clause. What did Jagielski mean about their 'ideological profile'? Does that mean the new unions are meant to be communist, for Christ's sake! Late in the afternoon the hall has somehow worked itself into a fury. Wałęsa hurries up to the platform. 'Listen,' he says, 'we're going to have our own building, with a large sign over the door saying IN-DE-PEN-DENT SELF-GOV-ER-NING TRADES UNIONS!' The pleonasm, 'independent, self-governing', incidentally, is deliberate, and Wałęsa is the first to grasp the rhetorical force of a pleonasm. His oratory is crude, but effective. The commotion subsides, and Wałęsa is able to call in some lesser actors—professionals, from the 'Theatre of the Coast'—to further soothe strained nerves, with readings from the great Romantic poets, and the strikers' own doggerel, before the Mass and the never-failing catharsis of 'Poland is not yet lost...'

*Subsequently reduced to three.

Wałęsa quietly instructs the pickets to check everyone entering and leaving the hall. From now on only delegates, the press and certain recognised supporters are meant to be allowed in. Those supporters are the subject of a no less bitter controversy. Should the Interfactory Strike Committee insist on the release of all political prisoners, including the detained KOR activists? Ewa Milewicz of KOR insists they should: it is, after all, a point of principle, and one of the 21 Demands. Mazowiecki and several of his colleagues are dismayed. If we get the Agreement, the KOR people will be released anyway, they say; if not, we will all be in prison. The argument is effectively decided by Gwiazda, who says, 'Of course we must get them free.'[31]

Later in the evening it is the even, reedy voice of Gwiazda which cuts through the confusion in the hall to restate the simple truth which the workers have learned since 1956. 'Will the new unions be totally free and independent?' he asks. No written agreement can ensure that. 'Our only guarantee is ourselves . . . we know that hundreds of thousands, millions of people think the same as us. There we have our guarantee . . . We know that the word "Solidarity" will survive . . .' So will Gwiazda's phrase: 'Our only guarantee is ourselves.'

Day Eighteen: Sunday 31 August

9 a.m. You could be forgiven for thinking the Pope has come again. In the same brilliant sunlight, the same vast, excited gentle crowd, and over the loudspeakers the sound of a Mass being celebrated somewhere up there on a platform. In fact the celebrant today is only Father Jankowski, but the Pope is here none the less, in a frame hung with flowers on the gate.

Shortly after eleven the government team returns for the last time: Jagielski, still tight-lipped, the Provincial Governor and pudding-faced Zbigniew Zieliński bringing up the rear. Once again they are led through the lines of shipyard workers, smiling and laughing now. Andrzej Wajda is here with a camera team to make a sequel to his portrait of a Stalinist hero-worker, *Man of Marble*. A striker has suggested the title *Man of Iron*. Was it Cybulski, I wonder.

In the glass room the two sides get briskly down to business.

There is another wrangle about the political prisoners, but then they pass on rapidly through the other seventeen points, reading and initialling the texts which have been agreed by the working-groups over the last few days. They break for lunch, and in the afternoon Andrzej Gwiazda has a secret meeting with Jagielski, to persuade him that the political detainees (including those from KOR) must be released.

When the two teams meet again in the glass room shortly after four, Jagielski reads out a signed pledge: the Prosecutor's Office will reach a decision on these cases by noon tomorrow; no one will be punished for taking part in or aiding the strike.[32]

Wałęsa, uncharacteristically, reads a short prepared statement. 'This is a success for both sides,' it says, diplomatically. Then he speaks from the heart:

> *Kochani!* [a word meaning literally 'beloved'] We return to work on 1 September. We all know what that day reminds us of, of what we think... of the fatherland... of the family which is called Poland... We got all we could in the present situation. And we will achieve the rest, because we now have the most important thing: our IN-DE-PEN-DENT SELF-GOVERNING TRADES UNIONS. That is our guarantee for the future... I declare the strike ended.[33]

Prolonged applause. The two delegations rise to sing the national anthem, Jagielski and Wałęsa facing each other no more than three feet apart across the formica tables.

Proceeding to the hall they assemble for the last time on the platform, between Lenin, the cross and the eagle, for the final signing ceremony. Wałęsa thanks 'the Deputy Prime Minister, and all those in power who refused to allow a settlement by force'. 'There are no winners and no losers,' he repeats, 'no victors and no vanquished... We have settled, as Pole talks to Pole' (*jak Polak z Polakiem*). In his reply, Jagielski picks up the phrase 'as Pole talks to Pole', and concludes, 'I think, and I deeply believe... that we wish to serve as best we can the cause of the people, the cause of our nation, our socialist fatherland—the Polish People's Republic.'[34] The state television cameras whirl. On the news this evening the country will be shown the packed hall enthusiastically applauding the title of the socialist fatherland. But they will also see Lech

Wałęsa signing the Agreement with an outsize plastic ballpoint pen, decorated with a photograph of the Pope.

Then more cheers, more ovations, a vote of thanks to the advisers, a speech of thanks from the advisers, as the gates are thrown open and the workers at last return to their families for one Sunday evening.

It is the end of the beginning.

2. A New Social Contract?

> And it isn't as if only people were talking. Stars and trees meet and converse, flowers talk philosophy at night, stone houses hold meetings. It's like something out of the Gospels, don't you think?
>
> Boris Pasternak, *Dr Zhivago*

Whatever Wałęsa and Jagielski said in public, both knew that the Gdańsk Agreement was in fact a tremendous victory for the workers. Communists as well as Christians, in Poland and in the West, greeted the 'Polish August' as a magnificent blow for human freedom and dignity. Milovan Djilas described it as 'the most significant development in eastern Europe since the Second World War'. Others placed it second only to the October Revolution in the history of the communist world. In eighteen days Poland's workers had blown a huge hole through the Leninist myth that the working class cannot see beyond immediate economic wants, and is therefore doomed to founder in mere economistic *tredyunionizm* until its sights are raised by a communist party. Here the roles had been reversed: the Party clung to economic issues, while the workers raised their own sights to the higher plane of human rights and political participation. It was the beginning of a workers' revolution against a 'Workers' State'.

Now a communist Party-state had conceded the right of independent representation to the working class which the Party itself claimed to represent, and which, according to Marxist theory, was moving inexorably upwards on the escalator of History. An independent trades union would be a far more dangerous element of pluralism than Poland's independent farmers and independent Church. No other Soviet bloc country had such a powerful Church or such a large agricultural private sector, but they all had young working classes. For the first time since 1945 the workers were set fair to become the vanguard, rather than the sporadic precipitator, of political change under communism. Poland seemed at last to be on the way to that *institutional* pluralism which western commentators and political scientists had so long wished on the Soviet system. The Gdańsk Agreement, the Agreement signed the day before in Szczecin, and that signed on 3 September with the miners' MKS in Jastrzębie, came to be known as the 'social accords'. They laid, it was hoped, the foundations for a new social contract.

What, however, were the terms of this new contract between the 'power' and the 'society'?[1] In the Gdańsk text, which the Party daily *Trybuna Ludu* described on 1 September as 'wise and sound', the people were promised a choice of trades unions: they could join the new, self-governing unions 'that would genuinely represent the working class', or the old unions which would continue to exist alongside them. The right to strike was to be guaranteed in a new Trades Unions Act. The new unions for their part agreed to recognise the 'leading role' of the Party 'in the state'—a formulation subtly different from the Constitution, where the Party is enshrined as the 'leading force in the building of socialism'. By specifying *'in the state'* the strikers' advisers meant to stress that the Party had no role at all to play inside the new unions, only in the state around them. In the more cursory Szczecin document it was agreed that the new unions would have a 'socialist character in keeping with the Constitution'. These political formulae were to assume immense symbolic importance.

Jagielski also promised that the new unions would have their own publications. A new Bill defining the limits of censorship, and providing the right of appeal to the Supreme Administrative Court, would be introduced in the *sejm* within three months (i.e. by the end of November 1980). The promises on the question of political prisoners and detainees—the subject of so much acrimonious debate in the Lenin Shipyard—were less precise: cases would be 'referred' and 'examined' within two weeks.

Running through all the agreements was the constant reiteration of the need for more information on which to conduct a genuine public debate about the appalling social and economic problems facing Poland at the end of a low, dishonest decade. 'The government will radically increase the areas of socio-economic information available to society, the trades unions and other social and economic organisations', it was agreed on point 6. The authorities would publish the 'basic principles' of an economic reform within the next few months, and these must include 'radically increased autonomy for enterprises and genuine participation in management by workers' self-government'. Virtually all economists agreed that a large measure of decentralisation (i.e. 'increased autonomy for enterprises') was vital for any economic reform.

Yet the combination of decentralisation and workers' self-government would strike directly at the jobs, powers and perks of the vast and immensely resistant central and local bureaucracy. One year later workers' self-government was to become the spearhead of Solidarity's direct attack on this ruling class. It is ironical that in Gdańsk the phrase was strongly supported by the government side, who hoped thereby to involve the new movement in a kind of co-responsibility for the economy which the workers' leaders were at that time anxious to avoid. They were, they protested, only trade unionists, their job was strictly to defend the interests of their members, no more and no less!

Wages were, of course, not the least of those interests. Gradual increases up to the zł. 2,000 demand were promised, the details to be worked out through individual factories and branches. Some workers were worried by the latter provision, rightly, as later emerged. If the new unions were to be organised on a 'branch' basis—all miners, metalworkers, transport workers, etc. in one unit—as they are so successfully in West Germany, then the clauses made good sense. But because the utterly discredited old unions were organised on this basis, and because of the way in which Solidarity was being born from factory and interfactory strike committees, Wałęsa might have guessed that the new unions would be organised on a regional not a branch basis. This discrepancy proved a source of much discontent, and an invitation to official manipulation.

On the other, specific social and economic demands more or less specific promises were made, from the bold 'Meat supplies to the public will improve by 31 December 1980' (point 10) to the vaguer 'The authorities will present a programme' on kindergartens (point 17), maternity leave (point 18), housing (point 19), etc., with deadlines at the end of November or December 1980. Special prominence was given to the demand for improved health services because, in the confusion of that last weekend, a long detailed appendix on this point was typed into the main text. So this historic document contains such resounding commitments as to 'recognise spinal conditions as an occupational sickness of dentists'! Comic though it sounds this was none the less a symbolic inclusion, for one of the remarkable things about the solidarity-strike was the way in which the industrially strong supported the claims of the industrially weak—a moral component seldom seen in strikes in the West. The MKS similarly tacked on to point 6 a demand for the security of private farming and paths to rural self-government (though an independent self-governing farmers' union was not explicitly suggested).

Another direct attack on the vital interests of the ruling class was contained in the agreement that 'cadres' should be selected on the criteria of 'competence and qualification', not Party allegiance. Moreover, the government promised (most explicitly in Szczecin) that family allowances would be brought up to the level enjoyed by the police and army, again by the end of the year. Finally, the government undertook to present a programme for more work-free Saturdays: and in Jastrzębie another Deputy Prime Minister agreed that *all* Saturdays should be work-free from 1 January 1981.

Such were the promises. But who would keep them? Five days after the Gdańsk Agreement was signed, Gierek fell. On Friday 5 September the *sejm*, ungagged by the workers' example, launched into fast and furious debate on the failings of the Gierek era. Professor Jan Szczepański, a well-known sociologist and critical member of the Establishment, averred that the Gdańsk Agreement was an example of 'good clean organisational methods' which the government should follow. In the late afternoon it was learned that Gierek had been taken to hospital after a heart attack. A Plenum of the Party's Central Committee (the sixth since the February Party Congress) was hastily called for later that night. It lasted just three hours, and at 2 a.m. on Saturday 6 September Poland had a new Party leader.

Stanisław Kania was a short, thick-set man with the broad, slab features of a Slav peasant but the fat and jowl of a functionary who has not lifted a spade in earnest for thirty years. Born the son of a peasant farmer in rural south-east Poland, he had worked his way steadily upward through the Stalinist Polish Youth Union (ZMP) and the central Party *apparat*, reaching the Politburo in 1971, where he soon took over supreme political control of internal security, later adding responsibility for relations with the Church. He was a man of the *apparat, par excellence*, and trusted by it. He promised a newly humble and consultative style of leadership, as had Gierek in 1971 and Gomułka in 1956; he promised a 'return to Leninist norms' and the correction of grave mistakes in the implementation of fundamentally correct policies, as had Gierek and Gomułka before him. It was all faintly reminiscent of a joke current in the late 1970s: 'What is the difference between Gierek and Gomułka?' 'None, only Gierek doesn't know it yet . . .'

Yet of course there were differences now as there had been then. With the good intelligence available to him from the internal security services, Kania seems to have been more closely in touch with the real mood of the country. He was apparently supported by Jagielski and Barcikowski, who had been confronted with that reality at first hand in Gdańsk and Szczecin, and, it seems, by Wojciech Jaruzelski, the powerful though indecisive Defence Minister (see below, pp. 150–1). These appeasers (probably a more precise description than 'moderates') had a strong, but not a dominant position in the Politburo. From what they said, and, more important, from what they did, it does appear that they genuinely sought some kind of political rather than military solution, some *modus vivendi* with the new unions, in the autumn of 1980. This meant that they would do everything in their power to *incorporate* the new unions into the Leninist Party state, as consultative rather than genuinely independent bodies. It meant they would try to give the workers' leaders responsibility without power; to divide and rule among them, and between different socio-economic groups; to isolate and repress the so-called 'anti-socialist elements' (like KOR and KPN). It meant a political *struggle*, this was clear; but still a *political* rather than a military one. It meant persuasion rather than unvarnished coercion. It therefore suggested a cautious and partial implementation of the 'social accords'.

Whatever the wishes of the new Party leader, however, there were immense obstacles to the implementation of the accords. First, the state of the economy made it impossible to meet the material commitments in the time-spans indicated. Only on the demand for lowering retirement age (for men to fifty-five and women to fifty) did the government state frankly in the Gdańsk Agreement that this was 'impossible to fulfil'. But in fact, with National Income shrinking by 5.4 per cent in 1980,[2] and the hard currency debt soaring above the $20 billion mark, a major programme for refurbishing the welfare state simply could not be produced within four months, as the agreement required. Nor could meat supplies be significantly improved by the end of the year, unless the West or the Soviet Union provided the means. As for economic reform, even the Hungarians had taken years to come up with their New Economic Mechanism, and the Poles began in 1980 from a far worse position. As a leading reformist Party journalist, Stefan Bratkowski, observed: 'With the system of economic management that exists in Poland, the Lord Himself would have to hand in his resignation at the end of three months.'[3] Nor was there full and detailed information available even, the Solidarity adviser Tadeusz Kowalik insists, to the top leadership. Such was the system of organised lying and fragmentation inside the economic apparatus, Kowalik argues, that in September 1980 no one, not even Kania, realised just how bad the economic crisis was.

Yet the withholding of economic information from the public was the result of a second and even larger obstacle: the political resistance to appeasement and reform. The resistance to appeasement came, overtly and covertly, from Moscow, Prague and East Berlin, while in the Politburo Stefan Olszowski led a group which pressed for substantial economic reforms to be pushed through by a revitalised, dictatorial Party. While objective constraints meant that the Kania leadership *could* not keep many of its economic promises, this group tried to ensure that the leadership *would* not keep its political promises—for example, on the mass media and censorship. At the same time the proposals for economic reform (some of which Olszowski had backed since the late 1970s) would be fought every inch of the way by that vast, entrenched bureaucracy which, since the Stalinist period, had so successfully resisted every major reform initiative from above. Their massive obstructionism was to be as important as any conspiracy at higher levels. In addition there was the large police and security apparatus, accustomed to manoeuvring between competing masters, and skilled in organising individual acts of repression, or provocations, which might please a particular patron. One should not, therefore, seek consistency where there is none. The appeasers were rarely able to impose a consistent 'line' on the whole apparatus of the Party-state.

This familiar inconsistency did not help Kania to win popular confidence. This was his greatest domestic problem. Most Poles greeted his appointment with indifference: 'Their musical chairs don't mean anything to us!' was a typical reaction. The commodity in shortest supply in Poland was trust, and as more information filtered through about the corruption of the Gierek era—starting with the sacked TV boss, Maciej Szczepański, with his luxury yachts and villas (one allegedly containing a resident harem of four black prostitutes), his hunting holidays in Africa and his London bank account—the supply of trust dwindled even further. 'The most important place today, tomorrow and the day after tomorrow, is taken by the word *credibility*,' the editor of the Warsaw weekly *Polityka*, Mieczysław F. Rakowski, pontificated on 6 September, in his influential column. In the same column just two weeks earlier—on the day Jagielski entered the shipyard—Rakowski himself had still been trumpeting the achievements of the Gierek era in the vainglorious accents of 'success propaganda'.

The Polish people, Bratkowski pithily observed, 'have taken socialism more seriously than the government ruling in its name. The question now is, will the government take the people more seriously, and will the people be able to take the government at all seriously.'[4]

Launching a Civil Crusade

Meanwhile, industrial workers across the country, in the coal mines, the sulphur mines, the steel mills and countless smaller concerns, launched their own local strikes—on the Lenin Shipyard model. Partly this was a point of honour: no one should say that they had not come out in the 'Polish August'! (even if it was actually September). Partly it was a result of the authorities' refusal to make the *nationwide* validity of the 'social accords' explicit. Perhaps the Politburo wanted to be 'forced from below' for the eyes of Moscow. If they also hoped to keep the independent workers' movements divided into disparate regions, however, they were soon disappointed.

On Wednesday 17 September delegates from some thirty-five embryonic independent unions met in the Hotel Morski, the shabby seamen's hotel which now served as the Gdańsk headquarters of the 'Founding Committee of Independent Self-Governing Trades Unions'. Two tough older workers who had led the strike committee in Szczecin, Marian Jurczyk and Stanisław Wądołowski, represented the second industrial stronghold on the coast. The veteran Free Trades Unions activist Kazimierz Świtoń was there for the Upper Silesian capital, Katowice. From Wrocław in Lower Silesia came Karol Modzelewski, co-author with Jacek Kuroń of a famous revisionist 'Open Letter to the Party' in 1964, but for the last few years living in comparative tranquillity as a medievalist (like Geremek). From Warsaw came the 26-year-old Zbigniew Bujak, catapulted into prominence from the Ursus tractor works. And so the roll-call went on, Poznań and Płock, Kraków and Lublin, Łódź, Elbląg, Wałbrzych, Jastrzębie, Opole... all the major industrial centres were represented in that grubby reception room of the Hotel Morski, with the world's press jostling in the corridors outside. Kuroń, too, was there. Soon after being released from prison he had travelled to Gdańsk, where (on 4 September) he was made welcome and issued with a special pass as an official adviser to the union, designed, amongst other things, to deter the security forces from further harassment. The more timid experts, like the authorities, were appalled.

'The review of organisational matters revealed that at the present moment over 3 million people from about 3,500 factories had joined or expressed the wish to join the NSZZ,'[5] the national delegates' meeting proudly declared at the end of its first, cheerfully chaotic debate. Three million in sixteen days!* 'Solidarity' (*Solidarność*) was formally adopted as the name of the new union. A Provisional Co-ordinating Commission was set up, with Gdańsk as its seat, and Lech Wałęsa—to nobody's surprise—duly elected its Chairman. His first task was to ensure the formal, legal registration of the new national union (or, more accurately, federation of unions), along the

*In Poznań I was told that 200,000 people had joined in the first week of September, pouring into the temporary office on... Red Square.

lines already indicated by a Council of State decree dated 13 September. Legal experts were nearly through with the drafting of new 'Statutes', and on Monday 22 September the National Co-ordinating Commission (KKP) met formally for the first time in Gdańsk to approve them. On Wednesday 24 September Wałęsa personally submitted the statutes and the application to the Warsaw Provincial Court in the course of a triumphal visit to the capital. The court employees, like almost everybody else he met that day—with the exception of the Deputy Prime Minister Jagielski and the Unknown Soldier—cheered him to the echo. So far so good.

Meanwhile, the young workers' leaders who had 'emerged' from strikes across the country began the herculean task of building completely new trades unions on no foundations except massive popular support. These local struggles were often overlooked in the breakneck development of the national drama, but they were crucial. In many regions the resistance of the local authorities was considerable. The new unions were granted only the most peripheral and squalid premises, they were refused cars, telephones, telex machines and funds. They had to fight, with the only weapon they had—the threat of strike action—to wrest anything from the hands of the old unions. This initial struggle was formative. In many regions the fragile goodwill of that last Sunday in Gdańsk never developed.

The structure of Solidarity also emerged from the organisation of the summer strikes. Factory strike committees became Solidarity's Factory Commissions (KZ). Where there were regional Interfactory Strike Committees (MKS) these became Solidarity's Interfactory Founding Committees (MKZ),* and other regions followed suit, establishing their own MKZs in a somewhat haphazard process of geographical self-definition. The third and highest level of decision-making, the National Co-ordinating Commission (KKP), was made up of delegates from the MKZs. As its name suggests, it was empowered only to co-ordinate the regional committees. This federal structure was in part a conscious answer to the 'branch' structure of the old unions, which had been exploited in the

*Confusingly, in Szczecin and one or two other regions the regional body was called the Interfactory Workers' Commission (MKR). I have used the abbreviation MKZ throughout, for clarity.

Gierek version of 'divide and rule'. But the stress on regional autonomy recalled earlier Polish traditions, like the *sejmiki* or 'little parliaments' of the Noble Democracy (see above, p. 4). Indeed, Solidarity's regions tended to follow older, historical boundaries, rather than the artificial lines of Gierek's new Provinces.

Though not themselves initially elected, most local leaders manifested an almost fanatical commitment to democracy—as pure as it was amateur, for of course they had no personal experience of democratic politics. In Szczecin the new union managed to organise an election as early as the second week of October, and the local Solidarity bulletin testifies to the intense excitement it generated. Moreover, they wished their elected representatives to function in the first place as defenders of the workers' interests in the work-place. Andrzej Gwiazda spelt things out with painstaking simplicity. People should not vote for 'Franek or Gienek' but for a programme

> . . . that protective clothing should always be provided, for example, or that proper cupboards should be fitted in the changing-rooms. And after six months people can say to Franek: 'What's happened about the cupboards then? You made a promise and we voted for you so that you would sort out the cupboards. But you haven't done anything, you creep. We're going to get rid of you.'[6]

When Wałęsa declared, 'I am only a trade unionist, I am not interested in politics', this was not solely a tactical disclaimer. In the subsequent months it was easy to forget that the Free Trades Unions activists had been originally concerned with such basic shopfloor problems. But of course they could not remain 'only' trades unionists.

For the flames of protest now spread throughout society, as quickly and irresistibly as they had among the workers. Private farmers launched their proposals for their own 'Independent Self-Governing Trades Unions'. Students were next off the mark, founding an Independent Students' Union (NZS) even before their term began officially on 1 October. Writers, journalists and historians flocked to excited extraordinary meetings of their professional associations where they passed resolutions demanding new officers, new statutes, less censorship, more truth! Film-makers were lectured by Andrzej Wajda on the need for more truth and 'national responsibility' in Polish film. Architects debated the renewal of Polish architecture. Doctors laid bare the sickness of Polish medicine. Economists dissected the even sicker Polish economy. If there had been a Polish association of belly-dancers they would certainly have held an extraordinary meeting, demanded changes in their statutes, less Party interference in the sport, more truth in the reporting of it...

It was as if the spirit of Pentecost had descended on Poland. No one had seen such a loosening of tongues since the 'Polish October' twenty-four years before. This October, though, the Party did not lead the debate: it straggled in the rear. It was through Solidarity that the younger generation rushed to articulate their frustrated aspirations. Solidarity filled that yawning gap between the family and the nation (see above, p. 30–1). Here at last was a secular organisation with which they could identify, and in which they would have a say.

The Hotel Morski, which, with its white railings and flagmasts, looked rather like a small ocean-liner, was both flagship and icebreaker of the movement. Although many more new 'Independent Self-Governing' organisations would be founded in the main union's wake, and old organisations democratically rejuvenated, it was the national leaders of Solidarity who bore the brunt of political responsibility. Because of their basic philosophy of solidarity between all social groups ('social self-defence'), they could not ignore the chorus of demands which rose behind them from every sector of the community.

> The... ideal should not be a trades union secretary, but *a tribune of the people*, able to react to every manifestation of tyranny and oppression, no matter where it takes place, no matter what class or stratum of the people it affects...

Did the Provincial Governor of Gdańsk have Lenin's definition in mind when he remarked of Lech Wałęsa, 'he is most certainly a tribune of the people'?[7] Certainly this is what Wałęsa swiftly became, almost willy-nilly, as every individual, association, stratum and profession turned with their grievances to Solidarity.

Talking to Wałęsa or Gwiazda in their tiny corner-rooms in the Hotel Morski—converted bedrooms, still with the rickety beds and washbasins—it was clear that they felt the pressure of popular expectations building up behind them, like steam in the liner's boiler. This was dramatically revealed in one public opinion poll. Whereas in July 1980 just 22 per cent of the sample believed that living standards would improve in the foreseeable future, on 2 September the percentage shot up to 70 per cent.[8] 'You see, they expect miracles of Solidarity,' one of Wałęsa's new advisers, the sociologist Andrzej Celiński, told me.

Already in October 1980, if one was asked, 'What is Solidarity?', one could not accurately reply 'a new trades union'. It was, at the very least, a massive and unique new social movement, a movement which was perhaps best described as a 'civil crusade for national regeneration'.

The Registration Crisis

At its second Monday meeting, on 29 September, Solidarity's National Co-ordinating Commission (KKP) resolved to call a 'nationwide warning and solidarity strike' for 3 October, because the authorities were 'not fully implementing' the summer accords. It had been agreed that negotiated wage rises would be introduced by the end of September: in many areas pay bargaining had not even begun. Though the Mass had been broadcast over state radio for the first time ever eight days before, the union itself had been given no access to the media. Thirdly, the construction of the new unions was being held back by local officials in many regions.

The obstructionism of local officials was confirmed by a commentator on Warsaw Radio, no less:

> Trust is prevented from growing by the news, which spreads like lightning, of difficulties encountered by the new trade unions, of difficulties deliberately exacerbated by people who do not sympathise with these unions ... Such people are not in favour of the new unions because they feel personally threatened.[9]

Such commentaries were a measure of how far the mass media had, in practice, improved in the last month: but Solidarity itself still had no direct access. On wages, clearly an important issue for Solidarity's reputation with its new members, the authorities were hamstrung by the sickness of the economy, quite apart from the tardiness of local apparatchiks and the real difficulty of negotiating on a branch basis with unions organised regionally.

Yet the attractions of a short, sharp strike were overwhelming to most regional delegates in the KKP. It would at once decrease the pressure (from below) on them and increase the pressure (from below) on the authorities. It would give their members who had not struck before a taste of participation and demonstrate the extent of the new union's national support and organisation. Despite the last-minute efforts of Barcikowski, who made another eloquent TV appearance, and Jagielski, who once again flew to Gdańsk to face the Solidarity leaders, these unwritten objectives were brilliantly achieved between noon and one o'clock on Friday 3 October. Across the country workers in selected factories, or in selected departments of larger works, laid down their tools for just one hour as instructed by their local Solidarity committee. In Warsaw the strike was sometimes symbolically represented by one man standing with a national flag at the factory gate. In Łódź all public transport came to a halt. Everywhere, loudspeakers, posters and flysheets brought the public reasons for the strike to the masses.

Next day Stanisław Kania stood up before a shaken Central Committee* to repeat that the August strikes had been genuine working-class protests caused by the grave mistakes of the previous government and Politburo (of which he was a senior member). Today, he went on, gradual but fundamental changes were needed in social and economic policy. The internal functioning of the Party should be democratised. He once again called for an extraordinary Party Congress at an early date. 'The policy of accord and co-operation', he concluded, 'is our country's only chance.'

The stormy debate which followed looked backward rather than forward: it was a reckoning and a bloodletting. Gierek's critics savaged the survivors of the Gierek clique who just nine years before had savaged the survivors of the Gomułka leadership who just fourteen years before . . . *plus ça change,* it seemed. 'The old truth has been confirmed once again,' Tadeusz Grabski fumed; 'nothing is more difficult for ham actors than quitting the stage.'

*It was formally the continuation of the Sixth Plenum, which had been interrupted after his election on 6 September.

'. . . we must cleanse our Party of dishonest, immoral and degenerate people . . .' General Moczar stormed, in the powerful voice which in 1968 had stormed against the Jews: 'We must also free ourselves from slippery and servile people, from sycophants and careerists.'[10] And so it went on, for two days and nights, ending only at 6.25 a.m. on Monday 6 October. Several heads rolled. A general commitment to Party reform was made, but without a deadline for the extraordinary Party Congress which alone might push it through.

Western commentators paid careful attention to these antics and nuances, recording a slight setback to the reformist cause. Most Poles paid little attention. For them, further revelations about the miasmic corruption of the Party in the Gierek era only sapped any residual trust they might have had in the Party leadership. Faced with the show-trial of another scapegoat, Kazimierz Tyrański, an Export-Import company boss officially accused of taking more than half a million dollars in bribes, they murmured, 'Well, if that is what the authorities are *admitting* to . . .' For them, the authorities could no longer regain credibility by brave words. But the next official deed which impinged on public opinion was an act of flagrant bad faith, quite in the *ancien régime* style.

On Friday 24 October Wałęsa arrived at the Warsaw Provincial Court in a sunny mood, a month after he had submitted the Solidarity statutes for registration. The crowd outside applauded, the Solidarity leaders filed into court, Judge Kościelniak declared the union formally registered, several spectators dashed out to give the good news, the crowd outside applauded some more. But inside, the Judge went on to read a new clause which the court unilaterally inserted into Solidarity's statutes, repeating the Gdańsk formula that the union recognised the leading role of the Party in the state and would not threaten Poland's international alliances. Wałęsa was visibly stunned. Recovering his breath, he led his delegation out of court (still moving at his early Chaplin pace), back into the coach and off to the Warsaw Club of the Catholic Intelligentsia (KIK) to debate this grave affront.

By this obvious political manipulation of the lawcourts to present a *fait accompli* the authorities goaded the new union's members throughout the country into fury. As Bronisław Geremek remarked a few days later, 'They have practically invited a general strike against the leading role of the Party!'[11] For, predictably, as angry messages came buzzing in from all the regional committees (MKZs), this is what the union's national leadership was compelled to threaten. Forgotten were all the last fortnight's gestures of goodwill—Solidarity's participation in a Joint Committee to draft the new Trades Unions Bill, Cardinal Wyszyński's meeting with Kania, the second meeting of a Committee for Economic Reform—and forgotten the patriotic unity of the last hours in the Lenin Shipyard.

On Monday 27 October the KKP in high dudgeon demanded that the Prime Minister come in person to negotiate at the Lenin Shipyard by 8 p.m. on Tuesday! Once again Jagielski hopped into an aeroplane for Gdańsk, and on Tuesday he managed to persuade Wałęsa, who then managed to persuade his comrades, that the KKP should instead go to Warsaw for talks on Friday. All over Gdańsk the posters which read 'We demand the registration of Solidarity' now had 'with unchanged statutes' neatly added in black crayon. 12 November was named as the date for a nationwide strike, if the Warsaw talks did not bring satisfaction. On Thursday 30 October, while the Solidarity leaders prepared their negotiating position in the Club of the Catholic Intelligentsia in Warsaw, it was learned that Kania and Pińkowski had flown to Moscow. 'Comrade Brezhnev expressed the confidence of Soviet communists and the working people of the Soviet Union that the communists and working people of fraternal Poland will be able to resolve the acute problems of political and economic development facing them . . .' declared the official communiqué at the end of this lightning visit. This meant, decoding the Newspeak, that Kania currently had the support of the Soviet leadership.

When the Solidarity team arrived at the Council of Ministers building on Friday 31 October they had added the private farmers' demand for an independent union to their own for unchanged statutes, and four other points from the summer agreements: access to the mass media, pay rises, supplies to the shops and an end to 'repressions' against union and opposition activists. When they emerged, after midnight, through a crowd of surly, half-frozen newsmen, they had agreed with the government to abide by a Supreme Court ruling on their appeal against the changes in the statutes, which was due on 10 November, but they had nothing in writing on the other points. At the very last minute the Prime

Minister had refused to sign a joint communiqué drafted by, among others, two of his ministers. (Pińkowski took his orders directly from Kania, according to Bronisław Geremek, who was in the drafting group.) 'What in God's name shall I say to my members,' one Gdańsk delegate exclaimed. Others shared his despair.

As they foresaw, their members were infuriated by this further sign of bad faith. On All Saints Day, Saturday 1 November, while the nation commemorated its dead, preparations began in earnest for a general strike on 12 November. Wałęsa and most of his advisers were less than delighted. Western observers now began to write about 'differences' in the Solidarity leadership and to play the labelling games ('hawks' and 'doves', 'radicals' and 'moderates') that they had so long played with the Politburo. And of course there were differences, as there had been in the shipyard in August. Andrzej Gwiazda, for example, had no doubts at all about the wisdom of the strike... 'and Wałęsa will have to go along if he wants to keep his position,' he said privately. The character of Gwiazda illustrated the problems of transition from persecuted opposition to leadership of a mass movement. Gwiazda was not a natural practitioner of the art of the possible: if he had been, he would never have begun the struggle for what seemed to everyone impossible in the late 1970s. He was a fighter for fundamental principles, with more than a streak of intransigence.

Yet no one who travelled around the country in this week could doubt that Gwiazda was more closely in tune with the mood of the workers than the counsellors of caution. In Gdańsk workers pounded with their fists on the windows of the conference hall where the KKP was meeting, to express their support for the strike call. In Szczecin a meeting of factory delegates voted 780 to 2 in favour of the strike (with 10 abstentions). A straw poll of the hundred largest factories in Warsaw showed just three against. Zbigniew Bujak commented that the regions which had been most cautious before, like Silesia, were now raring to show their mettle in an all-out strike. Everywhere, detailed strike instructions were drawn up, duplicated and distributed: what to take to the factory (sleeping-bag, food), how to react to police provocation, what if the authorities tried to use force? And as Solidarity was denounced in the Czechoslovak and East German press, as Polish television showed threatening film of joint Polish-Soviet military manoeuvres (military attachés said it was old film—there were leaves on the trees!), as a new hardline President, Ronald Reagan, was elected in America, Poland's temperature reached fever-point.

On judgment day, 10 November, a large crowd waited under a snow-filled sky before the grim façade of the Supreme Court. Photographers clung to the iron bars which covered the ground-floor windows, children were hoisted on to parents' shoulders, and an old man scurried through the crowd shouting 'Solidarity today, Soviets tomorrow!'—a play on the ubiquitous posters proclaiming 'Solidarity today, success tomorrow'. At about half-past one the Solidarity team finally emerged from the court and piled into their coach. Wałęsa shook his arms above his head like a footballer. 'We have got everything we wanted,' he shouted through a megaphone from the open side-window, but his words were lost in the commotion on the street below. Then he struck up 'Poland is not yet lost . . .', rocking slightly as the coach pulled slowly away, smiling, his eyes half-closed as if in a dream—a wooden mascot from the Land of Dobrzyn. Only the police refrained from singing with him. When the singing was over I noticed one man turn to his neighbour: 'Well, what *has* happened to the statutes?' he asked.

In fact the Supreme Court had ratified a compromise. Solidarity's appeal was upheld, the offending clauses removed, but instead, the first seven points of the Gdańsk Agreement—including the key phrase recognising the 'leading role of the Party'—were included in an appendix. This was a suggestion made by Solidarity's lawyers when they first appealed against the Provincial Court's ruling a fortnight before. 'No one has lost, it is not a "victory",' Wałęsa later, diplomatically, declared, as he had at the end of the shipyard strike: but once again, the workers and the nation celebrated it as a victory.

First the Solidarity charabanc drove down into town, to the Primate's Palace. There, Cardinal Wyszyński, who had already held Masses for Wałęsa and for the Warsaw region of Solidarity, received the delegation, handing out signed Bibles to pious Catholics and Jewish socialists alike. He reported on his trip to Rome: the Pope, he said, now possessed a large photo album of the Gdańsk strike; the Pope sent his greetings; and he talked about his personal experiences with Christian trades unions in pre-war Poland. Later in the afternoon, they moved on to a typically chaotic press conference in the 'Nowotko' factory on the outskirts of Warsaw. Then, climactically, to a grand gala variety performance in Warsaw's largest theatre.

I was privileged to be among the two thousand people who thronged into the plush interior of the Teatr Wielki that evening. A huge red SOLIDARNOŚĆ logo hung above an otherwise bare stage, like a crucifix over an altar. There were readings from the great Romantic poets and from the works of the exiled Czesław Miłosz, who had thrilled the nation by winning the Nobel Prize for Literature just a few days earlier. There were cabaret turns and skits on the TV news. In the interval Wałęsa scurried through the marble and gilt foyers, pursued by a train of photographers. Beside him his faithful bodyguard, stiffly buttoned up in Sunday suit and tie, rubbed shoulders with Marshal Piłsudski's granddaughter, in jeans and red scarf.

Then back into the auditorium for what was to become Solidarity's theme song. The song was already famous among the *cognoscenti* at Warsaw's best political cabaret, 'Under the Aegis', whose star, Jan Pietrzak, now stood on the empty stage. Its message could not be simpler. *'Żeby Polska była Polską'* ('So that Poland shall be Poland') runs its refrain, and as the audience took up that defiant, lilting melody I felt my own throat involuntarily contracting.

As I tumbled into bed, with a thousand voices still singing in my ear, 'So that Poland shall be Poland', I wondered for a moment how the Solidarity leaders were so sure that the Supreme Court would give them something to celebrate.

The next morning brought clarity. In effect, the compromise had been worked out between the government and Solidarity over the weekend. Top government leaders, including Jagielski, had privately appealed to the intransigent Gwiazda. When the KKP met in closed session on Sunday, only seven delegates voted against the (still hypothetical) deal. So much for the independence of the courts!

Yet it still seems to have been a close-run thing. At ten-thirty on the judgment day most visiting western correspondents were attending a summons to the Passport Office, where they were given twenty-four hours to leave the country. This order was rescinded a few hours later, by an exquisitely embarrassed spokesman for the Foreign Ministry, after the verdict had been made known. On the same day, a state of emergency was declared by the Provincial Governor in Częstochowa: typewriters and duplicating machines were confiscated from Solidarity offices and the local union leaders threatened with arrest. Was this part of a carefully co-ordinated 'war of nerves' right up to the last minute? Or was it rather a product of those deep divisions within the Party leadership? What we know is that Stefan Olszowski, who had a reputation as the Party's leading hard-liner, later claimed responsibility for the expulsion order to foreign journalists, and that the Provincial Governor of Częstochowa was close to Olszowski's tendency.

So That Poland Shall Be Poland

The Registration crisis did great damage. Solidarity's habits of political behaviour were formed in the mass mobilisation of that fortnight. The regions found that organising a strike was one thing they could certainly do well: it brought the people behind them and the government to its knees. Even where co-operation with the local authorities was good, usually because of the attitude of the Party First Secretary, as in Gdańsk and Kraków, union activists were still made militant by the national conflict.

There has been much argument about who in Solidarity was 'radicalised', when, why and to what extent. The argument is only useful if one first defines what one means by 'radicalisation'. For there is a sense in which the overwhelming majority of Polish society, and therefore of Solidarity, was from the start profoundly 'radical'. It is the sense expressed in 'So that Poland shall be Poland'. What did that haunting refrain mean? It meant that the Polish People's Republic in 1980 was *not* 'Poland', because it was bankrupt, sick, undemocratic, yes, but above all because it was not independent. We recall that for nearly two centuries the idea of independent sovereign nation-statehood had been the heart of that value-system which was—exceptionally in Europe—common to all the living generations of Poles. Many of them sung a subtly different version of *'Żeby Polska . . .'* which expressed this sense more clearly. *'Żeby Polska była polska . . .'* they sang, with 'a' (ah) instead of 'ą'; (nasal On) at the end of the line: 'so that Poland shall be *Polish* . . .' Polish, not Russian.*

*Apparently this was Pietrzak's original version, but the censor insisted on the change from 'a' to the less pointed 'ą'.

The day after the judgment was a good occasion to reflect on this aspiration, for it was from 11 November 1918 that Poland dated the restoration of her independence. The inter-war Independence Day had not been officially celebrated since the communists took power, but in the last two years fundamentalist national opposition groups had organised ceremonies before the Tomb of the Unknown Soldier in Victory Square. What we do know about the Unknown Soldier, incidentally, is that he was a Pole who fell fighting against the Russians in the Polish-Soviet war of 1918–20. This year the demonstration was bound to be larger than ever. After Mass in St John's Cathedral in the Old Town the congregation, and the people who had waited patiently outside in the icy wind, moved slowly off down the narrow, cobbled street. Banners and flags were raised, torches lit, and wreath-bearers appeared from nowhere at the head of the procession, which, passing the Royal Castle—reconstructed in Gierek's first bid for popular support—and the Column to Sigismund III, now flowed slowly along Krakowskie Przedmieście, Warsaw's Mall, between the beautiful seventeenth- and eighteenth-century town houses, and then sharp right into the bleak windswept expanse of Victory Square.

Before the Tomb, the white remnant of a colonnade which is all that is left of Marshal Piłsudski's General Staff headquarters, they halted. The crowd, now some ten thousand strong, was mustered into two halves, with a clear swathe down the centre to the Tomb, lined by young men wearing the khaki four-cornered caps of the pre-war army (where did they get them?). Lit by the flaming torches, held aloft against the night sky, the wreath-laying and the speeches began. They spoke of independence, they spoke of the Nazi-Soviet pact, they spoke of Katyń, they spoke of the imprisoned KPN leader, Leszek Moczulski, and then they spoke again of independence. They sang the national anthem, again and again they sang it, taut-faced young men and terrible old women,

> *'What the foreign power has seized from us,*
> *We'll recapture* with the sword . . .'

Suddenly a long-haired young man erupted inside the precincts of the Tomb; beating his head on the wreaths and scratching the flagstones he cried out, incomprehensible, frenzied, horrible. I glanced at my companion, a sensitive British Pole who lived and worked in Warsaw. His face was grey with distaste and foreboding. Then I glanced at the two soldiers who always stand guard at the Tomb. There they were, staring straight ahead into the frenzied crowd. What were they thinking? How would they behave in a crisis? Would they fight a Soviet invasion? Would they fire on a Polish crowd?

Here, before the Tomb of the Unknown Soldier on pre-war Independence Day, one saw the almost unbearable tension at the heart of the Polish Revolution. For Solidarity to limit its demands to those which did not challenge Soviet vital interests required an immense act of national self-denial. Those key political safety clauses—respecting socialist ownership of the means of production, the leading role of the Party, and Poland's international alliances—were, in effect, national self-denying ordinances. They were necessary, the communists were necessary, because otherwise the Russians would invade: that was what the Poles were meant to understand every time their communist politicians talked about the country's *'raison d'état'* (a sly code-phrase for Poland's strictly limited post-war independence). Yet here were Poles who did not see the limits, especially since their communist leaders had cried wolf so often before. Solidarity, with its central commitment to truth and democracy, therefore had to deny its own nature: opposed in principle to all censorship, it had yet to censor its own members. Like Bogdan Borusewicz in that first weekend in the shipyard, it had to remonstrate, '*That* we cannot demand, remember Czechoslovakia in 1968!' Already in November 1980, as regional branches demanded the sacking of named local officials, like the Provincial Governor of Częstochowa, the strain of political self-denial was beginning to show. The sociologist who coined the term 'self-limiting revolution' to describe what was happening in Poland was well aware of the contradiction in terms. Could one think of any European revolution since 1789 which had limited *itself*? 'An evolutionary revolution', as Jacek Kuroń wryly put it? Moreover, even those who knew there were limits did not know exactly where the limits were. The impossible, after all, had already happened.

Just a week later, before the country could take breath or stock, the capital was plunged into another crisis which was to remind everyone of those limits.

Timothy Garton Ash

The Naroźniak Affair

Predictably, Warsaw had rapidly become the centre of one of the most important and militant of Solidarity's regional chapters. It was called 'Mazowsze', that is, Mazovia, the historic name for the flatlands of central Poland, and it already boasted more than half a million members. Their affairs were chaotically administered from one small apartment at 5 Szpitalna Street, in the city centre—the City authorities were not forthcoming with larger accommodation. So an unending stream of visitors flowed through a damp courtyard, up worn wooden stairs to the three crumbling yellow-painted rooms where a crowd of foreign journalists elbowed the patient queues of worker-delegates and Zbigniew Bujak tried to make his voice heard above the polyglot hubbub. In a back-room, Witold Łuczywo, *Robotnik*'s bearded printing boffin, watched over the two battered roneo machines which pounded out material day and night. Every few seconds a long-haired young man would explode into the room with a piece of news, a joke or a glass of tea, and then explode out again carrying a brace of flysheets in his canvas shoulder-bag. Here everyone seemed to live at three times the normal pace.

Mazowsze spilled over into the coffee-house round the corner, where tablefuls of old women looked on approvingly as the excited young activists smoked faster even than they talked. Then you could walk back down Szpitalna Street, past a long shopping queue on the corner—'a *frivolous* queue', as your companion laughingly remarks, for gift-box chocolates—past the statue of Copernicus, to the second hub of Solidarity activity, the Club of the Catholic Intelligentsia. Here, in wood-panelled rooms vaguely reminiscent of a Cunard liner, the Catholic experts sat amidst middle-aged secretaries and pot-plants, tirelessly telephoning in the cause of compromise and occasionally pausing for a quiet grumble at the hotheads of Szpitalna.

As you walked on towards the old town you might see a temporary builder's hoarding plastered with Solidarity and other unofficial posters. 'We call it the Chinese Wall,' a student told me, and led me down into the University courtyard, past the glass-fronted display boards showing a 'Nowa' underground edition of Czesław Miłosz's great dissection of Polish intellectuals' submission to Stalinism, *The Captive Mind*, exhibited with the Rector's tacit consent—unthinkable three months before! Entering the beautiful Kazimierzowski Palace he took me to a table marked 'occupied', where the new independent students' union (NZS), though still unregistered, collected members and planned their own elections at the foot of the Rector's staircase. (Would an English Vice-Chancellor stand for this?) Two thousand of the University's thirteen thousand students had joined in a fortnight, they told me, oh yes, and they had founded a new jazz-band: its name, 'Strajk!'. Shades of Paris '68.

But the most important places to see were the city's largest industrial works, the FSO car factory, for example, the massive 'Huta Warszawa' steelworks or the MZK Public Transport depot. Here you could listen to the anger built up through the Registration crisis, and further fuelled by the surprising and provocative appointment of Stanisław Kociołek, the man widely held responsible for the shootings on the coast in 1970, as the new Party First Secretary for Warsaw. In the public transport depot I talked to the 28-year-old Solidarity leader (i.e. formally Chairman of the Factory Commission—KZ) Wojciech Kamiński. They founded their independent union on 1 September, he told me, and within five weeks they had 5,000 members. Kamiński had the air of a freedom fighter: long, flowing locks, deep-set eyes, moustache, leather jacket, and the characteristic Warsaw mixture of quick wit and quicker temper. He told me his father had been an officer in the Polish army in the West during the war. When he returned home to Stalinist Poland he, like many officers who served in the West, was arrested and imprisoned for three years. For Wojciech Kamiński the communists were his father's gaolers. He was spoiling for a fight.

Into this powder-keg the authorities now dropped a lighted match. On the afternoon of Thursday 20 November a bevy of police tramped up the wooden stairs to Mazowsze headquarters, which they proceeded to search until they found what they were looking for: a document issued to his staff by the Prosecutor General, Lucjan Czubiński, with the cumbersome title 'On the present methods of prosecution of illegal antisocialist activity' and an ominous covering note: 'to be used with care in political and professional work'.[12] This was a surprisingly inaccurate account of the development of political opposition since Kuroń and Modzelewski's 1964 'Open Letter to the Party', and the Prosecutor's somewhat feeble efforts to crush it. Solidarity was angered by the implication that the whole movement was simply an extension of the opposition's 'illegal antisocialist activity' and would be treated accordingly. In the document KOR was inaccurately but revealingly called the 'Committee of Social *Solidarity*'. Plainly the spirit of the 'social accords' had not penetrated to the Prosecutor's Office. Next day, one of Mazowsze's volunteer printers, a young mathematician called Jan Narożniak, was arrested together with one Piotr Sapiełło, a clerk in the Prosecutor's Office accused of passing the secret document to Narożniak.

Mazowsze exploded. That evening the regional Presidium (i.e. the inner cabinet of the MKZ) issued a statement threatening a strike alert if Narożniak was not released, and more: 'At the same time we demand that L. Czubiński's role in violating the law over the last decade be revealed, especially his responsibility for the persecution of the workers in Ursus and Radom after June 1976.' Bujak, himself from Ursus, felt the duty of securing justice against the Prosecutors of 1976 quite personally: this issue was for him and Mazowsze what December 1970 was for Wałęsa and Gdańsk. On Monday, the Prosecutor General's office curtly informed a Solidarity delegation that Narożniak was charged with 'disseminating state secrets'—maximum sentence, five years. That afternoon, the Ursus workers occupied their factory. Next morning Bujak held a press conference. He threatened a regional general strike if the two were not released, and he added five more demands: sanctions against those responsible for the document; an end to the harassment of people 'accused of anti-socialist activities'; an investigation into responsibility for the events of 1970 and 1976; the creation of a parliamentary commission to investigate whether the activities of the Prosecutor's office, the police and the security forces were in conformity with the law; and the reduction of these services' budget!

Down the road in the Club, the more cautious union advisers were appalled. Here was a direct challenge to the whole security apparatus, which clearly went beyond the summer agreements, for the first time. It would stiffen resistance to the Kania political line within the Party, and wherever else the security chiefs could pull strings. Desperately the middlemen of KIK leapt to their telephones in an attempt to find a compromise. Amongst themselves they blamed the dissident activists around Mazowsze, especially those connected with KOR, for this alarming escalation of demands. Certainly the opposition activists were the people most directly threatened by the document and the Narożniak arrest. Certainly they had a hand in drafting the demands. Yet it would be wrong to suggest that they were goading forward a reluctant rank-and-file. In Warsaw, as in Gdańsk, the conduct and privileges of the security forces had long infuriated the workers; in Warsaw, as in Gdańsk, the workers saw where the authorities' attempt to pare away the poisonous 'anti-socialist elements' from the supposedly healthy body of the workers' movement could lead. 'Today Narożniak, tomorrow Wałęsa, the day after tomorrow—you', as a flysheet circulated on Tuesday morning put it.

Meanwhile, the Prosecutor's office defiantly announced the charges which had now been officially preferred against Leszek Moczulski (whose release Solidarity once again demanded). He had 'denigrated the highest authorities of the Polish state by questioning the authenticity of their patriotism and their right to rule', they said. In an interview with *Der Spiegel* he had announced: 'We in the Confederation for an Independent Poland (KPN) do indeed want new political parties . . . which will in the end force the removal of communism from power.'[13] Elsewhere in the country other dangerous fires were still burning. A strike on suburban railway lines in Warsaw and Gdańsk had brought a menacing commentary from *Izvestia* about the threat to Poland's 'defence interests', a commentary which had not been made during the far more serious railway stoppages in July. The low-paid textile-workers of Łódź were striking for more money. But in the southern textile town of Bielsko-Biała, close to the Czech border, the local government headquarters had been occupied by Solidarity members demanding the sacking of all the top local officials. After the successful campaign against the Provincial Governor in Częstochowa, this kind of demand—a frontal challenge to the ruling class—seemed to be spreading.

On Wednesday some twenty Warsaw factories had already come out on strike. In the afternoon a stormy meeting in the Ursus works set the general strike for noon on Thursday, while the steelmen of

Huta Warszawa began to occupy their industrial fortress. The efforts of the mediators became frantic. According to Bernard Guetta of *Le Monde*, Stefan Bratkowski, newly elected Chairman of the Polish Journalists' Association, a moving spirit of DiP and probably the most outspoken reformist Party journalist, finally fixed a compromise in the presence of the top Party leaders in the late evening. He telephoned Gdańsk from the Central Committee building in Warsaw. The phone was answered by . . . Jacek Kuroń, *bête noire* of all official propaganda, and this famous 'radical' proved tireless in the cause of compromise. Did the Party leaders still believe their own propaganda? Guetta wondered. Whatever else passed behind the closed doors of the Central Committee, at about one o'clock in the morning of Thursday 27 November an exhausted Bratkowski was able to deliver Narożniak and Sapiełło in his car to the Ursus works. They were formally released on his personal guarantees, as Warsaw Radio hastened to announce at 2 a.m.

At this point Bujak received a nasty shock from Huta Warszawa. The steelmen had been slowly stoked up into a fury and now declined to end their strike. 'You raised the further five demands,' they said, 'you told us how important they were, now we want answers from the government.' More frantic telephoning. A promise, apparently from Mr Kania no less, that Deputy Prime Minister Jagielski would come to the Huta, as he had come to the shipyard, before noon. With this assurance, the general strike could at last be called off, and the leaders could at last stumble to bed, reassured that they had once again stepped back from the edge of the abyss.

Or so they thought. But on Thursday morning Jagielski refused point-blank to be summoned to Huta Warszawa. Negotiations, he said, could begin in an orderly fashion in a few days' time—*after* the Seventh Plenum of the Central Committee, which was due to open on 1 December. The steelmen were maddened. Bujak hurried out to plead with them, in vain. Lech Wałęsa was flown down from Gdańsk to throw all his eloquence and authority against a continued strike, in vain. Finally, Jacek Kuroń, who by now enjoyed considerable popularity with the workers, was hauled out of bed to help. He talked forcefully of keeping to the Gdańsk Agreement and recognising the 'geopolitical reality'—another code-phrase for the threat of Soviet intervention. Yet even then it was only after the date and details of the promised negotiations had been announced on the late-night news, only after the unfortunate newscaster had been dragged out of bed to produce his actual *text* ('Give us *proofs!*' shouted the steelmen), that the inflamed strikers finally voted to return to work, at 4 a.m. on Friday 28 November.[14]

That weekend the weary Solidarity leaders might congratulate themselves on another victory over the government, and another victory—by the skin of their teeth—for union discipline and self-restraint. The controversial phrase in point 3 of the Gdańsk Agreement which guaranteed the personal security of strikers and 'persons helping them' made a case for saying that the defence of Narożniak was in the spirit of the social contract.

With their other demands, however, Mazowsze had sallied far beyond the bounds of the social accords. By directly attacking the legitimacy, powers and economic position of the judicial/police apparatus they had broken another major taboo and made it all too easy for their enemies to argue that Solidarity was turning into a political party. Probably this was what the people who arranged the arrests hoped they would do. The whole security apparatus now mobilised, politically and professionally (as the Prosecutor had put it), with the added acerbity that always comes from defending your own privileges. The 'Narożniak Affair' was a significant milepost in the internal development of Solidarity, indicating how easily the revolution could run away from its leaders. It was, arguably, an equally significant milepost in the struggle within the Party-state and the resultant (never consistent) behaviour of the authorities towards Solidarity. As the next week's crisis indicated, the allies and patrons of the security apparatus were legion, by no means all agreed with the former security chief Kania, and their strings reached to Moscow.

The Warsaw Pact

Until December 1980 most Polish workers wanted to talk about everything except Soviet threats. Most western journalists, it seemed to the Poles, wanted to talk about nothing else. Indeed, every morsel of Soviet reaction was tirelessly chewed over in the western media. The fact that the Soviet media now prominently reproduced a menacing article from the Czechoslovak Party daily,

Rudé Pravo, comparing the situation in Poland with Czechoslovakia in 1968, rated as highly as the dramatic denouement of the Narożniak affair. In the first days of December, however, the inside and outside worlds came briefly closer together as two new choruses of alarm finally set Polish workers talking, rather than merely thinking, about the danger of a Soviet invasion.

One chorus came from the West. Through the Polish Services of Radio Free Europe and the BBC, people learned of two direct warnings to the Soviet Union from the outgoing Carter administration in Washington, and a trenchant declaration from the EEC summit in Luxemburg. This time the West was not going to be caught napping, as it had been in August 1968. CIA intelligence—together with other NATO and Swedish sources—indicated how far military preparations for a Warsaw Pact intervention had gone: East German, Czechoslovak and Soviet forces were fully mobilised on Poland's frontiers, while military field hospitals had reportedly been prepared in the Ukraine and Byelorussia. The Soviet Union was to be left in no doubt that an armed intervention in Poland would have disastrous consequences for East-West relations, far worse than after the invasions of Czechoslovakia in 1968 and Afghanistan in 1979. 'Détente could not survive another Afghanistan', one of the most powerful advocates of détente, the West German Chancellor, Helmut Schmidt, had already declared. The sustained and, it was hoped, preventive verbal barrage of December 1980 was the first major co-ordinated western response to the Polish crisis. At the same time the Poles were given no reason to believe—as the Hungarians had been given reason to believe in 1956—that the West would give them any military aid against the Russians. The Polish Service of Radio Free Europe was always cautious.

The other chorus came from the Polish authorities. The Seventh Plenum of the Central Committee began on 1 December with a careful, moderate speech from Mr Kania, reaffirming his commitment to the 'socialist character of renewal' and denouncing 'conservatism' (i.e. resistance to 'renewal' inside the Party) as well as 'anarchy'—the latter linked to 'counter-revolutionary' plans and 'centres of imperialist subversion'. It ended with a much tougher, fighting speech, which explicitly singled out and twisted a metaphor used by Kuroń. 'Imagine for a moment', Kuroń had written, 'that our railway system, whose timetables are all determined by a central authority, suddenly had to cope with an influx of trains whose schedules are to be worked out jointly by passengers and railway workers.'[15] This, he went on, was the current position of the Polish political system. Kania commented: 'In such a situation the logical outcome will be a collision between trains travelling according to different timetables . . .' And then the rhetorical twist: 'Who is it who wants to transform the new unions into trains set on a collision course?'[16]

This language still did not prepare the Poles for the unprecedented appeal launched by the Central Committee at the end of its meeting: 'Compatriots! The fate of our people and our country is at stake! The continuing disturbances are bringing our fatherland to the brink of economic and moral destruction . . .' it began, and went on to appeal in equally dramatic terms for the nation to rally round the Party. On the same day, Wednesday 3 December, a body of which most Poles had never heard, the 'Military Council'—sitting, apparently, in the Defence Ministry—announced that the 'situation' could adversely affect the country's defences. On Thursday, a Party spokesman told foreign journalists that if there was a real threat to socialism in Poland then 'Polish communists would have the right and duty to ask for assistance from other socialist countries.'

It is reasonable to assume that the main source of this Polish official alarm—more dramatic than in August—was not the CIA. But we have to admit that we do not know in any detail how and by whom the alarm was transmitted to and from Moscow. The crucial connections of the Soviet-Polish military–political complex are hidden in a black box. Most probably they will remain hidden from historians for generations to come, and they might not be exposed even when Soviet or Polish secret archives are finally opened. The few high-placed Polish defectors have thus far proved less than reliable witnesses. What we can see is many of the inputs and outputs of the black box, and these can be analysed in the light of a great deal of evidence about Soviet perceptions and behaviour since 1945. This informed speculation provides several tentative answers to the question: why the Soviet invasion scare in December 1980?

First, and obviously, the development of Solidarity. The Independent Self-Governing Trades Unions had proved, in three months, to be not merely an ideological anathema, but an anathema with revolutionary momentum. In the Narożniak affair they had directly challenged the security apparatus. General Oliwa, military commander of the Warsaw region, had declared publicly that military production was also threatened: and what did he say privately to his patrons in Moscow? Official propaganda in the Soviet, East German and Czechoslovak press concentrated obsessively on the activities of so-called 'anti-socialist elements', 'counter-revolutionaries', especially from KOR, who had sinister 'links' with 'centres of imperialist subversion' amongst which the Munich-based, American-run Radio Free Europe, the Paris-based Polish émigré monthly *Kultura* and the West German weekly *Der Spiegel* featured prominently alongside the CIA. Of course they could never have publicly admitted, as their Polish comrades had publicly admitted, that Solidarity was a genuine mass working-class protest. The Polish leaders were too weak and divided either to demolish the conspiracy theory or to lock up the supposed conspirators. (Instead, they contented themselves with detaining Moczulski and a few other KPN leaders, thus beginning the transformation of fringe national oppositionists into popular heroes.)

Secondly, the fear of infection. Would not the 'Polish disease' spread to Lithuania and the Ukraine, historically parts of the Polish commonwealth? To Czechoslovakia, seething with anti-Soviet resentment since 1968? To East Germany, even, the front-line of the Warsaw Pact? To Hungary? The answer to these questions was 'No'—at least in the short term. There were, in fact, remarkably few symptoms of 'Polish disease' beyond Poland's frontiers, for a number of reasons which included old anti-Polish prejudices, resentment of the Polish shoppers who had swarmed through the stores of neighbouring capitals, much less unhealthy economic situations and different political cultures. Poles joked that Lwów and Wilno (now inside the Soviet Union) were the only Polish cities not in revolt. In addition, both East Germany and Czechoslovakia had prophylactically closed their frontiers with Poland. None the less, the fraternal leaders were very worried, and perhaps in the longer term with good reason. At present Poland's economic misery deterred neighbouring peoples from following Poland's example. But if Solidarity brought economic recovery as well as democracy and freedom of speech, then neighbouring regimes really would have an example to fear.

Thirdly, the state of the Polish Party. It was the wilful independence of the Dubček leadership and the imminent democratisation of the Czech Party, analysts recalled, which had brought the Russians into Czechoslovakia on the eve of an extraordinary Party Congress like that which Mr Kania had now promised for the early spring. Until now, no one could have seriously accused the Party of leading the movement for reform and renewal in Poland. But now things were beginning to happen inside the Party. At the Seventh Plenum (on 1–3 December) no fewer than four old Politburo hands were eased out, including Andrzej Werblan, an 'anti-Zionist' ideologue from 1968, and Władysław Kruczek, the old trades union boss. Both were known as Moscow's men. The men who replaced them were hardly Czech-style reformers but they were not exactly Moscow's men either: Mieczysław Moczar, returning to the centre of power, was a national communist, with the emphasis on national; Tadeusz Grabski was Olszowski's henchman; Tadeusz Fiszbach (who became a candidate Politburo member) was a leading proponent of a new social contract.

Sophisticated westerners may underestimate the primitive importance to the Brezhnev leadership of having 'their' people, trusties, in the most important Politburo positions. Yet this is illustrated by the remarkable account of a former Czech Politburo member and close associate of Dubček. In Moscow on 26 August 1968, five days after Red Army tanks rolled into Prague, Brezhnev faced Dubček across a table in Moscow. Zdeněk Mlynář reports his tirade:

> 'From the outset, I wanted to help you out against Novotny,' Brezhnev said to Dubček, 'and immediately in January I asked you: Are his people threatening you? Do you want to replace them? Do you want to replace the Minister of the Interior? And the Minister of National Defence? And is there anyone else you want to replace? But you said no, they're good comrades. And then suddenly I hear that you've replaced the Ministers of the Interior, of National Defence, and other Ministers, and that you replaced secretaries of the Central Committee.'...

> Brezhnev was personally and sincerely angered that Dubček had betrayed his trust by not having every step he took approved beforehand in the Kremlin. 'I believed in you, and I stood up for you against the others,' he told Dubček reproachfully. 'Our Sasha is a good comrade, I said. And you disappointed us all so terribly.' At moments like this Brezhnev's voice would quiver with regret and he spoke haltingly, as though he were close to tears. The impression he made was that of a deeply wronged patriarch who fully believed it was entirely natural and proper that his position as head of the family entitled him to the unconditional subservience and obedience of all its members. . .[17]

We do not yet know what passed between Kania and Brezhnev. But we see here quite clearly the horns of Kania's dilemma. If he was to keep the confidence of Moscow, Kania could not behave independently like Dubček. If he was ever to gain the confidence of the Poles, he had to behave more independently than Dubček.

Moreover, this double crisis of confidence was compounded by a third: the Party's crisis of confidence in itself. For a start, the PZPR had shrunk to fewer than three million members as people simply handed in their Party cards. Of those that stayed, more than 700,000 had joined Solidarity, which now counted more than nine million members. Thus, more than a quarter of the Party made up about 7 per cent of Solidarity. Inspired by Solidarity, working-class Party members began to demand a radical democratisation of the Party itself. In the town of Toruń, north-west of Warsaw, workers combined with academics in the university Party organisation (who, like those in Warsaw, had expressed their dissent well before August) to produce first proposals as early as October. Their leader, one Zbigniew Iwanow, was formally expelled from the Party in November, but his local comrades refused to recognise the expulsion. From two factories in Łódź came stinging attacks on the leadership: 'The Dictatorship of the Proletariat must not be Dictatorship against the Proletariat,' they said. They demanded free, secret elections inside the Party, the rotation of offices (no one to serve more than two terms), and an early Party Congress in which to wrest control of the Central Committee from the bloated apparatus. More heretically still, they began to establish 'horizontal' links between themselves, thus defying the basic vertical power principle of Leninist 'democratic centralism'. In the Soviet Leninist model the Party has a pyramidal structure. In theory, suggestions are thrown up in free debate from below, a decision is made at the top, and orders then come down from above, orders as binding as in any army: in theory there is 'diversity in discussion, unity in action'. In practice there are orders from above: centralism defeats democracy. By December 1980 there were reported to be 'horizontal' initiatives in seventeen of the country's forty-nine Provinces.

In sum, the situation in Poland could be, and was, compared to that of Russia in summer 1917. Then the Soviets grew alongside Kerensky's Provisional Government in what Trotsky described as 'Dual Power'. Now Solidarity grew alongside Kania's Soviet-style, Soviet-backed government. The Party leader declared to the Plenum that a state of 'Dual Power' could not be tolerated. Yet it was already there, and Soviet intelligence could see it was there.

On Friday 5 December Poland was startled by the news that there had been a summit meeting of Warsaw Pact leaders in Moscow. The final communiqué declared:

> The participants in the meeting expressed confidence that the Communists, the working class, the working people of fraternal Poland will be able to overcome the present difficulties and will ensure the country's further development along the socialist path. It was repeated that socialist Poland, the Polish United Workers' Party and the Polish people can firmly rely on the fraternal solidarity and support of the members of the Warsaw Pact.[18]

We do not know what private assurances the Polish delegation, which included Stefan Olszowski and General Jaruzelski as well as Mr Kania, gave to secure this conditional vote of confidence. Polish sources later said that the East German State Security Minister, General Erich Mielke, had acted as an unofficial Prosecutor-General at the meeting, putting the case for an armed intervention against the 'counter-revolution' in Poland. East German sources went out of their way to deny this charge: the summit, they hinted, was actually a *substitute* for intervention, a means of exerting the maximum possible psychological pressure on Poland short of physical invasion.

Certainly this pressure was kept up in a chillingly convincing way for at least another week. On Monday 8 December NATO sources in Brussels announced that some half a million Warsaw Pact troops were fully mobilised on Poland's frontiers. The same day TASS carried a completely fabricated report that 'counter-revolutionary groups' in Poland were 'turning to open confrontation' and had 'arbitrarily dismissed the management and disarmed the works guard' at the Iskra works in Kielce. Polish official sources hastened to assure the world that the Iskra works in Kielce were working completely normally . . . The NATO foreign ministers' meeting on 11–12 December was largely taken up with the Polish question and concluded with another fierce warning to the Soviet Union. In fact it was not until just before Christmas that the invasion scare gradually subsided out of the world's headlines, as Mr Valentin Falin, a former Soviet Ambassador to Bonn, told *Der Spiegel* that the Soviet Union 'does not intend to interfere in Polish affairs', by which it was understood that the Soviet Union would continue to interfere massively in Polish affairs, but probably not, for the moment, with its own tanks.

Opinions differ widely on how close the Soviet Union actually came to invading Poland in December 1980. For some, Poland escaped the 'national tragedy' by the narrowest of margins; a 'creeping intervention' may even have begun at some border-points (hence the lurid rumours of troop movements inside Poland at this time); the West's warnings may just have saved her. For others, 'it is arguable whether the Soviet Union was ever really serious about an invasion, the political, military and economic costs of which would have been incalculable.'[19] The former tend to stress the 'Brezhnev doctrine' and the ideological outrage which was Poland in the Solidarity period; the latter, more pragmatic, traditional considerations of vital national (or imperial) interests, such as the security of strategic lines of communication with East Germany, a minimal stability, and the loyalty of the Polish armed forces. Probably both tendencies were represented at the highest level in the Soviet leadership. Mikhail Suslov, the powerful high-priest and guardian of ideological orthodoxy, apparently did plead for a rapid clamp-down in Poland, backed by a strong groundswell of indignation from within the Soviet Communist Party. The military leadership, on the other hand, for whom pragmatic considerations of imperial security are prima facie more important than ideological considerations, probably backed an internal Polish solution, reposing their trust in a man whom they knew extremely well, General Wojciech Jaruzelski, backed by an officer corps which they knew to have been intensively indoctrinated and skilfully purged in the 1960s.[20] The most frequent Soviet leader to Warsaw in 1981 was to be Marshal Kulikov, Commander-in-Chief of the Warsaw Pact.

This, of course, is no more than informed speculation. What can be charted with confidence, however, is the impact of these choruses of alarm on Poland.

Season of Goodwill

The effect was sobering. On the day of the Moscow summit Solidarity's KKP issued a statement pointing out that there were no strikes in Poland and none planned. Five days later it called for a 'social alliance representing wisdom, common sense and responsibility'.* Then the Episcopate came out with an immensely conciliatory communiqué, which the state media hastened to broadcast nationwide. It lauded the 'process of national renewal' (thus adopting the Party word, *'odnowa'*) and warned that the country 'first and foremost, needs internal peace in order to stabilise social life in an atmosphere of rebuilding mutual trust'. On Sunday 14 December prayers were said in all churches for national unity to ensure that 'the institutions of our state remain secure and the sovereignty of our nation is not threatened.' In mid-December a team of sociologists from the Polish Academy of Sciences asked a representative sample of Poles if they believed the 'present socio-political situation' in the country constituted a threat to 'the independence of our state'. 30.6 per cent answered 'yes' and another 17 per cent 'rather yes'.[21]

Faced with the threat of Russian invasion the Poles closed ranks. Like massed bands in a grand tattoo, representatives of all the major forces in the Polish nation came together for the ceremony

*Behind closed doors, however, they discussed what to do in the case of a Soviet invasion. They resolved that everyone should go to their workplace and practise 'passive resistance'.

to commemorate the December Dead in Gdańsk, all apparently marching in step and playing the same tune. On the evening of 16 December the nominal Head of State, Henryk Jabłoński, and the local Party secretary, Tadeusz Fiszbach, stood side by side with the Archbishop of Kraków and Lech Wałęsa, in front of the Lenin Shipyard gates. Through the dark and the drizzle they could discern a crowd of 150,000 people, assembled from all over Poland and controlled by Solidarity stewards. Above their heads towered the most extraordinary contemporary monument in Europe. Glistening in vertical shafts of light, three silver crosses, 140 feet tall, crowned with three anchors, recalled the three main post-war revolts of Poland's workers: 1956, 1970, and 1980. Around its base a crumpled metal relief showed the workers oppressed, then rising up and marching out of the cross, triumphant, under the banner of '*solidarność*'. Behind it, where in August the workers talked with their anxious families through the rusty railings, there now stood a plain, rough-finished concrete wall; in its centre a black tablet with words from the Polish Pope; to the right, set in letters of bronze, two lines from Psalm 29 (translated by Czesław Miłosz):

The Lord will give strength unto his people
The Lord will bless his people with peace.

The orchestra struck up the mournful chords of a 'Lacrimosa' chorale especially composed by Krzysztof Penderecki, the country's best-known living composer. The whole ceremony was designed by Andrzej Wajda. It was, in every symbol, in every word, a dramatic exhortation to national unity. When the chorale was over, the actor Daniel Olbrychski stepped forward. He read out the names of twenty-seven people who the authorities concede died in Gdańsk in December 1970. After every name the huge crowd intoned, 'He is with us.'

Just a year before, Lech Wałęsa had been smuggled to this spot past the noses of the security police. On what was then a squalid patch of industrial wasteland he had sworn that they would return in 1980, each carrying a stone, and build their own monument to the December Dead. The crowd had loved him for it, but no one had quite believed him. Yet here he was, stepping forward with an outsize blowtorch to light the flame in the base of this magnificent martyrs' memorial, and there below him was the Head of State, an admiral, a general, the local Party Secretary, and the Provincial Governor. Afterwards the Party leaders would stand with half-bowed heads and expressions of slight embarrassment while Cardinal Macharski, the Archbishop of Kraków, celebrated a solemn Mass. It was all fantastic, incredible. The spectator tried to imagine a monument in Budapest to the victims of 1956, or in Moscow to the victims of Stalinism.

Wałęsa's speech was quite uncharacteristic. It was an earnest, high-flown appeal for peace, order and responsibility, which clearly betrayed the drafting hand of his parish priest, Father Jankowski (the man who had blessed the original wooden cross outside the shipyard gates on the first Sunday of the August strike). Wałęsa read it, and he read badly. 'I charge you,' he said, 'to keep peace and order, and respect all laws and authorities'—was this really Lech speaking? He referred to the 'Polish People's Republic', the official communist title for the state, which only the government side had used in August. Tadeusz Fiszbach punched the message home: 'The memory of the December events, though painful, should not and must not divide us. It must unite the nation . . . to ensure that such tragedies never occur again. That is why, four months ago, we . . . chose the only correct way of solving the August conflict, the path of agreement.'[22]

Now, as on the last Sunday in August, the gates of the Lenin Shipyard were witness to a celebration of patriotic concord. But this time there was nothing spontaneous about it; this time it was an act of will, a carefully orchestrated public demonstration by the Church, Solidarity and the Party. Official commentators talked busily about a 'Historic Compromise' between these three powers. Many observers (myself included) saw another chance for Poland to begin to cement its new social contract. In the fortnight of national alarm the Church had partially recovered the mediating role (between the nation and the state, society and the authorities) which it seemed to have ceded to Solidarity since August. Perhaps it might enable the Party and Solidarity to find their way back to the common ground of the summer agreements. Wałęsa, Kania and Wyszyński, at least, were committed to seeking some kind of compromise, though their visions of that possible compromise were very different.

Yet all the theatre of Gdańsk could not conceal the fact that compromise was now more difficult to achieve—the nation more alienated from its rulers—than in September. On the side of the authorities, the pressure of the Warsaw Pact had further limited Kania's already narrow room for manoeuvre. In the invasion rumpus it was at first barely noticed that in the first week of December Stefan Olszowski took over supreme political control of the mass media.* His strong arm was soon glimpsed in an official ban on the public showing of *Workers '80*, a remarkable documentary film of the negotiations in Gdańsk, and it would be seen again and again over the next eleven months in the provocative mendacity of the TV news, and the authorities' long-drawn-out refusal to allow Solidarity any direct access to radio or TV, although an opinion poll conducted by state radio and TV researchers themselves showed that 82 per cent of those questioned wished Solidarity to have this access. The broadcasting of Masses was not enough.[23] Olszowski was reliably reported to have been in Moscow before the rest of the Polish delegation. It was now as difficult for Kania to oust him, as it was for the Politburo as a whole to tolerate the democratic ('horizontal') movement at the basis of the Party.

On the side of society, the recalcitrance of local officials, the Registration crisis and the Narożniak Affair had so shaped the perceptions and behaviour of many Solidarity regional chapters that they were no longer prepared to take anything on trust from the authorities. Even as the Poles celebrated *wigilia*, the Polish Christmas which begins when the first star shines on the evening of 24 December, tucking into *barszcz* and imported carp, another confrontation was looming. And all the time, the political conflict was exacerbated and complicated by economic collapse.

Economics

A few unreliable statistics give a rough measure of Poland's economic collapse by the end of 1980. National Income was estimated to have fallen by 5.4 per cent in 1980, on top of a 2.3 per cent fall in 1979, industrial output by 3 per cent and gross

*This was, however, promptly reported by Christopher Bobinski in the *Financial Times*. His reports were an invaluable source of information about Party and state affairs throughout the crisis.

agricultural output by 10.7 per cent. Coal production was some 14 million tons short of the Plan goal, which meant the loss of a potential $600 million in export earnings. According to a Deputy Agriculture Minister, the potato crop was just 26 million tons, as against 50 million tons in 1979. Ten million tons of grain had to be imported at a cost of over $1 billion. The country's western creditors, meeting in Paris, estimated her total hard currency debt at $24–25 billion; her gross financing requirement for 1981 was put at about $10 billion. In short, Poland was broke.[24]

The root causes of this collapse are to be found in the unreformed system, faulty strategy and inept management of the Gierek era. Since the failure of the Babiuch manoeuvre which led directly to the summer strikes, the government had been too crippled by external and internal conflict to come up with any significant economic initiative. Appeasement wage rises had further fuelled the inflationary spiral, so that more money chased even fewer goods. According to the independent economist Waldemar Kuczyński, between July and December 1980 wages increased by 13 per cent, while supplies to the domestic market fell by 2 per cent.[25] Strikes had certainly affected certain key industrial sectors: notably mining and shipbuilding, although it was estimated that just a third of the fall in coal production was due to industrial action. But by far the most important single cause of the continued deterioration was now Poland's dependence on the West.

As well as investing massively in white elephants like the 'Huta Katowice' steelworks and the 'Ursus II' tractor factory, Gierek had spread the dollar jam thinly across the rest of the country's industry, in the interests of 'modernisation' and satisfying the appetites of the managerial apparatus. Consequently, there were few major factories in Poland which did not require at least one input (component, substance, spare part) from the West,* to be paid for in hard currency: the so-called 'valuta portion'. When that currency was not forthcoming the whole production line had to stop, which, in turn, lamed three further factories, and so on. 'Poland's best

*Some of the wants were very simple indeed. According to Tadeusz Kowalik, about half the decline in the potato crop could be ascribed to the lack of pesticides. The chronic shortage of matches in spring 1981 was all for lack of a quantity of glue which ten men with twenty suitcases could have carried into the country.

product is bottlenecks,' Edward Lipiński pithily remarked. What western economists called the 'bottleneck multiplier' now wreaked its vengeance.

To break the vicious spiral, the Polish government sought $3 billion in emergency aid from the United States and some $5 billion from other countries. The outgoing Carter administration temporised, pleading budgetary restraint, the imminent adjournment of Congress, and its own imminent departure from office. Instead, western economic aid came in fits and starts—$670 million from a West German consortium in October, 400,000 tons of EEC surplus food promised in December, bankers lurching from one rescheduling agreement to the next—but not on a scale to halt the downward spiral, not co-ordinated in any significant way (as the diplomatic warnings against Soviet intervention *were* co-ordinated), and without attaching the conditions which just might have catalysed economic reform in Poland.

The domestic political effects of unchecked economic decline were legion. Worsening shortages increased popular frustration and anger. One had to queue for so much now, not merely for meat, but for butter, sugar, potatoes, rice, fruit, not to mention soap or washing powder, starting at five in the morning, and then again after working an eight-hour day, for another three or four hours until supper, the women's pale exhausted faces closed against the icy drizzle. The first words a foreign visitor learned were *'nie ma'*—'we haven't got it'. Since August the consumption of political jokes, like the consumption of alcohol, had dwindled—people had other, better outlets for their political energy and ingenuity—but in the queues they still joked tiredly:

> . . . A guy goes into a butcher's and asks for pork, 'nie ma'; for beef, 'nie ma'; for lamb, 'nie ma'; for veal, 'nie ma'; for chicken, 'nie ma'. Finally, he leaves, defeated. 'He was kind of crazy, wasn't he?' says the butcher's assistant. 'Yeah,' says the butcher, 'but what a memory!'
>
> Or the same recitative, but finally the infuriated customer asks, 'Well, what *do* you have then?' 'Eagle,' says the butcher, pointing to the white plastic national symbol on the wall.

That second joke makes a point which was made more ponderously by the German philosopher Ernst Bloch at the time of the Great Depression. 'Men do not live by bread alone,' said Bloch, '*especially* when they have none.' One response to economic distress was an almost chiliastic hope: people lifted their heads from the hopeless queues and the empty shelves to symbolic, patriotic, and utopian goals—to the cross and the eagle.

Poland had not yet reached the hunger level, although the estimated three million people whose income was below the 'social minimum' (*c.* zł. 2,400 monthly) came close to it.[26] Most city-dwellers could use some of their surplus funds to buy on the flourishing black market—in the 'bazaar' in Warsaw's tough Praga district, for, example, where Russian tourists swopped caviar for Polish jeans, and Poles haggled with Romanians over Czech shoes (it was, they joked, the one place where Comecon really worked). Most country-dwellers could feed themselves. But to be old and poor in a remote country town was misery. Moreover, people's anger was constantly inflamed by further revelations about official corruption and mismanagement. At the Ursus tractor factory, Solidarity compiled a fifty-two-page dossier on the massive piles of equipment rusting away in the snow. Brand-new Rolls-Royce spare parts were found on a scrap-heap. And again, the cry went up for the sacking of those responsible.

If the state of the economy increased the pressure from below on the Solidarity leadership, it simultaneously made the social and economic clauses of the summer agreements more impossible than ever to fulfil. True to its promise on point 6 the government did manage to come up with some suggested 'Basic Foundations of Economic Reform' in January 1981, but, as one might expect from a Commission of five hundred members, the 'project' was a rambling, vague document, a mere anthology of good intentions. In broad outline it followed the suggestions which the best Polish economists had made for the last twenty-five years: there should be decentralisation; enterprises should have more autonomy, but they should be required to be 'self-financing' (Newspeak for 'making a profit'); banks should be reorganised to give credits on a more strictly commercial basis; the tax and price structure should be drastically revised; investment should be stepped up in agriculture, and private farmers should no longer be discriminated against. The issue of workers' control (*samorząd*, literally, 'self-government') was fudged: the workers' self-government should play a far greater role, said the document, but the Director could veto any self-government resolution which might be against the 'social interest'.[27] And who would decide what was the 'social interest'? Why, the Party of course. Meanwhile, a 'small reform' was introduced in the New Year: the independence of enterprises was slightly increased, more funds were earmarked for private agriculture, investment in the white elephants was cut. New Trades Union and Workers' Self-Government Acts should be passed by the end of 1981, said the document.

Solidarity now faced a fundamental dilemma. Throughout the autumn its leaders protested that they wished only to be a trade union, defending their members' interests, no more and no less. 'We will not propose a programme of economic reform,' Bogdan Lis insisted in the Gdańsk union leaders' first interview with the official weekly *Polityka* (apparently the 'censor' in the case of this piece was Stanisław Kania in person) on 1 November 1980. The union should be 'consulted', it would 'control' the actions of the state. In this they were true to KOR's strategy of social self-defence. Jacek Kuroń was particularly insistent that the unions should 'refrain from playing any role in the organs of administration'; they should not be compromised by accepting co-responsibility with the communist authorities. As for workers' self-government, would it not be a nonsense for Solidarity to represent both the employees and the employer? Moreover, official propagandists already insinuated that Solidarity was responsible for the country's economic plight: they must not give any possible credence to these charges.

Yet how could they, as Poles, stand to one side while the Polish economy went down the drain? As the largest social movement in the land by far, a civil crusade for national regeneration, how could they not take responsibility for leading the country out of the economic crisis? Their members expected it of them.

Their economists, now formally working under the aegis of a Solidarity 'Centre for Socio-Professional Studies' (OPSZ) in Warsaw, told them what this would mean. Unless foreign sources came up with economic aid on a massive scale, they would have to support a stringent austerity programme. All the economic improvements in the summer agreements would have to be postponed. Instead, the workers would have to accept those drastic price increases (now in the order of 100 per cent plus) which they had effectively vetoed in 1970, 1976 and 1980. Moreover, the 'rationalisation' of industry would require the relocation of labour, which would mean putting up to one million people out of work, at least temporarily. In October an old Party member went to see the aged Władysław Gomułka, living in disgruntled retirement near Warsaw.'We will have to cut our standard of living by 25 per cent,' said the old puritan: and this time the doyen of independent Polish economists, Professor Edward Lipiński of KOR, and most of his colleagues, could only agree.[28]

In the New Year Solidarity's leaders began to accept that they would have to take some responsibility for an austerity programme to lift the country out of the crisis. But before they did so they wanted full access to all the available information: how much coal was produced? Where was it exported to? Who decided how food was distributed? These were explosive issues. Many Poles believed that the country's economy was bled by the Soviet Union, and food distribution was manipulated by the authorities to favour the army, security forces and party-state apparatus. Local Solidarity bulletins were filled with such stories, and you could not be in the country long without hearing rumours of shiploads of food diverted to Kaliningrad and trainloads of Polish goods bound for Moscow. Nor could the dockers understand why Poland continued to export meat at a time when there was none to be had in the shops. In vain did ministers explain that for every one kilogramme of meat they exported they could buy two kilos from Argentina. But full information the authorities would not give. It was to be another seven months before Solidarity representatives were allowed even partial access to food warehouses and distribution points. What was on offer, so far, was the appearance of participation, as that sly last clause on workers' self-government suggested. In the country, as in the enterprise, there would be all the machinery of consultation, but the Director would have the veto; the Director, not society, would decide what was in society's interest. What was on offer to Solidarity was responsibility without power.

To accept this offer as it stood would have been political suicide. Not to accept responsibility was unthinkable for a movement whose *raison d'être* was national regeneration. Therefore Solidarity leaders were compelled to seek a measure of power over the economy concomitant with the responsibility which they were being asked to take for it. But to seek power *in the state* was what they had resolved not to do, arguing that *this* must be unacceptable to the Russians. For the next year they would wrestle with this contradiction.

3. Inside the Rzeszów Commune: The Peasants Revolt

The peasantry is capable of becoming a wholehearted and most radical adherent of the democratic revolution . . .

V. I. Lenin, *Two Tactics of Social Democracy in the Democratic Revolution*

In the early hours of New Year's Day 1981 the headquarters of the already defunct Provincial Council of Trades Unions (WRZZ) in the south-eastern county town of Rzeszów was outwardly indistinguishable from all the other government buildings around Victory Square, indeed from countless public buildings in countless Victory Squares across the Soviet bloc from Magdeburg to Vladivostok and Gdańsk to Plovdiv. The flattened neo-classicism of the grey concrete façade and the clumsy balustrade around the flat roof* betrayed the imperial style of the Stalinist first decade after the War—what they call in Moscow the 'Repressionist Style'. What the exterior did not betray was the lavish New Year's Ball being enjoyed by communist functionaries within.

On Sunday 2 January a rare distinction was conferred on this establishment. A delegation of workers and peasants occupied it, initially to protest against the high-handed appropriation of the defunct Unions' funds by the local government. Soon, however, a large improvised banner appeared across the grim frontage: 'WE DEMAND THE REGISTRATION OF RURAL SOLIDARITY. The double doors were padlocked. Burly peasants in enormous felt boots and fur coats, identified as Solidarity guards by their red and white armbands, patrolled the snow-covered pavements. From their

*In Gdańsk the roof of the Party headquarters was specially flattened during reconstruction after the December 1970 riots, to facilitate the emergency evacuation of apparatchiks by helicopter. 'Like the American Embassy in Saigon,' an Interpress guide remarked.

precarious perch in a first-floor window loudspeakers broadcast communiqués and songs to the attentive crowd in the square below. Within days farmers arrived from other regions; food was brought in superabundance from the surrounding countryside; and it became clear that the protesters were there to stay.

By now the private farmers' national campaign for their own independent union had acquired some momentum. Activists from the Farmers' Self-Defence Committees had formed a pilot group in the first week of September. Draft statutes for an 'Independent Self-Governing Trades Union—"Rural Solidarity"' had been submitted to the Warsaw Provincial Court by Zdzisław Ostatek, a farmer from Zbrosza Duża, on 24 September, at the same time as Wałęsa submitted those of industrial Solidarity. A Solidarity delegation led by Wałęsa was present at the 22 October court hearing of Rural Solidarity's application, but the judge ruled that private farmers were not entitled to form a trades union since they were self-employed. 'Rural Solidarity' none the less went ahead with an All-Poland founding congress in Warsaw on 14 December, while they appealed against this judgment to the Supreme Court. On 30 December the Supreme Court postponed the appeal hearing on a feeble pretext.

'Rural Solidarity' was plainly going to be one of the major political problems of the New Year. The farmers enjoyed the unequivocal support of Solidarity and the Church. They faced the unequivocal opposition of the Party leadership, strongly backed by Moscow. On 8 January Solidarity's National Commission formally declared its support for the Rzeszów sit-in. Two days later Mr Kania roundly denounced the very idea of an independent farmers' union, in a speech to provincial Party Secretaries which was enthusiastically reproduced by Moscow Radio. Neither was the conflict confined to words. On Monday 12 January, farmers occupying another public building in Ustrzyki Dolne, a remote hill town some 100 kilometres south-east of Rzeszów, were cleared out by force. Photographs of the helmeted, truncheon-wielding riot police (no expense spared on their equipment) soon appeared in Mazowsze headquarters with ironical captions like 'dialogue'. Three days later the Pope, while receiving Wałęsa in Rome, went out of his way to endorse the aspirations of Poland's private farmers. There were some three and a half million of them, and they were now by far the largest unrepresented social force in the land. Moreover, the immediate economic future depended directly on them. Would they produce for the cities this spring? 'Agriculture', Wałęsa had told *Polityka* back in November, 'will be our point of honour.' But only with an officially registered 'Rural Solidarity'...

I arrived in Rzeszów on the eighteenth day of the occupation-strike. For most of the next week I was the only foreign witness of this extraordinary peasants' commune. I have therefore included here a personal diary, at slightly greater length than strict historical proportion might dictate.

Monday 19 January

By hired car from Kraków to Rzeszów, through a frozen, sunlit landscape, on a road which, although it is the main route from Berlin to the Soviet frontier, is not even a dual carriageway. You are constantly risking your neck to pass a horse-drawn wooden cart, a 'furmanka' loaded with timber, or swerving to avoid peasant women driving their gaggles of geese along the hard shoulder. The south-east is economically the most backward corner of Poland. You think, at first glance, that the patchwork-quilt landscape of tiny, fragmented fields must be a remnant of the medieval pattern of land holding. In fact this medieval landscape was created by the communists after the Second World War, when they redistributed over six million hectares of land (in holdings of, on average, five hectares) in a vain attempt to win the allegiance of a solidly conservative, Roman Catholic peasantry. It is these private farmers who are now demanding their own independent organisation—Rural Solidarity. The communist government sowed the wind. It is reaping the whirlwind.

A portly, middle-aged man flags me down. He is a small-time builder, a member neither of Solidarity nor of any political party. 'You know the winter is warmer this year,' he says. 'You see the Red Army is stamping its feet at the frontier and keeping out the wind from Siberia.' That is how the local population treat the threat of Soviet intervention.

Rzeszów is just 70 kilometres from the Soviet frontier. I dread to think what winter is like without the Red Army. At -20°C even the secret policemen—the 'UBeks'—don't stand around for long.

Parking the car down a side street some hundred yards from Victory Square I approach cautiously, stopping to buy a newspaper and glance behind. Across the road a fat man in a clean, white Fiat lowers the copy of *Trybuna Ludu* which he has been reading at the steering wheel, conspicuously inconspicuous. Warsaw friends have warned me that the place is crawling with UBeks. Western journalists have been summarily expelled from Poland after visiting the occupied building for just a few hours. And I have parked right in front of an UBek's nose.

Dismayed, I hasten through the crowd which stands in the snow before the old headquarters. At the door I am stopped by the Solidarity guards, who finger my identification card like some mysterious token. Then they knock and the doors are unlocked from within. Immediately my identity is checked for a second time by two fellows in the dark-blue jackets and peaked caps of Polish State Railways. In the tiny entrance-hall smelling of damp fur coats I am met by a small man who looks like Puck. His Solidarity lapel badge declares him to be the Press Spokesman. After a long wait I am issued with a 'Press Pass' for the 'Occupation-Strike in the building of the WRZZ in Rzeszów'. Very grand, with two rubber stamps of the Rzeszów Interfactory Founding Committee (MKZ) and my name given as 'Tim Garton'. This I have to show to a further railwayman, who peers at it with childlike suspicion before knocking on a second padlocked door; a repeat performance follows; in sum, four identity checks in so many yards.

The Press Spokesman, who turns out to be a historian of ideas from the Catholic University of Lublin, explains that they fear infiltration by *agents provocateurs*. Posters have been seen in the town with the text:

> 1981—Year of Blood and Glory.
> Down with the Party and Socialism.
> signed: Lech Wałęsa & John Paul II.

Well, as Herodotus remarked, my business is to record what people say—but I am by no means bound to believe it.

What hits you first are the smells: stale tobacco smoke and melting snow on pinewood, cabbage soup and six hundred peasant feet, all mingling with the last whiffs of incense from early-morning Mass. The large assembly hall is dominated by an altar, which stands up front in the middle of the stage where a bust of Lenin stood for the last thirty years. Behind the altar the heavy brown stage-curtain is decorated with images of the Pope, on a yellow and white papal flag, and the Black Madonna of Częstochowa, on the red and white national flag. In between them is a six-foot-tall cardboard representation of the Gdańsk monument: the three silver crosses and the three anchors. Beside the flower-decked altar a Christmas tree, complete with tinsel and candle-lights. And where is Lenin now? Slipping behind the curtain I discover a yet more extraordinary scene. Backstage, people are dozing, wrapped in blankets, surrounded by the remnants of that last, before-the-deluge, apparatchiks' beano. The planks are strewn with party streamers. A large expanded polystyrene clock face leans drunkenly against the wall, with the hands stopped at midnight. 'Happy New Year!' proclaims one bedraggled banner, and another, 'We will realise the goals of the Eighth Party Congress'. The strikers seem to have made a special point of trampling on that one. And here at last is Lenin: pushed away into the corner in disgrace with his face to the wall and his papier mâché nose stoved in.

In the Lenin Shipyard the workers left their bust of Lenin on the platform throughout the proceedings. Rzeszów is the peasants' Lenin Shipyard—without Lenin.

Certainly the strike committee sees it that way. They are set on achieving a Gdańsk Agreement for the countryside. Their three-page list of demands has been thrashed out by the strikers themselves, with very little help from intellectuals or 'experts', in a week of intense discussion. It includes, first and foremost, the registration of an Independent Self-Governing Farmers' Union 'Rural Solidarity'. 'Farming', the paper rhetorically declares, 'is after all an ancient trade which is inseparably bound up with the history and survival of the Polish nation and state.' (It was indeed the very survival of the nation which hung on the farmers' choice: to supply the townspeople, or not to supply them.) Far-reaching 'partnership' in government decision-making at the local, regional and central levels is demanded. State-requisitioned land should be returned to private hands. Private ownership and inheritance of property should be guaranteed. Fuel, machinery, building materials and improvement grants should be made available to private farmers and not exclusively channelled to the public sector. There must be free elections to self-governing organisations at the local level. The people responsible for the ruin of the national economy must answer for it by the confiscation of their estate! Bureaucracy must be reduced. The state should not hinder the building of churches. Schoolchildren must not be hindered in their religious observances. They should be allowed to choose freely which language they wish to study: 'English, German, French or Russian' (in that order). By 1982 there should be new history textbooks which tell the truth. And so it goes on—a detailed programme for a peaceful revolution in the Polish countryside. Or for a Restoration?

I talk to a member of the Presidium of the Strike Committee. Czesław Opolski is a small, wiry man in his fifties, with a weatherlined, nut-brown face, thinning hair and twinkling button eyes. He was born on his father's seventeen-hectare private farm in the neighbourhood of Lwów, which became Soviet territory at the end of the Second World War. His father fought in Piłsudski's army against the Russians. Mr Opolski fought first in the Polish army against Hitler's invading armies, then with the Partisans, then with the First Polish Army (organised in Russia) to drive the Germans out of Poland. He remained in the army until 1953. Subsequently, he worked the small five-hectare farm of his parents-in-law in a village near Lublin until, in the early 1960s, he moved to the new industrial centre of Radom so that his children should have decent secondary schooling. He became a so-called 'peasant-worker' with a job in a food-processing factory during the day and some ten hectares to cultivate in his own time. Ten years later much of his land was requisitioned by the state—for the Gierek years saw a renewed drive to collectivise Polish agriculture. In compensation he was given absurd postage-stamp plots of land scattered all over the town. After the June 1976 Radom protests against food price rises, many of his friends were sacked from the factory. Naturally he too went on strike in the summer of 1980.

How does he come to be here? The old face lights up, the hands come up in a cavalier gesture. *'Ale normalnie!'* ('But normally!') he replies, 'I came by train! I'm a Solidarity delegate from Radom. These people need our support. I come here and stay. I can stay here until next Christmas. My wife and friends will look after my farm—what remains of it.'

He talks of the need for free and secret elections, the right to buy and sell and inherit land, to speak out about violations of human rights . . .

But doesn't this mean the end of the communist system?

The face lights up, the hands come up: *'Ale jasne!'* ('But of course!') What idiotic questions these foreigners ask.

Mr Opolski's ideal, it seems, is a seventeen-hectare private farm in the neighbourhood of . . . well, preferably in the neighbourhood of Lwów.

Yet he illustrates in his own person how much has changed in Polish society since his father's day. He is, after all, a worker-peasant. In contemporary Poland, to steal some words from a Stalinist hymn, workers and peasants are one family. The peasant father has a daytime job in the factory. The son is a worker in the shipyards or the tractor factory. Their solidarity is beyond question, a matter of course, all in the family. 'We fed them in August,' remarks a farmer from the Gdańsk region, 'now they will support us.' At this moment someone rushes in with a telex message from the Szczecin Warski Shipyard: they will strike in sympathy if the Rzeszów communards want them to! 'So will we,' the man with a complexion the colour of curry powder says quietly, with authority. He is a miner from Jastrzębie. He speaks for Silesia.

Our conversation is interrupted by the first chant of a Mass. The peasants stand in rows at the front of the assembly-hall, the priest on the stage above them. In worship they are completely natural and unselfconscious, as if it was the most normal thing in the world to celebrate Mass in an occupied communist government building in the heart of the Soviet bloc. In a way all Poland is like this at the moment. From afar it looks like a vast conflagration. You think that panic must be the prevailing emotion. Come to Warsaw and you find excitement, theatre, suffering, tension—but panic, no. In Warsaw people tell you that in Rzeszów things are really burning. So you come to Rzeszów, step inside the burning house, and find . . . the family at prayer, the atmosphere of a village fête, a good vegetable soup on the hob downstairs, and Mr Opolski to shame you with his *'Ale normalnie!'*

'Be not downcast!' the priest admonishes his flock. 'The whole nation is behind you. The disturbance to the economy caused by your strike is nothing compared to the damage it has suffered under the communists since 1945. Right will prevail.' Under the Christmas tree another priest hears the strikers' confessions, though there can be few sins to confess within these walls. The peasants' discipline is perfect. Alcohol is strictly forbidden. There is a collection-box for the two-złoty fines imposed for any use of a swear-word.

The service ends with a deep, slow, spellbinding chant: 'We want God, we want God . . .', the elemental refrain of an old Polish hymn, rising on the first line, falling on the second, 'He is our King, He our Lord', and the peasants' faces—faces from a Breughel painting—speak of a faith as ancient and unmoving as the Beskid hills whence many of them come . . . 'He is our King, He our Lord.'

In the late afternoon we make our way through a blizzard to the small town of Kolbuszowa, where a local historian of the peasants' movement is said to live. Low, badly plastered houses cluster around the small central square with its pollarded trees and the inevitable monument to the Soviet liberators. I have seen few sights more instantly depressing than the dirty, ill-lit, joyless drinking-shop which gives on to this mournful square. Here is no Breughel jollity, no collective singing, no sense of solidarity: just a small crowd of cold, poor people buying a few hours' alcoholic immunity against the cold and the hardship, with the mute passivity of patients in a doctor's waiting-room, before stumbling to their beds.

The historian's ground-floor flat is decorated with enormous cheap pictures of the Virgin Mary, plastic wood, plastic flowers and a plastic Christmas tree. His parents greet us with unaffected warmth. They tell us about the state of the town: how the women queue from two in the morning, in temperatures of -20°C., for butter and meat. Then the grandmother brings in a tray groaning with bread, butter and meat, and, despite our protests, forces us to eat. Our conversation is punctuated by her clucking 'More! More!' and shovelling it on to our plates with clean, knobbly fingers.

Kolbuszowa, it emerges, is a Polish Clochemerle. The town has been dominated by the mayor, the Communist Party Secretary, and the curé. But now, in the wake of the revolution, the mayor is in gaol for corruption, the Party Secretary wants to resign, and nobody can be found to take their jobs. The curé is triumphant.

Little that this helps the peasant-farmers. The area, part of Austrian-ruled Galicia until the First World War, is one of the heartlands of Polish peasant radicalism. The first peasants' political organisation was founded in Rzeszów in 1895. The immensely popular inter-war leader of the Peasant Party, Wincenty Witos, was born in the neighbouring city of Tarnów. In August 1937 the Peasant Party organised a remarkable political strike against the authoritarian national government of the time. They refused to allow agricultural produce to be transported to the towns. At least forty-two people were killed by police. An earlier Polish August with a different, bloody outcome.

At the end of the war the Peasant Party, like the communists, favoured land redistribution. But they proposed a minimum size of twelve hectares, and wherever possible large, effectively modernised private farms. For our local historian this was the great missed opportunity. 'What we are saying now is: the last thirty-five years have been a catastrophe. Let us start again in 1945.'

Tuesday 20 January

There are three classes of road in rural Poland, bad, very bad and impassable. The road to Łowisko is very bad. At one point the remains of a collapsed bus make it impassable. Two wheels and most of the bodywork have been left behind in the snow like a discarded snake skin. *'Polska gospodarka!'* roars Stanisław Krasoń as we negotiate the frozen ditch: 'Polish economy!'

Stanisław Krasoń is a stocky, bright-eyed, vibrant man. A small square badge with the inscription *'Solidarność Wiejska'*—Rural Solidarity—and a larger round one with a colour photograph of the Pope leap out from the lapel of his dirty blue-grey jacket.

Łowisko, his native village, comprises an unmade road, 264 small farmsteads, and a church clothed in scaffolding and snow. The church will be a fine brick building when completed. It is being built, against the passive resistance of the communist local authorities, by the villagers with their own money and their own hands. Proudly, Krasoń points out the vicarage, a four-square red-brick house which was thrown up from foundation to gable one Sunday in an astonishing sixteen hours.

Krasoń's own house, like most others in the village, is made of wood. Its three small rooms are bare, gloomy, dank and low. Besides the tiled stove a comprehensive inventory would count seven wooden beds, six wooden chairs, two tables covered with plastic cloths, various pots and pans, one television, one radio and an incredible gallery of sacred images. There must be thirty of them at least in this tiny space: long reproductions of *The Last Supper* in heavy varnished frames, pallid pre-Raphaelite Virgin Marys, and, most of all, Popes. The Pope in Kraków, the Pope in Warsaw, the Pope with Wałęsa in Rome, the Pope in black and white, the Pope in colour, the Pope in gouache, the Pope rampant on top of the television, the Pope couchant on the stove, the Pope suspended in a perspex box on the wall and garlanded with plastic daisies.

Large dishes piled high with salted pork are laid on the table. 'Nothing for the communists!' Mrs Krasoń exclaims. Her husband shows his gold fillings in another eruption of laughter. Not so much as a trotter of Mr Krasoń's pigs has been seen on the official market for two years now. The price fixed by the state is too low to make it worth his while, and anyway, nothing which he needs can be had in the shops for złotys. As a 'peasant-worker' he earns enough money from working a forty-six-hour week in a factory which manufactures agricultural machinery. 'All sent to the Soviet Union,' he says with a grimace. He himself has been unable to buy the machinery he wants. It has all gone to the state-owned farms.

The latest of these unwanted additions to village life is an intensive beef-production station, built partly by Italians under licence: an extravagant complex of barrack-like buildings surrounded by a high wire fence. For this, the authorities required arable land to grow fodder. They attempted to requisition private farmers' fields, offering as compensation a good pension or fields elsewhere. Krasoń, however, resisted all blandishments. Finally, the local Party boss sent tractors on to his land, protected by a police guard. Mr Krasoń fought them off with sticks, stones and his wife.

The formidable Mrs Krasoń re-enacts her finest hour, waving the metal ladle with which she has been serving tea laced with honey and almost decapitating the Pope couchant. Of course Krasoń went straight to his curé for counsel. The priest went to his bishop—the flamboyantly radical Bishop Tokarczuk of Przemyśl—and brought back word that all would be well and all manner of things would be well. A few days later, four gentlemen from Warsaw arrived at dusk in the remote hamlet. One was a member of the Social Self-Defence Committee—KOR. They talked through the night, deciding to found a Farmers' Self-Defence Committee of the kind which had already been founded (with KOR's assistance) in the Lublin and Grójec regions.

Next day the story of the Battle of Łowisko was heard all over Poland through the Polish service of Radio Free Europe. Thereafter, the identity of all visitors to Łowisko was controlled. The farmers were threatened with reprisals. Krasoń claims the secret police (SB) told him he would be deported to the Soviet Union. His answer: 'I have always wanted to visit Siberia.' This was in the autumn of 1978. Just two years later he was in Warsaw, participating in the pilot group for Rural Solidarity. He joined the Rzeszów commune on 2 January and has been with it ever since.

In the early evening we drive to another hamlet. Tolstoyan farmsteads under thick snow in the light of the moon. Inside one damp and filthy farmhouse we find a whole family clustered on two ancient bedsteads, making baskets by hand: their traditional winter employment. Our host is an enormous young man in patched blue overalls. He stands before his hearth, back straight, head up, arms akimbo, talking with a slow fury about the chicanery of local officials, the impossibility of obtaining building material and agricultural equipment. With one great sweep of his arms he embraces the tiny, wretched room: *'To nie jest Polska!'* she says—this is not Poland!

He has joined Solidarity, of course he has. Two weeks ago he sold some baskets and bought a radio, to keep himself informed about the Rzeszów strike by listening to Radio Free Europe. There it stands on the rickety table: apart from the electric light and the wooden wall-clock (permanently telling twenty to eight) the only object in the room which could not have been there a hundred years ago.

Tonight I listen with the communards to the BBC Polish Service news. First item: the inauguration of Ronald Reagan as President of the USA and the release of the American hostages from Tehran. Second item: the Solidarity National Commission, meeting in Gdańsk, has resolved that nobody will work next Saturday. Applause in the hall.

I sleep backstage, next to Lenin, on a makeshift bed of kitchen chairs. About one o'clock a great commotion. An elderly peasant lady is waving her blanket like a matador's cloak. She is frightened of mice, she says. Anything would be better than mice, she says, even the riot police. The noise from the body of the hall, the noise of two hundred peasants sleeping, is incredible: it is not merely snoring, it is grunting and snorting, heaving and groaning.

Wednesday 21 January

The next sound I hear through the heavy stage-curtain is more melodious: women's voices rising and falling in the chants of a sung rosary at seven o'clock in the morning. A few minutes later the priest comes backstage, his expression changing from composed sanctity to shocked dismay as he sees what has been going on just behind the altar.

Loudspeakers are perched in the window of the washroom, booming out long screeds about agriculture in Sweden, articles from the uncensored press, and poems written by the communards. The poetry makes you cut yourself when shaving. Throughout the day the 'Strike Radio Service' broadcasts its bulletins. This morning they relay yesterday's National Commission resolutions declaring 28 January a Day of Solidarity with the farmers. Workers' Committees around the country are asked to send delegates to Rzeszów. Solidarity will treat all hostile acts against Rural Solidarity members as acts against its own.

Spirits are buoyed up, sustained by ample home-made bread, mounds of fresh butter, cheese and meat. People play chess and cards, watch the television, and engage in long, earnest discussions—apparently the greatest pleasure.

In the late afternoon an exotic group gathers in the snow before the double doors. There is an oriental king in a gorgeous black beard, a jester, a simpering Virgin Mary, and so on. This, it emerges, is the local fire-brigade, come to treat the strikers to a *Jasełka*, the traditional Nativity play.

This evening to the former committee room to sleep. A small crucifix hangs over a slightly darker rectangular patch on the wall. 'That', a communard chortles, 'was a picture of Lenin.' Here Lenin has actually been thrown out of the window.

As we settle down for the night a small man in shiny Terylene trousers kneels down to say his prayers beneath the plastic Polish eagle—silver on red—which has been left in its place behind the chairman's seat. To me this small man praying to the plastic eagle is one of the many strange and moving images which the revolution constantly throws up; to his mates, however, he seems simply ridiculous. How they laugh.

Thursday 22 January

This commune has opened a window on to a culture which is almost unknown even to my friends in Warsaw, the arcane, naïve, resilient culture of rural Poland. Again and again I am reminded of the superstitious peasant radicalism of the English revolution in the seventeenth century, a world opened up for us by Christopher Hill, a world turned upside down. It is as if I enter a time-warp every time I pass through those padlocked double-doors. Behind the doors the seventeenth and twentieth centuries rub shoulders in a quite familiar way. This sense of temporal dislocation is heightened by having a modern telephone and telex at my disposal, for the Provincial Council of Trades Unions has not skimped on their equipment and now the authorities apparently do not dare to cut the strikers' lines of communication as they tried to do in Gdańsk last August. So here at my left hand is a Polish Winstanley, with bowed back and Breughel face, telling some fantastic tale about a village miracle in the crude language of his forefathers, and here at my right is the new telex machine, buzzing expectantly with a direct line to London, where *The Times* awaits seven hundred well measured words to slot into the next day's news pages.

The foreign editor looks for signs of Soviet intervention. Winstanley gives me signs of divine intervention.

This afternoon the Chairman of the Rzeszów Interfactory Founding Committee (MKZ) visited the Provincial Governor, who offered negotiations in Warsaw. The workers' leader immediately refused, insisting that the Government Commission must come to Rzeszów and negotiate in public. They have learned from Gdańsk.

I return from a short shopping foray (hopeless) to find the young historian Adam Michnik lecturing to the assembled communards. Michnik is a charismatic figure who has breathed fire into the intellectual opposition ever since the students' protest at Warsaw University in 1968. He has dropped off here on his way back from a flying visit to Bishop Tokarczuk of Przemyśl (the same who supported the Łowisko Farmers' Self-Defence Committee). Unshaven, pale from too many empty nights in prison (and too many full ones outside it), stylishly dishevelled as ever, he talks with a compelling urgency, turning a slight stammer to devastating rhetorical effect, like a brilliantly articulate sub-machine-gun. He is speaking now about the January Uprising of 1863, when the Poles rose against the Russian occupiers and successfully resisted the Russian army for sixteen months. Then, the Russians were able to turn the peasantry against the Uprising by offering them major concessions. Now, says Michnik, the solidarity of the peasants with the workers is beyond question.

It is clear that most of the communards have only the vaguest notion who Michnik is. At one point he dilates on the mendacity of *Trybuna Ludu*—of which he has much personal experience, having been denounced in its columns as a Jewish *provocateur* and counter-revolutionary.

'Are you from *Trybuna Ludu?*' asks a peasant woman, to Michnik's evident delight.

Most of the questions are about the popular heroes of recent Polish history. What is the Sir Professor's opinion of Wincenty Witos? And of Marshal Piłsudski? Who killed General Sikorski?

Afterwards we go to a dim, sleazy restaurant in Heroes-of-Stalingrad Street. A Bulgarian striptease artiste is announced as a special attraction, but fails to appear. Even here Michnik's charm works its spell, teasing a smile out of the sullen, mustachioed waitress. He eats with the appetite of a man who knows what it is to live on a prison diet. We drink a lot of *korn*. There is in his hungry, sensuous enjoyment of every moment more than a hint of desperation.

'It's like a dream,' he says later. For all his adult life he has been persecuted. When he was twenty-two he was condemned to three years' imprisonment on trumped-up charges. Subsequently, debarred from the university, he was compelled to take unskilled labour in a Warsaw factory—until the authorities woke up to the influence he was beginning to exert on younger workers. Granted a passport and permission to travel to the West (on the intercession of Jean-Paul Sartre) he none the less decided to return to Poland in May 1977, after eight heady months of international discussion, well knowing that this was tantamount to readmitting himself to prison. A few days later he was arrested, along with other leading members of KOR. Released after two months he spent the next three years tirelessly active in the intellectual opposition, being periodically arrested, interrogated and detained for forty- eight hours. He wrote for the unofficial press. He lectured in the 'flying university', organised in private flats. He drafted and signed petitions. He established links with young workers. He published a book in Paris, pointing the way to an alliance between democratic socialists like himself and the Catholic Church. All this time he practised and taught one fundamental principle: behave here and now as if you lived in a free country. He, like Andrei Sakharov in Russia, defied reality—but he did not ignore it. The time when Poland would once again be free could hardly come in his lifetime.

Yet here he is, in January 1981, aged thirty-four, living in a country which behaves as if it is free. He travels unimpeded from meeting to meeting. He lectures to an audience of thousands in the main lecture-hall of the university from which he was expelled in 1968. His articles are published in the Solidarity press and distributed in the streets. He has just addressed a gathering which the Party leadership unequivocally condemns. Yet he is still at liberty to drink his *korn,* laugh at the Brylcreemed provincial Lotharios on the dance floor, and take the night train back to Warsaw. The UBeks are still just behind him, we saw them lurking in the shadows as we turned the corner, but they don't dare to arrest him now. It's like a dream.

Michnik is too much of a fighter not to hope that the dream will last. He is too good a historian not to know that, in Poland, such dreams sooner or later come to an end. 'The question is only if they lock us up before the congress [*przed zjazdem*] or before the invasion [*przed najazdem*],' he concludes, grins at the word-play, tosses back his glass of *korn,* and says farewell.

I will not forget this strange encounter. His voice and above all his face, pale, strained, split by that defiant grin, stay with me for a long time afterwards. Some lines of Orwell, one of Michnik's favourite authors, come into my mind, the lines which conclude 'Looking Back on the Spanish War':

But the thing that I saw in your face
No power can disinherit:
No bomb that ever burst
Shatters the crystal spirit.

What is it which makes this one particular individual an incorruptible defender of certain absolute political and cultural values, a resistance fighter against all the odds? What are the ingredients of the crystal spirit?

Friday 23 January

Hill-farmers from the Bieszczady region (the easternmost part of the Polish Carpathians) have told me a fantastic tale about the Arłamów government recreation estate which occupies, they say, some 60,000 hectares of spectacular mountain pasture. They call it 'the Red Principate'. Here, they say, the highest Party members entertain their guests to extravagant parties with night shows, western films and 'hostesses'. Here, President Giscard d'Estaing was accompanied by Edward Gierek on bison hunts such as have not been seen since the days of the Tarnowskis and Potockis. Here, a petty tyrant called Kazimierz Doskoczyński rules the roost. Doskoczyński, I am told, was a sergeant in the bodyguard of the Stalinist leader Bierut. During an assassination attempt on the hated leader, Doskoczyński received injuries which left him a eunuch. Promoted to Captain he was subsequently given control (on sound Turkish precedent) of this pleasure fief.

Mixed in with the tale of the Red Principate is the story of the Ukrainians. This area was long inhabited by Ukrainian mountain people, many of whom, at the end of the Second World War, supported the Ukrainian Insurrectionary Army (UPA) in its guerilla struggle against the new Polish communist authorities. After the UPA succeeded in assassinating the Communist Deputy Defence Minister, those authorities answered with massive reprisals. In the summer of 1947 the Ukrainian villages were systematically razed to the ground. The highland clans were dispersed to the new western territories, or deported to the Soviet Union. Thirty years later the Gierek regime delivered the *coup de grâce* by renaming the surviving 'Ukrainian' settlements, giving them purely Polish names. The village of Muczne, for example, was renamed in honour of the portly eunuch: Kazimierzowo. It is a remarkable fact that the Polish hill-farmers have included in their list of demands the restoration of the original Ukrainian names. Here, at least, there is no hint of that virulent, intolerant, racist nationalism which has too often marred the Polish record in the twentieth century.

As for the Red Principate, I might dismiss the tale out of hand, had I not talked to a West German businessman who spent, as he put it, 'the best hunting holiday of my life' in this very reserve. He confirmed that indeed the facilities were luxurious. New films and the latest western newspapers were flown down from Warsaw daily. Moreover the gross extravagances of the 'Red Princes' under Gierek are by now common knowledge (and in part officially admitted).

A trip to the hill-farmers' home town of Ustrzyki Dolne gives still more credence to the story. Sitting in the three spartan rooms which serve as Solidarity's headquarters, a long-haired young man explains in great detail how the funds voted for the development of the backward Bieszczady region were increasingly channelled, from the mid-1970s, into the apparatchiks' Xanadu. Next door a small assembly of gnarled sheep-farmers pour out their grievances, detailing all the improvements that should have been made with the money that went to the Principate, warming themselves with their fury. On the wall, alongside quotations from the inter-war peasants' leader Wincenty Witos, is a large banner in the national colours, with a large heart in the place of the eagle, and the text 'Everything which is great is great through the heart'. Next to it another text scrawled in an unlettered hand:

we don't care about life
the pig also lives
we want a life of dignity

The official chairman of the Rzeszów strike committee is a fat little man called Jan Ogrodnik. He is a mirror-image of the apparatchiks they are working to overturn: petty, bureaucratic, inflexible, and with a vastly exaggerated notion of his own importance.

Bureaucracy, rivalry, hierarchy—how swiftly they grow up again, and worse weeds with them. Our identity cards are constantly being changed (for fear of *provocateurs*), with childishly elaborate codes of different coloured inks, and privileged access for committee members. Yesterday I noticed a worker sitting in a corner carefully screwing a hinge on to a spar of wood. A few hours later there was a barrier across the main office: Committee Members Only Beyond This Point! This evening, returning late from Ustrzyki Dolne, I go down to the basement canteen. Here we have been served regular, ample meals, with equal portions for all. But now I come upon a rather different scene. At the far end of the room Mr Ogrodnik and the Chairman of the local Solidarity Interfactory Committee are entertaining Bogdan Lis to dinner. The table is covered with a white cloth and laid with far richer fare than we are ever served. No doubt the object is simply to pay tribute to a man who played such an important role in the Lenin Shipyard and in the subsequent development of Solidarity—to do Lis proud. No doubt that is one of the harmless ways in which the corruption of revolutions always begins. I suppose the next thing they will do is to smuggle in a crate of whisky, like the pigs in Animal Farm.

And so to floor. My place under the plastic eagle in the committee room has become quite familiar now. I no longer notice the snoring, heaving and grunting of the communards. As we settle down for the night someone brings news that Lech Wałęsa has promised to join us.

Saturday 24 January

The suffragan bishop of Przemyśl is here, a moon-faced Trollopean figure. 'Jesus the worker of Nazareth is here among you the workers of Rzeszów,' he preaches. 'Jesus gave his sacrifice for you. Now you sacrifice your comfort for Jesus, for equality, for freedom, to make sufficient food for all.' He talks of respect for human rights and quotes the Pope's encyclical. 'I am here because of what the Pope said.' There are, he goes on, three crises in Poland at the moment: the crisis of the economy, because no one will take responsibility; the crisis of confidence in the leadership; and the crisis of truth, because young people are growing up in an atmosphere poisoned by lies. Untruth is leading to the destruction of the Polish nation. 'You confess here. The government has never confessed.' Then he presents a detailed exposition, with statistics, of the superiority of private over state farming. 'You have the right to own your own land and to form your own trades unions,' he concludes.

No bishop ever spoke to the workers on the Baltic coast like this. Rural Solidarity enjoys the full and unequivocal support of the Church—far more so than the workers' Solidarity. The Holy Father himself indicated that support when he received Lech Wałęsa in Rome just a week ago. He would probably not have expressed it in quite such forthright, political terms as the Bishop. The clergy of the Przemyśl diocese practise a kind of radical commitment which the Pope has condemned in South America. There the clergy join with the communists, here against them, in both cases denouncing the corruption of the authorities.

After his astonishing homily the Bishop goes on a walkabout in the hall, with a microphone.

'Tell me how you sleep, are you hungry? Do you weep?' he asks.

'We were afraid,' says one old woman, 'but now we believe in victory.' She receives a holy picture and a blessing.

'We share blankets . . .' says another.

The Bishop somehow keeps his unctuous composure. 'Ah, this is indeed *a school of Christian life,*' he avers, 'this is *one great family.*'

'You ask "do we weep?",' quavers yet another, 'well, now I have tears of happiness in my eyes.'

'There are no tears unseen by Jesus. Suffering is always seen by God.' The unction is almost unbearable.

Wednesday 28 January

The Christ child says:
'I've had enough of those asses
Let's get rid of them . . .'

the voice of the Strike Poet booms from the Strike Radio. 'Let all Polish drunkards start decent work . . .' Then it breaks into ragged song:

We don't want
vodka or sausage.
The times are past
when they closed our mouths
with sausage.

The Poet has poems for all occasions: a poem to greet the Bishop, a poem to greet Lech Wałęsa, a poem to families at home, a poem against state farms, a poem against collective farms, a poem against the village co-operative, a poem against the police. Tirelessly he declaims these epics of earthy doggerel with the voice of a town-crier, to anyone who will listen. And they do listen. For the communards the Poet is quite as natural and necessary a functionary as the Press Spokesman. Indeed rather more so: at a pinch they would dispense with the Press Spokesman. The Poet here still performs his medieval function as custodian of the collective memory. His presence is appropriately hieratic. Clear blue eyes peer over an enormous handlebar moustache; the Pope and the Black Madonna gaze from the lapel; he sits upright and immobile, punctuating his delivery with slow, impressive gestures.

In secular life he has a tiny two-and-a-half hectare farm near Rzeszów. Like most others, it was originally a rather larger plot given to his father in the massive communist land redistribution of 1944–5. Like most others, it was subdivided between sons. Like most others, too, he has reduced his livestock holding to subsistence level—that is, from three cows to one—because it no longer pays to supply the market. He tried to sell his fruit through the village co-operative but they 'cheated' him, so now he either eats it himself or sells it through the private ('black') market.

As a good Catholic he has five children, but none of them would dream of taking over the farm. They live and work in the cities now, the eldest son as a surgeon, one daughter as a doctor, another at the huge new 'Huta Katowice' steelworks, and a fourth at college in Kraków. They are, in short, products of that industrial and social revolution which Poland has undergone in the first generation of communist rule. (Whether the country would have gone through such a revolution anyway, under capitalism as well, like Italy, is another question.) The cream of their peers, workers mostly between twenty and forty, and peasant sons, will be coming to join us tomorrow: the National Co-ordinating Commission of Solidarity.

The Strike Poet, this strange survivor of an ancient rural culture with its long tradition of oral poetry, and the solidarity of young workers with him and his kind embody a unique moment in the historical process. Perhaps only in this unrepeatable moment of social transformation, with nearly three million 'peasant-workers' and every third urban worker a peasant son, could this solidarity arise. For the objective interests of these two social groups, workers and farmers, are anything but identical.

The strikers' awareness of this problem is shown by a short visit to the main Rzeszów printing works, which is out on strike in sympathy. The workers here are nervous—it is their first strike ever—but also unusually well-informed. They explain that much of their information comes from the uncensored first proofs of the publications (including the local Party newspaper) which they print. We sit round a table with a few representative farmers and workers.

'What do you, as an enlightened farmer, say about the propaganda which attempts to divide farmers and workers?' asks one of the latter addressing one of the former. 'Can you feed us?'

The farmer, a dignified man from Toruń with a fine head of silver hair, rises slowly to his feet. 'I can assure you, *in the name of all enlightened farmers,* that we do not want more for our products than the fair price. We will feed you. Your struggle is our struggle.' And so on and so forth, thumping the table the while. 'I have written to my family,' he concludes, 'to say that if anything happens I want to be buried here in Rzeszów.'

And so they go on, consciously playing out their revolutionary theatre.

None more theatrical, of course, than Lech Wałęsa. Wałęsa has just arrived back from a drive into the Bieszczady mountains, where he attempted to visit the Red Principate. His car was shadowed all the way by UBeks and he was turned back at the gates of the hunting reserve. Now he stands in the snow by the side of his small Fiat and teases the crowd in Victory Square. His speech is impossible to reproduce, disjointed, full of slang, wildly ungrammatical, at times almost nonsensical: 'We went to look at our nice frontier, such a pretty frontier—amazed to see no guns—no

Russians either!—we looked for a villa but they seemed to have moved it . . .' And then the masterly common touch: 'Now it will be a long time while we're sorting things out here with the government, some of us will find a new child when we came home . . .' Has somebody told him that the wife of one of the main organisers of the strike has just had a baby, which the father has not yet seen? Or was he speaking off the top of his head? Either way, the crowd love it.

Thursday 29 January

In the private debates of the National Co-ordinating Commission, by contrast, Wałęsa is reserved and generally cautious. With more than fifty regional representatives assembled under the plastic eagle in my dormitory, it is Bronisław Geremek and then the younger workers who lead the discussion. Bogdan Lis from Gdańsk declares that the Rzeszów strike is comparable in importance with that in Gdańsk—not in scale, but in the weight of the issues.

Wałęsa proposes that the whole Commission goes down into the main hall to listen to the farmers. There they are joined by the Provincial Governor and the Minister for Trades Union Affairs, Stanisław Ciosek. As on the tenth day in Gdańsk the authorities have at last agreed to face the strikers on their own ground. And such language they have certainly not heard for many years.

'There was this idea thirty-five years ago, that here there could be socialism,' begins one farmer. 'But somehow the sun didn't come to this socialism! When somebody tells me he's a communist, I ask: for how much, for 80,000 złotys? Now if he would be a communist for 1,500 or 2,000 złotys, *then* I could believe him. Three times in my life there has been "renewal" in Poland. There is a chance for the fourth time, but the government doesn't take advantage of it. Without the realisation of our sixty-nine demands, and in particular registration [of Rural Solidarity], we won't move from here.'

'They taught me at school', says another, 'that it was forbidden to listen to [Radio] Free Europe. But how can we know what's going on in the country, when our press, radio and television lie?'

'We are gathered together here for all Poland. We have worked out a programme for securing food supplies. We are helped by expert advisers. If we do not win this battle, then the farmer will go into his field *and will produce only for himself and not for the workers.'*

With this plain language stinging in their ears the minister, the governor, and the National Commission rise to their feet and join in singing the peasants' sprightly anthem, the 'Rota':

We shall not yield our forebears' land,
Nor see our language muted.
Poles we are, our nation Poland
By Piasts constituted . . .
So help us then O God
So help us then O God

And so on for rousing verse after patriotic verse. Soon most of the workers on the National Commission are mouthing in an embarrassed, unconvincing way. Only Professor Geremek, the historian, is word-perfect all the way.

In private again the National Commission plunges into a long diffuse discussion which ends, as so often, with the threat of a strike. On the issue of registering Rural Solidarity, the government, in the person of the Minister for Trades Union Affairs, stalls again. 'This is a question for the court,' he implausibly protests. The assembled delegates pass a resolution reaffirming the farmers' right to form their own Independent Self-Governing Trades Union, and depart. Wałęsa's characteristic spontaneous promise, made on Wednesday, that 'we will stay here until everything has been sorted out' is quietly dropped.

By now, the Rzeszów strike was launched into the phase of face-to-face negotiation with the government. On Sunday 1 February a Deputy Agriculture Minister, Mr Kacała, arrived to take up the brief. Three days later the representatives of the three embryonic independent farmers' unions (for my dormitory-mates under the plastic eagle included such proud regional activists as Zdzisław Ostatek, who submitted the statutes in September) finally agreed to a formal merger under the title 'Rural Solidarity'. At approximately the equivalent stage in the Lenin Shipyard strike Cardinal Wyszyński proclaimed his ill-received warning from Częstochowa. Now, however, the Primate acted rather differently, for the peasants were without a doubt the Church's most faithful members, and correspondingly unfaithful to the Party. On 6 February he received a delegation of Rural Solidarity officials with all honours in his Warsaw palace. According to the subsequent Episcopal communiqué he 'confirmed that the right of the farmers to found freely their own associations... independently of existing structures, is a natural right that does not originate from any state authority...' Then, on 10 February, the Supreme Court finally heard Rural Solidarity's appeal and ruled that while the peasants, being self-employed, could not form a union, they could legally register as an 'association'. Walesa called this verdict a 'draw' and urged the farmers to register as the Court suggested.[1]

With the appointment of a new Prime Minister (see below, Chapter 4) the path was now cleared for an agreement in Rzeszów, which was duly signed by the government commission, by Lis and Wałęsa for Solidarity, and by the farmers' strike committee, on 18 February.[2] The communist government solemnly committed itself to passing a law guaranteeing 'the inviolability of peasants' private property, especially land, and the right to inherit it, as well as the recognition of private farming as a lasting and equal element in our national economy.' In cases of 'illegal or glaringly unjust' expropriation of private land for the 'socialised economy', the land would be given back to its owner: rolling back the socialised sector! The prohibitive restrictions on the sale and purchase of private farmland would be lifted. Having learnt from bitter experience, the strikers insisted on detailed and concrete promises in this agreement, for example: 'Beginning on 1 July grants and credits for land development will be given on an equal basis to all sectors of agriculture.' Greatly increased investment in private agriculture—tractors, building materials, credits—and radical revision of the price structure which deliberately discriminated against it was promised by the end of June, that is, in just four and a half months. Production of 'pitchforks, rakes, ploughshares, chains etc.' (Part II, point 5) would be increased, as would coal supplies (II, 12) 'until free market trade is fully restored'.

Thus, after thirty-five years of Soviet socialism, the Polish government solemnly blessed private property and free market trade, in a written agreement subsequently published in the official press. After this, the promise to supply 'full historical truth' in new history textbooks was almost an anticlimax. In the spirit of Solidarity, the farmers extracted a promise to reduce the number of 'facilities selling alcohol' in rural areas, and to annul the 'incentives encouraging shop personnel to increase alcohol sales' (a great money-spinner for the state). Most of their religious and educational demands were referred to the Government-Episcopate Joint Commission which had been active since October. Finally, the Rzeszów Agreement was made conditional on agreement being reached in Ustrzyki Dolne. The weary Minister drove off into the Bieszczady mountains, and, on 20 February, finally secured a kind of accord with the angry hill-farmers. The outstanding feature of this document was the government commitment to reduce its pleasure lands. By the end of June, it was promised, the Provincial Governor would decide how many of the Arlamów Red Principate's *c.* 60,000 hectares should 'from the point of view of rational use' (!) be sold or rented (back) to private farmers. (Some good arable land was indeed handed back, but there was still enough of the Red Principate left for it to serve as an internment camp for Lech Wałęsa in the spring of 1982.)

The peasants had won a great victory. What they had not won was a government promise of legal recognition for their independent unions, although the last part of the Rzeszów Agreement did specify: 'Whenever mention is made of farmers' representatives, this includes all legally active private farmers' organisations, *both present and future*' (Part VIII, point 1—my italics). But they reckoned with the Holy Father behind them the future would not be long in coming. And they were right. On 26 March the dying Primate, Cardinal Wyszyński, rose from his sick-bed to meet the new Prime Minister, General Jaruzelski. It is reliably reported that he insisted on legal registration of Rural Solidarity as a virtual precondition of the Church's continued mediation between the authorities and society. On Good Friday another government commission signed another agreement concluding another farmers' occupation-strike, this time in the town of Bydgoszcz, north-west of Warsaw.

It promised the registration of Rural Solidarity. But to understand how it came to these agreements we must return to the centre of the stage: to Warsaw at the beginning of 1981.

4. The Ides of March

Much Ado About Nothing?

The conflict which broke the Christmas truce in the first week of the New Year seemed, at first glance, trivial and unnecessary. Ostensibly it was about how many Saturdays people should be required to work each month. Solidarity, citing the Jastrzębie Agreement, insisted that in principle the government was committed to introducing the five-day week in 1981. The government said that two work-free Saturdays per month was the maximum Poland could afford at the moment. Like the Registration crisis and the Narożniak Affair, this conflict rapidly escalated out of all apparent proportion to the point at issue, until, with Solidarity on the verge of a general strike, the government once again retreated, under cover of a face-saving compromise. Many observers wondered which side had acted more reasonably. '. . . in the present crisis', *The Times*'s leader admonished, 'it is unreasonable of the workers to demand shorter working hours until productivity has improved.'[1]

Sound economics, no doubt—although the workers had been waiting ten years for the five-day week which Edward Gierek promised them in 1971, and which their East German and Hungarian colleagues already enjoyed. But fundamentally the Free Saturdays conflict was not about free Saturdays. Fundamentally it was about the meaning to be given to such words as 'partnership', 'consultation' and 'trust'—the buzz-words of 'socialist renewal' *(odnowa)*. What infuriated Solidarity was not the substance of the government proposal but the way in which it was made. In mid-November the authorities had suggested linking the introduction of free Saturdays to a lengthening of week-day working hours, making an average 42½-hour week. Solidarity rejected this offer. The next it heard of the matter was a unilateral declaration by the government at the end of December that two Saturdays would be worked every month in 1981. Solidarity's opinion was not asked.

Now if the government was not prepared to consult Solidarity seriously on this question—a purely trades union issue if ever there was one—then what was it prepared to consult the union about? 'Dialogue—yes, Monologue—no,' said the poster in Mazowsze's headquarters. If the government had made the offer in good time then, according to Bronisław Geremek, the workers' leaders might well have been persuaded to accept some variant of the 42½-hour week, in view of Poland's economic plight. Reform-minded Party men soon admitted the government's blunder: 'We must not conduct a policy of presenting society, and particularly the working class, with *faits accomplis*,' Mieczysław Rakowski wrote in an article entitled 'Respect your Partner'.[2] Meanwhile, both sides dug in their heels: Solidarity declared all Saturdays work-free until further notice; the government said workers who did not work on Saturday 10 January would not be paid. Many hundreds of thousands did not work, particularly in larger factories. The following week, while Wałęsa flew off with his delegation to be blessed by the Pope in Rome (and to meet Italian trades unionists), Warsaw public transport workers staged a four-hour strike, their depot adorned with a large banner proclaiming *'Polonia Semper Fidelis'*.

After fruitless negotiations, Saturday 24 January was another trial of strength. Officials claimed that just 40 per cent of the workforce stayed at home: Solidarity claimed between 70 and 90 per cent: but no one doubted who had won. Millions of workers had once again defied the government. As the temperature rose, a rash of new strikes spread across the country like bushfires starting by spontaneous combustion. On Wednesday 28 January the National Commission met in Gdańsk and, partly to regain control of these bushfires, threatened a one-hour nationwide general strike for 3 February if the government did not give satisfaction on three major issues: Free Saturdays, Rural Solidarity and freedom of information. Then they dashed off to join Wałęsa for the day in Rzeszów.

On Friday 30 January a delegation led by Lech Wałęsa once again entered the Council of Ministers building—as they had precisely three months before to negotiate with a delegation led by the Prime

Minister, Pińkowski. Once again they emerged after midnight, through a crowd of surly, half-frozen newsmen; but this time they had a signed agreement to brandish. On Free Saturdays it was a straight compromise: the government reaffirmed its commitment in principle to the forty-hour week, Solidarity agreed that one Saturday per month would be worked in 1981. This would be an eight-hour day (previously it had been only six), thus making an average working week of forty-two hours. On information policy, the government finally agreed in writing to the publication of a Solidarity national weekly with a print-run of half a million. Rather vaguer commitments were made to full radio and TV coverage of Solidarity National Commission statements, in consultation with the Solidarity Press Officer, and to Solidarity participation in a weekly trades union TV programme. Only on the thorny question of Rural Solidarity could no progress be made.

When the National Commission met in the Warsaw Polytechnic on Sunday 1 February, Karol Modzelewski was able to make a guardedly upbeat presentation of these 'concrete results'. For him, as for most Poles, the question of freedom of information was a vital one. Wojciech Kamiński, the fiery 28-year-old leader of the militant Warsaw public transport workers, made an important connection explicit. 'We would work a six-day-week', he told me, 'if we were fully informed about the country's economic position.' 'If the government gives us the gen and we reckon the position's really bad,' Wałęsa told a startled audience in Rzeszów, 'we will go to work on *Sunday!* Even if the priest shouts at us!'

Poland's appetite for truthful information was insatiable. Even the poor peasant farmer in his shack tuned in nightly to hear the news from Radio Free Europe and perhaps a BBC commentary. Astonishingly, there were queues in front of newspaper kiosks as long as those before the butchers'. After standing four hours in the drizzle to buy meat, people were still prepared to stand another hour or two to obtain a copy of *Polityka* or *Gazeta Krakowska.* In Warsaw, old women made a living by getting up very early in the morning, buying several copies of selected newspapers, and selling them at black market prices.

This reflected a great transformation of the official press. Until August it had been subjected to minute control by the censors' Central Office, which stipulated, for example, 'Absolutely no information is to be published about the Katowice mine disasters in which four miners lost their lives'; 'All publications presenting statistics of safety and hygiene at work or occupational diseases must be withheld'; and 'Figures illustrating the state and growth of alcoholism in the country are not to appear in the mass media'.[3] Since September, the press had been, in practice, much freer. *Polityka* was able to publish interviews with Solidarity leaders. The weekly *Kultura* (not to be confused with the Paris émigré monthly of the same name) printed a series of excellent reportages. Previously it had been forbidden so much as to mention the *name* of many exile and opposition writers, including the Nobel Prize-winner Czesław Miłosz. Now this long blacklist of literary unpersons was slowly torn up before the eyes of a delighted public, as the unmentionable were mentioned and the unpublishable published.

The supply of truth, like the supply of meat, varied greatly from day to day and place to place, although it was everywhere inadequate. Much depended on the attitude of the local Party Secretary. 'What I can write in Kraków I can't write in Warsaw, what I can write today I can't write tomorrow,' one Party journalist complained. The *Gazeta Krakowska* showed what an ungagged press might do. Under a new editor it took up an environmentalist campaign against the nearby Huta Skawina aluminium works, which had poisoned the air and ruined the facades of a city which once combined the charms of Oxford and Vienna. Within months, the aluminium works were closed.

But this new freedom was provisional, on sufferance. According to the Gdańsk Agreement a new Censorship Bill should have been presented to parliament by the end of November, but, as the literary critic and KOR member Jan Józef Lipski now informed the National Commission, there were still great differences between the draft prepared by the Justice Ministry, and the proposals of an independent committee representing producers of the word (writers, journalists, film-makers etc.). The Ministry wanted an almost infinitely elastic definition of 'interests of state', and a highly restrictive definition of those 'internal' union publications which would not be censored.

The Solidarity press was now booming. In every branch, news-sheets, circulars and bulletins were lovingly duplicated and distributed. There was the regular *Solidarność* (Solidarity) in

Gdańsk, *Niezależność* '(Independence) in Warsaw—both uncensored—and now the properly printed *Jedność* (Unity) in Szczecin, which was censored and sold at the state-run newspaper kiosks. A Solidarity news agency, *'Agencja Solidarność' (AS)*, had just been established to circulate detailed information on the latest strikes and National Commission meetings to all the regional headquarters. The volume and audacity of these alternative publications grew all the time, as imported offset and duplicating machines (mostly gifts from western unions) permitted increasingly professional production. By early May, AS could list eighty-seven Solidarity journals and bulletins. Even Nowa, the unofficial publishers (latest publication, Zbigniew Brzeziński's book on the Soviet bloc!) was being edged under the protective eaves of Mazowsze. In the Lower Silesian bulletins, poems by Miłosz were printed alongside detailed accounts of union elections. 'Have you got a spare copy of Brecht?' an engineer greeted the poet Ryszard Krynicki as he entered the Solidarity headquarters in Poznań to work on the union news-sheet, and Krynicki slipped another copy of his Brecht translations out of his canvas bag. It is hard to recapture the excitement with which these bulletins were read, but easy enough to understand the government's fears.

Moreover, some 40–50,000 of the country's print-workers were Solidarity members. In Szczecin they had already struck to protest at the way that *Jedność* was being censored. Their militancy had been nourished by years of reading the first proofs of newspapers before they went to the censors. Now they threatened to leave blank spaces wherever the censor had been at work, a tactic used to great effect by their predecessors against the Tsars.

Since December, however, there had been a perceptible squeeze on the official media, despite the protests of the Journalists' Association led by its outspoken new chairman, Stefan Bratkowski. Mr Olszowski's strong arm was most visible in the evening television news, a programme which did not have to be seen to be disbelieved. But to a western eye the comparative sophistication of the news presentation pointed up the absurdity of its content. On Saturday 24 January, for instance, there were twenty-five minutes' 'reporting' on how the Solidarity absentees had damaged Poland's economy, leaving just five minutes for the rest of the world, sport and weather. On Friday 30 January, as negotiations dragged on in the Council of Ministers building, a lugubrious newscaster read out a little sermon on civic responsibility concluding with a Polish proverb, 'The Pole is wise after the event'. On Sunday 1 February they actually showed ten minutes' film of the National Commission meeting in the Warsaw Polytechnic. Solidarity's national Press Spokesman, Karol Modzelewski, one of the unmentionables since his 'Open Letter to the Party' (with Kuroń) in 1964, was now shown reading a statement which included the decision to 'suspend' (not cancel) the 3 February one-hour general strike. This, presumably, was the main reason for showing it, as also, perhaps, the authorities' feeling that they could not break their promises the very day after making them. On Monday 2 February, none the less, it was back to normal, with the same lugubrious newscaster spending fifteen minutes, no less (half the news), reading out a tough speech by Stefan Olszowski, denouncing 'political strikes' and 'partisans of chaos and destruction' in a deadly monotone. With every major crisis in 1981 the news was to get worse until, in the autumn, Poland's walls were covered with the simple words 'The TV lies' and just 16 per cent of those asked by the TV Public Opinion Research Centre (OBOP) 'believed the TV reports'.[4]

The National Commission debate was stormy. The Solidarity news agency (AS) reported strong criticism of the way the negotiations had been conducted. 'We are working like the CRZZ [the old Central Council of Trades Unions],' said Wądołowski from Szczecin. Another regional chairman objected to the leading role of the advisers: 'We advise and they blather,' he commented. Several thought they should still go ahead with the general strike for Rural Solidarity. The men who made up the KKP (like the TUC, Solidarity's leadership was largely a male preserve) were mostly younger workers, generally with no experience of political organisation when they were catapulted into their present seats by popular acclamation.

There was Ryszard Kalinowski, for example, a 28-year-old electrician from Elbląg and now one of Wałęsa's two deputy chairmen. He was a worker's son, still completing his further education (the week before he had had to dash back to Elbląg to take an exam . . . in Russian). In August, he recalled, 'I just got up on a packing case and started to speak, and the people seemed to like what I said.' But five months in revolution is a very long time: and five months of confrontation had shaped Kalinowski's attitudes decisively. 'In September I really believed that the government was prepared to keep the promises it made in the social accords,' he told me. 'Now I only believe in the truncheon'—meaning, of course, the strike weapon.

Moreover, each of the fifty-two regional chairmen and delegates knew that he would soon be standing for election. Running through the discussion was an urgent awareness of the growing militancy of the rank-and-file in many regions, and a strong undertow of anxiety about the ability of the Commission—which was, as its name said, only a 'co-ordinating' body—to control the bushfires. Lech Dymarski, the delegate from Poznań (and, exceptionally, not a worker but an opposition intellectual) put it bluntly. They should not be so afraid of the word confrontation, he said, because the confrontation was going on one way or another, since the authorities 'have no other purpose but to destroy . . . the union. People intuitively feel this and that is why they are angry with the KKP.' . . . 'The government has its back to the wall, but so do we. Our walls are the rank-and-file.'[5]

Here, perhaps, was the answer to the question which many people were asking, in one form or another: 'Where are the Jacobins?' In every modern European revolution there had been at least one small, tightly knit, often conspiratorial group which deliberately drove the revolution to the 'left'. Official propaganda cast KOR in this role substituting, of course, 'right' for 'left' and 'counter-revolution' for 'revolution'. But in fact, as we have seen, KOR really did not fit the bill: typically, in this National Commission meeting it was Jacek Kuroń who cooled the heady discussion with the single sentence 'We must remember that we cannot overthrow the government.' So where were the Jacobins? 'Here there are only sans-culottes,' Karol Modzelewski smilingly replied, when I put the question to him. He was not referring only to the clothes shortage. It was the textile and car workers in the southern Silesian town of Bielsko-Biała who were demanding the heads of the Second Estate—the 'Owners of People's Poland'. It was the Catholic peasants in Rzeszów who would overthrow the ruling oligarchy at the drop of a Cardinal's hat. KOR were among the Girondists now. It was a looking-glass revolution.

In Bielsko-Biała the MKZ had already rushed into a regional general strike, without the assent of the National Commission. The whole Province had been paralysed since 27 January. Their aim was to unseat top local officials whom they had found guilty of the abuse of local government funds. 'We have twenty names on our blacklist,' their Chairman proudly reported to the National Commission. In the remote south-eastern county town of Jelenia Góra they were threatening a regional general strike for Monday 9 February. Here, they demanded the resignation of the Minister for Trades Union Affairs, Stanisław Ciosek, who had been an unpopular Party First Secretary in Jelenia Góra. They also wanted a sanatorium reserved for employees of the Interior Ministry (i.e. mostly security forces and police) to be handed over to the public health service. Like so many other local demands, when you were on the spot—when you had seen the dreadful state of the public hospitals—this seemed only just. But it was also, like Mazowsze's demands in the Narożniak Affair, the kind of frontal challenge to the security apparatus which Wałęsa's advisers begged him to avoid. Meanwhile, in Łódź, students continued a sit-in strike, demanding university reforms and the recognition of their nationwide Independent Students' Union. The peasants' commune continued in Rzeszów. And every few days another bushfire would break out, now in Białystok, now in Olsztyn, now in Wrocław . . .

Wałęsa hurried down to Bielsko-Biała, but even his magic could not put out the flames. Negotiations broke down. Wałęsa issued a dramatic telex calling on workers across the country to occupy their factories if force was used in the strikebound Province. Privately, he telephoned desperately to Mazowiecki and Geremek in Warsaw. They in turn succeeded in securing the assistance of Bishop Bronisław Dąbrowski who, after meeting a very senior Party official, and with the blessing of the Primate, raced down to Bielsko-Biała to give his personal 'guarantee' that the local officials would indeed resign—after a decent interval. Only then did the workers agree to leave the factories which they had now been occupying for ten days.

Fireman Wałęsa dashed off to Jelenia Góra, but here too his frantic diplomacy could not prevent them going ahead with the regional general strike on 9 February—the day the Eighth Plenum opened in Warsaw. Next day the government gave in and agreed to hand the police sanatorium over to the public health service. You see, said the local Jacobins, the truncheon is the only language they understand. The National Commission drew a rather different conclusion. Meeting in Gdańsk on 12 February it appealed to the membership:

> The plethora of local and regional strikes pursuing disparate aims without the consent of the National Co-ordinating Commission, often against its advice, not only made little impact; they have also sometimes been provoked by advocates of confrontation among those in authority as a means to disrupt our unity. As a result we are threatened with dismemberment into 50 regional organisations. This would mean the destruction of our movement ...[6]

Moreover, they at last created what was in effect a kind of provisional cabinet. For five months the union had no permanent executive at all: between one National Commission meeting and the next there was no formally constituted central authority. Now there would be a group of between six and twelve top leaders—the 'Presidium' of the National Commission—empowered to act for the union at the national level between meetings. No longer could officials refuse, as the state radio and TV boss, Zdzisław Balicki, had just outrageously refused, to negotiate with ad hoc Solidarity committees (in this case on the promised weekly union broadcast—an obvious delaying tactic). This Solidarity cabinet could deal afresh with a new government cabinet: for that same morning the *sejm* had confirmed the replacement of the discredited Pińkowski as Prime Minister.

A General for What?

A flat inscrutable face. Thin lips clamped shut above a sharp, clean jaw. The small head set bolt upright, as if fixed to the spine by a steel pin. A trim figure looking fragile inside the heavy uniform. The eyes, perhaps, might betray some emotion, but they are hidden behind large rectangular dark glasses which give the whole an expression of almost inhuman blankness—faintly menacing. General Wojciech Jaruzelski, the new Prime Minister who stood before parliament on 11 February, was an enigma. Minister of Defence since 1968 and a Politburo member for the last decade, he was one of the two or three most powerful men in the country. Yet little was known of him, and what was known could bear two very different interpretations.

At the age of twenty, in 1943, he was already training in a Soviet officers' school at Ryazan, some hundred miles south of Moscow, whence he joined the Soviet-organised Polish First Army which took part in the liberation of Poland. In the immediate post-war years he distinguished himself in the brutal military campaign to wipe out anti-communist guerilla resistance. He joined the communist Polish Workers' Party in 1947. In 1960, at the exceptionally young age of thirty-seven, he became chief political commissar of the army: a certain sign of the Party's and Moscow's trust, as was his promotion to Chief of Staff five years later. In 1968 he stepped into the Defence Minister's shoes just in time to oversee Polish Army participation in the Soviet invasion of Czechoslovakia. He arrived in the Politburo as a candidate member with the riots of December 1970. Since December 1971 he had been a full Politburo member. All this suggested a communist soldier completely loyal to Moscow.

On the other hand he was the scion of a Polish gentry family, with a patriotic tradition of military service. He had attended a rather exclusive Jesuit boarding school. At the age of sixteen he had been deported, like so many others, to work for the Soviets as a forced labourer. He had been promoted to General (the youngest in the army) in 1956, at the time when Gomulka was purging the officer corps of Soviet stooges. As Defence Minister he was known to have modernised and 'cleaned up' the armed forces. He was himself undoubtedly 'clean', in the sense of materially uncorrupted: his was one of the very few Politburo faces without that characteristic, tell-tale apparatchik's jowl. On taking office in 1968 he promptly transferred an opulent mansion inherited from his predecessor to welfare uses. More important, he was widely reputed to have opposed the use of force against the workers both in December 1970 and in August 1980. Subsequently he was seen to have been a staunch supporter of the Kania line: the search for a political, rather than a military, solution. All this gave some credence to his claim to be a Polish patriot.[7]

After the military takeover of 13 December 1981 most Poles were suddenly certain of the first interpretation. Of course he is a puppet and a traitor, they said, of course he has been preparing this 'war' ever since he became Prime Minister! In a limited sense they were almost certainly right. Like any good communist general, Jaruzelski would have had *contingency* plans for that internal use of the military for which men like Olszowski had repeatedly pleaded ever since August. No doubt he had the plans before he became Prime Minister and no doubt he developed them greatly afterwards. The record of the next few months, however, does not support the thesis that Jaruzelski had *decided on* a military solution when he took office in February. Rather does the evidence of his words and deeds suggest that at this stage he still hoped to find a political solution acceptable to Moscow. It also suggests, what some who knew him have remarked, that he was not a very decisive man.

At the time, most Poles seem to have given him the benefit of the doubt. 85 per cent of those asked by the Radio and TV Public Opinion Research Centre (OBOP) in early March approved of his appointment.[8] The popular myth of the army became stronger with every month soldiers were not used against the people. Wałęsa told Bernard Guetta of *Le Monde*, 'I like soldiers . . . but, seriously, I have respect for him [Jaruzelski]: I think he's all right, that he's a good Pole.'[9] A diplomatic answer, perhaps, for Wałęsa was well aware that the Jaruzelski government would be the 'last card' before the use of force.

In fact the tone of the Eighth Plenum which nominated Jaruzelski had been very tough indeed. Grabski had thundered against KOR, mentioning three of its most active members (Kuroń, Michnik, Macierewicz) by name (a 'judicial investigation' of KOR had been announced the previous day). Barcikowski, though a reputed 'moderate', had been only slightly more restrained. All had categorically rejected 'Rural Solidarity'. The word '*odnowa*' (renewal) was hardly mentioned. Kania rounded up with a commitment to kill 'counter-revolution' 'in the egg'. His speech next day to the *sejm* was mild by comparison, commending Jaruzelski as a man who had always favoured 'political solutions'. The General himself claimed to see 'evil and hostile political forces . . . opposed to socialism' as the main source of conflict in Poland, but his inaugural address (on 12 February) went on to call for 'a three-month, ninety-day, moratorium on strikes... so we could... undertake the most urgent social programmes... take the first steps towards the introduction of a programme for economic stability, and... prepare wide-ranging economic reforms'. In return for their co-operation, Solidarity was offered a 'Permanent Committee' for government-union relations. This would be headed by Mieczysław Rakowski, the Party reformist editor of *Polityka*, who now entered the government with the rank of Deputy Prime Minister. Jaruzelski was unyielding on the Censorship Bill and silent on Solidarity's access to the mass media, but he did promise that new Trades Union and Workers' Self-Government Bills would be submitted to parliament by the end of June.

It was not much, neither was the subsequent government reshuffle as far-going as they had hoped: Rakowski's new responsibilities, for example, were relations with the trades unions and the press but Mr Ciosek was still Minister for Trades Union Affairs, and, more important, Stefan Olszowski was still Central Committee Secretary for Propaganda. Some semi-official sources suggested that the offer was meant to look like this: a *government* leadership set on finding a *modus vivendi* with Solidarity, while the *Party* leadership kept up the ideological struggle. If so, this was a wholly implausible distinction. The Party-state could not be cut in two any more than Siamese twins, and the Poles would not have believed it even if it happened.

None the less, Solidarity cautiously welcomed the new government and the truce offer. On 12 February the National Commission established its own permanent committee, and reiterated its willingness to refrain from industrial action if the authorities kept their promises. On the 16th, an interview with Karol Modzelewski was published in *Życie Warszawy*. Speaking as Solidarity Press Spokesman he said:

> ... the establishment of a new government, its personnel composition and its policies as outlined in Prime Minister Jaruzelski's speech create real opportunities to turn back the dangerous course of events that became particularly visible during the last weeks...

Solidarity wanted a strong government, he went on, for only a strong government could be a reliable partner. As the advisers commented privately, they *had* to believe in Rakowski's professed desire for genuine 'partnership', in Jaruzelski's good faith, and in their ability to push through their policies against the resistance of the political bureaucracy and the security apparatus. For without them what chance was there of a *modus vivendi*?

For the moment, the surge of goodwill worked marvels. Messages of support for the General's appeal came from Solidarity committees in Silesia. The miners of Jastrzębie even sent a telegram offering to work *all* Saturdays for the next three months. Within a week all the major outstanding disputes had been settled. The Minister for Higher Education reached a kind of agreement with the student strikers in Łódź, after their Inter-University Co-ordinating Committee had allowed a wave of student sit-in strikes to spread from Łódź and Kraków to Toruń, Olsztyn and several other cities. It was a wide-ranging document, vague on many crucial points, but the Minister was forced to promise a much greater autonomy for universities (which were rather more tightly controlled by the Ministry than an English state secondary school is by its Local Authority). Students would no longer be obliged to learn Russian and to sit through compulsory courses in Marxism-Leninism.[10] The same day agreement was reached in Rzeszów, and two days later in Ustrzyki Dolne.

The General had his truce. Like a ceasefire after prolonged fighting the silence which descended on Poland seemed unnatural. It came in the nick of time, for two days later Poland's fraternal allies solemnly declared their kind of solidarity with Comrades Kania and Jaruzelski, at the 26th Congress of the Communist Party of the Soviet Union in Moscow.

The Bydgoszcz Crisis

The truce lasted just ten days. It was broken in Moscow. On Wednesday 4 March, as soon as the Soviet Party Congress was over, the Polish delegation was hauled into the Kremlin for talks. Kania, Jaruzelski, Żabiński (Katowice First Secretary) and Emil Wojtaszek (a Central Committee secretary) found themselves facing seven of the most powerful men in the world, the same seven who had formed the Soviet delegation at the Moscow summit of the Warsaw Pact in December. Beside Brezhnev there were Yuri Andropov, KGB boss, Marshal Ustinov, the Defence Minister, Mikhail Suslov, supreme guardian of ideological orthodoxy, Tikhonov, Chairman of the Council of Ministers, Rusakov, Central Committee secretary for relations with other ruling communist parties, and the Foreign Minister, Gromyko. This formidable team proceeded to read the riot act. One of them (Suslov?) apparently brandished copies of the Łódź and Rzeszów Agreements. Why was Russian no longer compulsory? he demanded. How dare they guarantee private land ownership! The Soviet leaders, said the final communiqué, 'voiced their conviction that the Polish communists have both the opportunity and the strength to turn the course of events and to remove the peril hanging over the socialist achievements of the Polish people'.*[11] At five o'clock the next morning Jacek Kuroń was detained in Warsaw. He was held for six hours and informed that he was under investigation on suspicion of 'slandering the Polish People's Republic' (maximum sentence: eight years). On Friday 6 March they tried to do the same to Adam Michnik in Wrocław, but Michnik politely declined to be arrested and the local Solidarity immediately gave him a Workers' Guard. At the same time charges were formally laid against the four KPN activists already in prison.

The timing could hardly be a coincidence. The evidence for the effects of Moscow's pressure is, however, circumstantial. We cannot document precisely the chain of links of cause and effect. We have no log books of telephone calls from Moscow. We do not know from whom and to whom such calls, if at all, were made. We are in doubt whether and how much each of the Polish leaders knew in advance of the series of police actions which were now to bring Poland to the edge of the abyss. Moreover, as Leszek Kołakowski pertinently observes:

> ... in a political system pervaded by obsessive secretiveness and with an incredible number of built-in barriers blocking the flow of information, the rulers themselves are often incapable of properly controlling their own apparatus of repression: not only is the security police never 'neutral' in factional squabbles which, with varying intensity, tear the Party asunder, but, having vested

*In Poland it sounded even more alarming, since it was translated as 'to reverse the course of events'.

> interests of its own, it sometimes uses repressive measures for its own purposes and not on the orders of higher political authorities. Which of the police brutalities are in fact ordered by the Party leadership, and which are not, is, however, almost impossible to verify and indeed, *the question is not very important: whoever initiated them, they serve the same purpose of perpetuating the oppressive power system* [my italics].[12]

The worker delegates to Solidarity's National Commission might not have expressed it so subtly, but they seem to have grasped this point no less firmly, almost intuitively. Speaker after speaker at the National Commission meeting on 7 March recounted the harassment of union workers and advisers by security officials in their region. A tear-gas canister had been hurled into a Warsaw shop where the assistants wore Solidarity armbands; delegates to the 'Rural Solidarity' National Congress which was due to begin in Poznań the next day had been 'warned off' by plainclothes men; in Nowy Sącz a local Solidarity chairman had been found dead—hanged—in mysterious circumstances; in Łódź five Solidarity members had been quite unfairly dismissed from a hospital run by the Ministry of the Interior. And now there were Kuroń and Michnik and the KPN men . . .

Most of their advisers preached caution: the empire of the Interior Ministry must be another taboo, they said, like the nation's defences. The workers were insistent. Those from Radom and Ursus, in particular, felt a personal debt to KOR, which had, after all, been established in 1976 to help them against lawbreaking courts and lawless police. 'KOR protected the workers, the workers protect KOR,' read a poster which soon appeared around Warsaw. Radom's MKZ shot off a protest telegram to General Jaruzelski. In Radom, too, the demands for justice for the dead and injured of 1976 were once again boiling over. For the worker-delegates, a fundamental principle was at stake: everyone should be equal before the law, no one could be above it. Mazowiecki and Geremek pleaded the primacy of politics—the imperative of self-denial. But the workers had a political argument too. For them, every arrest was the thin end of the wedge. Faced with the 'salami tactics' of the security forces they could allow no distinction between 'dissidents', who might be sacrificed, and 'unionists' who might not. If it was Kuroń today it might be themselves tomorrow. This kind of solidarity was not merely an ethical commandment: it was a political necessity.

From afar, Solidarity's reactions often seemed exaggerated, unreasonable, irresponsible. What, for example, could justify the whole city of Łódź going on strike for one hour on 10 March, to secure the reinstatement of just five workers! And this despite Lech Wałęsa's appeal, and on a day when Wałęsa was due, for the first time, to meet the new Prime Minister! But the case looked rather different from close to. In early February five employees of a Łódź hospital for police and security officers discovered that the Hospital Director (with the police rank of colonel) had set aside more than 5 kg of the 10 kg of ham delivered to the hospital canteen, for the personal use of management. When the employees protested, they were sacked. For more than a month the Colonel, acting, he said, 'on orders', flatly refused to reinstate them. Only the strike brought reinstatement, and permission for Solidarity to operate in the hospital.

The meeting between General Jaruzelski and Lech Wałęsa was clearly intended to diminish the tension, to advance the 'political solution'. But on the very same day an 'unknown assailant' attacked one of the senior members of KOR, Antoni Pajdak, a well-known pre-war socialist and wartime resistance leader, on the street outside his Warsaw home. The 'unknown assailant' used a kind of gas canister normally available only to the police and security forces. The 86-year-old Pajdak was taken to hospital, badly bruised and with a shattered pelvis.

On the most favourable interpretation, the Prime Minister and Party leader were not in control of all the arms of the security 'state within a state'. Yet it was also clear to Solidarity's leaders that the swarming denizens of the security underworld were being encouraged by Polish politicians at the highest level. That week, they could read in the AS bulletin extracts from a secret speech given by the Politburo member Andrzej Żabiński to his security and police chiefs in Katowice (a tape-recording was smuggled out and passed to Solidarity: there is no reason to doubt its authenticity, though every reason to doubt the motives of those who passed it). The MKZ in Katowice played the tape of this speech over and over again. It was a remarkably frank exposition of the 'hardliners'' tactics for fragmenting and corrupting Solidarity:

> Firstly, there must be a political attack on the concept of regional organisation, which is supported by Mr Wałęsa, or rather by his souffleurs . . .
>
> The aim of the struggle is to divide the leading KOR people from the factories, that means also, to destroy the new union structure and impose a branch structure on them . . . Then we will have an easier game. The trade traditions are tremendously strong. Tell a railwayman that he is to be in the same union as a fashion designer! . . .

The wisdom of Solidarity's regional structure, as a defence against the deliberate 'divide and rule' tactics of the authorities, could hardly have been better confirmed. Here, too, the workers could taste the cynicism and contempt with which a man like Żabiński spoke about them:

> We must involve these people in a thousand affairs—I sympathise with them, because some of them are nice young lads, but they've let themselves in for big time politics (laughs) so there's no other way. They must get the taste of power. We should give them offices—as luxurious as possible. I've said it before but I'll say it once again in this group: *I don't know anyone who is not corrupted by power, the only question is how far and how fast* (laughs again). [my italics][13]

He obviously spoke from personal experience.

One must know this evidence for the real intentions of the 'hardliners' in the Politburo, and for the counter-offensive by the security apparatus, to understand Solidarity's reaction to what came to be known as the 'Bydgoszcz crisis'.

On 16 March, Wałęsa, Kuroń and a priest once again took turns on the same platform, deploying all their combined magic to pull yet another region—this time, Radom—back from the verge of a general strike—this time, with the sacking of local officials held responsible for the violent repression in 1976 at the top of the list. The same day, private farmers' representatives occupied the headquarters of the

United Peasant Party (ZSL)* in Bydgoszcz, to press for full recognition of Rural Solidarity. They were joined by the regional Solidarity leader, Jan Rulewski, already well-known as a 'militant' on the National Commission. On 19 March, six of them were invited to a local council meeting where, they were told, they could air their grievances at the appropriate point on the agenda. However, shortly before two o'clock the meeting was abruptly adjourned. The Solidarity representatives—some thirty-five by now—protested, and about forty-five councillors stayed on with them in the chamber. Five hours later they were still there, still debating, and working very slowly towards a final communiqué. About ten-past seven, after the Mayor and the Deputy Provincial Governor had failed to persuade the Solidarity group to leave, a force of some two hundred uniformed policemen entered the room. Like so many other crucial moments in the Polish revolution, what followed was recorded on tape.

The police Major quite politely asked the occupants to leave the room. One unionist said this reminded him of the attack on the Spanish parliament. Rulewski himself taunted the Major: 'You're not one of those western policemen who truncheon people at the behest of the bourgeoisie!' The police several times gave them 'fifteen minutes' to finish their communiqué and leave the room. Finally, around half-past eight, just as they were reading out their communiqué, the police re-entered the chamber, accompanied by plainclothes men.

> The Major: Gentlemen . . . I beg your pardon, I overlooked the Ladies . . . Ladies and Gentlemen, I ask you to leave the room. Otherwise we will use force. Tumult . . . cries of 'Make a circle . . . women in the middle!'

A circle was formed, the occupants linking arms and swinging into the first verse of 'Poland is not yet lost/So long as we live'. One by one they were pulled from the circle and roughly ejected from the building. Some were apparently pushed down a corridor of truncheon-wielding police—like the Radom 'paths of health'. A shout was heard from the police ranks: 'Get Rulewski!'[14]

*One of the façade parties hitched to the PZPR in the so-called 'National Unity Front' in the *sejm*.

When they had all been hustled from the courtyard, it was found that three people had been badly hurt. A 68-year-old farmer called Bartoszcze—original leader of the peasants' sit-in—had contusions to the skull and ribs, and suspected brain damage. Rulewski and one other were concussed with bad bruising; bad enough to put them in hospital for several days.

The news was flashed across Poland: Solidarity exploded. The Presidium of the National Commission even had to hurry out a communiqué stating that, contrary to rumour, Rulewski had not been killed. On Saturday the streets of Bydgoszcz were thronged by a furious crowd chanting 'M—O—Gestapo'. It was not in fact the MO (the ordinary police) who had done the worst beating, according to most reliable reports, but the hatred was general. By Sunday, most Solidarity headquarters displayed dramatic black-and-white photos of the three injured men, headed, in large blood-red letters: 'PROWOKACJA' (Provocation). From the very beginning, Solidarity took the line that the beatings were a deliberate provocation by 'hardliners' in the Party and security apparatus who sought confrontation, even at the risk—or perhaps even in the hope—of Soviet armed intervention. It was, said Wałęsa, an obvious provocation against the government of General Jaruzelski.

Of course such a claim is almost impossible to verify (as Kołakowski suggests, any such claim would be). Yet, again, the circumstantial evidence is strong. The Deputy Provincial Governor may just have decided on his own authority to send in the uniformed police. Rulewski's behaviour was certainly itself high-handed and provocative. But Rulewski was singled out for special treatment by the plainclothes men of the SB—and from whom did they receive their orders? People's thoughts turned immediately to Olszowski and Grabski. It was soon remarked that most of the 'appeasers' in the Party leadership were otherwise engaged on this particular day. Kania was paying a lightning visit to Budapest. Jaruzelski was tied up with the latest and largest round of Warsaw Pact manoeuvres on Polish soil, codenamed 'Soyuz '81', which began (*could* it be a coincidence?) that same day. Rakowski was receiving the West German Foreign Minister, Hans-Dietrich Genscher, in Warsaw. It was noted, too, that Bydgoszcz lay near the important railway junction of Inowrocław, on the strategic line of communication to East Germany which a strike might have been expected to cut. Bydgoszcz was Olszowski's parliamentary constituency. Olszowski and Grabski were rumoured to have been pleading once again for a state of emergency or martial law. At the time it was reported that this threat was averted only by a counter-threat of resignation by General Jaruzelski, who returned to Warsaw hotfoot from another meeting with Marshal Kulikov. The Politburo none the less issued an uncompromising statement, denouncing 'extremism' and 'adventurism' and declaring, absurdly but infuriatingly, that 'the organs of law and order in Bydgoszcz' had 'acted in accordance with law and order'.

Perhaps the most important support for the provocation thesis came from Stefan Bratkowski. The day after the Politburo meeting he published an unprecedented Open Letter to all Party members. 'Let us have no illusions,' he wrote, 'this is a crisis of the last chance for those who would like to drive our Party from the path of social agreement, bringing our state and society to an inevitable catastrophe.' And he did not mean Solidarity . . .

> Our hardliners stand for no programme except the concept of confrontation and disinformation . . . Today they are trying to involve the whole Party leadership and government in a clash with the entire society. With incalculable consequences, they are trying to provoke society to behaviour justifying the use of force.

And more:

> I say it openly: we are all counting on Comrade Kania, on Barcikowski. Nor do we see any alternative to the government of General Jaruzelski.[15]

A Party member and Chairman of the Journalists' Association could hardly be more explicit than that. It was a broadside directed straight at his own political boss, the Propaganda chief, Stefan Olszowski. Olszowski meanwhile pulled out all the media stops he could: 'Bydgoszcz was really two provocations,' a Warsaw writer commented at the time, 'the first was the beatings, the second, the subsequent television coverage.'

It was the most serious political crisis since August: of that the

National Commission delegates who assembled in Bydgoszcz on Monday 23 March had no doubt. For most of them the question was not *if* to respond with a general strike, but only when to call it, and whether to preface it with a 'warning strike'. They felt personally insulted and threatened: if it could happen to Rulewski it could happen to any of them. In vain did the advisers beat against the flames of their anger. Indeed, several of the worker-delegates did not think the advisers need be heard at all. Only late in the evening could Mazowiecki remind them that, in his view, the Jaruzelski government was 'the last chance for a peaceful solution in Poland'. The historian Geremek's appeal was still more dramatic: the decision for an unlimited general strike, he said, would be a decision for a National Insurrection. It was an angry, fractious meeting, marred by the personal recriminations which were becoming a familiar feature of the National Commission, and it was adjourned in disarray at three o'clock in the morning.

After a few hours' sleep tempers had cooled, and the majority voted for Wałęsa's moderate proposal: a four-hour nationwide warning strike on Friday and then, if no agreement had been reached with the government, the general strike from Tuesday 31 March. On the now familiar pattern a list of negotiating demands was drawn up. In addition to the immediate punishment or suspension of the people responsible for the Bydgoszcz incident, they included the recognition of Rural Solidarity, guarantees of security for all union members, annulment of a government directive giving only half-pay to strikers, and the closure of all cases pending against people arrested for opposition activity between 1976 (founding date of KOR) and 1980. A strike steering committee of ten was elected and the telex lines to regional headquarters were soon humming with their instructions.

In contrast to the messy National Commission debate, Solidarity's subsequent mobilisation of its members was extraordinarily swift and effective. Indeed what followed was the most impressive democratic mass mobilisation of any modern European society in peacetime, against its rulers' wishes. Like a country going to war, Poland decked itself out in the national colours: red and white flags bloomed on every facade, red and white were the inks for the ubiquitous strike posters, the women made red and white armbands for the men who were to guard the occupied factories. When you arrived at Warsaw airport the second person you saw sported a Solidarity badge, and from then on you saw the badges everywhere, large and small, square and round, red (for workers) and green (for peasants), with prison bars for the memory of Radom and Ursus, silver on black for the Gdańsk monument—a miniature gallery of graphic ingenuity. (The first person you saw was a soldier. He wore no badge.) In Mazowsze they ran off a poster with one of Krynicki's Brecht translations: above a crowd of determined workers with Käthe Kollwitz faces, the text:

> *When things remain as they are,*
> *You are lost.*
> *Give up what you have, and take*
> *WHAT IS DENIED YOU.*

Solidarity was by now a formidable *organisation*, with *c*. 9.5 million members, of *c*. 12.5 million employees theoretically eligible. It had some 40,000 regular staff—formally seconded from their workplaces (like one L. Wałęsa, an electrician in Section M-4 of the Lenin Shipyard), or employed directly by Solidarity and paid out of the regular union dues (1 per cent of pay). In Poznań, the offices had an air of Prussian efficiency: responsible men in suits and ties dictated cautious letters to businesslike secretaries. In Wrocław, industrial centre of Lower Silesia, they had organised a library for their half-million members: all the union press, unofficial publications and *Gazeta Krakowska* (a tribute to its independence). Most important, there were telex and telephone links between all regional centres.

Down the lines from Gdańsk, where the National Strike Committee had established itself in the Lenin Shipyard (for safety), came the Instructions: no. 1, *In case of a General Strike*, no. 2, *In case of a State of Emergency*, no. 3, *In case of a Foreign Intervention*. These were swiftly duplicated on the union presses and distributed to all the factories and offices where Solidarity had Factory Commissions. In Wrocław, they had a 'Solidarity Radio': the day's news and instructions recorded on cassettes and 'broadcast' over the works radio at 7 a.m. Every MKZ moved to a large factory for the strike period: Mazowsze to the Ursus tractor factory, Szczecin to the

Warski shipyard again, Kraków to the Nowa Huta steelworks. Instruction no. 1 specified a countrywide occupation-strike on the Lenin Shipyard model. Worker guards would be on a twenty-four-hour watch. 'It is forbidden to possess or consume any alcoholic beverage. All offenders should be expelled from the enterprise (including the Director)'. In the event of the arrest of the union's national leadership, a general strike should commence automatically. Instruction no. 2 explained the possibility of the authorities declaring a 'state of emergency' (*stan wyjątkowy*), militarising all enterprises, and urged the formation of shadow strike committees in case the first rank of leaders should be captured.

Instruction no. 3, most dramatically, suggested a few possible means of passive resistance to 'foreign troops'. Signposts should be reversed and street names obliterated (as in Czechoslovakia in 1968), all attempts at requisitioning food should be 'made impossible'.[16] Not even in August had so many Poles been so aware of the danger. In December the threat of the Warsaw Pact mobilisation had been somehow remote from their own activity: 'There's not much we can do about it,' they had said. Now the threat was directly related to their own activity. It was up to them: to strike or not to strike. A new poster appeared in Warsaw. It showed a sign usually seen on building-sites: 'NO ENTRY! BUILDING IN PROGRESS'—behind the sign, an outline map of Poland.

With this full awareness Wałęsa and a delegation met Rakowski on Wednesday 25 March. Rakowski launched into a long and, it seems, personally embittered attack on the politicisation of Solidarity, before giving some convoluted hints at possible compromise on the first Bydgoszcz demand. Any apology for the beatings was almost lost in the convolutions. Marian Jurczyk, the Szczecin chairman, a tough, plainspeaking docker, but so far by no means a 'radical' in Solidarity, was stung to fury. 'If your wife deceives you, and deceives you, and deceives you again,' he shouted across the table at Rakowski, 'would you have confidence in her? . . . Well, we no longer have confidence in you!'[17] After little more than an hour they were out on the street again.

At eight o'clock on Friday 27 March the factory sirens sounded from Gdańsk to Jastrzębie and Poland stopped work. For the next four hours Polish society demonstrated its unity and self-discipline in the largest strike in the history of the Soviet bloc.* Essential services and industrial plants such as steelworks, which it was dangerous to stop, were kept in operation, as were armaments factories: they would only stop work, Solidarity announced, 'in the event of armed intervention'. The nation's television screens were filled with the words *'solidarność-strajk'*. Wałęsa toured Warsaw factories, reiterating his confidence in General Jaruzelski: 'This is a uniform we can trust . . .' One participant in the Ursus works wrote that these were the calmest moments she had experienced for weeks.[18] At noon precisely the sirens sounded again and Poland went back to work.

For the Party leadership the most shattering feature of this national demonstration was the almost universal participation of Party members, against the explicit orders of the Politburo. ('The strikes that have been called are clearly political. Party members should not take part in them.')[19] By now the base of the Party was in open revolt. The leadership was deluged with protest letters and resolutions against the hardliners' confrontation course.

On Friday evening Rakowski presented Solidarity with the final version of a report prepared by a government commission on the Bydgoszcz incident. 'It is the opinion of the commission', it said, 'that medical expertise concerning the extent of the injuries [of the three Solidarity activists] does not provide grounds to assert that these injuries were self-inflicted'—as if Rulewski and Bartoszcze were likely to have beaten themselves unconscious! This was the kind of Circumlocution Office absurdity with which Solidarity constantly had to deal. The government commission did, however, go on to acknowledge that 'Rulewski was being hit by persons in plain clothes . . .' and that the 'forces of order' . . . 'had a duty to protect the people who had been led out of the hall against the possibility of being beaten up . . .'[20]

What the authorities were prepared to do about it depended on the Ninth Plenum of the Central Committee which met on Sunday 29 March. As if to nudge it in the right direction, TASS that morning 'reported' from Poland:

*The largest, in terms of numbers participating, and the best organised, but not the longest. In Budapest in 1956 the general strike lasted for some two months following the Russian invasion.

> Subversive elements operating in Kielce Province have set up road-blocks, specifically on Motorway E-7 between Suchedniów and Łączna; all road signs in that region have been destroyed. In Warsaw . . . and other cities anti-socialist forces tried to seize post offices. In the Polish capital, for instance, they managed to seize a television transmitter for some time.

This amazing 'report' was pure fiction, every word, and Radio Warsaw issued an exhaustive rebuttal (though of course not naming TASS as the source). But the message was plain, as was the message of the 'Soyuz '81' manoeuvres still continuing on Polish soil. Yet despite the lies and the tanks the worker members of the Central Committee spoke up as never before. 'I know no anti-socialists in my factory,' said a man from Kielce (for some mysterious reason Kielce was twice the subject of TASS's fictions). A woman worker from Wrocław described the Bydgoszcz beatings as 'a brutal violation of constitutional and civic rights and freedoms'. 'The use of force', declared a Party First Secretary, no less, from Siedlce, would 'discredit the idea of Socialism in the world'. In the early hours of Monday 30 March, the meeting took a Byzantine turn. Olszowski and Grabski, along with one other candidate Politburo member, Roman Ney, offered their resignations. A little later the First Secretary from Włocławek stood up to propose that Olszowski and Grabski should be asked to stay . . . and then voted against his own resolution! There are times, he subsequently explained to his local newspaper, when political reason must take precedence over conscience. Political reason (i.e. Moscow) demanded that Olszowski and Grabski should stay. At four o'clock on Monday morning the reformers had at last got a date for the Party Congress—not later than 20 July—but they had not much more to offer Solidarity.

Meanwhile, the pressure on Wałęsa mounted. His closest advisers, Geremek, Mazowiecki and the Primate's representative, Professor Kukułowicz, told him that a general strike would mean civil war: the risk was too high. The Primate had personally urged restraint when he met Wałęsa again on Saturday. He apparently produced a letter from the Pope which said that Polish working people wanted to work not to strike. As a matter of fact most Polish working people were preparing, with nervous determination, for the general strike. Lorryloads of bread, sausage and jam rolled into Huta Warszawa. Workers, typists, students, teachers, all brought their sleeping-bags to their workplaces over the weekend. In some plants, acetylene torches, gasoline and chemicals were readied for possible defence against the 'forces of order'—the visible determination was greatest amongst younger workers in the largest factories. Meanwhile many members of the National Commission wanted to come to Warsaw to take part in the negotiations, although Wałęsa had told them at the beginning of the last meeting that in his view the situation was so grave that 'democracy must be limited'.[21] On Sunday evening he telephoned desperately to Gdańsk from Mazowsze headquarters: Lis and Bujak must stay there, he bawled down the line, they must oversee the strike preparations, he, Wałęsa, would deal with the government, he would get them a good deal.

We do not yet have a full, reliable account of the negotiations which followed, but democratic they were not. Much of the time Wałęsa and Rakowski seem to have been closeted with a few of their advisers. Other members of the Solidarity team were left in a state of nervous confusion. Marian Jurczyk subsequently described his own bewilderment to his regional Solidarity paper, *Jedność*. If the government threatened Wałęsa and his advisers with total confrontation and bloodshed, those advisers hastened to elaborate the warnings to men like Jurczyk and Gwiazda. According to Jurczyk's account, every few hours an adviser would appear at their hotel with some new tale of imminent violence. Geremek and the lawyer Olszewski effectively drew up the text of the proposed agreement for Solidarity, and (again, according to Jurczyk) at the time of signing, there were only two copies of it: one for Rakowski, one for Wałęsa.[22]

When millions of Poles turned on their television sets for the seven-thirty evening news, they were fully prepared for this to be their last evening at home for some time. Tomorrow they would be spending the night at their workplace, and the day after tomorrow... who knew? They swapped the old jokes about remembering your fur coat for Siberia. Instead, they saw Andrzej Gwiazda—Gwiazda of all people—hesitantly, almost apologetically, reading out a summary of the agreement, with Wałęsa standing next to him, looking nervous and foxy. After all that organisation, all that psychological preparation, the strike was 'suspended'.

Western leaders, who had been watching developments in Poland with mounting alarm—on 26 March the White House once again warned of imminent danger of Soviet intervention—at this point breathed a sigh of relief. Was it Balzac who said that a Pole cannot see an abyss without jumping into it? Certainly that view of the national character was widely held. Yet the Poles seemed to be behaving in a quite 'unPolish' way. This was the fourth time in eight months that they had rushed seemingly to the very brink of the abyss—and then stepped back.

Within Solidarity, however, the 'Warsaw Agreement', as it soon came to be called, was only the beginning of a major storm.

Moment of Truth?

The storm broke when the National Commission met the next afternoon in the Lenin Shipyard 'Health and Safety' hall. At issue was, first, the decision itself—to 'suspend' the general strike on what seemed, to many, quite inadequate promises from the government. But what angered the delegates even more was the way in which the decision had been taken. The angry recriminations against Wałęsa and his advisers which this same hall had witnessed on the last evening of the August strike (see above, p. 69), were compliments when compared with the accusations which now rained down upon them. In the corridors, workers grumbled about the 'cowardice' of the advisers: 'They were frightened by the tanks!' None the less, a clear majority of the Commission voted formally to call off the strike before they dispersed at one o'clock in the morning.

On Wednesday they reassembled in the Hotel Morski, to continue the debate behind closed doors. Now Andrzej Gwiazda, looking more than ever like an El Greco saint, declared that he had sinned against the fundamental principles of union democracy, for which he had so long fought, and accordingly offered his resignation. Andrzej Słowik, the tough-talking workers' leader from Łódź, said that the Warsaw negotiations had been 'a farce' and everything had been fixed between the advisers and the government beforehand. Lech Dymarski from Poznań launched a furious personal attack on Wałęsa, accusing him of being 'anti-democratic' and even paranoid. Wałęsa retorted that Dymarski was paranoid. Geremek and Mazowiecki defended their own role with habitual eloquence and dignity. The sociologist Andrzej Celiński carried the can for the intellectuals, being temporarily ousted from his 'secretaryship' of the National Commission. But the speech of the day came from Karol Modzelewski.

Solidarity was beginning to resemble a feudal monarchy, the medievalist Modzelewski remarked. The King, Wałęsa, governed with his Court and his Parliament, the National Commission. But too much power was concentrated in the hands of the King and the King's men. He personally could not go on putting his name, as national Press Spokesman, to undemocratic decisions with which he disagreed. Therefore, he tendered his resignation. But, he went on, Wałęsa must not be dethroned: for in the eyes of millions of Poles he was the symbol and lynchpin of the union's unity.[23]

As so often, Modzelewski had cut straight to the heart of the matter: the conflict between the ideal of democracy and the necessity of unity. Much of the history of Solidarity can be understood in terms of this fundamental conflict. Solidarity had to be strong and united if it was to survive against a regime which would do everything in its power to 'divide and rule'. But Solidarity defined itself against that regime precisely by being genuinely democratic. 'Is there really no unity in Solidarity?' asked a contributor to the new national Solidarity weekly, *Tygodnik Solidarność*, which was at last allowed to appear in early April. 'No,' she answered herself. 'There is only *democracy*.' . . . The attacks on Wałęsa should be welcomed because 'distrust of authority is the most valuable sign of democracy (the Americans are proud of the fact that they never trust their government)'![24]

From March onward, democracy increasingly gained the upper hand over unity, and Solidarity's Congress, unlike the American Congress, would not be counter-balanced by a strong administration. It is from the aftermath of the Bydgoszcz crisis that one can chart the rapid growth of those factions and divisions which were to weaken the union so visibly in the autumn. From March, too, one can date the growing public challenge to the personal authority of Lech Wałęsa. Wałęsa's own understanding of democracy was, like most things about him, singular.

'But how do you see yourself—as a real leader or more as a symbol?' two Polish journalists asked him in the summer of 1981.

'Symbol indeed! What a thing to say! You know very well that I have no wish to be any kind of symbol.'

'How much of the decision-making process is in your hands? What specifically needs your participation?'

'Almost everything does. Especially the very crucial questions. Nobody is prepared to take decisions without me.'

'Do you always know what you have to do? How do you come to your decisions?'

'It take seconds. Split seconds. Those are the best decisions. The ones you make in a split second are best. Those that are weighed up, chewed over, compromised on—they're no good.'[25]

Well, take a large pinch of salt. In practice, Wałęsa would often 'weigh up, chew over and compromise on' the widely differing advice that was offered him. In practice, he seems to have regarded himself rather as one of those sixteenth-century Polish elected kings—while the National Commission, like the sixteenth-century nobility, cried 'Nothing about us without us!' In an interview he gave to the Solidarity Weekly he declared 'democracy is invaluable', but, he went on, it would not be 'democratic' if 'when the Prime Minister asked "how are you?" eighty of us would reply at once "we're well". When, after voting, we would all together gaggle "Mr Prime Minister, give us shoe-laces"!'[26]

'When I say "democracy" I don't mean the gaggling of geese,' he told the two journalists. And, of course, *he* would decide what was 'gaggling'.

In defending the Warsaw Agreement he used another argument: 'I saw what society wanted, and I do not know in whose name those who say otherwise speak.' And later, 'Society is tired, and does not want a confrontation.' A slippery concept, 'what society wanted'. Solidarity polls conducted in the run-up to the strike suggested massive support for it. In the petrochemicals town of Płock, for example, 79 per cent of those asked were definitely in favour of the general strike. First reactions on the evening the strike was called off were very mixed, with anger and dismay foremost amongst those who had already occupied their factories—who had screwed their courage to the sticking-place. Wałęsa had begged Gwiazda to make the television announcement for him, because he feared for his own popularity. The messages which poured into Gdańsk from regional and factory committees the following day were also mixed. Wałęsa claimed that most were in the spirit of the Poznań Cegielski works (starting-place of the 1956 riots) who telexed: 'Leszek, we support your position . . . the rank-and-file have complete trust in you . . .'[27] But several of the largest regions, including Mazowsze and the Silesian centres of Katowice and Wałbrzych, were fiercely critical of the King's 'manipulation'.

Two days later Solidarity's Centre for Social Research (OBS) began an inquiry among 270 employees in twenty-five enterprises in the Warsaw area (80 per cent of the sample were Solidarity members). 91 per cent of those asked thought 'in general, the decision to suspend the strike was right'.[28] Many people only now admitted how frightened they had been. In late April and early May a larger sample of Solidarity members was asked if they would have signed the agreement on each of the five points. Their answers reflected the extreme vagueness of the government's promises. Only 40 per cent said 'yes' without reservations on the question of bringing those responsible for the Bydgoszcz incident to justice. 57 per cent said 'yes' on 'security for Solidarity workers', although Rakowski had merely promised to speed up the new Trades Union Bill.[29] My own straw polls reinforced this impression of general assent, after the event, mixed with major reservations in detail.

With hindsight one can see that March was the most important single turning-point between August 1980 and December 1981. The decision of Wałęsa and his advisers dealt a fatal blow to the credibility of Solidarity's ultimate deterrent. For of course a general strike is not a missile which can be kept almost indefinitely in its silo, ready for action at the press of a button. Some Solidarity activists came to believe it was such a weapon: they were proved wrong on 13 December. From March onward the divisions within the national and regional leadership, and the increasingly bitter criticism of Wałęsa by militant activists and 'fundamentalists', weakened Solidarity organisationally and politically. More important, never again would they approach the extraordinary degree of mass mobilisation, popular resolution and preparation which they achieved on 30 March. Over the next eight months the Poles' strength, unity and determination was steadily sapped by political frustration and economic decline. On 1 April the rationing for which Solidarity, too, had pressed was introduced, covering meat, butter, cereals and flour. A cartoon in the first number of the Solidarity Weekly (TS) showed a woman standing in a queue before empty shelves, reading an official newspaper: 'They write that Solidarity is pouring oil on the flames. But where do they buy the oil?'

At the time, Wałęsa believed what the government and the Primate and his most experienced advisers and (indirectly) even the White House told him: that the risk of bloodshed was too great. Moreover, the actual negotiating demands did not have the clarity and self-evident importance of those first two demands in the Lenin Shipyard. But he instinctively grasped the historical importance of the decision. A few days later he told his interviewers:

> The Pope wrote to us, and the Primate, pleading for reason and reflection. Tomorrow we may achieve more, but we may not go to the brink. At the same time I know that what is good today, may turn out tomorrow to be bad. And the historians, when they come to judge, may say: but he was crazy, the authorities were bluffing, they were weak, their bark was worse than their bite, it would have been possible at last to put the country straight, they could have won, and they flunked it. They can judge me like that in 10 or 50 years. And we don't yet know if I was right, or those who took another view. In my opinion the risk was too great.[30]

Was it? Was this the greatest blunder of the Solidarity leadership or was it the moment of truth for the 'self-limiting' revolution? What would have happened if they had gone ahead with the general strike? We can do no more than speculate on three possibilities. The first is that Solidarity would have won a decisive victory. As in the previous three major confrontations the authorities would have retreated behind a face-saving compromise, while Solidarity would have been immensely strengthened by the experience of actually deploying its ultimate deterrent. However, the then Polish Ambassador to Japan, Mr Rurarz, reports that he was sent a secret telegram warning him that a 'state of war' would be declared in the event of a general strike.* Marian Jurczyk, relaying Rakowski's threats to the National Commission on 1 April, uses the specific phrase 'state of war' (*stan wojenny*). The National Strike Committee had prepared their members for a 'state of emergency' (*stan wyjątkowy*). The second possibility is therefore that Kania and Jaruzelski would have decided to use their contingency plans for a 'state of war', and that they would, in fact, have succeeded in using the army and security forces to crush resistance as they did after 13 December. However, Solidarity was, as we have seen, fully prepared for such a danger, the workers were occupying their factories and the whole society was mobilised in a way it definitely was not by December. At the same time, there can have been little of the highly professional, detailed and secret planning, not to mention the political and psychological preparation of the army and security forces, which preceded the brilliantly executed coup of 13 December. In December, the loyalty of the conscript army was not put to the hardest test, since flying squads of security thugs and professional soldiers were sufficient to break the pockets of workers' resistance. Large numbers of conscript soldiers were not ordered to fire on their brothers. In March, it would almost certainly have come to that. The third possibility, therefore, is that the authorities would have tried *and failed* to crush Solidarity with the Polish forces at their disposal.

In the third case, obviously, in the first case, sooner or later, the Russians would have had to decide whether or not once again to assert the 'Brezhnev doctrine' by armed invasion—on a scale larger than any military operation they had mounted since 1945.

We know now that the German troops who moved into the demilitarised Rhineland in 1936 had orders to retreat if a shot was fired against them. We can see that if the French troops had fired those shots, the subsequent retreat and humiliation might have

*Mr Rurarz repeated his version to ITV's 'TV Eye', in an interview broadcast on 26 February 1982. Mr Rurarz, who defected to the West after the declaration of a 'state of war' in December 1981, is not the most reliable of sources. He has tended to tell his questioners what they want to hear.

changed the whole course of Hitler's dictatorship, and therefore of history.

Perhaps in ten or fifty years, as Lech Wałęsa said, we will have documents which enable us to judge Russian intentions in 1981 as we can now judge German intentions in 1936. Or perhaps we will not. Perhaps the Soviet leaders themselves do not know how they would have decided.

5. Democratic Communism?

For the next four months, from April to July, the most urgent questions in Poland concerned not Solidarity but the Party. How far would the *fronde* inside the Party spread? What would happen at the Extraordinary Party Congress? How would Moscow react?

The 'loyal opposition' still hoped that, given time, the Party could reform itself sufficiently to begin to lead the country out of the economic crisis, as it had promised to do in point 6 of the Gdańsk Agreement. Then Solidarity might still be held to the terms of the summer's 'historic compromise'. Then, with Solidarity pushing from behind and the Party pulling from the front, the rickety cart might yet move up instead of downhill. As one of them subsequently explained, they felt that KOR's 'New Evolutionism' was not enough: Poland needed a New Revisionism as well. Only the *combination* of pressure from a society which had organised itself (as in 1980) *and* a Party which was reforming itself (as in 1956) could bring the country through.

Now was the time for all good men to come to the aid of the Party. Privately, the Church leaders closest to Cardinal Wyszyński took a rather similar position. 'You know this may sound strange coming from a Cardinal of the Church,' the Primate himself reportedly told a government adviser in January 1981, 'but what we need now is a strong Party leadership.' Wyszyński, much more than Kania or Wałęsa, could still set a clear 'line' and expect to have it followed by most of his activists. Yet even within the centralised, authoritarian structure of the Church the revolution had exacerbated disagreements about how much to render unto Caesar. At one extreme there was the Church militant of Bishop Tokarczuk, supporting KOR, or Józef Tischner, the moral philosopher of Solidarity. At the other, there was an ecclesiastical cabal around the aged Wyszyński in Warsaw, steered by Bishop Dąbrowski, secretary of the Episcopate, and spoken for by one Father Orszulik, sometime Episcopate press spokesman. They advocated close, cautious co-operation with the authorities, and, at the height of the December invasion scare, Orszulik had directly attacked 'irresponsible' people in KOR, mentioning Kuroń by name.

Ever since the war the Party had tried to use puppet lay Catholic organisations to divide and weaken the Church, and it was in lay Catholic circles that the divisions were now most apparent. On the one hand the Club of the Catholic Intelligentsia in Warsaw was a Solidarity centre; leading Catholic intellectuals like Mazowiecki, Cywiński and Wielowieyski were editing the Solidarity Weekly (TS) and organising the union's Centre for Socio-Professional Studies (OPSZ); the original Kraków-based 'Znak' group were no less explicit in supporting the civil crusade for national regeneration. On the other hand, Jerzy Ozdowski, from the collaborationist 'neoZnak' splinter group, had, in November 1980, accepted the post of Deputy Prime Minister—a gesture much celebrated, in the West. Now he sat, a small apologetic man in the corner of a large empty government office, shuffling papers and receiving foreign journalists.[1]

The Pope had discreetly but unmistakably distanced himself from the 'neo-Znak' collaborationists when he returned to Kraków in the summer of 1979. Tischner and members of the Kraków 'Znak' circle were among his closest associates. Yet in November 1980 he received Ozdowski in private audience a week before the appointment was announced. His Christmas message, broadcast on state radio and television, extended greetings to 'everyone in Poland without exception' and used the Party's catchword *'odnowa'* (renewal).

Since the sixteenth century, when the Primate had governed as *Interrex* between the death of one king and the election of the next, the Church had been regarded, and regarded itself, as the one true guardian of Poland's national sovereignty. The more Church leaders felt that sovereignty (however limited) was threatened, the more they were drawn into the political arena, and the more they felt compelled to throw their authority on the side of *'odnowa'*, though they talked of 'national' rather than 'socialist' renewal, of 'calm' and 'responsibility' and 'restraint'.

Poland now presented the paradoxical spectacle of a Church

leader and the communist Party which had imprisoned him both silently praying that the other should recover strength. The Party knew that this Primate might sway Wałęsa, as he had in March, to the side of caution. Wyszyński, now seventy-nine years old and a dying man, exacted a price for his support. Beside direct concessions, such as permission to build new seminaries in Koszalin and Szczecin, he had, for instance, made Jaruzelski promise to register 'Rural Solidarity'. But developments inside the Party were one of the few things in Poland which the Church could not directly influence. It could attempt to create the social conditions in which the Party would have the best chance to reform itself. And then it would watch and pray. 'For thirty years the Party had Democratic Centralism without the Democracy,' commented Jerzy Turowicz, editor of the Catholic *Tygodnik Powszechny* (catholic with a small as well as a large 'c', and consistently the best weekly in Poland). 'Now the rank-and-file Party members want Democratic Centralism without the Centre. We hope they will end up somewhere in between.'[2]

Western eyes were also focused on the Party, in fear and hope. It was observed that the Soviets had intervened in Czechoslovakia just before an Extraordinary Party Congress which threatened to become a reformist rout. Could the Polish communists 'seize the torch of reform and run forward with it' while yet appeasing the Russians?

The people least interested in the Party were the men and women who worked in Solidarity. For most of this period they once again displayed great self-restraint, matched by a new sensitivity on the part of the authorities, who had seen how quickly local disputes could explode into nationwide conflagrations. There were public celebrations on 3 May, anniversary of the famous 1791 liberal constitution which precipitated Russian intervention, and pointed abstinence from celebration on 1 May. There was an ugly incident in the small town of Otwock, where a mob burnt down a police station and a policeman was saved from lynching only by the personal intervention of Adam Michnik ('I am an "Anti-Socialist Force",' he shouted at the angry crowd—and then they began to trust him).[3] There was a march through Warsaw on behalf of political prisoners, organised by the Independent Students' Union, but the Solidarity leaders persuaded them to change their route so that it did not pass Party headquarters. Otherwise, the months of April and May were remarkably free of public conflict.

Solidarity's self-restraint was due partly to the pleading of the Church and the advisers. Partly, it was a response to Jaruzelski's renewed appeal for a moratorium on strikes, this time for a period of two months and backed by a *sejm* resolution passed on 10 April under the threat of Jaruzelski's resignation. But it was also the outward symptom of a prolonged 'identity crisis' which began with the cancellation of the general strike. As Solidarity, like the Party, plunged into regional elections, both turned inwards for a time of intense self-examination.

None the less, though most Solidarity members could hardly be less interested in the Party, it was Solidarity which had precipitated the Party *fronde*. According to official figures, between October 1980 and March 1981 the Party lost 216,000 members, bringing total membership below three million.[4] Of those who stayed, at least one million (there are no precise figures) became members of Solidarity. Some did so on Party instructions, following the principle of the Trojan horse: but the trouble with this Trojan horse was that Greeks tended to become Trojans the moment they got inside the city walls. On 27 March they had followed Solidarity's orders against the Party's. Furthermore, the revolt of the Party rank-and-file was often most visible in those factories where Solidarity was strongest, partly because worker-members felt impelled to regain their honour, partly because Party Secretaries saw the need to make a splash before their support evaporated altogether.

The *locus classicus* for this phenomenon was the Lenin Shipyard. Here the Party Secretary, a worker called Jan Łabęcki, became more Polish than the Pope and more democratic than Wałęsa. During the Ninth Plenum at the end of March, Party members at the Lenin Shipyard occupied that same 'Health and Safety' hall which had been the centre of the August strike, declaring a 'Party alert' and shooting off telexes of protest to the Central Committee in Warsaw. On 9 April, Kania came to see them, and sat through seven hours of angry criticism. 'Who is the Party?' one worker demanded. 'Is it three million members who think the same? Or is it the small circle of the leadership who think otherwise? . . .'[5]

Across the country the basic grievance was the same: the Party leadership represented the apparatus not the Party. 75 per cent of the Central Committee was drawn from a group representing less than 5 per cent of the Party—*c.* 50 per cent from the apparatus and 25 per cent of managers.[6] In this sense the Party had indeed become, in Adam Michnik's striking phrase, 'a trades union for the rulers'. Every week brought new revelations about the privileges, the gross corruption and inefficiency of this ruling class which had brought Poland to ruin. Now the issue was clear: would the Party seize control of the apparatus, or would the apparatus keep control of the Party?

To challenge the power of the apparatus the Party rebels had to organise themselves—but the very fact of independent organisation inside the Party was, since Lenin, the capital offence of 'factionalism'. The organisation of what became the anti-apparatus movement nevertheless began immediately after the August strikes, not in Gdańsk but in the handsome university town of Toruń. Here, as in Szczecin, many of the strike leaders were Party members. One of them, Zbigniew Iwanów, was promptly elected Party Secretary at his factory, the 'Towimor' marine engineering plant, and proceeded to establish a 'Consultative Commission' which brought together other Party Secretaries from other factories in the region on the model of Solidarity's Interfactory Strike Committees. These 'horizontal' links were anathema to Leninist Democratic Centralism (see above, pp. 104 ff.). 'An attack on the apparatus is an attack on the Party,' as the Warsaw Party Secretary, Kociołek, succinctly put the Soviet view.[7]

In November, Iwanów was duly expelled from the Party because he had challenged the Marxist-Leninist World Outlook—the local Party Control Commission had a picture of him taking communion at the factory gate in August—and on the grounds of 'factionalism'. Iwanów replied that for him the Party leadership was the 'faction' and carried on regardless, with an overwhelming vote of confidence from his members. The 'horizontal' movement grew apace. One key to its progress, as to that of Solidarity, was the alliance with intellectuals. Lech Witkowski, a 29-year-old philosophy lecturer from Toruń University, was instrumental in elaborating the Toruń demands. In Warsaw, a bevy of Party intellectuals who had privately been developing revisionist ideas with increasing urgency in the late 1970s (in DiP, in the Warsaw University 'Sigma' club, in the Party High School) now broke cover. In the pentecostal excitement of that autumn they began to draft and debate new statutes which, if accepted by the Extraordinary Party Congress, would transform the Party beyond recognition. Horizontal structures would be permitted. All Party officials would be elected on a free, secret ballot with a real choice of candidates. They would be directly accountable and there would be strict limits to the time they could hold office, and the number of offices they could combine. In short, the Party would control the apparatus.

By April 1981 the emancipation of the Party had gone further than anyone would have predicted. New democratic elections were already bringing new representatives into the basic Party organisations: in Bydgoszcz, for example, 322 out of 393 basic Party organisations elected new First Secretaries.[8] These organisations would democratically elect new local committees, which would democratically elect new regional committees, which would democratically elect delegates to the Congress, who would democratically elect a new Central Committee, who would appoint a new Politburo, who would preside over the dismantling of the pyramid at the top of which they now sat . . . This, at least, was the perspective of the 750 delegates from thirteen Provinces (they claimed to represent some one million Party members) who gathered in Toruń for an independent pre-Congress forum on 15 April. To their surprise, a senior Party official, not renowned for his 'moderate' views, extended a cautious blessing: 'Your movement', he said, 'represents life-giving capital for our Party.' This was tactical trimming, but the Soviet guardian of ideological orthodoxy, Mikhail Suslov, was sufficiently alarmed to fly to Warsaw the next week. Prague television meanwhile thundered that this gathering of 'right-wing revisionist currents' was preparing the ground 'for the transformation of the PZPR into some kind of social democratic party'.[9]

For once, Prague television was close to the truth. If the Toruń forum had been the Party Congress, the Polish United Workers' Party (PZPR) would have broken the Leninist mould. Though there were many opportunists who bent with the wind, at all levels of the Party, the activists of the horizontal movement genuinely sought this transformation. Typically, they were men in their twenties and thirties, with a university or higher technical education—Iwanow was a 32-year-old engineer. There is a sense in which this movement and Solidarity were two faces of the same phenomenon: a new generation's bid for political participation. As they could see in Prague, it was the most radical attempt to reform a Soviet bloc communist Party since 1968.

Between mid-April and mid-July the attempt was defeated. The most fundamental internal Polish cause of this defeat was the absence of popular support for Party reform. The Polish reformists could never claim, as the Czech reformists could in 1968, that the hopes of the nation were vested in them. They had no democratic mandate from society. Just 3 per cent of those asked in a poll conducted for *Paris Match* in autumn 1980 said they would vote for the communist party in a free election. On 21 June the Warsaw weekly *Kultura* published an opinion poll which asked what institutions people most trusted. The Church came first on the list, Solidarity second, and the army a surprisingly good third. The Party came fifteenth on the list, lower even than the police.[10]

From the earliest basic Party organisation meetings it was noticed that manual workers were extremely reluctant to stand for Party office. In fact, of the 1,964 delegates finally elected to the Extraordinary Party Congress only 393 were blue-collar workers, although no fewer than 365 delegates were elected directly from large factories.[11] This was the most devastating vote of no confidence. The Party daily, *Trybuna Ludu*, made the extraordinary admission that the workers felt 'strangers in the Party's ranks'.[12] Those workers who looked for authentic, democratic political activity found their fulfilment in Solidarity: and we recall that Solidarity was strongest among young workers in the large factories. By another paradox of this looking-glass revolution, the worker who stood for office in the PZPR was treated as a blackleg by his mates. This robbed the reformers of their most important potential power base.

At the end of April the Tenth Plenum of the Central Committee finally set the opening date for the Congress: 14 July, Bastille Day! It also provisionally endorsed the kind of genuinely democratic elections, that is, with a free choice of candidates and a secret ballot, with which the lower echelons of the Party were proceeding willy-nilly. Kania reiterated that the horizontal movement 'type of activity must not lead to the weakening or the replacement of the *Leninist structure of the Party* . . .' (my italics). This was a crucial phrase. Otherwise he restated his middle-of-the-road line, emphasising collective responsibility and the need for Party unity, a line which was essentially tactical and intended to keep the Party from falling apart over the next few months. 'Horizontal' activists from eighteen Provincial organisations had appeared at the door demanding admission, and, when this was refused, withdrew to the nearby headquarters of the Journalists' Association to form a lobby.

It was on the Provincial conferences which would elect most of the delegates to the Congress that attention now focused. And it was here, in elections which could be only marginally manipulated, that the horizontal activists were defeated, even in regions like Kraków, Gdańsk and Toruń where they had appeared strongest. 'We have already lost the Congress,' Iwanow said at the end of May. Ironically, the super-democratic electoral method—to be successful a candidate had to get more than 50 per cent of the total vote—worked against the men who had campaigned for it. In practice it meant that both 'extremes', reformist and reactionary, were eliminated.[13] Characteristically, and fatally, the Party concentrated on personalities rather than on structures. The Lenin Shipyard, for example, unanimously adopted Tadeusz Fiszbach as its delegate. Kania himself was elected almost unanimously in Kraków, while the steelworkers of Nowa Huta surprisingly adopted Rakowski. Beside them, there was row upon row of unknowns, whose facelessness was their fortune. The safest candidate was the one who had no political track-record at all. 'Say two sentences criticising the past and the party apparatus and you get 90 per cent of the votes,' a Kraków official reported to Mark Frankland of the *Observer*.[14]

Measured against the hopes of Toruń this was already a defeat. Measured against the Soviet standard model for a Party Congress, the minutely orchestrated demonstrations of 'spontaneous' unanimity which had passed off so satisfactorily in Prague and East Berlin in April, it was appalling, heretical, unpredictable. On 28 May the declaration of an anonymous Party group called the 'Katowice Forum' was published in the youth daily *Sztandar Młodych*. It contained a splenetic assault on the Kania leadership. This had lost its political and ideological bearings, said the statement, while the Party was becoming infected by 'Trotskyite-Zionist views, nationalism, agrarianism, clericalism, and anti-Sovietism'! Most Poles were far more concerned with mourning Cardinal Wyszyński, who died that same day, than in discussing this ugly throwback to the language of his Stalinist persecutors. In his will, Wyszyński counted among his life's blessings the fact that he had been permitted 'to bear witness to the truth as a political prisoner'[15] (from 1953 to 1956). A huge cross appeared in Victory Square for his funeral. The Pope asked for thirty days of peaceful mourning for the Primate—an appeal which certainly contributed to Solidarity's self-restraint in the run-up to the Party Congress.

Inside the Party the 'Katowice Forum' declaration provoked such a torrent of criticism that just five days later the Politburo publicly disowned it. At a press conference Kazimierz Barcikowski described it as 'harmful'. His listeners returned to find on their desks a TASS 'report' warmly approving the views of the Forum. Significantly, no senior 'hardliners' dared to express public support for it, and on 4 June it 'suspended' itself until the Party leadership would take an 'unambiguous stand' on its activities.

Their variety of communist ideology none the less continued to be expressed through the sinister 'Grunwald* Patriotic Union' and a new political weekly called *Rzeczywistość* (Reality). The 'Grunwald Patriotic Union' was a mysterious organisation which had announced its existence on the anniversary of the March 1968 events, with a grotesque ceremony commemorating the 'victims of Zionist terror' in the Stalinist period. Their virulent mixture of communism, anti-Semitism and nationalism recalled the Party factions which had led the anti-Semitic campaign in 1968, but not even Olszowski and Grabski were prepared to associate themselves unequivocally with 'Grunwald'. Its Chairman, one Bohdan Poręba, contrived to suggest 'a continuum stretching from the security service interrogators in the 1950s to Solidarity activists in the 1980s'.[16] 'Grunwald's' baffling longevity (it was not suspended even under martial law) testified to powerful backers.

In the short-term, however, the 'healthy forces' of reaction inside the Party failed in their objectives—and when they failed, the Soviet

*At the Battle of Grunwald in 1410 the Poles and Lithuanians routed the Teutonic Knights.

Union once again intervened directly in Poland's internal affairs. On 5 June an unprecedented letter from the Soviet to the Polish Central Committee was learned to have 'arrived' in Warsaw. Its first sentence expressed 'profound anxiety for the fate of socialism in Poland and the freedom and independence of the country'. The Polish Party had withdrawn 'in the face of pressure from counter-revolution which relies on the support of foreign centres of imperialism and subversion'. 'Enemies of socialist Poland' were 'conducting a struggle for power and winning.' There followed a direct attack on the Kania leadership:

> We wish to underline that in all these questions Comrades Kania and Jaruzelski and other Polish comrades expressed agreement with our point of view, but in fact everything remained unchanged and there was no correction whatever to the policy of concession and compromise. One position after another is being surrendered.
>
> Recently the situation inside the PZPR itself has become the subject of our particular concern. There is not much more than a month left before the congress, yet increasingly forces hostile to socialism are setting the tone of the election campaign.

After expressing concern at the shortage of working-class delegates it singled out 'the so-called "horizontal structures" movement' which, it said shortly, 'is an instrument for dismantling the Party . . .' Then came the expressions of brotherly love:*

> Respected comrades, in writing to you we not only have in mind our anxiety about the situation in fraternal Poland and the conditions and future prospects of Soviet-Polish co-operation. Like other fraternal parties, we are also concerned that anti-socialist forces, the enemies of the People's Republic of Poland, are menacing the interests of our entire community, its cohesion, its integrity and the security of its frontiers—yes, our common security! . . .
>
> We believe that a possibility of avoiding a national

*'Are the Russians our brothers or our friends?' asks an old Soviet bloc joke. Answer: 'Our brothers—you can *choose* your friends.'

> catastrophe still exists . . . Our point of view was expressed with precision in the declaration of Comrade L. I. Brezhnev to the twenty-sixth congress of the CPSU. We will not permit any attack on socialist Poland and we will not abandon a fraternal country in distress.[17]

They could hardly be more threatening.

Unavoidably, a Plenum of the Central Committee had to be called to discuss this bombshell. It is occasionally suggested that the Soviet Letter was actually designed to reinforce Kania's and Jaruzelski's position, since being attacked by the Soviets would obviously enhance their standing with most Party members! This is almost certainly too Machiavellian an interpretation, and the course of the Eleventh Plenum belies it. For Tadeusz Grabski, one of the two most prominent hardliners in the Politburo, took the Letter as his cue for an open attempt to depose Kania:

> In the light of the situation in the Party and the danger threatening our people, I want to answer the question whether the members of the Politburo are capable of leading the country out of its political crisis. I do not see such a possibility in its present composition under the leadership of Comrade Stanisław Kania, the First Secretary.

The battle for the leadership was joined. In the event Kania survived, partly through his own clever tactics: at one point he proposed an individual vote of confidence on each Politburo member, adopting the super-democratic '50 per cent plus one vote' method which originated with the anti-apparatus movement. But what finally saved him was the support of Jaruzelski and the military. One in every ten Central Committee members wore an army uniform, and now the Generals 'expressed their confidence' in Kania and Jaruzelski. In the light of the military's subsequent role, it is interesting to speculate whether and whom Jaruzelski consulted in Moscow (his military superiors?) before this open defiance of the Soviet Party.

Kania survived—indeed, his position was apparendy strengthened—but he now had to 'fix' the remaining Provincial election conferences. As his concluding remarks about the 'need to retain continuity' in the leadership showed, he fully understood the primitive importance which the Brezhnev leadership attached to having 'their' people—faces they knew and trusted—at the top (see above, pp. 103 ff.). In the past this had presented no problems: the Central Committee member would arrive at the Provincial conference, produce a list of names from his briefcase, and the chosen members of the central apparatus would be adopted as delegates to the Party Congress with a nod and a wink. But now things were different.

In Katowice, for example, the conference was declining to elect its own Provincial First Secretary as a delegate! The well-hated Andrzej Żabiński (of the 'power corrupts' secret speech, above, p. 158) was blamed for tolerating the presence of the 'Katowice Forum' in his fief. Kania and Jaruzelski had to hurry down to Silesia in person—for all the world like Wałęsa dashing down to quell a Solidarity bushfire. Kania twice pleaded with the conference to accept a man who everyone knew opposed his conciliatory line, and then Żabiński just scraped through with 60 per cent of the vote. In Poznań, Grabski brusquely attempted to foist four central candidates on the meeting. He was sharply told that only candidates who had been elected at a lower level could stand (even Solidarity did not have that democratic rule in all its regions!) Eventually, he was reduced to telephoning for help to Kania, the man he had tried to oust. Only when Kania had personally appealed to the conference by telephone were the four grudgingly accepted as candidates—and then only two of them were actually elected (but those two were the police chief and an Air Force general).[18] In Warsaw itself, seat of the apparatus, the hardliners were most successful. Olszowski and Kociołek passed into the ranks of delegates, albeit with slim majorities, as did the Interior Minister, General Mirosław Milewski, and a hatchet-jawed Warsaw building foreman called Albin Siwak, who looked and talked as if he had just stepped down from the Stalinist frieze of gigantic Hero-Workers on Warsaw's Marszałkowska boulevard. Most of the prominent reformists, including Stefan Bratkowski, were eliminated.

In sum, slightly fewer than a third of the Central Committee made it to the Congress. 90 per cent of the delegates who assembled in the Warsaw Palace of Culture—an appalling Stalinist wedding-cake given to an ungrateful Polish people by their Soviet liberators—on the 192nd anniversary of the storming of the Bastille were there for the first time. No one could be certain how they would behave.

The Extraordinary Congress

From the moment they met at half-past eight that Tuesday morning it was clear that this Congress would indeed be 'Extraordinary'. The leadership proposed they should accept a report prepared by a commission under Tadeusz Grabski, on the errors and crimes of the Gierek leadership. This was a bad tactical mistake, for they should have known that most Party members were almost obsessively concerned with 'settling accounts'. The delegates said no, they would pass judgment on the guilty men themselves. Grabski reportedly stormed out, declaring that the delegates were behaving 'like Chinese'.[19] Then the leadership proposed that Kania should be re-elected as First Secretary at the outset; no, said the delegates again, by a vote of 925 to 872, they would elect the Party leader at the end of the proceedings, and the whole Congress would choose him from a list of candidates proposed by a newly elected Central Committee. And so it went on.

Wednesday morning brought Mieczysław Rakowski to the red-carpeted podium with a powerful, fighting speech in favour of reform, hitting equally hard at 'conservatives' in the Party and 'radicals' in Solidarity. As he left the platform to rapturous applause the arch-conservative Albin Siwak leapt to the microphone, but the delegates kept up the deafening ovation for Rakowski until Siwak was forced to retreat, looking like a wounded buffalo. When it came to the elections, they threw out all but four members of the old Politburo, all but eighteen of the Central Committee. True, they did re-elect Mr Kania as Party leader, but no fewer than 568 of them gave their votes to Kazimierz Barcikowski, the man who agreed to stand against him. All this under the impassive gaze of Soviet Politburo member Viktor Grishin, dressed (Mark Frankland reported) 'as though for a funeral'.[20]

By Soviet standards this Polish Congress was shocking: at first glance the leadership change seemed almost as complete as in a western democracy. At first glance. When the new fifteen-member Politburo had been nominated by Mr Kania and accepted by the Central Committee, however, it looked rather less startling. Gone, it is true, were Grabski and Żabiński, but gone too were several of the most prominent appeasers, Jagielski and Fiszbach, co-signatories of the Gdańsk Agreement, and Moczar, a victim of his own murky past. Of the four Politburo survivors, three might still be considered appeasers (Kania, Jaruzelski, Barcikowski) but the fourth was none other than . . . Stefan Olszowski. They were joined by two men who already held ministerial office, Józef Czyrek, Foreign Minister, and the Interior Minister, General Mirosław Milewski. Milewski was a career security man. He had commanded the Interior Ministry 'state within a state' since October 1980, and he had certainly not hindered the security police actions from the Narożniak Affair to the Bydgoszcz incident. Co-operation with Solidarity was not his strong suit. Worse still, the arch-conservative Siwak became a full Politburo member. The rest of the fifteen were either moderate conciliators, like Hieronim Kubiak, from the Jagiellonian University in Kraków, and Jan Łabęcki, from the Lenin Shipyard, or unknowns like one Zofia Grzyb, for whom a triple distinction was claimed: she was a worker; she was the first woman ever to sit in the Politburo; and she was a member of Solidarity.

How was this unlikely mixture arrived at? What seems to have happened was essentially what happened at the Provincial conferences. The delegates first concentrated on eliminating almost everyone compromised by their political past. Then, helped by the '50 per cent plus one vote' method, they eliminated men from both extremes. Then they put back several highly compromised figures from the conservative extreme, to keep the Russians happy. Thus they cheered Rakowski to the echo; but it was Siwak who made it to the Politburo. This was precisely the kind of result which the Toruń reformist leader Zbigniew Iwanów foresaw already in May. Asked about the unknown delegates he said, '. . . they are people into whose minds the fear of invasion is encoded. This will cause half-measures again, and the crisis will be repeated in a few years hence . . .'[21] What he did not foresee was that the Russians would directly transmit the threat of invasion, almost uncoded, to bring the delegates into line.

The composition of the Politburo alone spelt disaster. Firstly, the presence of Olszowski, Siwak and Milewski made it certain that they, like their predecessors, could never agree on, let alone consistently pursue, a strategy. Instead, they would continue to be paralysed by their own divisions. The enfeebled right hand of the Party-state would continue to try to take from society what the enfeebled left hand was trying to give it. Secondly, a Politburo containing Olszowski and Siwak could not possibly regain the trust of society. Once again, the minimum needed to satisfy Moscow was more than the maximum most Poles would accept. Ordinary Poles, like the Brezhnev leadership, attached immense symbolic importance to the presence or absence of particular individuals. *'Nowe wraca'* ('The new comes back again'), they shrugged, seeing Olszowski still in charge of radio and television, and wrote off the Party's vaunted *'odnowa'* for good.

More important in reality than the faces were the structures of the Party. As the horizontal movement had understood, if this was to be the hoped-for breakthrough to 'democratic socialism' then the internal organisation of the Party would have to be so radically altered that the leadership was directly answerable to the rank-and-file, who, moreover, would be able to organise themselves pluralistically (i.e. to agitate in 'factions').* The new Party statutes adopted by the Congress did contain some dramatic changes: all Party officials should in theory be elected on a multiple-choice secret ballot, and limited to a maximum of two five-year terms in office (on which rule Comrades Brezhnev, Honecker, Husak and Ceausescu would all be out on their ears). But they did not transform the basic Leninist structures. The Democratic Centralist pyramid remained. The apparatus remained at the top of the pyramid. Their day-to-day, executive decisions could not be controlled by the rank-and-file. New human material had been poured into the mould; but the mould itself was unbroken.

If 'democratic socialism' meant internal Party democracy, then the breakthrough had not come. Instead, 'socialism' as the word was used in the Soviet Central Committee's letter (what in the West is more usually called 'communism'), had once again proved incompatible with democracy, on any except the Soviet definition of 'democracy'. This is not to say that 'democratic socialism' is everywhere and always a contradiction in terms, since the word 'socialism' has so many different meanings in different mouths and

*Iwanów himself used the phrase 'a multi-faction Party' in an interview for the Toruń Solidarity paper.[22]

in different places. It is to say that no one has yet managed to combine a Leninist Party with pluralistic democracy. If 'democratic socialism' meant a ruling Party which was answerable to the majority of the electorate—or at least responsive to their clearly expressed wishes—then the failure was complete. So bad were the food shortages now, that Solidarity could only with the greatest difficulty prevent people going on the streets to protest. Solidarity had waited patiently, observing an industrial truce, for three and a half months, giving the Party time to reform itself. It could wait no longer. If the Party was to begin to lead the national renewal then the Congress had to come up with, first, a clear programme for getting out of the economic crisis, and, second, a clear statement of the kind of 'partnership' with Solidarity it envisaged. Sealed in the windowless hall in the Palace of Culture, devoured by its own internal struggles, it proved incapable of either. Tadeusz Fiszbach was one of the few speakers to make what was, one might think, the obvious connection with the aspirations of the great majority of Poles outside:

> . . . an historic union is taking place between democracy in the Party and the independence of the trades union organisation of the working class. In the long run none of these important factors can function independently . . . I think the trades unions must be guaranteed the right to co-participation in taking strategic decisions . . .[23]

In other words, the Party must *share power* in certain areas of social and economic policy. But Mr Fiszbach was not re-elected to the Central Committee.

The much-praised 'reformer' who was re-elected to the Central Committee, the Deputy Prime Minister directly responsible for relations with Solidarity, Mieczysław Rakowski, did not go as far this, for all his stirring rhetoric of reform. He talked of a 'new authentic formula' for the parliamentary Front of National Unity (containing the 'United Peasant' and 'Democratic' parties in harness with the PZPR) including 'Catholic circles and social movements', an 'alliance of reason'; but he made no proposals at all for 'co-participation' or 'partnership' with Solidarity.

Just three weeks later he would break off negotiations with Solidarity, while Stefan Olszowski masterminded a propaganda barrage against it. Thus did the Party celebrate its democratic renewal.

6. What Partnership?

PARTNER: co-participant (games, talks etc.); comrade, associate; actor playing with someone else.

W. Kopaliński, *Dictionary of Unfamiliar Terms*

July Debates

When Solidarity's National Commission met in Gdańsk for an extaordinary three-day conference, one week after the end of the Extraordinary Party Congress, its overwhelming concern was not the state of the Party but the state of the country. Solidarity found itself, as Zbigniew Bujak had remarked, like 'a union of seamen on a sinking ship'.[1] Its leaders knew that this was not the time to argue about wages which would be paid if the ship reached port. But their members demanded that they should do something to prevent the ship from floundering while the captain was paralysed and the officers fought among themselves on the bridge. Why, indeed, some demanded, did they not take over the running of the ship? As Jacek Kuroń pointed out, that is what, on the model of previous European revolutions, they would already have done. The revolutionary power would have taken over state power. The question now, said Kuroń, was should this revolution, the Polish revolution, continue to *limit itself*?

As the National Commission talked, hundreds of people marched through the central Polish city of Kutno with banners proclaiming 'We are tired of being hungry', 'We are tired of queueing' and 'We demand life on the level of a civilised country'. They carried empty pots and pans. Three days later some 30,000 women took to the streets of Łódź, Poland's Manchester, where butter and flour were the only rationed foodstuffs still regularly available. These hunger marches were organised by the local Solidarity committees 'to channel people's anger into acceptable forms and in this way to help maintain law and order'. Unchannelled, that anger could soon explode into the violence which until now had been so conspicuously absent from this peaceful revolution. 'Poland faces hunger uprisings' wrote Adam Michnik.[2]

According to official statistics released at the end of July, meat supplies had fallen by 17 per cent in the first half of 1981.[3] On 23 July the Minister for Domestic Trade announced that the meat ration would have to be cut from 3.7 kg to just 3 kg per person per month for August and September. 3 kg, that is, if you could find it. The textile-workers of Łódź, young women with complexions ruined by the sweat-shop air, dressed in dirty, torn cotton dresses (on their wages they could not afford new ones: washing powder and thread were unobtainable), told how they joined the butcher's queue in the evening of one day on the chance (just the chance) that they might get some meat at two o'clock the next afternoon. Those who had been given wage rises found less and less to buy with them even on the black market, where the exchange rate for the dollar soared from around zł.120:$1 in August 1980 to *c.* zł.250:$1 in August 1981.[4]

To understand the anger, however, one must understand the subjective context in which people lived through these shortages. It was not just the fact of the queues. Of course tempers frayed—there were petty squabbles, degrading fist-fights between exhausted middle-aged housewives. But over two centuries the Poles had developed a genius for self-defence in adversity, which was now displayed in the organisation of the queues. A long-standing queue, for furniture, say, would be established weeks or even months before a delivery was due. A Head of the Queue would be nominated, who drew up a list of those waiting in front of the empty shop-window. Every week, at an appointed time, they would reassemble: anyone who failed to turn up lost his or her place. 'Queue Social Committees' were formed, and the Warsaw daily *Życie Warszawy* actually carried an advertisement from the state car distributors inviting the 'Social Committee' to control the distribution of the latest delivery. In shorter-standing queues certain conventions developed: for instance, the handicapped, the elderly and mothers with young children might be allowed to move forward five places for every one place the queue advanced.

Small wonder they joked that a new Professorship was to be established at Warsaw University, the Chair of Codology (from Latin *coda:* queue). Already, there were distinguished essays on the sociology and psychology of queues. And then there was the oral literature: the tale of poor Bogdan, for example, faithful husband and father of two, out queueing for a wedding anniversary present for his wife. In front of him, alas!, stood a young blonde from Warsaw, and . . . well, they did take a very long time, those queues.[5]

No, it was not just the fact of queueing. It was that while they stood in those queues they could read in the local paper, or, even more, in the uncensored Solidarity news bulletins, the latest scandal of corruption or maladministration. Here, 3,000 lb. of butter had gone rancid due to official neglect; there, lard had been used to feed animals; while people could obtain neither in the shops. Truckloads of cigarettes were found on a rubbish-dump, while people queued for two hours to buy one packet at the tobacconist. In Silesia whole consignments of letters from Britain, France and Sweden (centres of Polish emigration) were found at the bottom of a lake. On one page the housewife would read about a hospital in Lower Silesia where fourteen babies died from a serious infection caused, incredibly, by a shortage of water—the local authorities having failed to invest adequately in the municipal water system. On the next, she could read about the pasha-like lifestyle of the men responsible for this mess. The Solidarity news agency (AS) supplied a graphic description of the villa until recently occupied by Edward Gierek: situated on an attractive hillock in 4,000 acres of parkland, with a dining-room to seat forty, billiards room and private cinema.[6] Even the official Grabski Commission, which had investigated 26,000 charges of official misconduct, upheld the charges in no less than 12,000 cases.[7]

The starkness of these contrasts between private opulence and public squalor, and the fact that people were being fully (and sensationally) informed about them for the first time, go far to explain why the commodity of popular trust was unavailable to the political bureaucrats—even on ration cards. Having been lied to for so long, the Poles did not believe their rulers even when they were telling the truth. Thus many people were convinced that the regime was deliberately withholding food in order to wear down their powers of resistance. There were rumours of secret government hoards and gargantuan underground larders. Into these, I was told, western food aid was diverted—when the cargo boats did not carry straight on past Gdańsk to Leningrad!

What was the proportion of truth in these rumours? Certainly, priority supply arrangements were made for the army and security forces.[8] Certainly, the authorities were sometimes able to improve supplies to the shops overnight when it was politically expedient: as, for instance, in Łódź at the time of the hunger marches and in much of the country immediately after the military takeover. In some rural areas the state purchaser did not arrive even when the private farmers had meat which they wanted to sell on the official market. In Łódź, Solidarity actually went out to the surrounding countryside and bought it themselves. In the nature of the problem, it is virtually impossible to establish how much of the collapse of the official marketing and distribution system was intentional. Sins of omission are the hardest to detect. However, it must be said that with bad harvests and almost no foreign currency to pay for food imports, only a large-scale programme of external economic aid could have cut the queues dramatically. It is important for the evolution of Solidarity, none the less, that a great many people *believed* the conspiracy theory.

It was the combination of hunger and distrust which was high explosive. 'A hungry nation can eat its rulers' proclaimed one banner in the demonstration which blockaded Warsaw's equivalent of Piccadilly Circus for two days in early August. Those rulers, meanwhile, blamed Solidarity for the economic disorder and the 12.5 per cent decline in industrial production in the first half of 1981. It must be stressed once again that this charge was largely unfounded. In the first year of Solidarity's existence, at most one working day per worker had been lost through strikes.[9] A western economic expert not over-sympathetic to Solidarity, Professor Domenico Mario Nuti, gave this balanced assessment:

> The sheer scale of economic collapse can only in small part be imputed to labour militancy and the August settlement. The combination of wage increases and lower supplies is responsible for the widening inflationary gap, queues and rationing, and disruption in the consumption market; the

> miners' free Saturday has cost precious export earnings,* with multiplier effects on the rest of the economy. But the main causes of the 1981 collapse are the combination of Poland's extraordinary *import-dependence on the West*—from distilled water for car batteries to steel cans for food-processing—and the loss of short-term credit facilities (of the order of $2 billion) on which Poland had been relying for essential imports, following the suspension . . . of debt repayment and pending negotiations for debt rescheduling. Other contributory factors have been the continued disintegration of central planning and administration, the paralysis of decision-making at all levels; the political stalemate that blocks even obvious emergency measures.[10]

Solidarity's members saw this paralysis of a 'government which did not govern'. They turned to their local and regional Solidarity leaders for action. The record of the July debates of the National Commission is shot through with the urgent awareness of this social pressure—that is, the growing impatience of its members. Something had to be done, and be seen to be done. And whatever this 'something' was it could not be 'pure' trades union activity: arguing about wages on the sinking ship!

From Self-Defence to Self-Government

On food distribution the answer was simple and generally agreed. Solidarity wanted full information about the country's internal and external trade, and they wanted their representatives to have direct access to government stores, where they would control (in the sense of 'check' or 'audit') the distribution of meat, butter, cigarettes, etc. Solidarity's leaders did not endorse the conspiracy theory. '. . . we cannot say that the market [is] . . . deliberately disorganised, you need to be well organised to disorganise,' Bujak wryly commented.[11] And whatever the administration was, well organised it was not. But they quite rightly insisted that most Poles would only *believe* the government when a Solidarity leader could

*Coal output fell by 22 per cent in the first half of 1981.

say to them: 'We have seen the stores, we have seen the figures. It is true. The cupboards are bare. The Russians are not eating it all.'

On industrial production the answer was far more difficult and controversial. The debate within Solidarity had crystallised around varying conceptions of workers' self-government (*samorząd*).* The movement for workers' self-government was, in fact, the most important initiative spawned by Solidarity during the three and a half months of the Party's abortive attempt at self-emancipation. As we have seen, mention of 'genuine participation in management by workers' self-government' was made in point 6 of the Gdańsk Agreement with the support of the government side. In the autumn Solidarity's leaders emphatically declined the kind of responsibility without power which the authorities repeatedly urged upon them. Their objection to any kind of managerial role weakened only gradually under the pressure of economic collapse (see above, pp. 110–16). By early March, however, a survey conducted among Solidarity activists showed strong support for new self-government groups, quite separate from the discredited, Party-controlled Conferences of Workers' Self-Government (KSR) dating from 1958. Once again, large factories took the lead: 95 per cent of respondents in factories employing more than 1,000 people were in favour of new self-government structures, and 68 per cent of the whole sample thought Solidarity should start building them at once.[12]

Late March saw the formation of an embryonic interfactory 'Network' (*siec*) of self-government initiatives. By early May the largest enterprises in Poland—the Lenin and the Warski Shipyards, the Ursus works near Warsaw and the Cegielski in Poznań, the Wujek mine near Katowice—were all represented on an *ad hoc* basis in this spontaneous movement. The 'Network' spread rapidly, elaborating both its own regional structures and its alternative proposals for the new Workers' Self-Government Bill which General Jaruzelski had promised to introduce by mid-1981. By 8 July it linked over 3,000 enterprises. Another independent initiative of self-government groups then emerged in Lublin, and the 'Lublin group' was soon busily competing with the 'Network'.[13]

So self-government was not an initiative 'from above', and

*The translation 'self-management' is less accurate (*rząd* = government) and loses the wider associations of the term.

certainly not from the National Commission. The first draft of the union's programme, published in April, emphasised that self-government and union organisations 'must be clearly separated'. At the end of May the National Commission rather grudgingly accepted the 'Network' as a 'consultative body'. On 19 June the Presidium (the National Commission's cabinet) issued a communiqué objecting to the government's draft Bill on self-government; but it elaborated no alternative proposals.[14] It was only after the July debates that the National Commission finally adopted the demand for authentic self-government as a spearhead of its strategy.

In so doing Solidarity's leaders were aware of crossing another Rubicon. Since Bydgoszcz they had passed through regional elections; they had regularized their weekly cabinet meetings and improved the union's internal administration; they had engaged in numerous rounds of negotiation, with the Education Ministry on language and history textbooks, with the Ministry of Justice on legal reform, with the Ministry of Mining, with government spokesmen, with Rakowski, all faithfully recorded in the AS bulletins, and most with few concrete results; they had inaugurated another monument, to the victims of June 1956 in Poznań. For the first year of the revolution they had remained within the strategic conception of 'social self-defence'. Theirs was a self-governing (*samorządny*) union for the defence of society's interests against the authorities. Now they were going beyond that conception: now they proposed to control the very process of production. To go for 'self-government' in the factories as well as the unions was to go decisively beyond the terms of the previous summer's agreements.

It would be wrong to seek too sophisticated or Machiavellian explanations for the popularity of the self-government idea. In part, it was a quite basic workers' notion that they could run their factories better than the bosses they read about in those Solidarity bulletins. As I heard someone say at the gate of the Lenin Shipyard in August 1980: 'If the whole economy was organised as well as this strike . . .' In part, it was a means of circumventing the paralysed central economic apparatus, and beginning to introduce that decentralisation which the economists agreed was essential. It was a device for wresting management from the hands of incompetent managers—Party placemen. Younger members of the technical intelligentsia, engineers, administrators and so forth, were noticeably active in the self-government movement. They were the potential managers. To these directly economic considerations Solidarity's leaders added a consideration of social psychology, and an anxiety about the internal dynamics of the movement.

'In a decaying economy,' Bronisław Geremek perceptively observed, 'there is also a decay of human activity, yet the way out of the crisis needs increasing efforts, despite deteriorating material conditions. Self-government is, it seems to me, the only means of generating an active attitude. And this argument, I believe, refutes all the objections raised against self-government.'[15] As a poster outside Huta Warszawa had put it, the workers needed to feel that they were 'making a difference by their own action'. But since the mass mobilisation of March they had been largely deprived of this feeling. They had been compelled to watch impotently as their standard of living further declined. If they were not actually disappointed in Solidarity, they had to be shown the point of further active commitment to it. 'Our movement grows weaker,'[16] Bujak commented. So Solidarity could not stand still: if it did not go forward it would surely go backward. The adoption of workers' self-government was an attempt to give new dynamism to the movement in a way which was also economically constructive.

The Network's proposals were sweeping. 'Social ownership of the means of production', it said, 'should now mean just that: ownership by society, not the state.' Enterprises would become 'social enterprises'. 'The self-government administers the property of the enterprise, lays down the general lines for its activity and development, and *decides how profits should be distributed*' (my italics) said the Draft Bill on Social Enterprises produced by the Network (Article 10, section 5). 'The managing director...' explained Article 36, 'carries out the resolutions of the workers' self-government' and the workers would have the right to hire and fire him (Article 42)![17] Ideologically, the Network proposals contained important elements of French Syndicalism and even Bennite industrial democracy. The Solidarity leadership did not all endorse the ideology, but they certainly wanted a share of *power* inside the enterprise, not merely (as the government offered) improved *consultation*.

Yet this, as Bronisław Geremek warned the National

Commission, would be perceived by the apparatus as a direct threat. Even if in practice workers' self-government did not go so far as the Network proposed and merely ensured the selection of managers on grounds of professional competence rather than Party allegiance—as promised in point 12 of the Gdańsk Agreement—*nomenklatura* jobs and privileges would be lost. Even if it only extended initially to heavy industry, as Solidarity proposed (explicitly excluding *armaments* production), the whole Party-state apparatus—some quarter-million strong—would see this as the thin end of the wedge. The ruling class, the Second Estate, as it were, the greater part of which had survived the Party Congress, would now return with acerbity to the defence of its power and privileges.

The notion of 'workers' self-government' in 'social enterprises' was, moreover, logically incomplete. It left open the whole fundamental question of how economic choices were to be co-ordinated between the enterprises. Solidarity's economic advisers came up with a range of answers. At one extreme was the old-fashioned economic liberalism of Stefan Kurowski, leaving regulation to the market; at the other the pragmatic marriage of flexible and decentralised planning with market mechanisms advocated by Ryszard Bugaj, a pupil of the exiled economist Włodzimierz Brus. But every answer would require profound, structural changes in the institutions of state.

Jerzy Milewski, intellectual co-ordinator of the Network, suggested this change should come progressively from below: '. . . our next step after self-government,' he explained in the pages of *Robotnik*, 'would be to go on to local self-government, and finally, a self-governing state . . .' They should start building political parties, as they had built the Network, from below, to be ready for the local government elections which were due in February 1982.[18] Geremek and Kuroń, by contrast, both argued that it was too early to found political parties. Kuroń favoured a movement of Self-Government Clubs—Clubs, not parties, he emphasised—to prepare people for political participation. (Had he forgotten what developed from the 'Clubs' in the French Revolution?) In the July Debates he talked in terms of free elections for 1984: only to be rebuked by Wladysław Frasyniuk, a 27-year-old mechanic newly elected as MKZ Chairman in Wrocław. '. . . we should not talk about whether and when we take power . . .' said Frasyniuk. His earnest appeal for self-censorship could be read just a fortnight later in half a million copies of the Solidarity Weekly![19]

A New Deal?

So was it true, after all, what official propagandists were so often to reiterate, that a certain (typically unspecified) 'tendency' or 'faction' in Solidarity wanted to 'take power'? Indeed, were conspiring to seize it? As the above detail indicates, if this was a conspiracy it was one of the most open conspiracies in history.

The differences between Solidarity activists had certainly multiplied since the Bydgoszcz crisis, and they are difficult to characterise briefly, not least because they varied from region to region. None the less, there were lines of division which were common to all regions. By now, the Solidarity press was identifying two broad tendencies, which it labelled 'fundamentalist' and 'pragmatist'. Fundamentalists insisted on the absolute primacy of first principles: honesty, democracy, dignity, sovereignty. If 'politics' mean compromise with the communists and speaking Newspeak, then they were against 'politics'. Pragmatists, by contrast, recognised the political necessity of compromise, including verbal compromise. The recognition of the 'leading role of the Party in the state' in the Gdańsk Agreement may be taken as a paradigm of pragmatism. For the division was there in embryo in the Lenin Shipyard in August 1980. Now, however, it had become an open split. In the row after the Warsaw Agreement (see above, p. 168 f.) Wałęsa and Gwiazda had exchanged Open Letters: Gwiazda, the 'fundamentalist', reminded Wałęsa of the moral imperative of democracy inside the union, Wałęsa, the 'pragmatist', stressed the *political* imperative of unity. 'I will fight dictatorship,' Gwiazda dramatically declared during the Gdańsk regional elections early in July—and he meant the 'dictatorship' of Wałęsa and the Wałęsa faction.

On the whole, 'fundamentalists' were likely to take a 'tougher' line with the authorities, although their first concern was often with the morality and democracy of the movement's internal affairs. But there is no simple correlation between 'fundamentalist' and 'radical', 'pragmatist' and 'moderate'. In the July Debates Gwiazda spoke *against* Solidarity's adoption of self-government as the spearhead of its strategy. Neither were there anything like clear party lines: in the debates on the Solidarity Programme at the Solidarity Congress in September Gwiazda would be counted among the 'pragmatists'. But the distinction between 'fundamentalists' and 'pragmatists' is an important and revealing one.[20]

Plainly, there is a sense in which all Solidarity activists 'wanted' power for Solidarity. Their *ideal* was a free Poland (So that Poland shall be *Polish*) in which their political differences could be expressed through a multiplicity of parties, and, as Kuroń indicated, were it not for the Red Army they would long since have taken state power. Every single Solidarity member carried around this inner tension between the ideal and the possible. Fundamentalists insisted on articulating the ideal: they wished to end the *self-censorship* which their Catholic and 'loyal opposition' advisers urged upon them.

Yet when Kuroń posed the question, 'Should the revolution continue to *limit itself*?' there was only one man—Jan Rulewski of Bydgoszcz fame—who effectively answered 'No' (and stop worrying about the Russians . . .).[21] The other speakers in the July Debates may have disagreed about how far they should go in words (Kuroń, for example, argued that they should drop the self-censorship in order to facilitate self-limitation: you could not hold back the workers at Huta Warszawa unless you told them clearly why they had to restrain themselves). But they all agreed that the revolution must continue to limit itself in deeds.

With the demands for self-government and control over food distribution the National Commission would stake a claim to a *share* of power over economic and social policy. With self-government they opened up a perspective in which larger areas of social, economic and cultural life would gradually be placed under increasing social control through democratically elected bodies: first, local councils, then perhaps even the national parliament. There was much discussion of a possible second chamber of the *sejm*, filled with genuine representatives of Polish society, to exist side by side with the present sham representatives in the *sejm* 'National Unity Front' (containing the 'United Peasant Party' and 'Democratic Party' in harness with the PZPR). But the National Commission had no intention of overthrowing the

Party, or of laying a finger on foreign and defence policy, which 'fundamentalists' and 'pragmatists' alike still recognised as Soviet vital interests in Poland. The revolution was, and would remain, self-limiting.

At the end of July they hoped that this new initiative might therefore lead to a new deal with the authorities. There was talk of renegotiating the 'social accords' on more (economically) realistic terms. 'We say the authorities have no programme . . .' Kuroń lectured the National Commission, 'but at the newspaper kiosks we can buy a Programme for Overcoming the Crisis and Stabilising the Economy [published by the government in July]. I bought it and I want to tell you that it's worth discussing, that it's a significant document.' However, said Kuroń, this programme was a 'letter to nobody' . . .[22] it was meaningless and pointless unless society agreed to it. On the strictly economic merits of the programme Kuroń was kinder than Professor Mario Nuti, who described it as 'vague and short on policy measures'. Yet, without massive western aid, the best possible programme would still have required almost wartime austerity: food price rises of more than 100 per cent, continued rationing, 'greater intensity and length of labour' and, in Nuti's judgment, 'massive redundancies of the order of 1.2 million'.[23] This was what the government would ask the independent trades union Solidarity to sell to its members.

Seen in this perspective the price which Solidarity proposed to demand was not exorbitant. Yes, they said, we will support the necessary price rises, but only when you give us full information about food production and distribution. Yes, they said, we will try to offer more and better production for less reward, but only if our members can have a measure of control over their own work (as you suggested a year ago) and the shape of economic recovery. *Sharing* power—but not over the guns or bridge—the crew and the captain would work together to save the sinking ship.

'We want to see the authorities [*wladza*] working energetically, unambiguously on the basis of partnership with Solidarity,' declared a leading article in the Solidarity Weekly of 7 August, 'and we want our union to co-operate energetically to overcome the crisis.'

The question was: did the captain or his officers want to work in partnership? And were they capable of it even if they wanted to?

August Rupture

The noises from the bridge were not encouraging. True, on 31 July the *sejm* finally passed the Censorship Act which had been promised in the Gdańsk Agreement for the end of November 1980. It was the first piece of legislation implementing the Gdańsk Agreement, and, though Solidarity was not entirely satisfied, an incredible document by Soviet bloc standards. For thirty-five years the authorities had had *carte blanche* to censor what and how they liked (by virtue of a 'special decree' issued in 1946). Now the Act laid down in detail what could and could not be published or performed, together with a long list of publications and performances (parliamentary speeches, scholarly works, internal union bulletins) which would not be pre-censored. (Solidarity insisted its bulletins should not be censored at all.) Censored persons were given the right of appeal to administrative courts. It was a remarkable achievement, on paper.[24]

Yet at the very time that this was passing through the *sejm*, the official media, still under the supreme command of Stefan Olszowski, were launching a violent propaganda offensive against Solidarity. It was not merely Solidarity which said this. On 10 August the Polish Journalists' Association issued a statement deploring 'the strongest campaign of disinformation since August last year'. It referred to cases of the Censor's Office blocking news items on the grounds that they were 'objectivist in an abstract way'. 'The Polish Press Agency (PAP) published, on 1 August, a text which was a clear falsification of a telex from A. Gwiazda to the government, concerning talks between the two sides', the Journalists' Association reported.[25] Those talks were set for Monday 3 August.

It was with no high hopes, therefore, that the Solidarity delegation gathered on the evening of Sunday 2 August. They stayed in the Hotel Solec, a good (but not luxurious) modern establishment with a reputation for serving the best tripe in Warsaw. On Monday morning they made their way to the Council of Ministers building through a besieged city centre. On the initiative of the militant public transport workers, Mazowsze had organised a motorcade to protest at the shortages and the ration cuts. A fantastic procession of buses, taxis, building trucks and rubbish-disposal lorries converged on Marszałkowska (Warsaw's Regent Street), intending to turn into al. Jerozolimskie (Jerusalem Alley) and so parade past Party House. But they were stopped by the police, whereupon the protestors declared that they would stay right there; and stay there they did, blocking Warsaw's equivalent of Piccadilly Circus for the next fifty hours!

Meanwhile, in the Council of Ministers building (also cordoned off by police) Rakowski had launched into his own protest *démarche*, shooting accusations at Solidarity from a note-card held in his hand: Solidarity was damaging the atmosphere by organising street demonstrations; the slogan of 'hunger' was demagogy (said the well-fed Deputy Prime Minister); Solidarity was organising 'anti-Soviet, anti-government, and anti-Party' actions. He then offensively speculated that this was the result of pre-Congress electioneering on the part of 'factions' inside Solidarity, naming Wałęsa, Gwiazda and Kuroń 'factions'. Their ultimate goal was to liquidate the authorities. Their aim was to deepen the economic crisis. He accused 'Comrade Słowik' (Łódź Solidarity leader) of lying. The Students' Union had a clearly anti-communist character . . . and so it went on, a bitter, provocative torrent of recrimination. After an interval he returned to 'report' on the news from the city centre. The way to the Central Committee and the Council of Ministers would not be unblocked, he said, and special forces had been ordered to Warsaw.[26]

The tone was set. After some sharp exchanges—Wałęsa recalled Jurczyk's remark about the government as adulterous wife—Solidarity managed to present their points for negotiation. Rakowski said he must discuss them with the Prime Minister, and another round of talks was set for Thursday 6 August. In the intervening three days the 'hunger marches' spread to several other cities, and short warning strikes were announced (for example in Kielce) to protest at the ration cuts. It was against this background of almost uncontrollable popular anger that Solidarity outlined its proposals for supervision of food production and distribution, on the Thursday morning. Rakowski reacted with a histrionic speech, wondering aloud about the 'motives' for this proposal. 'In Poland', he said, 'he who controls the production and distribution of food, possesses power' . . . ergo: 'This is a programme for the takeover of power!'

In the afternoon, Rakowski asked the Minister for Trades Union Affairs, Ciosek, to read out a prepared list of the authorities' demands to Solidarity. Solidarity should 'give up political activity beyond its statute' (including the defence of 'so-called political prisoners'); 'stop spreading false information about the government allegedly hampering the economic reform'; 'conduct [its] international activity in accordance with Poland's foreign policy'; 'act for social support of the price reform—an integral part of the economic reform'; 'stop strikes... dangerous street demonstrations and... false messages about hunger in Poland'; 'support the efforts undertaken to increase coal production' and more. (Quotations from the official media version.) When he finished, there was a moment's shocked silence.

One must recall the reality concealed behind such bland phrases as 'act for social support of the price reform'. In effect, Solidarity was being asked to function like a trades union in an orthodox Leninist system: that is, as a 'transmission-belt' (Lenin's metaphor) for the communist authorities' plans. Here was this Programme for Overcoming the Crisis, passed unanimously by the *sejm*, the government side expostulated, and now it was Solidarity's leaders' patriotic and civil duty to sell it to society. Their reward? Well, their reward would be the knowledge that they had nobly contributed to the process of 'socialist renewal', sacrificing their own popularity and their members' jobs and standards of living for the greater good of the Party. History would record their sacrifice!

Of course it was unthinkable that Solidarity would accept these terms, and Rakowski knew it. The most sanguine of Solidarity's advisers now had to acknowledge the painful truth that, following the Party Congress, the authorities were not more but rather less prepared to share power with Solidarity in the social and economic fields. Tired, hungry and dispirited, they none the less set about trying to draft a joint communiqué. About 11 p.m. they returned to find that the text of the joint communiqué had been unilaterally altered by the government side. They refused to sign this, but, rather than allow the talks to collapse without any joint statement, swiftly drafted a short neutral communiqué which Andrzej Celiński read out when both delegations had reassembled in the conference room.

'That is not the joint communiqué. I won't sign it because I didn't write it...' Rakowski reacted furiously (according to the report in the Solidarity Weekly). 'That joint communiqué was accepted, and then General Jaruzelski and I made certain improvements, having in mind the interests of the state, as we understand them. Good night.' Bujak quickly rose to protest about a police house-search which had been carried out that morning in the flat of a KOR activist, Wiesław Kęcik. Rakowski interrupted him: he wouldn't accept the protest but he knew what Bujak was talking about. Then he theatrically conducted the Solidarity delegation into a neighbouring room, where the opposition literature confiscated at Kęcik's flat was laid out on tables. 'Interesting where the paper comes from,' Rakowski remarked, darkly. 'I bid you farewell, gentlemen.' And out he swept into the night.[27]

Within hours PAP was informing the world that Solidarity 'unilaterally broke off the talks . . . in a manner insulting to the government . . .'

The August breakdown was not the end of the talking between the government and Solidarity. But it was the beginning of the end. There were to be no top-level, general talks for three whole months, until mid-November. This experience dashed any residual hopes among the 'loyal opposition' and pragmatists that the Party, having re-formed itself, would now go forward to a new, authentic, negotiated partnership with Solidarity, as Tadeusz Fiszbach had suggested at the Party Congress. The Congress had been a turning-point at which the Party failed to turn. From now on, the positions of the two sides would slide rapidly apart.

The 'partnership' was ended for the government by the man who, seven months before, had launched the slogan 'respect your partner' in the columns of *Polityka*. No man enjoys being compared to an adulterous wife, and Rakowski had to put up with some round abuse from angry Solidarity leaders. Yet the circumstantial evidence—his prepared *démarche* on 3 August, the government's exorbitant list of demands, the unilateral changes in the joint communiqué, the confiscated books carefully laid out in a neighbouring room—all this does suggest very strongly that the breakdown was premeditated. The time has come to examine more closely the role of this major actor.

Rakowski and the Vision of 'Partnership'

Mieczysław F. Rakowski was the best-known advocate and apologist of communist Poland in the West. In Warsaw they called him 'Mr Poland for Foreigners'. His chubby, boxer's face was a familiar sight in Washington and Bonn, where he long enjoyed the reputation of an outstanding 'liberal' among Polish communists.

Now the distinctions between 'hardliners' and 'moderates', 'hawks' and 'doves' in a ruling communist Party—the ornithology of Sovietology—should always be treated with care. You can find 'moderates' and 'hardliners' in any power élite if you look hard enough. (British diplomats in Nazi Berlin backed the 'moderate' Hermann Goering.) Moreover, such differences are deliberately played up for western consumption, and by none more skilfully than by Mr Rakowski. Often this takes the form of a 'Spenlow and Jorkins'. (Mr Spenlow in *David Copperfield* habitually attributes his own hard dealings to the pressure of his relentless hardline partner, Mr Jorkins, a figure all the more fearsome for being invisible.) We in the West are particularly susceptible to this kind of suggestion precisely because our own politics *are* pluralist. And Mr Rakowski was so used to playing on this susceptibility that (under pressure from the Italian journalist Oriana Fallaci, in an interview conducted after the military takeover) he even explained: 'You see, there is a double tendency in the Soviet Union, one pro-Polish and one anti-Polish, and Brezhnev belongs to the first one. He loves Poland, believe me.'[28] Therefore the West should support Poland-loving Leonid Brezhnev, since otherwise there were really 'hardline' Comrade Jorkinses waiting in the wings to do really beastly things to Poland (you see, believe me . . .). Mr Rakowski knew this because 'Some of my best friends are in Moscow—I spend exquisite nights drinking vodka and talking with them.'

It is worth recalling what a 'liberal' like Rakowski has in common with his most 'hardline' comrades. His record is, after all, one of survival in that predatory company.[29] Beginning as a nineteen-year-old political education officer in the army in 1945, the bright, ambitious son of a peasant from Pomerania rose steadily through the central Party apparatus in the Stalinist period—getting his hands dirty, but not too dirty. He joined in the reformist surge of October 1956, but not too wholeheartedly, and when the genuinely radical and outspoken weeklies were closed down in 1957 his career took off on *Polityka*, of which he soon became Editor. Under his editorship, *Polityka* became critical, but not too critical (although it played an honourable role in refusing the anti-Semitic filth of 1968). In the late 1960s he cautiously distanced himself from the failing Gomułka. He launched into the 1970s with a burst of enthusiasm for the Gierek great leap forward. Becoming critical (but not too critical) in mid-decade, he distanced himself in good time from the doomed Party leader. The advancement of Kania and then Jaruzelski brought him Deputy Prime Ministerial office and the job of negotiating with Solidarity. Now, in August 1981, he was distancing himself from Solidarity and working more and more closely with General Jaruzelski. The reader will not be surprised to learn that Rakowski stayed in office after 13 December, still the artful apologist for the existing regime, still the would-be 'liberal' Mr Spenlow confounded by the evil Comrade Jorkinses.

This record goes some way to explain why Solidarity leaders did not respect him, as he complained to Ms Fallaci: 'None of those demagogues and anarchists ever gave me credit [for struggling for reform in the Party]. None of them ever said: "Mr Rakowski, we know that you were a fighter". None! None!'

A couple of his other comments on Solidarity leaders go still further to explain their shameful ingratitude. On Wałęsa: 'His peasant nature intrigued me. As a peasant he cheated his interlocutor and one could never find a common language with him.' And again, in a secret speech to Warsaw party functionaries after 13 December: 'I have no resentment against the blockheads in Solidarity, against those who were serious about it, little shits like this Zbigniew Bujak . . .'[30]

So much for respecting your partner! It may be objected that the former remark was an expression of bitter disappointment after the failure of a reformer's hopes, that the latter was part of a tactical speech at a time when he was struggling to defend his own position in the new military-Party-state.

Yet his profound contempt for those men from the lower classes who made the Polish revolution, the 'peasant-natured' worker Wałęsa, the 'little shit' Bujak, is all of a piece with his social position as a prominent member of (what he himself calls) 'the Warsaw Establishment' and Poland's communist ruling class. Thirty-six years previously he was himself, like Wałęsa and Bujak, a peasant's son: blond, well-built, energetic, free of religious prejudice, the perfect human material for the new élite. Recruited, like half a million other peasant sons, he prospered through the system.

He studied journalism, history and political science; he acquired knowledge and some sophistication; he added position and influence as Editor of *Polityka*; in the 1960s he began to travel, was feted as the coming man in America and West Germany; his clothes became smarter, the haircut more stylish, the car a Peugeot now; and then, to comfort, position, authority and influence was added . . . power. And now these peasants, these 'little shits', wanted to share it with him, Mieczysław F. Rakowski, the toast of Washington and Bonn, he who spent 'exquisite nights' drinking vodka with his friends in Moscow.

None the less, he was a clever, clear-sighted man, and in Party terms he was definitely a reformer. He had written a book which could only be published after August 1980 (thanks to Solidarity!). In it he proposed a wide range of reforms, initiated and carefully controlled from above by a strong, vital, Leninist Party. His vision of reform communism is, to simplify, a Polish national version of Kádárism. Economic planning would be made more decentralised and flexible, with more elements of the free market inside the official economy. Government would be more responsive to public opinion, which, to be heard at the top, required more freedom of information. The Party would set up institutions for regular and genuine consultation with major interest groups: technical intelligentsia, Church, farmers, workers, etc. These views earned him the opposition of a great part of the apparatus, whose vested interests they put in question. If they had been implemented, the power of the Party would have been exercised in a very different way.[31]

It is important to stress, however, that the vision was *not* one of political pluralism, but rather of what might be called consultative authoritarianism (as in Hungary). On offer to the various interest groups, to Polish society, would be a measure of consultation, not a share of power. The difference was precisely the difference between Solidarity's and the government's draft on 'workers' self-government'. All decisions would still ultimately lie with the Party ruling class. It would be as at that 6 August meeting: joint communiqués would be accepted, and then the General and he would make 'certain improvements, having in mind the interests of the state, as we understand them'.

The word 'partnership', therefore, did not mean for Mr

Rakowski what it means for us, even when he was using it sincerely. The implication of equal (or at least contractually binding) rights and liabilities was never there in his dictionary. It was not there in January 1981 when he 'launched' the slogan ('I was the one who . . . launched the idea of partnership. I believed in it so,' he told Ms Fallaci), and it was not there when he ditched it in August. It is strange that so many people in the West still somehow half-believe or assume that Soviet bloc leaders use words like 'democracy', 'peace', 'freedom' or 'partnership' in the same sense as we do. It is still stranger that some Solidarity leaders half-believed that they and Mr Rakowski meant the same thing by 'partnership'. But the myth of national understanding was very powerful: the belief that, taking *'jak Polak z Polakiem'*, 'as Pole talks to Pole' (the slogan given out from the gate of the Lenin Shipyard on 31 August 1980), they must find a common way.

In his secret speech Rakowski explained, 'The horse which is galloping wildly must be brought back to a trot, and it must be made clear to it that it has to obey.' Polish society in the autumn of 1981 was the horse, the communist apparatus the rider. This metaphor says more than a thousand public interviews. Rakowski and his comrades disagreed furiously about how the horse should be ridden, and who should hold the reins. But on one thing they were all agreed: their place was on top and the horse's underneath. Democratic socialists who objected that Polish society is not a horse were no longer riders.*

'At a Crossroads'

Amid a hailstorm of mutual recriminations—each side accusing the other of breaking off the talks—the National Commission and the Central Committee met in their respective capitals. The Central Committee's Second Plenum (i.e. the second after the Party Congress) was marked by intensified efforts to divide the Solidarity leadership from the rank-and-file. Zofia Grzyb, the Politburo Solidarity member, accused Solidarity's leadership of betraying the workers, and the Plenum's final resolution attacked 'certain

*Stefan Bratkowski, for example, was expelled from the Party in October.

irresponsible advisers and activists in Solidarity'. On the same day, Bronisław Geremek and Karol Modzelewski explained to the National Commission in Gdańsk what seemed to them to be the new, post-Congress, Rakowski 'scenario'. Solidarity would be blamed for everything that was wrong with the country. 'Extremists' and 'factions' devoured by political ambition would be blamed for everything that was wrong with Solidarity. Under the relentless pressure of this propaganda, the exhausted, frustrated society should be gradually prised away from its loyalty to Solidarity's leaders.[32]

Their considered response was to issue, on 12 August, a remarkable 'Appeal to union members and the whole society', printed in bold type on the front page of the Solidarity Weekly.[33] The main challenge of the moment, it said, was the deepening economic crisis, which was caused not merely by the blunders of the Gierek team but by the *system* of government and economic administration. Conceived to function in the absence of democratic freedoms, this system failed completely in the present situation 'where a decision from above might face social objections'. Consequently a 'democratic reconstruction' of these institutions was necessary. To this end, Solidarity now supported not merely enterprise self-government but also 'territorial self-government; the transformation of local councils and the *sejm*, by way of democratic elections, into authentic representatives of society with increased powers over the state administration'. At its First National Congress (due to open on 5 September) the union faced the task of 'designing a model of social life' in which enterprise and territorial self-government would be guaranteed.

Meanwhile, the National Commission proposed two immediate ways of working 'to save ourselves with our own hands'. First, they created a Social Control Commission to supervise food production and distribution. Second, they appealed to all their members to work on eight of their newly-won work-free Saturdays by the end of the year (that is, on virtually all their free Saturdays). In particular they appealed to workers in four areas: mining, export concerns, factories producing goods vital for farmers, and food production. If their members agreed, then production on these days would be controlled by the factory Self-Government Founding Committees and (Solidarity) Factory Commissions: it would be the 'first great test/rehearsal' (*próba*) of workers' self-government. Solidarity would do everything in its power to ensure that the extra efforts of working people would not be wasted. The extra coal produced would go to the private farmers, who would supply potatoes to the miners in return. At the same time it appealed for an end to hunger marches, and, indeed, to all 'isolated protest actions'.

'We will reply to attacks' (i.e. government propaganda attacks), concluded the Appeal, 'by refusing to print the daily press.'

This lucid statement of medium-term goals, strategy and tactics was the public declaration of the new phase of the revolution whose gestation has been traced in this chapter. 'We find ourselves at a crossroads,' Wałęsa declared at a press conference to launch the Appeal. Now they were compelled by the state of the nation to become, professedly, more than a union.

Of course the attacks did not cease, and on 18 August Solidarity printers went ahead with two 'Days without Papers', occupying their works but printing no official papers. *Trybuna Ludu* and the hardline army daily *Żołnierz Wolności* were printed none the less, in smaller than usual editions on reserve and military presses, but the newsagents did not sell them. When the papers came back, so did the attacks.

The reaction of Solidarity members to the rest of the Appeal was mixed. 70 per cent of miners asked by Solidarity's Centre for Social Research said they would go to work on their free Saturdays in response to the Appeal, but researchers noted that the approval was cautious. According to a paper produced during the Solidarity Congress, on Saturday 5 September—a free Saturday—the miners dug 236,000 tons of coal. The paper did not say where it went to. In Lower Silesia, where food supplies were especially bad, many respondents felt that the union should demand more for its co-operation. (The Silesian delegates had voted against the Appeal in the National Commission.) In the Warsaw region, 70 per cent of those asked said they would have a more positive attitude to working free Saturdays if Solidarity was given access to the mass media. Once again, this poll suggests that the accusation of politicisation and radicalisation from above turned the truth on its head. The pressure came from below. It was the young coal-miners at the pithead who raised the slogan 'No coal without freedom'. The sans-culottes were the Jacobins. At the same time, the researchers inquired if the members' trust in the National Commission had been diminished by the events of the last three weeks. 7 per cent of the miners said, yes, their trust had been diminished (in other Silesian enterprises the figure was 17 per cent). 45 per cent said it was unchanged. 35 per cent said, on the contrary, their trust had been *increased*.[34] With such a vote of confidence, the National Commission could look forward to their Congress rather more than the old Central Committee had to theirs.

While the Party leader flew off for his traditional meeting with Mr Brezhnev in the Crimea, accompanied—uniquely and significantly—by General Jaruzelski (who on 8 August had once again been host to Marshal Kulikov), another major actor edged his way reluctantly on to the political stage. Before the announcement of his appointment to succeed Cardinal Wyszyński, on 7 July, the new Primate, Józef Glemp, then Bishop of Warmia, explained that 'the Church wants... to approach its contacts with Solidarity primarily in a pastoral spirit, but it refuses to be drawn into politics and will continue to do so in the future.'[35] Now the Church, like Solidarity, was being inexorably sucked into the vacuum of political power. In the coming winter, the personality and views of Archbishop Glemp would be of vital importance for Solidarity and the communist authorities.

Glemp was a man marked by the experience of terror. Born in 1929 at Inowrocław (central Poland), where his father worked in the salt-mines as well as on the land, he was just ten years old when the Germans invaded. At thirteen he was designated by the Nazi authorities for 'heavy labour'. In an interview before his elevation he spoke movingly about this back-breaking child-labour in the fields. He grew up amid stories of the arrests, internments and shootings which cost the lives of at least 3,500 Catholic clergy. By the time he entered the seminary at Gniezno, the cradle of Polish Catholicism, several hundred priests and eight bishops had been imprisoned by the communist authorities. Archbishop Wyszyński was himself under house arrest in a remote monastery.

After studying as a Church lawyer he joined the Primate's office in Warsaw in 1967, soon becoming Wyszyński's private secretary, chaplain and acknowledged 'spiritual son'. It was at Wyszyński's express request (some say his deathbed wish, communicated by telephone to the Pope, lying wounded by the assassin's bullet in Rome) that Glemp succeeded him, at the relatively young age of fifty-two, after just two years' pastoral experience as Bishop of Warmia.

This personal formation was immediately visible in his pronouncements. As before, the Main Council of the Episcopate continued to be much more outspoken than the Primate in its support for Solidarity. In a statement read from all pulpits on Sunday 16 August it declared:

> We believe that the public is ready to make... sacrifices [necessary to resolve the crisis] if it can be certain that its efforts will not be wasted, if the expected structures of workers' responsibility in the management of their place of work are created, if all social forces take part in the preparation of economic reform and if its programme is acceptable to the entire nation. Working people rightly wish to have the opportunity to control what was jointly produced, the manner in which the fruits of common work are shared.

The Church for industrial democracy! You might think you were in Latin America, except that here it was the clergy agitating for the workers *against* the communists. And again:

> Those who are using [the mass media] at present ought to abstain from stirring the feelings of the masses and from irritating propaganda. A matter of tremendous importance is to give access to radio and television for the new trades unions, the Church, and all centres of public opinion in Poland.

But then came the personal touch of the new Primate, who, like his predecessor, was also Chairman of the Main Council: 'May none of us clench his fist. Let each of us abandon hatred and desire for revenge...'[36] The theme of 'love your enemies, do good to those who hate you' was to become a *leitmotif* of his homilies:

> You only have to switch on the television or the radio to hear how one virtuous and saintly side is condemning the wrongdoing and arrogance of the other. The other side, in

> turn, deprived of access to the same media, specialises either in caricatures or, not infrequently, abusive words... Let us look at ourselves truthfully. We shall then see our own sins... and this will allow us to see the good done by the other side.[37]

This he declared at the most sacred shrine of Jasna Góra on 26 August, exactly one year after Cardinal Wyszyński's ill-fated warnings to the strikers from the same pulpit. Indeed it soon became apparent that, despite the transformed state of the country, his message differed only in the bluntness of its language from that of his predecessor. (Wyszyński would never have made such a crude equation of the two sides.) It was a constant plea for caution and reflection and moderation and sobriety and forgiveness and national understanding and, above all things, peace. From Jasna Góra he called explicitly for a month of peace. In every crisis the first question Glemp seemed to ask himself was: what would Wyszyński have done?

But in August 1980 the workers had ignored the warnings of that grand and venerable Prince of the Church. Would they now, after a year of revolution, heed the warnings of his secretary, a short, dumpy figure, with none of Wyszyński's accumulated authority?

7. Noble Democracy

> One leaves Poland today with the impression that the most beautiful flowers sometimes bloom on the edge of the abyss.
>
> Czesław Miłosz, summer 1981

The formidable Soviet naval manoeuvres which began in the Gulf of Gdańsk on Friday 4 September had, of course, nothing whatsoever to do with the scheduled opening of Solidarity's First National Congress in Gdańsk on Saturday 5 September. Only the most perverse Anti-Socialist Element or CIA agent could suppose that these manoeuvres, combined with land operations in Byelorussia (on Poland's eastern border) and code-named 'West '81', were anything other than a direct response to increased American aggression, as the Soviet Defence Ministry newspaper *Red Star* so convincingly explained. Fortunately the nearly 900 Solidarity delegates who gathered the next morning in the Oliwa district of Gdańsk, its wooded slopes giving a splendid view of the sea, were neither perverse Anti-Socialist Elements nor CIA agents, and therefore did not give the intimidating manoeuvres a second thought.

Whether they gave many more thoughts to the sermon preached by Archbishop Glemp at the Mass in Oliwa Cathedral which preceded the official Congress opening must, in view of their subsequent behaviour, also be doubted. It seems rather that, as a year before, they tended to hear from the Church what they wanted to hear, and disregard the rest. Glemp dwelt on the theme of do as you would be done by; he spoke of patriotism, the 'Christian love of the fatherland'; he proclaimed that the Congress had the task of shaping 'the situation of working people, and also *the future of our Fatherland*' (my italics), and then he spoke again of peace. The whole society, he said, expected the Congress to be conducted in that peace which began the previous year in the Gdańsk shipyard and which both the country and Europe needed.[1]

The delegates obviously appreciated that this was more than a Trades Union Congress: it was a patriotic gathering, an alternative parliament without precedent in the Soviet bloc, a National Assembly—and not merely of the Third Estate. Predictably, the symbolic politics of this Polish National Assembly were superb. From the moment when the electronic scoreboard lit up with the sign of the cross and the words '*Polonia semper fidelis*', while Wałęsa rose to intone yet again, 'Poland is not yet lost . . .', and 'God who protects Poland . . .', the usually soulless Olivia sports hall was filled with the spirits of the national martyrs. No chance was lost to demonstrate that here were the true heirs of the great tradition of Polish ideals, of the other, the real People's Poland, whose history is remembered by months. On the second day the hall rose to its feet in a storm of applause as a middle-aged man slowly made his way up to the platform, walking with crutches. He was a leader of the Poznań workers in June 1956. 'Those people gave their lives so that such a Congress could take place,' he said.[2]

Later, in the second half of the two-part Congress, the delegates would give an equally rapturous reception to General Boruta-Spiechowicz, the last surviving General of Marshal Piłsudski's army, a smart, upright old man who marched into the hall with a troop of veterans, all resplendent in their pre-war uniforms. The General recalled his three wars: two against the Germans, one against the Soviets. He repeated the words on his regimental flag: GOD, HONOUR, FATHERLAND. 'Do not allow yourselves to be intimidated,' he admonished, 'fear is a bad counsellor.'[3] '*Sto lat, sto lat . . .*' ('Let him live for a hundred years') the delegates sang, hopefully. Then they cheered a slim, dark-haired Jewish doctor among the delegates from Łódź, Marek Edelman, who, as a teenager, had been a leader of the Warsaw ghetto uprising.

They welcomed and applauded the representatives of all those who had joined the civil crusade for national regeneration in the pentecostal excitement of a year before. Andrzej Wajda, representing Polish film-makers, told them about his problems making *Man of Marble* and *Man of Iron*. The Polish Writers' Union (ZLP) signed a formal agreement on co-operation with Solidarity.

Rural Solidarity was present, of course, as was the small Artisans' Solidarity—since, formally, the self-employed were not eligible for membership of the main union. Polish journalists were represented by Stefan Bratkowski, greeted with an ovation, who spoke about the difficulties of writing the truth in the official media, and then a socialist echoing the words of the Primate, wished the delegates 'thirty days of wisdom and cool blood'. And among the delegates from Toruń was Zbigniew Iwanow, the man whose efforts to democratise the communist Party had been repaid with his expulsion from it.

They welcomed foreign guests too—some more warmly than others. Most major western trades unions were represented, except for the American AFL-CIO whose leader, Lane Kirkland, was refused a visa. The head of the West German trades union federation (Deutsche Gewerkschaftsbund) made a strong speech. The East German trades union federation, ironically distinguished from the West German by the adjective 'Free' (Freie Deutsche Gewerkschaftsbund), was not represented; neither were other official Soviet bloc unions. One L. Murray spoke on behalf of 11.5 million members of the British Trades Union Congress, explaining that British unionists also had to fight constantly for their rights. However, in their relations with the government both sides understood that the one could not demand from the other what the other was not in a position to give, Mr Murray soberly lectured the Polish delegates. Then he presented Lech Wałęsa with a 'plaquette' commemorating the English Peasants' Revolt of 1381.[4]

With tradition—the democracy of the dead—the delegates had long experience and few problems. The dead can usually be persuaded to agree. The democracy of the living was more problematic. More than half the delegates were under thirty-five, and therefore had no first-hand experience of democracy before August 1980 (unless, like the Press Spokesman Janusz Onyszkiewicz, they had spent some time living in a western country). Yet they were determined that the one-year-old in a Solidarity T-shirt shown romping out of the Congress poster should grow up to be a perfect democrat. This was to be their 'school of political culture', as Tadeusz Mazowiecki put it.

Ultra-democratic rules of procedure ensured that every delegate had the right to intervene in the debates at almost any point. Every regional platoon of delegates on the floor of the Olivia sports hall had its own microphone. A bevy of messengers circulated around the floor like ball-boys at a tennis match, carrying proposals for resolutions, protests and apologies from group to group and from the floor to the platform. When it came to elections, the urns were upturned and shaken over the heads of the delegates, to show that they had not been 'fixed'. Loudspeakers broadcast the debates outside the hall, where large crowds came to listen, bringing folding chairs, dogs and children. 'Cool-blooded' the proceedings were not, despite the admonitions of Glemp and Bratkowski. In fact, the debates on the future structure and statutes of the movement, and the electoral procedures, were heated, protracted and often—it must be said—chaotic. So addictive were the new drugs of free speech and democratic politics that the National Congress, like many of the regional ones which preceded it, far out-talked its scheduled time. The plan was to have a first three-day 'round' in which the leadership would report on the year's work, and the Congress would debate the internal structure and constitution (statutes) of the movement. After an interval in which working-groups would redraft the Solidarity Programme, a second 'round' of seven or eight days would pass the Programme, elect a new leadership, and set the course for the next year. In the event, the first 'round' boiled on for six days (5–10 September) and the second for twelve (26 September–7 October). 'You know, we are just learning democracy,' delegates remarked apologetically.[5]

Internal union democracy was the subject of the first major Congress debate, on Monday 7 September, as it had been of the regional conferences and of many articles in the union media for months. Two broad conceptions of the union's central authority were presented. One, favoured by advisers like Bronisław Geremek, suggested a clear distinction between an 'executive' and a 'legislature'. A large representative Supreme Council would act as the union's parliament, while a smaller Presidium—elected directly by the Congress—would act as its government. This would concentrate executive power in the hands of national leaders, and, in particular, of Wałęsa and his advisers. The second, favoured by most regional chairmen, was to have one enlarged National Commission in which the regions were represented proportionately to their membership. This would be both executive and legislature:

a straight majority vote of the whole Commission would decide on all major issues, and the Presidium would be elected (as previously) from its numbers, for the day-to-day running of the union. Here, more power would be concentrated in the hands of the regional 'barons' rather than the 'King' and the King's men. In the former system, Wałęsa and his advisers could, for example, decide to call off a general strike as they did in March over Bydgoszcz; in the latter, the decision would lie with the whole Commission.

'DICTATORSHIP OR DEMOCRACY' was how the Congress daily newspaper *Głos Wolny* (The Free Voice) melodramatically summarised the nub of this debate, following a startling speech by Wałęsa on the last day of the first 'round'. In four years' time, he said, they would have democracy, yes, he was sure of it, he promised them, in four years they would have democracy: but now, now they faced a power which still had the police and the security men (he did not mention the armed forces), now they needed a strong, decisive central authority for the struggle against it, and therefore, for the time being, he must continue to be a dictator—and he repeated the phrase 'my dictatorship' . . . 'and that is why I am a dictator here'.[6] Loud and prolonged applause: almost as rapturous for the 'dictator' as for 'democracy'. This was Wałęsa at his best and worst: Wałęsa the orator, Wałęsa the manipulator: and it was disturbing to find that the delegates in the Olivia sports hall seemed no less volatile and easily swayed than the delegates in the Lenin Shipyard a year before. Then as now, however, there was a real political point behind Wałęsa's slippery rhetoric. Now, faced with a power which was more than ever determined to divide and weaken Solidarity, anyone who thought politically could see the imperative of a strong, centralised executive able to respond rapidly and decisively to attacks on the movement.

There were many motives and reasons for the opposition to this quasi-monarchic executive: personal resentment of Wałęsa's high-handedness; the personal ambitions of the regional barons; very real differences of interest between their constituencies; but perhaps the most important single reason was that many of the delegates were not, in the first instance, thinking *politically*. When they thought, rather than emotionally reacted, they tended to think first in moral and symbolic rather than political categories: they listened to the voices of the dead and the promptings of the national conscience, and then they voted for what should be, rather than what could be: politics, for them as for their ancestors, was the art of the impossible. In everyone, the fundamentalist urge fought with the pragmatic understanding.

On Tuesday 8 September the fundamentalist urge swept the field. The most immediate political question before them was, of course, self-government. The most recent Central Committee Plenum had restated the authorities' position, contained in the new draft Bill on Workers' Self-Government, that, though the workforce would be consulted about management appointments, the ultimate *power* to hire and fire must remain in Party hands. Karol Modzelewski now proposed a resolution demanding a referendum on this issue. If the 'organs of state' refused to organise this referendum, the resolution went on, the union would organise a referendum itself. A *frisson* passed through the hall as the delegates raised their hands to pass this resolution with just one vote against, then they stood as one and applauded. A little later a 'Message to the Working People of Eastern Europe' was proposed:

> The delegates greet the workers of Albania, Bulgaria, Czechoslovakia, the German Democratic Republic, Romania, Hungary and all the nations of the Soviet Union.
>
> As the first independent self-governing trades union in our post-war history we are profoundly aware of the community of our fates. We assure you that, contrary to the lies spread in your countries, we are an authentic ten-million strong organisation of workers, created as a result of workers' strikes. Our goal is to improve the condition of all working people. We support those among you who have decided on the difficult road of struggle for free trades unions. We believe that it will not be long before your and our representatives can meet to exchange our trades union experiences.

This was magnificent, but it was not politic. It was not politic at all: particularly that telling phrase about 'all the nations of the Soviet Union'. None the less, it was passed—almost casually—by a show of hands. Later still came a Letter to Poles in the whole world:

> Here, on the Vistula, a new Poland is being born . . . Born of the whole nation's will, Solidarity is not only a trades union of working people, but at the same time a civic social movement of people conscious of their rights and their duties towards the Fatherland and its independence . . .

Bravo! bravo! bravo![7]

Next morning they woke up to the shocked reaction of the world's press, East and West. Now Solidarity really *has* gone too far, western observers commented. Soviet propaganda yelled about unwarranted interference in the internal affairs of sovereign states. Wałęsa retorted that they were only following Marx's advice ('proletarians of all countries, unite!'). In the Olivia hall the Message had seemed quite natural. In that atmosphere there was little question of not saying what they wanted. This did not mean they now imagined they could *do* what they wanted. The barriers which had fallen were ones of self-censorship, not of self-limitation in political action. Neither was a complete end made to self-censorship: a delegate from Gdańsk who proposed that Solidarity should cease to recognise the leading role of the Party was coolly received, even by those most 'drunk on democracy'. When they dispersed on 11 September, the only immediate, substantive political challenge to the regime—apart from the very existence of such an alternative parliament—was the resolution on self-government.

In the interval between the two rounds Wałęsa used his executive power to defuse this challenge. After ten days of haggling, against a background of heated government propaganda and an extraordinary diplomatic *démarche* delivered to the Polish government by the Soviet Ambassador, a compromise was finally reached between the Solidarity and government proposals for the Bill on Workers' Self-Government. On Tuesday 22 September Wałęsa, backed strongly by Kuroń and Mazowiecki, persuaded the National Commission Presidium to accept the compromise. Unusually, there were only four voting members of Solidarity's cabinet present, and one of them, Jan Rulewski, voted against the compromise. Then, on Wednesday morning, Mr Kania suddenly informed the communist Party deputies to the *sejm* that the compromise was not, after all, acceptable to them, and the government proposed to revert to its original form of words for the appointment of managers.

At this point, the members of the *sejm* started behaving like members of the other national parliament in Gdańsk. On Wednesday evening, General Jaruzelski had the dubious pleasure of receiving an envoy representing the deputies of the Democratic Party, most of the United Peasant Party, the two regime-backed lay Catholic groups (Pax and 'neo-Znak'), and those 'without party'. They would not vote for the Party version, the Prime Minister was informed. The Bill was due to be voted next morning, but when the General rose to speak the *sejm* commission was still obstinately refusing to return to the Party version. Fevered negotiations continued all day, until Mr Kania once again retreated. The Act which the *sejm* triumphantly passed on Friday 25 September was a compromise distinguished only by a few turns of phrase from that which the Solidarity cabinet had approved on Tuesday.[8]

The behaviour of the *sejm* was without precedent in the history of Poland since 1947. For the first time, infected with democracy after a year of revolution, the deputies had directly and publicly rejected the communist Party whip.

Yet when the Solidarity parliament reassembled the next day in Gdańsk, it did not celebrate this as a victory. Instead, a tremendous thunderstorm of criticism broke over the head of Lech Wałęsa, partly because of the unsatisfactory nature of the compromise, but mainly because of the undemocratic way in which it had been reached. It was an action replay of the controversy after the Warsaw agreement, but on a much larger field. The delegates demanded that the protocol of the Presidium meeting (recorded on tape) be read out to them. They lauded Rulewski for what he grandly called his *'votum separatum'* and they scourged Wałęsa for being a 'dictator'. Finally, after the storm had rumbled on for four days, they passed by 348 votes to 189 a formal motion criticising the Presidium's conduct, and especially the role of the advisers.[9]

No sooner had this storm subsided but another blew up. On Monday 28 September the venerable and witty Professor Edward Lipiński (a Polish A. J. P. Taylor) read from the platform a statement in which the Social Self-Defence Committee—'KOR'—formally terminated its activities on the fifth anniversary of its foundation. The task of 'social self-defence', the statement explained, was now being carried out by Solidarity, which represented 'the whole society':

> When several years ago we began this open and unequal struggle we could never have foreseen that our vision would so soon materialise...
>
> Before our eyes we had the vision of that Poland whose glory was once tolerance and freedom, which was the common motherland of Poles, Byelorussians, Ukrainians and Jews...

Lipiński capped the statement with a personal plea for democratic socialism. 'We are not all socialists like me,' he said, 'but we are all fighting for the same goals.'[10]

'Sto lat, sto lat...' they sang—but in the fierce debates which followed it was often hard to discern that essential unity. Moreover, little tolerance was shown by the small group of delegates who called themselves 'True Poles', and cast dark aspersions on the 'Polishness' of KOR's Jewish intellectuals. When, following Lipiński's speech, a vote of thanks to KOR was proposed, a 'True Pole' rose to his feet and objected that the Congress should not thank KOR particularly. What about the Church? And KPN? And so on. In the end the Congress did, on its last day, pass a resolution specially thanking KOR. It is plausibly suggested that this particular 'True Pole' was working with the security services (SB), who had a long record of attempting to manipulate anti-Semitic sentiment*—but the support which the 'True Poles' received cannot simply be explained away as police 'provocation'.

Western observers expressed surprise and dismay at the political divisions which surfaced during the Congress. Yet it is hardly surprising that a democratic mass movement with nearly ten million members, and a brief for 'national regeneration', should reveal differences of view. Would anyone expect an assembly which contained democratically elected representatives of all employed people in Britain to agree in the space of ten days on the leaders, organisation and strategy to carry through a fundamental transformation of the country's economic, social and political systems?

*Anti-Semitic flysheets were also found in the Congress hall—a familiar secret-police device.

Of course they would not. And of course the differences in such an assembly could not be reduced to any simple polarity: 'radicals' versus 'moderates', for example. To approximate to the shifting positions of individuals and groups on different issues within Solidarity we would need a graph with at least five co-ordinates: regional, social, strategic, ideological and, last but not least, personal. In this five-dimensional picture, regional differences were very important. Solidarity now had thirty-eight regional organisations (MKZs). The largest, Upper Silesia, had fifty-four times more members than the smallest: 1.4 million to 26,000.[11] Like the nobles in the sixteenth-century *sejm*, however, the least regional baron considered himself the equal of the greatest. Conflicts of interests between regions were not blunted by a fiery local patriotism. Social differences were probably less important by comparison. According to a survey conducted at the Congress, 47 per cent of the delegates were of working-class origin (71 per cent for Upper Silesia) while 32.8 per cent came from the intelligentsia. Only 7.7 per cent were women—an imbalance remarked less by Poles than by the western Left.[12] Strategic disagreements were myriad, but they revolved essentially around the question: how far and how fast could the movement go in its struggle with the authorities? The inadequate heading of 'ideological' differences must serve to cover the delegates' differing visions of the ideal shape of that free Poland which was their common goal. Personal differences, finally, as in all democratic politics, were both expressed through and reinforced by all the other kinds of difference. In the case of Wałęsa and Gwiazda, for instance, it was hard to separate their growing personal antipathy from their diverging views on strategy and internal democracy.

In the debates about ideology and strategy, three areas of polarisation could be identified. First, the Confederation for an Independent Poland (KPN) opposition group was gaining increasingly vocal support. Weary of Solidarity's self-censorship and peering into the apparent power vacuum, many workers were drawn to the KPN's clear, explicit programme. The authorities, by persecuting the KPN activists instead of KOR, had unwittingly turned them into heroes. In its most unsavoury variant, the 'True Poles' carried on the intolerant, racist tradition of the pre-war National Democrats. They could accurately be described as 'nationalists', unlike the vast majority of Solidarity members who were simply patriots—that is, their love of their country and desire to see it free from foreign occupation was not mixed with intolerance, hatred of other peoples, or the desire to see other nations occupied. (The essential distinction between nationalism and patriotism is made by George Orwell in his 'Notes on Nationalism'.) KPN's brand of nationalism clashed most directly with the agnostic, tolerant democratic socialism espoused by many KOR members. The fact that some of the most active younger KOR members were the children of Jewish communists was obscurely held against them. Here, alas, the 'two nations' of pre-war Poland began to resurface. Here, too, ideological differences were both reflected in and a vehicle for personal differences: in Mazowsze, for example, a challenge to Bujak's leadership from firebrands like Wojciech Kamiński of the public transport workers.

Secondly, there was the divide between 'fundamentalists' and 'pragmatists'. In the Programme working-group on 'the attitude of the union to the state and Party', the fundamentalists and pragmatists formed two distinct groups, whose projects for the Programme could not initially be reconciled. Instead they were presented to the delegates as alternatives. The fundamentalists' draft said the 'Party apparatus has become a new ruling class'; the power monopoly and the *nomenklatura* were 'immoral'; the present state apparatus could not be a credible partner for society; and though it concluded, 'Solidarity does not struggle for power for itself, nor to become a political party', the implication was clear. One leading fundamentalist, Andrzej Rozpłochowski, a thirty-year-old mechanic from Huta Katowice, later told the Congress that Party committees at the enterprise level should be liquidated. The pragmatists, in this strategically vital discussion, included not only the advisers but also Bogdan Lis, Karol Modzelewski and Andrzej Gwiazda. Their draft referred cautiously to the August agreements and the Constitution; it talked of 'supervising' the authorities; it did not question the position of the Party. The union's struggle, it declared, was the struggle for bread, not the struggle for political power. Pragmatists accused fundamentalists of threatening the unity of the movement by encouraging the development of rival political parties inside it. Fundamentalists retorted that the pragmatists were out of touch with the increasingly radical masses.[13]

Thirdly, there was a spectrum of views on economic reform, ranging from the economic liberalism of Stefan Kurowski to the 'realistic' proposals of a group of economists led by Ryszard Bugaj, who envisaged a far less radical dismantling of the socialist planned economy.

On many issues it was possible to observe a loose alignment of KPN supporters, fundamentalists, Kurowski fans, on one side, 'secular leftists' (Michnik's *lewica laicka*), pragmatists (from both KOR and KIK), economic 'realists' on the other. Thus it was Kurowski who broke another pragmatist taboo by suggesting, in a powerful speech, that the 'fruitless sector' of armaments production should be limited . . . 'We are for disarmament' . . . 'Since our press prints resolutions of the Labour Party or the English Liberals in favour of unilateral disarmament, why should we be worse than them?'[14] As this example suggests, the labels 'right' and 'left' do not explain much in Solidarity.

Most of these tensions and cross-currents were visible when, on the evening of Thursday 1 October, the Congress finally proceeded to elect the Chairman of the National Commission. Three candidates stood against Wałęsa and the procedure was ultra-democratic to the point of parody. First, the candidates delivered their prepared speeches. Marian Jurczyk, the tough, straight-talking warehouseman from Szczecin, talked about the need for discipline in the union—discipline but not dictatorship. He had closely observed the Party Congress, he said, but 'only the people had changed', the 'methods' and 'mechanisms' remained the same; and that was why the union must take a strong and decisive line. He was in favour of free elections to the *sejm* 'so that power should be in the hands of the people of Town and Country.' A calm, deliberate speech, warmly received. 'For a year we have talked to the government . . . like blind men talking about colours', Gwiazda said, and primarily for this strategic reason he, too, urged a strong line. The bowed, bearded prophetic figure, and the familiar, quiet reedy voice of Gwiazda were greeted with affection. Wałęsa, for once, was right off form: visibly exhausted, irritable, and actually running out of things to say. We underestimate our partner, he said, the authorities are deliberately, step by step, sapping the trust of society in Solidarity. It was a salutary warning, but a very odd electioneering speech, and poorly received. Jan Rulewski, finally, the hero of Bydgoszcz, gave a fiery speech, declaring, in effect, that they should forget about the Soviet threat. They should express their opinion on foreign policy, and look into the budget to see how much went to the military and how much to pay a basic wage to seven million starving Poles (a wild figure).

Then each candidate was put up for half an hour's questioning from the floor. Gwiazda was asked what influence his wife had on his work. A delegate from Lower Silesia asked Wałęsa, 'What do you consider most important for (a) Solidarity (b) Poland, (c) the world?'! (Wałęsa replied, 'Peace.') But there were also more serious questions about their attitude to internal democracy, economic reform, and how they would react to the declaration of a 'state of emergency'. Both Gwiazda and Wałęsa were asked directly about differences between workers and intelligentsia; both denied they were significant. By now it was after midnight, and everyone was exhausted, but perfect democracy must be seen to prevail so the four candidates were invited to stand up on the platform and ask questions *of each other*, by turns. Wałęsa asked Gwiazda if he would continue to be late for everything. 'Lech,' Gwiazda reedily retorted, 'when I am Chairman, and have a car, chauffeur, secretary and servant, why should I be late? You could travel on a tram for a change.' Laughter and applause.[15]

After this verbal riot, the voting was comparatively straightforward. The results, announced next evening: Wałęsa re-elected Chairman with the surprisingly small majority of 55 per cent (462 votes), Jurczyk a strong second with 24 per cent (201), Gwiazda third with nearly 9 per cent (74), and the firebrand Rulewski fourth with 6 per cent (52).[16] Once again, the photographers swarmed around the little man with the large moustache; *'sto lat, sto lat . . .'* the delegates sang, once again. But the vote against him was, amongst other things, a vote against the Personality Cult, the high-handedness, the undemocratic methods.

All candidates for the new National Commission (KK) and Audit Commission—an internal control agency, to prevent corruption or abuse of power—were subsequently submitted to the same ultra-democratic scrutiny. The Congress decided on the federal rather than the centralised solution, with the new National Commission (KK) to be both legislature and executive between Congresses. Sixty-nine members of the National Commission were elected directly by the Congress after no less than six rounds of balloting, while the thirty-eight regional chairmen became members *ex officio*. The federal nature of the organisation was emphasised by a resolution on the distribution of the large funds which had accumulated from the regular monthly membership dues: just 3 per cent would be disposed of by the national leadership, 22 per cent by regional offices, and 75 per cent by Factory Commissions directly.[17] As after the Party Congress, these structural changes (or the lack of them) were quite as important as any personnel changes.

The Congress was noticeably reluctant to vote for delegates who were also Party members (nearly 10 per cent of the total according to one survey),[18] and even Bogdan Lis only scraped on to the National Commission on the sixth ballot. But otherwise it is not possible to say that the new national leadership was predominantly 'radical' or 'moderate', 'fundamentalist' or 'pragmatist', let alone 'left' or 'right'. The Presidium which it elected on 8 October was composed of two elements: a permanent cabinet of twelve, based in Gdańsk and each with a special departmental responsibility, and the chairmen of the six largest regions who would 'commute' to Solidarity's capital. Naturally enough, Wałęsa wished to have in his cabinet people with whom he could work, so Gwiazda and Rulewski were not among his proposed 'ministers'. But his nominees were by no means ciphers: Janusz Onyszkiewicz, the former National Press Spokesman, Stanisław Wądołowski, one of the August strike leaders in Szczecin, Grzegorz Palka from Łódź, now to hold the vital portfolio for economic reform, were all men of independent views—and stature. Moreover, the six regional barons, including Bujak from Warsaw and Słowik from Łódź, would ensure that Wałęsa could behave like a 'dictator' only in his dreams.

How can we characterise the democratic politics of the Congress and the structures it endorsed? What was the *Demokratieverständnis*—the 'understanding of democracy'—of these men who, in August 1980, had no personal experience of democracy? If the fundamentalists had had their way, then the spectrum of political views inside Solidarity would already have been translated into political parties. 'Pluralism', for them, meant a multi-party system. In a year's time—if allowed to develop freely—Solidarity's parliament would probably have begun to look like the Polish parliament in that first 'explosion of democracy' sixty years before, when, after the country had regained independence, 'the proliferating profusion of possible political permutations among the pullulating peoples and parties of the Polish provinces... palpably prevented the propagation of permanent pacts between potential partners', as Norman Davies jocularly explains in his Oxford *History of Poland.*[19] Polish parliamentary politics then were, if possible, slightly more unstable than Italian parliamentary politics are now.

But on this the fundamentalists did not have their way, because, as the pragmatists argued, such a profusion would fatally weaken the unity and therefore the fighting strength of the union. None the less, the Congress did not produce a strong, orderly, centralised democracy. It produced a decentralised, disorderly and at times anarchic democracy. The fundamentalist urge broke down almost all the barriers of self-censorship—the verbal taboos of a year before—and this allowed all the differences which inevitably existed in a mass movement representing *a whole society* to be freely expressed, at the cost of unity. Fragmentation was warmly encouraged by the authorities.

The nearest historical parallel to the state of Solidarity in its last months is the Polish Noble Democracy of the sixteenth to eighteenth centuries. The regional conferences were Solidarity's *sejmiki* and the Congress its *sejm*. The delegates to the Congress, like those to a seventeenth-century *sejm*, were aware that in a few days they would have to return to their region and answer for their conduct to their peers, who had 'instructed' them. Wałęsa was the elected monarch, afflicted now, as then, by the fierce independence of the regional nobility, their profound distrust of any strong central authority, their liberal enjoyment of an almost unlimited right to disagree—endlessly, riotously—among themselves. Many a time would a regional chairman make what in the seventeenth century was called a *'rokosz'*: a kind of legalised revolt. All they lacked was the *Liberum Veto*.

Poland's Noble Democracy was unique in the Europe of its time. The right of resistance, the respect for individual liberty, the principles of government by consent, free speech and religious tolerance earned it the epithet of 'Golden Freedom', and prefigured the liberal democracy which in later centuries and more fortunate lands would be extended to all citizens, not merely to the nobility.

Yet this 'Golden Freedom', this anarchic democracy, by keeping the central government weak, poor, and therefore inadequately armed, ensured its own eventual destruction. By 1800 it had been devoured by the hungry autocracies which were its neighbours. It succumbed to what would now be called the 'geopolitical reality'. But it left a rich legacy of ideas and memories; ideas which were cherished and cultivated, memories which seeped into the deep subsoil of the national conscience.

'Historical parallel' is not an adequate description. Perhaps it was only a few intellectuals among the delegates who were fully conscious of the continuity from the noble to the workers' democracy. The historian Karol Modzelewski, for example, compared his instructions from his members in Wrocław to the seventeenth-century *instrukcja sejmowa*. But the continuity was there in the behaviour of the worker-delegates. As the aristocratic forms of address (*pan* and *pani*, 'Sir' and 'Madam') are preserved in the everyday speech of working people, so the aristocratic political culture of two centuries before re-emerges, like some underground river, in the workers' 'school of political culture' in Gdańsk, in the mouth even of a Jan Rulewski, proudly explaining what he calls his '*votum separatum*'.[20]

Solidarity, too, was unique in the Europe of its time. The right of resistance, the respect for individual liberty, the principle of government by consent, of free speech and tolerance . . . these had not been proclaimed by so many for so long in eastern Europe since 1945. But, like the Noble Democracy, its own, internal 'golden freedom' was a partial cause of its destruction. 'We are going to war . . . so we need generals,' Wałęsa is reported to have said in an early Congress debate. He did not get them, nor a strong central executive, nor an 'army'. Wanting peace, Solidarity failed to prepare for 'war'. It succumbed to the 'geopolitical reality' (or, some would say, to the same hungry autocracy). But it left a rich legacy of ideas and memories; more, it left a 'Programme' . . .

The Programme

The Programme, like the leadership, was the product of a long and ultra-democratic process. First proposals had been drafted by a group of intellectual advisers under the aegis of the union's

Centre for Socio-Professional Studies (OPSZ) and published in April,[21] at the beginning of that period of 'identity crisis' which followed the Warsaw Agreement. In a protracted discussion these 'theses' were fiercely criticised, elaborated and refined into another draft document prepared for the first round of the Congress. A 'Programme Commission' was then formed under the Chairmanship of Bronisław Geremek, and, in the interval between the two rounds, more than a hundred delegates organised in thirteen working-groups spent several hundred hours thrashing out a final draft Programme comprising eight 'chapters' and thirty-seven 'theses'. The second round of the Congress then debated and voted on each individual chapter, incorporating numerous amendments proposed from the floor. And even then, several individuals and (usually regional) groups felt impelled to record their protest *'votum separatum'* on this or that paragraph.

If ever a programme was democratically arrived at, this one was. It is therefore all the more astonishing, in view of the myriad representative differences already mentioned, that the end product is a document of remarkable coherence and power.[22] The first two chapters contain Solidarity's self-definition, starting from the great strikes of August 1980:

> What we had in mind was not only bread, butter and sausage but also justice, democracy, truth, legality, human dignity, freedom of convictions and the repair of the republic. All elementary values had been too mistreated to believe that anything could improve without their rebirth. Thus the economic protest had to be simultaneously a social protest, and the social protest had to be simultaneously a moral protest.

Now Solidarity combined the features of a 'trades union' and 'a great social movement'. It drew from 'the values of Christian ethics, from our national traditions and from the workers' and democratic traditions of the labour world.' Because of the Party-state's failure to reform itself in the year since the summer agreements, the second chapter explained, and the resultant 'national tragedy', Solidarity could no longer restrict itself to exerting pressure on the authorities to fulfil those agreements. The union had a 'fundamental duty to take every possible ... step to save the country from downfall and society from misery, apathy and self-destruction.' This required 'reforming the state and the economy on the basis of democracy and universal public initiative.' The 'geopolitical reality' was acknowledged, explicitly and clearly, without adopting the Newspeak formulas of the socialist state: 'Responsibility demands that we recognise the system of powers that emerged in Europe after the Second World War. We want to continue the work of the great change initiated by us without violating international alliances.'

True to the enlarged definition of its role, just one of the next six 'chapters' concerns Solidarity's action as a trades union in the strict sense. Chapter III treats Solidarity's 'attitude to the crisis and economic reform', Chapter V 'social policy', and Chapter VI bears the key title 'The Self-Governing Republic'. Chapter VII lays down principles for the internal organisation of the movement, while the short, concluding Chapter VIII demands a 'New Social Accord'. Short- and medium-term aims are spelt out side by side, rather as if the election manifesto of a western political party was to be dovetailed into its programme. In the economics chapter, for example, immediate practical suggestions for 'emergency measures' to survive the coming winter rub shoulders with proposals for improved production, macro-economic adjustments and the fundamental, structural reform of the whole economic system. Thesis 21 demands that new local-government election rules be presented to the *sejm*, after consultations with Solidarity, by the end of the year (31 December 1981). Thesis 22 looks forward to the longer-term possibility of a second parliamentary chamber. While theses 23 and 24 enunciate the basic principles of equality before the law and an independent judiciary, thesis 26 deals specifically with those responsible for repression in 1956, 1968, 1970, 1976 and those who 'through their activities in 1970–80, brought the country to economic ruin'. 'If penal proceedings in the aforementioned cases are not instituted by 31 December 1981,' it concludes, 'the National Commission will appoint a social tribunal which, having held a public trial, will pass judgement on and brand the guilty.'

Though we may glimpse the outlines of several utopias behind it, the programme was not utopian in conception. The vision of a sovereign, independent, nation-state 'Poland' expressed, for instance, in that Letter to Poles in the whole world, the dream that

Poland might once again be free, was deliberately excluded from the document, although this painful self-limitation did not pass without protest. Far-reaching as the proposals for a Self-Governing Republic were, they yet remained within what the delegates perceived as the limits of the possible. 'We regard censorship in the mass media as an evil we tolerate only for the time being and out of necessity', thesis 31 declares: the geopolitical 'necessity' is still recognised.

Defence interests were referred to only tangentially, in thesis 3, devoted to finding ways of increasing production: 'In the crisis period, armaments expenditures should be restricted to the absolute minimum, and the funds and facilities freed in this way should be used to raise production.' On foreign policy, the one paragraph on respecting the existing system of alliances concluded with a hopeful message which independent Polish publicists had long endeavoured to get through to Moscow: '. . . our nation can be a valuable partner only when it assumes obligations voluntarily and consciously.' Why anyone should assume that a democratically governed Poland would 'voluntarily and consciously' assume burdensome obligations for the defence of Russia was not clear.

None the less, this was the perspective within which the delegates operated. Jerzy Milewski, secretary of the Congress Programme Commission, confirms that, incredible as it seems, they genuinely imagined that the greater part of the Programme should and could be realised in a matter of years: not decades, or generations.[23] This Self-Governing Republic of Chapter VI, with its institutional pluralism, enterprise self-government, free local elections, representative parliament and independent judiciary would somehow flourish inside the Warsaw Pact. Even 'Finlandisation' was beyond the horizon of the Programme, for Poland's geopolitical position would not allow more benevolent neutrality, as Finland's does. But the Poles, like the Finns, would win for themselves the freedom to shape their own domestic affairs (almost) as they wished, and the Russians would accept this because, as in the case of Finland, the cost of destroying it would be too high.

What would have been the shape of this new republic? The question of Solidarity's ideological orientation exercised and distressed ideologists of all tendencies in the West. One day the delegates cheered the professed socialist Edward Lipiński; the next they resolved to adopt the sermons delivered by Father Józef Tischner as official Congress documents. Red was mixed with white, ice with steam.

The word 'socialism' does not appear in the Programme. The intellectuals' first draft had acknowledged a debt to 'socialist social thought' beside Christian ethics, national traditions and democratic politics: the democratic debate dropped the adjective 'socialist'. For the vast majority of Poles the word 'socialism' was utterly discredited by what the Soviet Union and their authorities since 1945 had done in its name. Professor Lipiński lectured the delegates:

> According to the classics, socialism should mean a better economy than the capitalist, a greater freedom than in capitalism... the liberation of the working class, the creation of conditions in which every human being... may have unhindered access to the goods of culture and civilisation.
>
> What was created, however, was a socialism which meant a rotten, inefficient, wasteful economy. It was precisely the socialist economic system which led not to economic crisis, but to an economic catastrophe without parallel in the history of the last one or two hundred years [Applause].
>
> Perhaps there are similar conditions in Cambodia, where the socialist system [Applause] shot three and a half million people in defence of their socialism.
>
> This socialism of rotten economy, this socialism of prisoners, censorship and police, has destroyed us for thirty years, as it has destroyed other nations.

Loud and prolonged applause. If 'socialism' was what General Jaruzelski meant by 'socialism' then he could keep it. But the delegates applauded, too, when Lipiński insisted that he was a socialist since 1906 and directly addressed what, for a Marxist, must be the crucial question:

> There are no forces in Poland who struggle for the privatisation of the means of production [Applause], a

> privatisation of Huta Katowice or Huta im. Lenina [Nowa Huta, near Kraków]...
>
> We all understand that so far as light industry, small-scale commerce, restaurants or handicrafts are concerned, there must be private initiative, for only private initiative is capable of running such concerns properly. To nationalise them means bureaucracy, destruction of the creative factor... In these cases private ownership is better. But there are no counter-revolutionary forces! Only those who demanded a privatisation of heavy industry would be counter-revolutionary. In Poland there are no such forces.
>
> But there are forces who demand freedom, who demand conditions of normal life for the Polish nation [Applause]. And those are not anti-socialist forces.[24]

This was not merely a magnificent answer to the official (per)version of socialism. On all the evidence, it accurately reflects the broad limits within which most Poles thought about the ownership of the means of production. Since the late 1950s Polish sociologists had found a large and growing majority of their respondents against free enterprise in medium and heavy industry.[25] Now the Solidarity Programme envisaged the encouragement of private agriculture 'Because private farms are more efficient than socialised ones' (thesis 3, point 4)—and, for example, private builders to help combat the housing shortage (thesis 17), alongside the public sector. Three rival proposals for economic reform were appended to it, and the most radical of these (drafted by Stefan Kurowski) did argue the need to 'activate private capital' and to seek to employ an additional one million people in the 'non-agricultural private sector' (industry, construction and services). Kurowski, an accomplished orator, was very popular at the Congress, especially because he held out the prospect of a rapid and relatively painless economic recovery. But even he did not propose a simple return to 'capitalism', in the sense of large-scale privatisation.

No, the majority was still for 'social ownership of the means of production'. But they restored to this socialist principle a literal meaning: 'social ownership', they said, means 'ownership by society', not ownership by the socialist state; and we are society. Thesis 1 demands 'a new socio-economic system combining the plan, self-government and the market'. The concentration of economic power 'in the hands of the Party and bureaucratic apparatus' and the 'command system, must be smashed.' Instead, 'The socialised enterprise should be the basic organisational unit in the economy'; its managing director should be hired and fired by the workers' council.

The 'socialised enterprise' would 'act independently on the basis of economic accountancy' (i.e. making a profit). 'The state should influence its activity through regulations and economic means—prices, taxes, interest rates on credits, currency exchange rates and so forth.' Further, 'Bureaucratic barriers hampering market activities should be abolished', and firms should be able to conduct their own foreign trade. 'The union duly appreciates the importance of profitable exports for collectives and the country.' The 'socialised enterprise' thus had two faces. Workers' control was an ideal which was particularly attractive to a generation of workers who had received a socialist education, and to some extent internalised socialist values. At the same time it was a practical means to achieve the decentralisation and flexibility which all competent economists agreed were prerequisites for a successful economic reform, but which the socialist Party-state was unwilling and unable to introduce itself. To some, 'self-government' meant primarily workers' control; to others, it meant primarily strong, independent, competent non-Party management. It is, of course, impossible to know what would have been in practice the mix of plan, self-government and market, of private, social and state ownership, in this new kind of mixed economy. Of course, many vital questions were left unanswered—or rather, were answered in several alternative ways. But the outline of the economic base, as it were the infrastructure for the Self-Governing Republic, is there, and it is neither utopian nor incoherent.

Another socialist value—one of the few, basic values common to all the myriad varieties of socialism—which many of the delegates had imbibed from the system was that of equality. Curiously, 'equality' does not appear beside 'justice, truth, democracy, legality . . .' in the introductory list of 'what we had in mind', although the growing inequalities of the late Gierek era had been a major cause of workers' discontent in 1980. None the less, there is a strong egalitarian strain in the Programme. Thesis 6 demands compensation for the 'less prosperous'; index-linked pensions, family allowances and other social benefits; and the increase of incomes to (what the socialist state already recognised as) the 'social minimum'. 'The union will resist the growing social differences among enterprises and regions,' declares thesis 8. And part of thesis 15, demanding that all hospital places should be allotted exclusively by the national health service, reads as if it had been lifted from a Labour Party manifesto. (The target here being the privileged 'private medicine' enjoyed by the communist ruling class, their policemen and, incidentally, those Party trades union functionaries with whom the official representatives of western trades unions so happily hobnobbed.) Thesis 9, in the chapter on 'Labour protection as the union's basic task', proposes nationwide 'equal payment for equal work' and standardised fringe benefits.

If there was a certain tension between this demand and that for independent enterprise management, the insistence in the same thesis on preventing unemployment could even less be reconciled with the necessities of economic reform. How, for example, was the suggestion that workers should not be fired but 'work shorter shifts without loss of wages'(!) to be reconciled with the suggestion that socialised enterprises should be profit-making? This is an area of inconsistency, if not outright contradiction, within the Programme. The delegates did not face up clearly to the fact that Solidarity, the movement for national regeneration, was demanding an economic reform requiring redundancies, which Solidarity, the trades union, would refuse to accept. It had this in common with most socialist programmes (and all Soviet socialist ones), that it postulated both full employment and economic efficiency ('profitable exports') but did not explain how the two could be combined.

The *political* groundplan of the Self-Governing Republic, moreover, is not distinctively 'socialist' at all. Rather does Chapter VI enumerate the basic principles of a liberal democracy: free elections for local governments which should have the right to levy taxes (thesis 21); free elections to a parliament which would be 'the supreme power in the state' (22); equality before the law (23); an independent judiciary (24); freedom of information, conscience, speech and science (23, 25, 30, 31). The emphasis on community self-help in the chapter on social policy—thesis 12, for instance, proposes 'residents' self-government groups' on housing estates—recalls the proposals of contemporary west European liberal parties. To the dismay of some western socialists, Solidarity looked to existing liberal democracies and to Poland's own liberal and democratic traditions, rather than to any socialist utopia, for the blueprint of their new political system.

Yet the 'ideology' with which Solidarity was most obviously identified was, of course, Christianity. Not even the Church wanted it to be a confessional union, but the debt to Christianity, unlike the debt to socialism, is explicitly acknowledged in the first chapter: 'John Paul II's encyclical about human labour is for us a new stimulus to work.' A direct influence may be detected in thesis 13, on the rights of the family, and in thesis 28 which begins:

> 'The history of our nation—condemned many times to death—proves that it has survived and preserved its identity, not because of physical strength, but exclusively because of its own culture.' (John Paul II) That is why the authorities' present policy, which has brought education and culture to a state of catastrophe, must be changed.

Solidarity's approach to education and culture can perhaps best be characterised as conservative-restorationist. It wished the values and teaching which had been conserved in the Polish Church, the family and the unofficial counter-culture, to be restored to their proper place in the schools and the media.

One should, however, beware the automatic equation of Catholicism and Conservatism. Poland defies this as it defies so many western equations. If few of the delegates troubled to read the Pope's Encyclical, or even the account of it which appeared in the Solidarity Weekly, they certainly listened to the Pope's close friend and intellectual associate, Father Józef Tischner. Although, like the Pope, steeped in phenomenology, Tischner yet retained an almost Lutheran pastoral directness and natural vividness of language. The world of Polish work, he preached on the first day of the Congress, was as broad and filthy as the River Vistula . . . 'Let the water in the Polish Vistula become as clean . . . as the water in the five Polish lakes in the Tatra mountains.'[26] In a remarkable cycle of short essays, published as *The Ethics of Solidarity*, he gave a special Polish

Catholic interpretation of concepts like 'exploitation', 'democracy', 'revolution' and 'socialism'. To strikes, under the existing economic system, he attributed the positive significance of an existential act:

> Senseless work is the most extreme form of the exploitation of man by man. It is a direct insult to the human dignity of the worker. When work becomes senseless, the strike is the only kind of behaviour which makes sense.[27]

As for socialism, one must distinguish between 'open' and 'closed' socialism. Closed socialism

> . . . allows of only one possible form of exploitation—that which is a result of private ownership of the means of production. When, therefore, after the abolition of private property, the workers come to the conclusion that they are being exploited, closed socialism concludes that they have fallen victim to an illusion. Their consciousness does not properly reflect objective reality . . .[28]

For closed socialism a strike is an impossibility: how can the workers strike against themselves? But not for open socialism. For open socialism the workers' consciousness of being exploited is part of objective reality. Between the ethical inspiration of this open socialism and the ethical inspiration of Christianity, writes Tischner, there is a profound difference, but not necessarily an opposition. 'The views are different. Different views open the possibility of mutual enrichment. With all the differences, the common ground is visible . . .' and it is visible in Solidarity. Polish Catholicism (the open Catholicism of Tischner, not the closed Catholicism of the 'True Poles') and Polish socialism (the open socialism of Lipiński, not the closed socialism of Olszowski and Jaruzelski) had come a long way from their bitter enmity of half a century before.

When the Programme proclaims, 'The union will accord particular solicitude to the poorest', is this a socialist or a Christian aspiration? When it proposes to defend the rights of the family by abolishing night work for women, 'in accordance with ILO Convention 89', is the inspiration socialist or Christian?

The peculiar interest of the Solidarity Programme is precisely that it overflows the banks of these ideological canals. It cannot be fitted whole into any of our existing political categories. In 1978 Leszek Kołakowski published a 'Credo' entitled *How to be a Conservative-Liberal-Socialist,* in which he noted conservative, liberal and socialist goals which are by no means mutually exclusive and even complementary.[29] The Solidarity Programme was a conservative-socialist-liberal manifesto: predominantly socialist (and Christian) in its approach to social questions, predominantly liberal democratic in its political vision, predominantly conservative in its cultural goals, and borrowing freely from all three in its economics. This eclecticism brought down the charge of rag-bag incoherence on the Programme. Apart from some of the economic proposals, which were not so much incoherent as inchoate, the charge is unfounded. All political programmes contain inconsistencies, all promise more than they can deliver, but the Solidarity Programme will stand comparison with any other political programme produced at the time. Compared with the programme of a social movement whose members had lived all their lives under parliamentary democracy—the West German 'Greens'—it is a miracle of coherence and lucidity. Its mixture is unique, like the democracy which produced it. Perhaps, like the Noble Democracy, it is also ahead of its time.

Parting Shots

'The Programme', Geremek declared at the outset, 'should be close to the daily life of working people; such, that a nation living in a nightmare of queues can see what people can do for themselves, how to survive the queues, but also, that they should not accustom themselves to them.'[30] It is hard to say how far this goal was realised. According to Jadwiga Staniszkis, the idea of 'settling accounts' with the bosses of the Gierek era was 'one of the few things in the programme . . . which actually [had] some resonance at the base'.[31] The larger perspectives of institutional reform were too remote for most people in the queues. The last chapter appealed for three new social accords: an 'anti-crisis accord' to 'enable society to survive the coming hard winter', an 'accord on economic reform', and an 'accord for the Self-Governing Republic'. In addition, thesis 5 demanded the setting up of a 'Social Council for the National Economy' to control and push forward the economic reform. So long as they were not mobilised for a nationwide confrontation, however, there was not much most Solidarity members could do about this. Such demands hardly gave them that vital sense of participation, of 'making a difference by their own activity'. Moreover, as the Programme despairingly remarked, 'hundreds and hundreds of accords signed by the government have remained bits of paper'.

Just how little the government was prepared to collaborate with Solidarity (or even consult it) on economic reform was demonstrated in the last week of the Congress. On Saturday 3 October the government unilaterally announced price increases which nearly doubled the cost of several popular brands of cigarettes. If this was not a deliberate provocation, it was another act of Bourbon stupidity. Of course the Congress exploded: Wałęsa shot off a protest telegram to General Jaruzelski; Jaruzelski shot back his Finance Minister to Gdańsk; and on Sunday evening the delegates laid into the hapless Mr Krzak with a vengeance. His explanation of the reasons for the increases was greeted with stony silence. Gradually the temperature in the hall rose, and the discussion acquired the character of a class confrontation. 'I get eight and a half thousand [złotys per month],' said a miner, in broad Silesian dialect, 'I have two kids and a wife who has no job. And I live. And Sir Minister...?' After two angry days, the Congress passed a resolution proposed by Karol Modzelewski demanding a price freeze until the economic reform programme was agreed with Solidarity. If a satisfactory agreement was not reached, it went on, the union would, within the next two weeks, declare a general warning strike. Meanwhile, local branches were asked to refrain from unco-ordinated protests.[32]

Apart from this, the only immediate initiative which the delegates could bring back to their members concerned self-government. On 3 October the Congress approved a resolution[33] proposed by Łódź, where self-government was strongly supported by the local Solidarity leaders. This did not reject the new Act outright, but called for a referendum in enterprises on those points where the Act differed from Solidarity's conception: for example, on the appointment of managers, and on the industries which would be excluded from self-government (according to union experts, government proposals might exclude nearly half the country's productive capacity from this 'resocialisation'). Meanwhile, workforces were urged to continue building 'authentic workers' self-government' the way Solidarity had planned it. Battle would now be joined on each individual shopfloor.

The immediate prospect, therefore, before they could begin to implement their remarkable Programme, was a familiar one: local, regional and national confrontation. This did not visibly dampen the spirits of the delegates at the end of their eighteen-day 'storm of democracy'. On the evening of Wednesday 7 October the Olivia sports hall was wreathed with smiles as they rose yet again to intone 'Poland is not yet lost...' and hurriedly exchanged souvenirs while the electronic scoreboard proclaimed its last hopeful message: 'See you at the next Congress.'

8. Confrontation

In mid-October the 44th bulletin of the Solidarity news agency (AS) carried a small news item under the regular rubric 'Against Solidarity':

> 30.09 A. Siwak informed members of the branch trades unions at a meeting in Krosno that a six-man Committee of National Salvation had been formed, with Generals Jaruzelski and Kiszczak at its head. Special units of the army and police had also been established to put down popular resistance. The Party and government leadership would wait another two months before using them, while popular support for Solidarity weakened. A decision to rescind the registration of Solidarity should be reckoned with.[1]

Two months later, on Sunday 13 December, General Jaruzelski announced the formation of a Military Council for National Salvation while special units of the army and police crushed popular resistance to the suspension of Solidarity.

When was the decision taken on the *coup de force?* Why was Solidarity unprepared for what actually happened? On the answers to these questions hinge several possible interpretations of Solidarity's development. The regime's answers were given most clearly, and artfully, by Mieczyław F. Rakowski. The decision, he claimed, was taken at the very last minute. On the afternoon of Friday 11 December, the General called Rakowski into his office.

'Jaruzelski looked very serious, more serious than ever. He raised his eyes and said: "The day has come. It's for the day after tomorrow the 13th." I answered, "I understand." There was nothing to add.'

It was a purely Polish decision. Referring to 'our Soviet friends',

Rakowski said, 'We have not done the job for them.' It was the result of an open bid for power, for the destruction of the state, for a general strike, chaos and anarchy, by Solidarity: ' . . blood would have flowed like rivers if we hadn't imposed martial law on December 13.'[2] Solidarity, as western commentators less melodramatically put it, 'went too far', and brought martial law upon its own head.

At the other extreme there is the testimony of Jaruzelski's former fellow-officer, General Leon Dubicki, a senior adviser in the Warsaw Defence Ministry until he defected to West Germany in August 1981. After the coup Dubicki told *Der Spiegel* that when Jaruzelski became Prime Minister, 'he said he would crush Solidarity with force. The top military leadership knew in February about what has now happened in December. Since then, the military was being prepared to crush Solidarity with force.' In other words, the decision was already taken in February. However, Dubicki immediately adds a rider: 'It was decided: *if Solidarity could not be destroyed by other means,* it would be destroyed by force at the beginning of the winter [my italics].'[3] A significant if.

That a military takeover of such magnitude and precision could not have been planned overnight is beyond reasonable doubt. Dubicki claims that the troop selection mentioned by Siwak began in March. We have seen that Rakowski himself threatened Solidarity specifically with the 'state of war' *(stan wojenny)* at the height of the Bydgoszcz crisis. An intensive campaign of political purification was reported by the army press in the spring. Western military observers noted that the Warsaw Pact manoeuvres had, by the early summer, established a formidable military communications network: the network that was used in December. Obviously the Polish army could not have been logistically prepared without the knowledge and active support of the Soviet high command. The list of interned opposition activists which was broadcast by Warsaw Radio after the coup included the names of people who had left the country several months before. The fact that martial law posters (undated) were printed in the Soviet Union is but one detail more of the direct Soviet participation without which the dispositions could hardly have been concealed from Solidarity's twenty million eyes. After the massive mobilisation on Poland's frontiers during the invasion scare of December 1980, the main thrust of Warsaw Pact 'fraternal aid' was to prepare Polish domestic forces for the battle with their own people. In this sense, Dubicki's judgment that from February the Polish military 'was being prepared to crush Solidarity with force' is surely correct.

This does not, however, necessarily support his (hastily qualified) assertion that Jaruzelski had already *chosen* to use force. A professional soldier will polish his weapon; but he may still hope not to have to use it. From the very beginning, from well before August 1980, the Polish communist leadership had the military option as a last resort: Gomułka had pleaded for it against the workers on the Baltic coast in December 1970, and Olszowski had pleaded for it in August 1980. Jaruzelski was not known to have done so; he was reputed to have done the opposite. Not merely his public statements but also his policies in the first months of his premiership suggest that he was still trying 'ineffectively' to find a 'political' solution. Of course, like Rakowski, he never intended to share power with Solidarity: at best, Solidarity would have been tamed, becoming a strictly consultative body on purely trades union questions, in the Rakowski model of 'partnership'. Certainly he wanted to 'destroy' Solidarity as an authentic, independent, representative mass movement. Yet his 'drift' was such that in June 1981 the Soviet Central Committee felt impelled to criticise him directly by name. Unless one accepts the implausible Machiavellian interpretation of the Letter (see above, pp. 184–5) then it suggests very strongly that there was not yet a secret, definite agreement between the Polish and Soviet leaderships. On the contrary, the fact that Jaruzelski and Kania were directly criticised and *none the less survived* suggests that both the Soviet and the Polish leaderships were still confused, uncertain and divided on how to cope with the unprecedented challenge of Solidarity. It was all Jaruzelski and Kania could do to contain the revolt within their own Party.

Yet contain it they did, and more: in retrospect the Party Congress was their one really successful piece of crisis management. In that windowless hall in the Palace of Culture, everything changed and nothing changed. They emerged still on top of what was still a Leninist Party, but with the new legitimacy given by democratic elections never before seen in the Soviet bloc. With their rear secured, they returned to the struggle with Solidarity. The offensive which immediately followed the Congress

(Olszowski's propaganda, Rakowski's 'negotiation') may, with hindsight, be seen as the Polish leadership's last serious attempt to achieve a 'political' solution. When the proffered terms of an unequal partnership were (predictably) rejected by Solidarity, Rakowski broke off the talks. His hope of taming Solidarity abandoned, he accused the workers' leaders of destroying the 'partnership'. The idea of partnership has been buried in Gdańsk, he said after the first round of the Solidarity Congress.

The crucial shift of probability from the political to the military option must therefore be placed between late July and late September.

Clearly, the operational planning had to proceed in the utmost secrecy, and the authorities would do everything in their power to put Solidarity (and the world) off its guard. They had learned the lessons of Bydgoszcz: given just a week's notice, Solidarity could organise the whole working population in a general occupation strike, which Polish forces might not be able to break without help from their friends. It is not therefore surprising that Albin Siwak's reported indiscretion is almost the only piece of *direct* evidence for the planned *timing* of the coup which has reached us, or is likely to reach us, unless another General defects or the most secret archives are opened.

There is, however, a good deal of indirect evidence. On 24 September Prime Minister Jaruzelski informed the *sejm* that army units would be deployed to assist the Interior Ministry in keeping law and order. Then, on 23 October, four days after Defence Minister Jaruzelski had met with the 'Military Council' at the Defence Ministry, and five days after Comrade Jaruzelski had replaced Stanisław Kania as Party leader, the government announced that military operational groups would be sent into the countryside to assist local government administrators in improving food supplies and enforcing law and order. These groups would be led by professional soldiers but would include conscript NCOs and privates. The conscripts' two-year period of national service had just been extended by two months.

This last detail is particularly significant. So far there had been no reports of Solidarity infecting the army in the way it had infected the police, where the Solidarity organisation, despite the sacking of its leaders and non-recognition by the courts, claimed some 40,000 would-be members out of a total *c.* 150,000. But could the Generals be certain of the next batch of conscripts? Young men were visibly the most enthusiastic and militant supporters of Solidarity. Now the *c.* 154,000 conscripts in Poland's *c.* 207,000-strong army would not be in the first line of those called upon to shoot or truncheon Poles who resisted the imposition of the 'state of war'. For the purposes of internal repression the regime had a total of some 130,000 specially trained and excellently equipped paramilitary forces and riot police. The most important of these would be the *c.* 65,000 Internal Defence Forces (WOW) and the 20,000–25,000 men in motorised units of riot police (ZOMO), but in addition they could call on the 22,000–25,000 men of the Army Security Service (UTSW) and some of the 20,000–22,000 Frontier troops (WOP). The Internal Defence Forces and the ZOMO had already been used against the workers on the coast in 1970. They were carefully selected, often from poor rural backgrounds, isolated from society, exceptionally well fed, housed, medically treated, indoctrinated and brutalised. Their equipment was of the best, the Internal Defence Forces being armed with tanks, armoured personnel carriers and sophisticated weaponry. The regime could certainly rely on them to fight the workers. None the less, in the best case (for the Generals), reliable, well-trained conscripts would be needed to patrol the streets and break all lines of internal communication. In Gdańsk in 1970 regular units of the local garrison had in fact been called upon to reinforce the Internal Defence Forces, and they inflicted some casualties.[4]

There was thus a distinct military logic behind the two-month time-frame indicated by Siwak, since national service could hardly be extended indefinitely. On purely military considerations, furthermore, the winter was plainly the best time for a takeover. Workers could hold out longer in balmy August weather than in the freezing snow of a Polish December. Moreover, such was the collapse of the whole system of distribution and administration that a hard winter was likely to bring either multiplying local disturbances—hunger marches, food riots—or the dramatic growth of social self-government, as prefigured in the Solidarity Programme, or both. This indicated a date in the early winter. Nor is it without significance that the government's plans for an intermediate economic reform, including more spectacular price increases, were due to come into effect on 1 January 1982. In the event Jaruzelski forced through the price increases with the first shock of martial law.

On 25 October the military operational groups were ordered into 2,000 villages. The television news showed officers investigating grain stocks, supervising tractor repairs, and generally 'earning the confidence of the people'. This intensive propaganda build-up of the army as popular and patriotic extended to the highest level. When a group of independent intellectuals went to see Jaruzelski a book about Piłsudski lay on his desk: Marshal Piłsudski, national hero and author of a military *coup d 'état* in May 1926 . . . At the same time the military groups served to test the popular response, while their officers became acquainted with the administration they were soon to control and perhaps also with a few of the Solidarity activists they were soon to intern. One month later, at the end of November, they were withdrawn from the countryside and slightly larger groups (ten to fifteen men) were sent into larger towns and cities, where they appeared in the most important industrial enterprises. This was the immediate preparation for the takeover on 13 December.

At first glance this analysis of the military logic of the regime's behaviour in the two months between the end of the Solidarity Congress and the military takeover may seem to ignore, or even to contradict, the apparent political logic of General Jaruzelski's public quest for a Front of National Agreement including the Church and Solidarity. The contradiction is only apparent. The most salient feature of this period was the continued 'collapse of the system', as Solidarity leaders accurately described it. Factory after factory, supply after supply, institution after institution, broke down like lorries crossing a desert. In mid-November it was officially announced that the National Income would fall by about 15 per cent that year. Józef Kuśmierek, one of Poland's best-known investigative reporters, estimated that up to 30 per cent of farm produce was being 'spoiled' between the producer and the consumer. How much spoilage was sales under the counter or official rake-offs it was impossible to say. Every day brought new stories in the press about food parcels from abroad rotting away on heaps, or whole factories standing idle for want of one spare part. And the state seemed to do nothing about it; indeed, as people commented in Warsaw, the state seemed to exist only on the television. Here was the power vacuum into which Solidarity was being sucked.

For a very long time Solidarity leaders were reluctant to endorse the popular opinion that this collapse was part of a deliberate strategy. Thus the 'realistic' economic reform proposal appended to the Programme comments:

> As for the authorities, they are torn by internal struggles, the overwhelming majority of their members are ill-disposed towards the changes initiated, and an even greater majority are incompetent inefficient people. As such, they have proved unable to draft an anti-crisis programme and to implement it in co-operation with society.

The power of the bureaucrat to sabotage unwelcome improvements by the simple expedient of doing nothing has rarely been used to more devastating effect. One small example must stand for many. Fifteen hundred people at a washing-machine factory stood idle (*Życie Warszawy* reported on 12 November) for want of one special tape costing *c.* $2,000. A group of individuals offered to lend the necessary money from their private savings, interest free, as a patriotic gesture. The offer was refused. As the *Życie Warszawy* journalist commented, 'We prefer to get loans abroad, paying fat interest charges . . .'

Now, if the top Party leadership were seeking a political solution based on an economic reform agreed with Solidarity, or if they were merely seeking to stem the economic collapse, one would expect some attempt to overcome this bureaucratic resistance. But in the late summer and autumn of 1981 there was no evidence at all of such a determined attempt. Constructive social initiatives, like that private loan proposal, were consistently rejected. Rather than concede enterprise self-government or social control over the national economy, they let things slide.

Such an attitude makes political sense only if the military option was taking shape as I have suggested. By now it was clear to most observers that continued economic collapse was not working to the benefit of Solidarity. The people 'living in a nightmare of queues' were physically exhausted and desperate. 'There is a perceptible inclination towards the idea of strong government', Kuroń cautioned already in August, 'even if it were to impose some restrictions.'[5] The worse things became before the introduction of martial law, the better the General's reforms would look by comparison. Moreover, the Party leaders could see that the more Solidarity was drawn into a wider political arena, the more it had to think about how it wished to use power, the more ground there was for dissension and disarray among its leaders.

No doubt General Jaruzelski did not originally 'plan' these developments as he planned the takeover.* It was more like 1812 in Russia. What began as a headlong retreat turned gradually into a strategy of scorched earth withdrawal: *reculer pour mieux sauter*. The exhausted enemy was drawn out on to the abandoned plains, but denied a pitched battle. Then General Winter came to the aid of the defenders. By the autumn, Poles with sources high up in the Party were talking about a deliberate *'politique du pire'*—the politics of allowing things to get worse.

This is not to argue that Jaruzelski was acting as a free agent, in total command of the Party-state as of his army, nor that dissension and disarray were confined to Solidarity. In March 1982 a Warsaw Solidarity underground journal published a remarkable transcript from a tape-recording made at a meeting of the military commissar for Polish radio and TV, one Colonel Wiślicki, with the organisation's Party group.† One exchange was particularly significant:

> VOICE: Comrade, what happened to Kania?
>
> COMMISSAR: As far as Kania is concerned there are suggestions . . . for example . . . um . . . er . . . by the Soviet comrades who judge him very critically, not directly of course, but at meetings, you know what sort of meetings. That's why he isn't First Secretary any more. Personally, I was very critical of his activities at the time when he was First Secretary. But . . . It won't be for another good few

*And as some of his hardline colleagues certainly did. Andrzej Żabiński told his police chiefs in early 1981: 'Let them go on striking, that will compromise the strikes. We shouldn't be in such a hurry to end the strikes.'[6]

†When *Le Monde* published excerpts from this transcript the Polish authorities protested, denying its authenticity.

> years, not before certain archives are open, that we will be in a position to answer the question whether the state of war was introduced at the right moment. Perhaps too late, perhaps too early. Certainly not too early. But too late? Because all of us, as we sit here, demanded decisive action from the beginning. Only history will tell who was right: us or Jaruzelski.[7]

'Us or Jaruzelski', says a Colonel talking with Party activists. If the 'us' refers to senior officers then the evidence for impatience with Jaruzelski's cunctation is not, for obvious reasons, going to be easily available. Warsaw Establishment gossip attributed greater 'toughness' to General Florian Siwicki, Chief of the General Staff, who was brought into the Politburo as a Deputy Member at the end of October, making a total of three Generals in the Politburo and five in the government.

If the 'us' refers to Party activists then the evidence is there in abundance. The same Central Committee Plenum which elected Jaruzelski with a majority of 180 to 4, charged the Party block in the *sejm* with the task of pushing through an Extraordinary Powers Bill giving the government the right to ban strikes for three months, suspend free Saturdays, etc. As the communist ruling class felt its privileges and positions directly threatened by self-government schemes, so the urgent message was communicated to the Party leadership: clamp down, now! But the non-(communist) Party Deputies in the *sejm*, having stood up to the Party in unprecedented fashion over the Workers' Self-Government Bill, were not going to act as a rubber-stamp on this licence for counter-revolution. After some wrestling behind the scenes, the Party had to be content with a mere appeal for an end to strikes, such as the *sejm* had made once before in April. The scene was repeated at the end of November. Again, the Central Committee ordered the Party delegates to 'initiate immediate measures' with regard to the Extraordinary Powers legislation; again the non-communist Deputies would not be stampeded.

The reluctance of the *sejm* members was as genuine as the impatience of Party activists. It was another constraint on Jaruzelski's freedom of action, and another, important facet of the 'collapse of the system'. Both the Democratic and Peasant Parties had come through traumatic—because democratic—elections. At the Democratic Party Congress in March just three of the 120-strong Central Committee had been re-elected. The 'Pax' group of Catholic collaborationists was striving to re-establish a modicum of credibility with the Catholic population. The small group of delegates 'without party' had always been the most independent. Finally, in December, their resolve was strengthened by an unprecedented and extraordinary letter from the Primate addressed individually to all *sejm* Deputies, urging them in the name of the Episcopate not to vote for an Extraordinary Powers Bill. Instead, Jaruzelski had to fall back on the Council of State to give the appearance of legality to his coup, and even there Ryszard Reiff of Pax voted against.[8]

Yet it may be doubted if the resistance of the *sejm* was entirely unwelcome to Jaruzelski. He did not use his full authority to urge the Bill upon the Deputies. Arguably, they helped him to hold off the pressure from the Party and hold on to the time-frame which military logic suggested. What his coup would have gained in legality from a *sejm* vote it would have lost in surprise. Moreover, we cannot automatically assume that his Soviet patrons were all and solely urging him to clamp down as soon as possible. In November, the Soviet Union's most important single business deal for the next decade—the Siberian gas pipeline to western Europe—was just being finalised. In late November Brezhnev visited Bonn with his message of peace. Of course what passed between Warsaw and Moscow, and specifically between Jaruzelski and Kulikov, is still secret. But it is not obvious that Soviet foreign policy interests would have been better served if the military clampdown had come a few weeks earlier.

Jaruzelski used the interval to develop the idea of a government of national unity. The new Democratic Party leader, Edward Kowalczyk, apparently undeterred by the example of impotence given by Mr Ozdowski, the ('neo-Znak') lay-Catholic Deputy Prime Minister appointed in December 1980, in his turn accepted the dubious honour of that prolific office. Zenon Komender of Pax took on the unenviable job of Minister for Internal Commerce, while Mr Jan Kamiński, a Deputy 'without party', became Minister of Transport. These changes were overshadowed by the promise of a Front of National Agreement which would include the Party,

Church and Solidarity. On Wednesday 4 November, General Jaruzelski met Archbishop Glemp and Lech Wałęsa for a much-lauded summit. The General subsequently described it as a 'momentous' meeting creating 'favourable conditions' for overcoming the crisis.[9] Yet Church and Solidarity leaders soon discovered that what was offered to them now was little better than what Mr Ozdowski had accepted a year before. The new Front was to be a revamped version of the old. Church and Solidarity would be *consulted* and symbolically represented, but all vital posts and crucial decisions would still be taken by the Party. (We recall that Ministers in a Leninist system cannot be compared with Ministers in a western one. They may propose; it is the Politburo which disposes.) They would have responsibility without power. In short, Jaruzelski made them an offer they had to refuse.

None the less, from his point of view the offer had a distinct political logic. If it failed, it was still a useful contribution to the white book: furnishing further 'proof' of his patriotic feelings and the communist authorities' good intentions. Meanwhile, it kept Solidarity guessing, and while there still seemed to be even a slim chance of a negotiated 'national agreement' they might not prepare wholeheartedly for the pitched battle. In both these objectives the National Front manoeuvre was successful.

If one scrutinises the last month of Solidarity's overground existence, it becomes clear that Jaruzelski, taking account of all the restraints on his freedom of action, turning forced retreat (economic collapse, *sejm* recalcitrance) into strategic advantage, was able first to slow and then to force the pace of Poland's descent into martial law, while at the same time convincing many in the West that Solidarity was primarily responsible for that descent.

In late November, the authorities launched their final pre-coup offensive. On the 22nd, police broke up a meeting at Jacek Kuroń's flat (see below, pp. 267–8). On the 23rd, the government revealed that the military operational groups would now be sent into the cities. On the 24th, Jaruzelski was once again host to Marshal Kulikov. On the 25th it was announced that the workforce of a factory in Żywiec had resolved that the Party committee should vacate its premises by 8 December. Although the elimination of factory Party committees was a genuine and popular fundamentalists' demand (see above, p. 226), the official media were certainly delighted to give this proposal immediate publicity. On the 28th, the Sixth Plenum of the Central Committee concluded with a demand for the Extraordinary Powers Bill in a resolution which Bernard Guetta of *Le Monde* at the time described as closing the door to 'national agreement'.[10] On 1 December, while Warsaw Pact Defence Ministers met in Moscow, the government presented to the *sejm* the limited economic reforms which it proposed to introduce on 1 January 1982—a so-called 'Provizorium'. A government team was still theoretically talking to a Solidarity team about economic reform, but Solidarity's suggestions were ignored in the decrees now laid before the *sejm*. On 2 December students occupying the Warsaw Fire Officers' Academy were cleared out by riot police (ZOMO) who broke through the gates and landed on the roof from helicopters: the most serious use of force since Bydgoszcz.

This offensive partially succeeded in provoking Solidarity into a violent reaction which would furnish the pretext for the military takeover—but only partially. On the 2nd, Wałęsa shot off a telex from the Hotel Solec declaring a 'state of extreme emergency' in the union. On the 3rd, the National Commission Presidium met in Radom with most of the thirty-eight regional chairmen for an emergency debate behind closed doors. Three days later Warsaw Radio started broadcasting carefully edited extracts from a secret tape-recording of this meeting. Poles woke up to hear what was allegedly the voice of Kuroń saying, 'The ground must be well prepared to overthrow the authorities . . .'; what was allegedly the voice of Palka (Solidarity's shadow economics minister) saying 'We must set up a so-called workers' militia, groups of people armed with helmets and batons . . .'; what was allegedly the voice of Bujak saying, 'The first action of the workers' militia will be aimed at liberating the radio and television headquarters . . .'; and, most important, what was unmistakably the voice of Wałęsa saying, 'Confrontation is inevitable, and it will take place. . . .' In the week before the coup, the official media deployed these 'Radomgate' tapes to demonstrate that Solidarity had 'revealed its true face . . .'[11]

They did not, however, print the official statement issued by Solidarity at the end of that heated debate. This would have rather disfigured their argument. It declared, first, that 'Talks on national agreement have been used as a screen, concealing preparations to attack the union.' A very accurate assessment. Secondly, it threatened a twenty-four-hour general strike if the *sejm* passed the Extraordinary Powers Bill, and an unlimited general strike if those powers were used. Thirdly, it rejected the proposed economic 'Provizorium' for 1982 in which '... society would have to pay for an economic reform which is not to be. The union will not agree to price increases without economic reform.'

What they understood by a genuine economic reform had been spelled out in outline in their Programme, in more detail by their negotiating teams, and therefore needed only to be indicated in their fourth and final point:

> The national agreement cannot be reduced to the incorporation of the union in a repainted Front of National Unity, as the government intends. To decorate the facade of the old system of state power, which has brought the country to ruin, with the symbol of 'Solidarność', would not ease the crisis, but would only rob the union of its independence and credibility.
>
> The union will not give up the following demands:
>
> (a) the authorities should stop all anti-union reprisals
> (b) the draft Bill on Trades Unions should be presented to the *sejm* in the form agreed with Solidarity representatives
> (c) the authorities should withdraw the so-called 'provizorium' and introduce an economic reform based on workers' self-government and agreed with the union
> (d) the holding of democratic elections to local councils at all levels (including early elections to Provincial councils), and the subordination of local administration to those councils
> (e) the implementation of union control over the economy and especially over food supplies. To keep these a secret from the nation is unacceptable
> (f) to give the Social Council for the National Economy powers which would enable it to exert a real influence over government decisions and control over the socio-economic policy of the state
> (g) that Council, Solidarity, the Church and other

> centres of public opinion must be guaranteed access to radio and television.
>
> These are the minimum conditions for a national agreement which would permit a common, effective struggle against the crisis. We are for such an agreement[12]

These were the demands of the Radom meeting which Mieczysław F. Rakowski would later describe as 'the moment of rupture', telling his interviewer in February 1982:

> Then they called the general strike for December 17. Undoubtedly, this would have meant the confrontation they had exposed in Radom. The bloodshed. The civil war. At this moment, the only alternative to martial law was to raise our arms and let ourselves, the state itself, be destroyed.[13]

What in fact happened was that the Mazowsze region of Solidarity called (on 6 December) for 'a day of protest against the use of force to solve social conflicts' on 17 December, the twelfth anniversary of the authorities' use of force against workers on the Baltic coast. The demonstrations, declared the resolution, should begin at 16.00 hrs—that is, after normal working hours. They called on other regions to join the protest action.[14]

When the National Commission gathered in the Lenin Shipyard on Friday 11 December, the precise date and time of the *coup de force* had (by Rakowski's own account) already been decided: Sunday 13th, in the early hours. Marshal Kulikov had arrived secretly in Warsaw.

Why Was Solidarity Unprepared?

Why were Solidarity's leaders not prepared for what hit them on that snowy winter's night? Most had ignored Wałęsa's repeated warnings that they underestimated their opponent, or, as he put it at the Congress, their 'partner'. 'The authorities [*władza*] do not have sufficient forces' to enforce a 'state of emergency [*stan wyjątkowy*],' a delegate from Łódź confidently assured the National Commission on 22 October. Gwiazda said reedily that one could not talk about an *external* threat to the union; the main threats were internal.[15]

This fatal underestimate of the authorities' potential powers of coercion was rooted partly in semantics. Solidarity operated with a simple dichotomy: *'władza'* v. *'społeczeństwo'*, literally 'power' v. 'society'. Now the 'power' was seen to be almost powerless, the Party continued to haemorrhage, the state to wither away. The workers' leaders were not alone in this analysis. Western analysts commented that 'those who govern are without power, those who have power are not allowed to govern'. They talked about Jaruzelski's trinity of offices as 'a concentration of powerlessness'. So far as the civil administration of the Party-state was concerned, this analysis was perfectly correct: 'the power' was increasingly powerless. But so far as the forces of repression were concerned, it was quite wrong. 'The power' was only powerless so long as it refrained from using force.

Many Solidarity leaders failed to make this elementary distinction. But even those who did distinguish the components of power were still loath to believe that Jaruzelski would use the army against the workers. The popular myth of the patriotic army was traditionally strong, since Piłsudski's army had won the country's independence. Surprisingly, the popular myth survived the shootings on the coast in 1970, even though Solidarity's own investigation in 1981 concluded that army units were definitely involved. People still told me that the 'soldiers' had actually been police or security men in army uniform. Many Solidarity activists were remarkably naive on this point. On Army Day, 12 October 1981, a little delegation from the Gdańsk shipyards walked up Grunwaldzka street from the Hotel Morski to the local army barracks, to pay their respects. An officer greeted them warmly and sat them all down in the guardroom for vodka. *You* wouldn't shoot us, would you? No, of course not, it's not even worth asking; *'na zdrowie'*, then, 'your health'... AS bulletins printed letters from conscripts in Jelenia Góra and Kołobrzeg, protesting at the extension of their military service. Soldiers in Lublin sent an Open Letter: 'We declare that we do not propose to fight workers. We wish to and we will serve them.'[16]

Ironically, what might be described as a more 'extreme' or 'radical' tendency in Solidarity, the 'True Poles' and KPN supporters, were most emphatic in their approval of the army which was being prepared to crush them. In Łódź, where this tendency was strong, Solidarity members put the army third only to Solidarity and the Church in their hierarchy of trust. 32.8 per cent of a sample asked at the end of October declared their confidence in it. In Wrocław, a referendum in one enterprise where 'True Poles' were strong revealed a 90 per cent vote for excising the 'leading role of the Party' from the constitution, an 88 per cent vote for a new parliament, but also an 82 per cent vote of confidence in Jaruzelski![17] From Wrocław, too, was reported an affectionate graffito in response to Jaruzelski's unprecedented concentration of offices: Defence Minister, Prime Minister and Party leader. It read, 'Wojtek, when will you become a Cardinal?'

No, the General was the last man they expected to break the unwritten commandment of the national tradition. Polish soldiers would not shoot Poles.

This terrible misassessment was the main reason why Solidarity leaders were not prepared. Bujak, who managed to escape his captors on 13 December and go underground, later explained to the New York Times, 'It was becoming clear that the authorities were planning a sizeable operation against the union. But we never thought it would be as serious as this . . .' Kowalewski from Łódź, abroad on the 13th, said he expected the confrontation later in the winter, when the *sejm* had finally consented to give the stamp of legality. A few technical preparations for resistance were made in a few regions: printing materials were hidden and, in Łódź at least, rough contingency plans for the arrest of the regional leadership were drawn up. But there were no such plans nationally, neither were there any attempts to set up an alternative radio communications network between factories and regions, though the experience of August 1980 showed how crucial communications would be for the chances of a general strike. Most national leaders were over-confident after fifteen months of doing the impossible. Conspiratorial preparations were anyway very difficult for a movement which was 'obsessed with openness'. Finally, and the point is no less important for being banal, they were so overwhelmed with immediate problems that they simply never got round to detailed, technical planning for a contingency they did not seriously anticipate.[18]

Immediately after the Congress another tidal wave of strikes and protests began to spread across the land. In many provinces even the meagre allocations on the ration cards were no longer honoured; on the black market dollars changed hands for fourteen times the official exchange rate; the queues lengthened until they disappeared into the twilight. This was the first and major cause of protests. In Żyrardów, some twelve thousand textile workers—mostly women—occupied their factories to demand better food supplies. By the end of the month the sulphur mines of Tarnobrzeg were out too. It was estimated that there were disputes in half of Poland's forty-nine Provinces. On this sea of discontent ugly squalls were blown up by ever more frequent police actions against union activists.

The reason or pretext for these actions was usually the distribution of material which the Soviet Union would characterise as 'anti-Soviet'. Certainly there were few taboos left. City walls were covered with large white graffiti proclaiming simply, 'TV LIES'. At night the police would attempt to remove them. Next day a young man would appear with a paint pot and a workers' guard to restore the message (it was the state which had to work by night). From Solidarity posters the mournful features of Karl Marx looked out over the text 'Proletarians of all countries, forgive us!' In Katowice a vendor had a regular stall on Market Square, selling photographs of Marshal Piłsudski and the graves at Katyn, KPN badges and a booklet entitled *Under Soviet Partition*, as well as regular union publications. At noon on 20 October five car-loads of plainclothes police arrived to arrest him. The result (predictably) was that an angry crowd gathered, demanding his release. Riot police responded with tear gas to chants of 'Gestapo', while Solidarity unionists attempted to calm the crowd and at one point actually formed a cordon between the police and the demonstrators. Katowice was, of course, a bastion of Party reaction, and most unionists were convinced that this arrest—like the daubing of Soviet war memorials (which the authorities also blamed on Solidarity)—was another crude provocation. Next day police seized a Solidarity van in Wrocław.[19]

When they met in the Gdańsk Old Town Hall on 22 October, therefore, Solidarity leaders found themselves fighting on several fronts. They decided to call a one-hour general strike on 28 October, as much to bring the nationwide protest actions under control as to apply pressure on the government. The Presidium issued a dramatic statement the day before the strike: 'The decisions of the congress and the appeals of the National Commission are not meeting with understanding. In this situation... the name "Solidarity" is beginning to be an empty term.'

The day after the strike it appealed to all members to refrain from unco-ordinated protests and preserve 'the unity and discipline of the union'. Wałęsa—the fireman once more—dashed down to Tarnobrzeg to try to end the near-general strike which had continued there for ten days. But on 3 November when the National Commission met again, some quarter of a million people were still on strike. 'Enough!' An angry woman from Żyrardów interrupted their wearisome debates: 'Enough of your discussions and your projects for resolutions!... *Do* something! Are you men or not?'[20]

Two contrasting views have been expressed about public opinion in these last months. Several outside observers, and Polish officials, suggest that a growing proportion of the public was increasingly disgruntled with the recurrent strikes, disillusioned with the histrionic feuding of Solidarity activists, who, it is further suggested, were much more 'radical' than the rank-and-file. Solidarity activists say that, on the contrary, rank-and-file members were much more 'radical' than they. They felt themselves under constant pressure from the thousands of workers shouting, like the woman from Żyrardów, '*Do* something!' Evidence for both attitudes was in fact presented to the National Commission. Andrzej Słowik from Łódź, for instance, reported that his members felt the Solidarity Commission on food supplies had brought no results. Mazowsze reported an opinion poll by their research centre in which one-third of respondents thought that most recent strikes should have been avoided and no less than 26 per cent supported the initiative of the last Central Committee Plenum to ban strikes.[21] Yet it was from the large enterprises of Łódź and Mazowsze that the most radical proposals for self-government, 'active strikes' (see below, p. 265) and free elections came. The fact is that both sets of attitudes were present in what was now a confused and a physically exhausted public. Radicalisation and disgruntlement were two faces of the same predicament: what becomes desperation in one becomes despair in another.

Their behaviour, however, was open to only one interpretation. The turn-out for the one-hour general strike on 28 October was as massive as for the last such manifestation, on 27 March, seven months before. Once again, Poland had decked herself out in the national colours like a country going to war. From the shipyards in the north to the mines in the south the workers wore red and white armbands and laid down their tools at noon for one hour precisely. In the roadside café and the small town bar the waitresses hurried to add up their bills before closing the doors at twelve. Students guarded the university gates. Party members participated, of course. It may be true that popular support was less wholehearted, less unanimous, less resolute than in March. A union opinion poll in Łódź revealed that while 90 per cent of those asked supported the strike, only 57 per cent were absolutely certain that it was necessary.[22] But if there was an erosion of Solidarity's popularity it was the erosion of Mount Everest. It is hard to think of any other union or social movement in the world which could command such massive disciplined, voluntary, popular support.

Small wonder the union leaders were overconfident! And being so, they provided a poor example of unity and discipline for their members. Not a National Commission meeting passed now without a public row between Rulewski and Wałęsa. Things were even worse in some of the most important regions. In Gdańsk, where it all began, Gwiazda and fourteen other members of the MKZ actually resigned in protest at Wałęsa's weakness with the government, just three weeks before the coup. To extend Bujak's metaphor, this was not a union of seamen on a sinking ship, it was a union of seamen fighting each other on a ship which was about to be torpedoed. Yet the differences, as well as being about power and personalities, were precisely about how to save the ship from sinking. It was clearly intolerable that a movement which enjoyed such overwhelming legitimacy should be powerless to prevent the economic collapse: but how could it convert legitimacy into power?

Three main tendencies are apparent in these last weeks. The first may be described as fundamentalist, nationalist and (in a special Polish sense) populist. Its standard-bearers were the KPN and a new group which emerged one week after the Congress under the title The Club for the Service of Independence (KSN). On its right wing swarmed the relatively small but disproportionately vociferous bands of 'True Poles'; anti-Russian, anti-intellectual, anti-Semitic, speaking the language of the pre-war National

Democrats. Behind it there rallied the kind of angry young man who remarked to someone crippled in the Warsaw Uprising, 'How lucky you were to take part in that...' It was most visible, of course, on pre-war Independence Day, 11 November. In 1980 a crowd of some ten thousand gathered before the Tomb of the Unknown Soldier on Victory Square (see above, p. 92 f.). In 1981 it was twenty thousand. Again the young put on their four-cornered khaki caps; again the torches fizzled in the first winter snows. A roll-call of national martyrs was read out. 'They fell on the field of honour,' intoned the crowd. 'Everything is possible,' proclaimed a message from the imprisoned KPN leader Leszek Moczulski, 'everything is possible if we have the will to act...'[23] The KSN handed round their patriotic song-sheets: 'Poland is not yet lost...' (with all the verses), 'God who protects Poland', the Confederates' Song, and the defiant marching song of Piłsudski's First Brigade.

There is no doubt that anyone who spoke, wrote, or (best of all) sung about national independence could be sure of a great and growing response. In one poll conducted in September a thousand Solidarity members were asked what should now be top priority issues for the movement. 'National Sovereignty' came top of the list, being mentioned by 44 per cent of respondents, while, by comparison, 43 per cent mentioned economic reform, 32 per cent curbing censorship, and just 21 per cent self-government.[24] Partly this reflected the disappearance of fear. After fifteen months of Solidarity fewer and fewer people were afraid to say what they really wanted. But it was rather for lack of any more positive ways of expressing their anguish that people fell back into the traditional theatre of national defiance.

The fundamentalist nationalists' political programme could be expressed in two words: free elections. There could be no compromise with the existing power, they said: such a compromise was both immoral and impossible. Therefore, the power must be replaced. Solidarity should form political parties which would stand in free elections. Legitimacy would then be translated into state power. This programme enjoyed the popularity of its simplicity. It was quite realistic given two small assumptions, both of which Rulewski and others made explicit: (1) there was no need to worry about the Polish army and police; (2) there was no need to worry about the Russians.

However, it must be stressed that both the KPN leader in his message from prison and the KSN emphatically rejected the use of force. 'The Polish striving for independence has taken different forms,' the KSN declared in its founding statement. 'There was the time of great romantic poetry and the time of armed struggle. "The key to independence today is the independence of Polish work."'[25] The fine-sounding quotation is from one of Father Tischner's sermons to the Solidarity Congress. The intellectuals in KSN, who included the economist Stefan Kurowski and Aleksander Hall from the Young Poland paper *Bratniak*, plainly did not share Rulewski's simplistic certainty about free elections. Neither can it be said that this tendency, visible and vociferous though it was, managed to impose its priorities on the official policy of Solidarity: witness the final statement of the Radom meeting quoted above.

The second main tendency, and the one which gave most substantive meaning to Tischner's phrase about the 'independence of Polish work', was the development of the self-government idea. The new Act on Workers' Self-Government (Article 51, para 1) set a deadline for establishing self-government bodies in state enterprises: 31 December 1981. An article in the Solidarity Weekly revealed, however, that by the end of November only 15–20 per cent of enterprises had even embryonic self-government committees. In the Łódź region (one of the most advanced in self-government theory) just 150 out of 1,500 were counted and in Mazowsze some 250–300 out of approximately the same total.[26] But these were generally the largest factories and their share of total production was much greater. The 'Network' meanwhile was already moving on to the organisation on paper of territorial self-government, and the tireless Jerzy Milewski had founded a 'Polish Labour Party' to stand in the February 1982 local government elections (for which they also drew up new draft election rules!). Given the infant nature of the self-government cells this might seem to be trying to run before they could walk. Yet on closer examination it is apparent that they had to.

In the Lenin steelworks at Nowa Huta, for example, the Founding Committee of Workers' Self-Government was led by an energetic young engineer called Edward Nowak, a man who would almost certainly have risen to managerial responsibility in a system not dominated by the *nomenklatura* and Party graft. He had several bright technical suggestions for improving production at the steelworks, and, in particular, for extracting metal from the waste which was currently polluting the Kraków landscape. His ideas, however, needed imported machinery, and who would allocate the foreign currency? Who would authorise the import?[27] It is true such constructive self-managerial initiatives were rare: but when they came, they were invariably confounded by the existing system of central planning and central control. Without decentralisation, enterprise self-government would remain a purely symbolic achievement. The self-governmentalists therefore came back to the imperative of reforming the system, fundamentally, at the top.

The most radical development of workers' self-government was the idea of the 'active strike'. The 'active strike' was to be a strike in which the workers continued to work, but controlled their own output. Like the original ideas of self-government in the spring, the ideas of 'active strike' spread from below (that is, from one or two particularly active groups in one or two regions) and were only gradually accepted by the national leadership. Here Łódź was the pathbreaker. It was Łódź's resolution calling for a shop-floor referendum on the most controversial parts of the new Act which had been adopted by the Congress. Łódź activists were instrumental in creating a Founding Committee for a National Federation of Self Government Bodies on 17 October (together with activists from the 'Lublin Group') and in pressuring the National Commission to challenge the government directly through the shopfloor referendum. One of them, Zbigniew Kowalewski, suggests a major theoretical difference with the 'Network' militants: 'They were believers in parliamentary democracy rather than the democracy of workers' councils.'[28]

The popularity of the 'active strike' slogan, however, had less to do with the finer differences of political theory than with the fact that it promised to give the workers in larger factories the feeling once again that they could 'make a difference by their own action'. The National Commission threatened an 'active strike' in 'selected economic sectors' in its statement on 23 October. Wałęsa used it as a rhetorical device when he addressed workers in the Warsaw 'Róża Luksemburg' factory during the one-hour general strike:

> We must find more effective forms of protest, ones which help ourselves. There are not enough underpants and washing powder. OK. Let's have active strikes in those factories and distribute the goods to those most in need of them.[29]

All this sounded very attractive in theory. In practice it was hardly tried. The most successful and characteristic example of a Solidarity 'active strike' was conducted in the secondary schools of Lublin. Here the pupils declared an 'active strike' in which the teachers who had joined Solidarity gave them lessons in recent Polish history! But Kowalewski does not produce one example of a major factory where the workers actually took control of their own production and distribution. How could they in an unreformed state socialist system? He does reveal that, from October 1981, Solidarity in the Łódź region was allowed to take over the printing and distribution of ration cards, and for that purpose had access to most major foodstores. He claims that in Łódź the queues then got shorter, and food supplies improved.[30] This is a singular and (if true) impressive achievement; but it is scarcely evidence for the feasibility of a bloodless takeover of economic power from below via 'active strike'. For the achievement depended entirely on the local authorities allowing unionists to print ration cards, giving them access to abbatoirs and warehouses, permitting them to supervise the wholesale distribution network.* In other words, it depended on a compromise with the authorities.

The third main tendency, the 'pragmatists', continued explicitly to recognise the necessity for compromise with the communist authorities. Still in the mainstream of the 'self-limiting revolution', still seeking the 'Historic Compromise', was, first of all, Lech Wałęsa himself. In this he was supported by most of his advisers and by the Church. Kuroń was one of the first people to suggest the formation of (what he then called) a Committee of National Salvation, in which representatives proposed by the Party, Church and Solidarity would share power. By November this was one of the two main forms in which Solidarity pragmatists proposed to

*So far as we know this happened only in Łódź: a city whose women had taken to the streets *en masse* in the August hunger marches and might be expected to do so again as the first in the country.

institutionalise compromise. The other was the Social Council for the National Economy, a body which would control the implementation of that economic reform on the basic outlines of which there was far-reaching agreement between government and Solidarity economists. This Social Council was now Solidarity's main *quid pro quo* for supporting the austerity programme which their advisers recognised as necessary.

It cannot be said that all National Commission members appreciated the necessity for austerity. On 23 October Andrzej Wielowieyski patiently explained to the Commission that the drastic price rises for alcohol, petrol and luxury goods proposed by the Finance Minister were absolutely vital to mop up part of the inflationary ocean of surplus money which now flooded the Polish economy. There were, he said, an estimated 500–600 thousand million złotys with no outlet on the market! His report provoked chaotic and, at times, childish criticism. Some fundamentalist nationalists were impatient of these Warsaw intellectuals with their uncomfortable truths couched in incomprehensible language. Yet Grzegorz Palka from Łódź, Wałęsa's shadow economics minister, defended Wielowieyski's presentation with a worker's clarity: 'It's an illusion to think the costs can be borne by the rich or the Party.' There was no other way: either the price rises or devaluation. If the National Commission saw another possibility, said Palka, they could choose a new negotiating group.[31]

When, on 17 November, a Solidarity delegation met with a government team under Minister Ciosek (Rakowski no longer...) for the first major Solidarity–government talks since August, this remained essentially their negotiating position: they would 'sell' the grim austerity deal to society so long as they were given a share of power over its implementation. There were six main points on the agenda: strike pay, access to the mass media, self-government, the local council elections in February, the Social Council for the National Economy and the National Agreement. The government stalled on every point.[32]

There is no doubt that at the level of policy-making the pragmatist tendency remained the predominant tendency in Solidarity, even under the extreme provocation of the authorities' last pre-coup offensive.

This began, as we have seen, with the police raid on Jacek

Kuroń's flat on Sunday 22 November, just five days after the opening of the 'talks'. An official statement explained that the objective of the raided gathering was 'the setting up of an organisation of a political character, which was to adopt the name: "Clubs of the Self-Governing Republic—Freedom, Justice, Independence". The organisation . . aspiring to the role of a political party . . .' The Clubs' founders explained it rather differently. They were very much aware that the tremendous urge to express political aspirations through Solidarity was threatening to tear the movement apart. In order to preserve Solidarity's unity, self-discipline, and therefore strength vis-à-vis the authorities, these political aspirations must be drawn off into other forums, such as the Clubs. 'There are', said their Founding Declaration, 'the nuclei of future political parties in a democratic state.'

After criticising some other political tendencies in Solidarity the Founding Declaration spelled out its vision of the Self-Governing Republic: an extension of the discussion in the Solidarity Programme. The suggested combination of a welfare state with parliamentary democracy might best be described in western political terms as 'social democratic', although the emphasis on direct democracy and social control ('co-operative movements and consumer associations' are specifically mentioned) would fit more easily into the programme of a western liberal party.

How exactly the Clubs of the Self-Governing Republic were intended to work was not clear. The Declaration talked of 'the substantiation and enrichment of the vision of a self-governing Poland' but also of 'putting the idea of a self-governing Poland into practice' specifically through workers' and territorial self-government. (Did that mean their representatives would stand in the local government elections in February or not?) The Declaration acknowledged that there was a threat of Soviet intervention but 'we think that Soviet intervention can be avoided'. A relationship with the Soviet Union, giving Poland a greater degree of self-determination, should be negotiated 'by an authentic national delegation'. Finally, it looked forward to the 'demilitarisation of central Europe' (i.e. the 'Finlandisation' of Poland which Kuroń had long considered the ultimate possible goal).[33]

Were these not, then, the Jacobin clubs which would drive the revolution still further to the 'left' (or was it 'right'?), carrying on the 'radicalisation' perpetrated by a small conspiratorial band of KOR activists? This was to be the claim of official propaganda. Of course historians cannot be certain what would have happened if... But two observations can be made. First, radical as the Founding Declaration was, it was a great deal less radical than the voices which were raised in many large factories, voices which no longer recognised the necessity for compromise. Secondly, its tactical objective was not to increase political agitation inside Solidarity, but, on the contrary, to siphon off the political steam into a forum where it would not obscure the immediate search for a national compromise between Solidarity and the government.

It is on its behaviour in that search that Solidarity must first be judged. One cannot deduce Solidarity's policy from the wilder statements of individual leaders or the manifestos of this or that tendency, any more than one would be justified in deducing the policy of the Jaruzelski government from the anti-Semitic pronouncements of the nationalist communist Grunwald league (though its members, like the 'True Poles', were increasingly visible and vociferous) or articles in the hardline Party papers. In fact rather less so. For articles in, say, *Żołnierz Wolności*, do indeed show traces of the Generals' secret plans. No articles in the Solidarity press show any traces of Wałęsa's and the Solidarity leadership's secret plans, because they did not have any secret plans. In mid-November the authorities were preparing to crush their partner by force while pretending to negotiate in good faith; Solidarity was negotiating in good faith while making no preparations for the use of force.

Meanwhile the ship continued to sink. On 19 November Wałęsa appealed to the West for immediate food aid to avert the danger of 'spontaneous eruptions of popular discontent... for the next five months'. 'Negotiations at government level', said his appeal, 'will define the means of financing and crediting this aid in a way that takes into account the present possibilities of the Polish state. For our part we wish to assure you that we shall do everything in our power to see that the aid will be subject to public control and that the resulting financial liabilities will be met as soon as possible.' Rural Solidarity's leader, young Jan Kułaj, addressed an even more dramatic—not to say melodramatic—Open Letter to Polish farmers, suggesting that Poland was 'threatened by famine'. His organisation, however, had so far been able to achieve few material improvements for private farmers, while its own internal discipline was considerably worse than that of industrial Solidarity. On 22 November its National Founding Committee tabled a vote of no confidence in the entire Presidium (with the exception of Kułaj). At the same time they voted to convert themselves into a national strike committee with the aim of obtaining the 'full and prompt implementation of the Rzeszów-Ustrzyki and Bydgoszcz agreements'.[34] In Siedlce there was to be a replay of the Rzeszów Commune. The students, too, were settling in for another round of sit-ins, partly to protest at the non-realisation of their February Agreement, and partly to reverse the undemocratic appointment of a colonel as Rector of the Radom Engineering College.

It is important to note, however, that thanks to repeated appeals from Wałęsa and the National Commission, the students' and farmers' protests were not matched by workers' protests. Ironically, the Solidarity leadership managed to put out the main fires of industrial unrest just in time for the military crackdown. None the less, as blow followed provocative blow, more and more people became aware that—as Wałęsa said in Radom—confrontation was inevitable. The Church made one last, desperate attempt to avert it. Stepping further than ever before into the political arena, the Primate sent a letter to all *sejm* Deputies, warning them not to pass the Extraordinary Powers Bill; he wrote to the Independent Students' Union, urging them to end the rash of university strikes; and he wrote to both Jaruzelski and Wałęsa, urging the resumption of their tripartite summitry. In vain.

To present Solidarity's reactions in that last desperate fortnight in a lucid and logical way would be to distort a chaotic reality. Men who are about to be torpedoed on a sinking ship do not usually react lucidly and logically. There were exceptions: the historian Bronisław Geremek retained to the end his extraordinary capacity to assess the position with crystal detachment while yet remaining passionately involved. Kuroń told a friend on 4 December that he thought the authorities would declare a 'state of emergency', and when she objected that the whole country would rise up in protest he replied that people were tired and that it would be easy to frighten them. 'They'll strike for a short while,' he said, 'then they'll give in.'[35] Like Danton in Büchner's *Danton's Death* these exceptional individuals walked with open eyes into a confrontation which they knew they could no longer avoid—it was written in the logic of the revolution—and which they sensed they would lose.

Perhaps Wałęsa, too, belongs among the Dantons. On 10 December he told reporters that the authorities were attempting to provoke a confrontation bloodier than December 1970. The union's ultimate weapon was strikes, he said, the authorities' . . . bullets. Opening the National Commission meeting next day in the Health and Safety hall of the Lenin Shipyard, the same from which he had led the strike sixteen months before, he repeated once again, as if for the historians, 'I declare with my full authority: we are for agreement . . . we do *not* want any confrontation. The National Agreement must become a reality.'[36]

Yet most of the National Commission were still blindly confident of the movement's strength. In Łódź a union poll found:

> 88.3 per cent of those interviewed stated that they will actively support the union leadership, whatever the dangers involved, if it decides on action to confront the authorities for the purpose of achieving the demands of August 1980. [Note that the demands of August 1980 are still the reference point.] The active strike is the form of confrontation most frequently mentioned.[37]

Attack, they therefore argued, was the best form of defence. Self-governmentalists from Kraków suggested an active general strike in which the union would implement its own economic reform—a fantastic scheme. Łódź activists supported the notion of active strike and urged the necessity of forming workers' guards. Seweryn Jaworski from Mazowsze argued that the general strike to be called in response to the *sejm* passing an Extraordinary Powers Bill should be converted into an active strike. Mazowsze's appeal for 17 December to be a nationwide day of protest *against the use of force* was endorsed by a large majority.

On Saturday 12 December, as the debate thundered on, the telex machines in the Lenin Shipyard began to chatter with alarming messages from Solidarity branches across the country: extraordinary troop movements were reported, Solidarity headquarters were being sealed off. Jan Rulewski rose to propose the most radical resolution of all: Solidarity should organise a referendum, before the local elections in February, on 'the authorities' methods of government', the methods of combatting the crisis, and 'the renewal of all representative bodies' (i.e. free elections to the *sejm*). If the referendum brought a vote of no confidence in the authorities, then the union should organise its own provisional government. Hardly was the resolution adopted before the rumours began to filter into the hall: the shipyard's telephone and telex lines had been cut (shades of August)—no, the whole of Gdańsk had been cut off from the rest of the country... And yet, when the meeting broke up after midnight, the delegates strolled out of the safety of the shipyard and back to their hotels, joking about the awful things that the authorities might try in the night. Wałęsa went home. He refused to hide himself.[38]

9. 'War'

In that freezing winter's night the Polish army and security forces invaded their own country. Tanks advanced into the centre of Warsaw. Troops set up road blocks in and between all major cities. Civilian telephone and telex lines were cut everywhere. Radio and television stations were taken over. Within hours, Poland was partitioned and blockaded, internally and externally sealed off. Neighbours were woken by the sound of crowbars smashing doors as thousands of Solidarity activists, advisers, intellectuals and even critical Party members were carried off to 'internment' camps. All but a handful of Solidarity's national leaders were caught in their hotel rooms, like doves in a cote, between 2 and 3 a.m.

At 6 a.m. General Jaruzelski broadcast his declaration of war: a dramatic, plangent speech prefaced by the national anthem. The 'state of war' (*stan wojenny*), he said, had been introduced, in accordance with the Constitution, by the Council of State at midnight. (In fact the hastily summoned Council met at the Belweder Palace around 1 a.m., when the first doors were already being smashed.) Its supreme organ would be a Military Council for National Salvation (Polish initials WRON). This institution was nowhere envisaged in the Constitution. Plenipotentiary military commissars had been appointed 'at all levels of the state administration and in some economic units'. This had to be done—he spoke in sorrow—because Poland was 'on the brink of an abyss'. Solidarity's leaders had revealed their intentions to overthrow the socialist state. 'Yesterday evening many public buildings were occupied'. Now 'the adventurists must have their hands tied, before they push the homeland into the abyss of fratricide.'

The speech contained two main kinds of appeal for popular support, and in particular for the support of 'the healthy trend in Solidarity . . . the working-class trend'. First, the General promised that there would be no return to the 'erroneous methods and practices' of before August 1980. 'Socialist renewal' and economic reform would be forced through in the orderly and disciplined conditions of martial law. 'Sharks of the economic underground' would be brought to book. So would all those responsible for the crisis. Besides unnamed 'extremist Solidarity activists', Edward Gierek and the most notorious leaders of the 1970s had been 'interned': 'We shall consistently purge Polish life from evil,' he commented. Just one short paragraph was devoted to the role of the Party. It was the army which would restore law and order, clean living, high thinking and prosperity.

Linked with this Cromwellian or Bonapartist appeal was a straight appeal to Polish patriotism and the myth of the patriotic army. 'We are but a drop in the stream of Polish history,' he declaimed . . . 'Our soldiers have clean hands . . . They have no goal other than the good of the nation.' Poland should be restored to her proper, honourable place in world esteem. No more should it be said that 'Poland stands by anarchy' (*Nierządem Polska stoi*), he quoted the old motto of the Noble Democracy. 'Poles! Brothers and Sisters! I appeal to you as a soldier who remembers well the horrors of the war. Let not another drop of Polish blood be spilled in this tormented country . . .' And at the end he repeated the 'immortal words' of the national anthem: 'Poland is not yet lost, so long as we live . . .' Then they played the anthem again. The speech did not merely dress up the takeover in patriotic uniform: it paraded the whole threadbare wardrobe of patriotic arguments for popular submission.

It was rebroadcast on radio and television throughout the day. Between bouts of solemn and martial music announcers read out the long lists of martial law decrees. All gatherings, processions and demonstrations, except for religious services, were banned. All trades unions and student organisations were 'suspended', as was the right to strike. All mail and telephone communications would be censored. A curfew from 6 a.m. to 10 p.m. was imposed. Everyone over the age of thirteen had to carry an identity card. No petrol could be sold to private motorists. Anyone who was thought to threaten the interests of the state could be immediately interned for an indefinite period. In a long list of 'militarised' enterprises the workers came directly under military discipline. Absenteeism or disobedience would be punishable by court martial sentences 'from two years' imprisonment to death . . .' And so on, and on. In some details the 'state of war' regulations were, on paper, more ferocious even than those of the Nazi occupation, as older Poles soon pointed out. About all a Pole could now legally do in company was to work, to stand in a queue, and to pray. In the evening you could sit at home and watch television: the news announcers were in army uniform now, and the screens were filled with bloody epics of war . . . the Soviet 'Liberation' of Poland, the suppression of the Hungarian Uprising in 1956 . . . no chance was lost to heighten the war psychosis.

But war against whom? The Military Council in its first proclamation talked of 'already overt preparations for a reactionary coup' and described its task as 'to foil a coup d'état'. The 'extremists' in Solidarity who had presumably prepared this 'coup' were zealously identified by the only two official newspapers still published, *Trybuna Ludu* and *Żołnierz Wolności*: Geremek, Kuroń, Modzelewski . . . the intellectuals, the men of KOR, the anti-socialist elements. Radio Warsaw 'revealed' Professor Geremek's Jewish origins and *Trybuna Ludu* 'revealed' his conspiratorial links with 'revisionist-Zionist centres' abroad. All was suddenly clear. Of course—this patriotic war was a war against the Jews . . .

The first popular reaction to the self-invasion was shock and incredulity. 'People could not have been more taken aback if the Martians had just landed,' one eye-witness on the streets of Warsaw reported. But within hours the protests had begun, and from the start the protesters stated clearly—on posters and hastily duplicated flysheets—who the war was really against. Thus the Strike Committee at the Polish Academy of Sciences in Kraków:

> . . . for the third time during the 20th century Poland is in captivity. The last two times were under a foreign occupier but now we are faced with a *self-occupation*. Let us not be deceived. It is not important what language the occupier speaks, German, Russian, or Newspeak! What is important is how the occupier behaves. In the middle of Europe, in the late 20th century, 35 million people have been stripped of their fundamental civil rights.[2]

The undeclared war was a war against the Polish people. Poles would shoot Poles in order to restore the monopoly powers (and privileges) of a communist ruling class which the Kremlin regarded as indispensable for the protection of its vital interests. Now, if ever, the people must resist. All the achievements of the revolution were at stake.

'MEMBERS OF SOLIDARITY, COMPATRIOTS!' the Solidarity branch at Ursus appealed in a broadsheet rushed out on Sunday afternoon, 'the purpose of this attack is to liquidate our union . . . our answer must be—in accordance with the statutes—an immediate general strike in the whole country.'[3] Although there could be no nationwide co-ordination, the same appeal came from the Lenin Shipyard, signed, for 'the National Strike Committee' by one of Wałęsa's Deputy Chairmen and three other members of the National Commission who had evaded capture; from the shipyards in Szczeczin; from the steelworkers in the mighty Hutas of Katowice, Warsaw and Nowa Huta; from the miners of Silesia; from teachers and students; from Wrocław and Łódź, Lublin and Poznań . . .

For the next two weeks Solidarity members across the country, though surprised, unarmed and for the most part leaderless, fought a series of desperate isolated defensive actions on the model of the occupation-strikes of August 1980. Because of the communications block only the military authorities could know how many people took part, how many were interned, how many arrested under the new 'laws', how many killed; but they were naturally determined to play down resistance and bloodshed. Yet enough information gradually filtered through the blockade, first from travellers, diplomats and western correspondents, later from participants, for us to gain some idea of the scale and quality of resistance in at least some of the major cities.

Among the quickest to respond were students and academics. Sit-in strikes began in most universities. On Tuesday 15 December the world watched on its television screens as armoured personnel carriers pulled up in front of the Polish Academy of Sciences in Warsaw and police hustled its distinguished members out into the snow. The intellectuals' solidarity was expressed in open letters of protest and in a massive refusal to collaborate with the martial law authorities. But everyone knew that the crucial battles in these first days would have to be fought by the workers. Poles turned again to

Radio Free Europe and the BBC (both heavily jammed) for news from the score of really powerful factories which have figured so large in our narrative, because they were both the largest in the land, and the strongest in support of Solidarity.

In Gdańsk the gates of the Lenin Shipyard were once again decked with flowers, the hymn-singing crowds gathered before them. This time the Strike Committee had just two demands: the release of all those detained and the end of the state of war. 'In the course of the strike we must maintain discipline and calm,' their first communiqué declared, in the spirit of August, 'respect public property, and avoid unnecessary clashes with the security forces'.

Next day army tanks with less 'respect for public property' crashed through the metal gates but the workers threw up a makeshift barricade in front of the shipyard hospital and the strike continued with the next shift. On Wednesday 16 December the tanks moved in to stay, closely followed by more military vehicles, red-beret paratroopers, and the specially trained professional toughs of the Internal Defence Forces. Inside the yard the workers offered only passive resistance, but the authorities could not be certain that the next shift would not simply start the occupation-strike all over again, so they closed the yards down—and they remained closed until the first week of January.

It was the eleventh anniversary of the bloody riots in December 1970, the memory of which, the local Party secretary had declared, standing in front of these gates a year before (see above, pp. 108–9), 'must unite the nation . . . to ensure that such tragedies never happen again.' Now the tragedy was happening again. The anniversary was marked by furious rioting on the streets of the Tri-City and even around the base of the martyrs' memorial. Officials said more than three hundred people were wounded: unofficial estimates put the figure nearer 1,000 with ten killed. Police used tear gas, watercannon and long lead-lined batons to disperse demonstrators in Warsaw, Kraków, Lublin and other towns. In several cases people were pursued into the churches where they had taken sanctuary.

In Solidarity's other industrial fortresses the General's battleplan was becoming clear. The occupied works, Huta Katowice or Ursus or the Gdańsk oil refinery, were cut off and surrounded by the army. For a few hours or days the army and police attempted to frighten, cajole or starve the strikers into peaceful evacuation. If they did not succeed then the army used their armour to smash the strikers' defences. The ZOMO riot police then stormed through the breach and hounded out the workers, where possible isolating and arresting the strike-leaders. In the next weeks and months the word 'ZOMO' would become a world synonym for police brutality. By this method the Generals did not put the loyalty of their regular or conscript troops to the ultimate test of shooting brother-Poles. The dirty work was done by hardened thugs of the special police and security forces, who were moved rapidly from one factory to the next.

This pattern of repression was seen most clearly in Silesia, where resistance was probably best organised and longest sustained. In Wrocław, where Władysław Frasyniuk and his two deputies were still at liberty, the battle resembled an extremely violent game of musical chairs. As the ZOMO 'pacified' one factory the strike leaders moved on to the next. In Huta Katowice—monument to Gierek's Heroic Modernisation—more than 2,000 workers held out until 23 December, supported by a small group of students and sustained by Masses said by a 'priest-worker'. An army Major came to ask them what they wanted: the end of the 'state of war', they said, the release of all those detained, and *free elections*. The Major replied that the Party would never relinquish power. (85 per cent of the officer corps were Party members, as western analysts now belatedly noted.) After helicopters dropped leaflets threatening to use chemical weapons the strikers finally accepted the army's offer of safe conduct. Outside the gates several were arrested by the ZOMO.[4]

On the 17th (the anniversary) Warsaw radio admitted that seven miners had been killed at the Wujek colliery near Katowice. Strikers had armed themselves with crowbars, pickaxes and hatchets, said the report: police had fired 'in self-defence'. There is every reason to believe that the official figure of eight deaths in this first fortnight—seven at Wujek and one in the Gdańsk riots—is an underestimate.

Silesia's, and Solidarity's, last bastion of resistance was an extraordinary occupation-strike some 1,600 feet underground in the 'Piast' mine near Katowice. Here, on the evening of Monday 14 December, more than 1,300 miners decided to stay down the pits, until the 'state of war' was lifted and Solidarity's leaders freed. For five days their families and well-wishers were able to send down food: then the police stopped the supplies. On Christmas Eve two priests were allowed down to try to persuade them to give in. Wives and parents pleaded with their relatives down the pit telephone. And still the men refused to capitulate. By now their rations were reduced to a third of a sandwich, a tiny piece of sausage and two cups of water per day. On Christmas Day they hunted for crusts on the pit floor. At night they huddled together for warmth. It was a scene from Zola's *Germinal*. Finally, on 27 December, the Strike Committee (led by a member of the National Commission), seeing their men weakened by hunger and learning that the strikes had ended in all the other mines, decided to surrender if they were given a promise of safe conduct. Most of the strikers were in fact permitted to leave a pithead swarming with soldiers and police, but the strike leaders were arrested.[5]

The general strike, Solidarity's ultimate weapon, was broken. It was a shattering defeat, and one not less bitter because the victorious forces wore Polish uniform. General Jaruzelski's two-week *Blitzkrieg* in December 1981 was to Solidarity what the three-week *Blitzkrieg* of September 1939 was to the Second Republic. That had meant the end, for the foreseeable future, of Poland as a fully sovereign, independent nation state. This now meant the end, for the foreseeable future, of Solidarity as a genuinely independent self-governing mass organisation.

Some commentators have taken the apparent ease with which the first phase of Solidarity's resistance was crushed as further evidence for the weakening of rank-and-file support. If the movement really had ten million people behind it, how could it be so swiftly defeated? This is as illogical as it would be to deduce from the rapid defeat of the Polish Army by the *Wehrmacht* in 1939 that there had been a weakening of popular support for Polish independence.

The reasons for Solidarity's defeat in the first battle of the 'war' are simple. Only in very exceptional circumstances does an unarmed workers' movement, however massive and well-organised, stand a chance of resisting the repressive power of a modern police state: witness, for example, the defeat of the German labour movement in 1933–4. Such exceptional circumstances may just have been present in March 1981. They certainly were not in

December. The military takeover was planned and executed with remarkable secrecy and skill. Surprise was total. General Winter proved a staunch ally of the army, with temperatures between -5° and -10° Centigrade. Technically, because Solidarity had prepared no alternative communications network, the strikers had only the vaguest idea what was happening in other cities. Each workers' fortress could be isolated and picked off at the ZOMO's leisure. Psychologically, the stage management of the coup was also brilliantly effective. According to Jan Józef Lipski, who joined the strikers in the Ursus tractor factory, the words *'stan wojenny'* had an almost hypnotic effect on this nation which had suffered so much in war. Jaruzelski deliberately and successfully perverted the first commandment of the national tradition. Pole should not kill Pole meant, in his exegesis, resistance is treachery!

One further, psychologically crucial actor must be mentioned: the Church. According to one reliable source the Primate, Archbishop Glemp, was woken in the early hours of Sunday 13 December by the 'liberal' Politburo member Kazimierz Barcikowski with the news of martial law. The Russians, Barcikowski explained, had given an ultimatum: if the Poles did not do it, they would.[6] What is certain is that when Archbishop Glemp climbed into the pulpit later that day he preached a sermon which the military-controlled TV and Radio were pleased to broadcast several times. 'The authorities', said the Primate, 'consider that the exceptional nature of martial law is dictated by a higher necessity, it is the choice of a lesser rather than a greater evil. *Assuming the correctness of such reasoning the man in the street will subordinate himself to the new situation* [my italics].' The Church 'received with pain the severance of dialogue' but the most important thing now was to prevent bloodshed. *'There is nothing of greater value than human life*. That is why I, myself, will call for reason even if that means I become the target of insults. I shall plead, even if I have to plead on my knees: *Do not start a fight of Pole against Pole*' [my italics].[7]

It is not for the historian to judge whether the sentence 'there is nothing of greater value than human life' accurately reflects the teaching of Jesus Christ, or whether the late Cardinal Wyszyński or Karol Wojtyła would have spoken in precisely this manner in this critical and incomparably difficult moment. He can only record that the sermon seems to have played a part in reducing the immediate (passive) resistance to martial law, and that the Primate's words were bitterly resented by many Christian Poles who were, at that moment, preparing to risk their own lives for what they considered greater values. A week later the Episcopate would come out with a much clearer defence of Solidarity; but that week was decisive.

The outcome of the *Blitzkrieg* therefore says very little about the quality of popular support for Solidarity. It is, rather, a devastating reminder of the power of a state—so long as its forces of repression are obedient and intact—to survive despite an almost total lack of legitimacy, trampling on the rights, confounding the wishes and destroying the hopes of the great majority of its population.

With the New Year, 1982, the Poles entered a new period with new terms of struggle: new, but yet terribly familiar. For the younger generation it was their 'war', and they used the word immediately, without inverted commas. They nicknamed the Military Council for National Salvation (WRON) the 'crow' (Polish *wrona*): the crow, they said, would never defeat the eagle. In Warsaw, martial law posters were captioned, at night, with one word, *Bekanntmachung*, the word used by the German authorities to head their terror regulations during the occupation. The experience of unfreedom was as familiar as that of freedom had been strange: the responses to occupation were stored in the collective memory, and the smoke-screen of a Polish self-occupation only bewildered for those first days.

If the authorities imagined they could bribe or cajole Solidarity leaders into collaboration they were soon disappointed. Only three national figures agreed to buy their liberty by some form of public recantation: the Press Spokesman, the young leader of Rural Solidarity, Jan Kułaj (he subsequently claimed his televised speech had been cut without his knowledge to exclude any reference to Solidarity), and an official from Poznań, who subsequently recanted his recantation in front of foreign journalists. Lech Wałęsa set an example for the rest. Flown to Warsaw early on the morning of the 13th to talk to General Jaruzelski he refused to negotiate (let alone to go on television and appeal for calm) without his advisers and colleagues from the National Commission. Held under house arrest (an 'internment' order dated 12 December was first delivered to him on 26 January) in a villa near Warsaw, he managed to smuggle out messages encouraging peaceful resistance. Later he was moved to the Arłamów hunting reserve, that 'Red Principate' where Edward Gierek had once lavishly entertained Giscard d'Estaing, diverting funds from the poor farmers whom Wałęsa had met in the Rzeszów commune (see above, p. 132 f.). He steadfastly refused all offers of collaboration or conditional release. 'He was asked if he wanted to emigrate with all of us to the west,' his wife reported. 'He replied by yelling at Deputy Prime Minister Rakowski, who ran from the interview room.'[8]

He and the internationally known Solidarity leaders and intellectuals were interned in relatively decent physical conditions. The same could not be said about the unknown worker activists freezing behind barbed wire on the Hel peninsula near Gdańsk, or the farmers herded into a crude camp at Uherce in the forests of the south-east. Only the military and police authorities know how many of the *c.* 50,000 (industrial and rural) Solidarity activists were interned in the first fortnight. By January they were claiming that the number was down to less than 5,000. Those arrested while trying to organise resistance after 13 December fared much worse. Courts martial handed down harsh sentences. Andrzej Słowik and Jerzy Kropiwnicki were caught on the first day, as they rode around on a lorry asking the workers of Łódź to come out on strike. They were sentenced to four and a half years' imprisonment. Kropiwnicki was the man who had assured the National Commission in October that 'the authorities do not have sufficient forces' to suppress Solidarity. Another man from Łódź was sentenced to three and a half years for the 'audacious theft of a fur hat' (i.e. snatching a soldier's or policeman's hat); another to three years for 'distributing leaflets from a company car'. The organisers of the strike in Huta Katowice received up to seven years.[9]

Moreover, thousands of workers were sacked for participating in strikes or demonstrations—and in Poland, being a socialist country where by definition there can be no unemployment, there is no unemployment benefit. Public service employees, and workers in many enterprises, were threatened with dismissal if they did not sign a 'loyalty pledge', declaring their resignation from Solidarity and their loyalty to the socialist state. So it went on, as the regime deployed its whole panoply of physical and non-physical coercion.

Despite the terror, Solidarity activists who managed to escape arrest and go underground were soon producing duplicated news-sheets (the most regular in Warsaw, called the War Weekly) and debating how best to continue the struggle. Those who found themselves abroad attempted to convert the world's indignation into acts of practical solidarity. The incredible claims of official propaganda were swept away in a torrent of popular jokes—the acid political humour which returned with martial law, for this kind of humour is an expression of impotence as much as defiance. Every new demonstration, strike or protest was ascribed by the TV news to tiny groups of Solidarity 'extremists'. The Poles translated this with the 'TV Dictionary':

2 Poles: an illegal gathering
3 Poles: an illegal demonstration
10 million Poles: a handful of extremists.

The gulf between 'the power' and 'the society' (to use Solidarity's terms) was wider than the Gulf of Gdańsk. Even the Church could not begin to bridge it.

PART II:
REFLECTIONS

10. What Revolution?

All revolutions are failures, but they are not all the same failure.

Orwell

Can the Polish events from August 1980 to December 1981 properly be described as a revolution? At the time, participants and observers from all sides used the term. As late as autumn 1981 the Provincial Governor of Gdańsk went to print with enthusiastic reflections on Lech Wałęsa as leader of a 'genuine revolutionary movement'. His comrades in the Soviet Union preferred the term 'counter-revolution', which in this case was a way of saying the same thing.* Before December, Mieczysław F. Rakowski described what was happening in Poland as a 'profound revolution'. After December, Mieczysław F. Rakowski described it as 'counter-revolution'.

Yet every major modern revolution has either taken over or destroyed the existing state apparatus, and radically transformed the political system. Solidarity, however, neither took over nor destroyed the existing state apparatus. In Marxist terms, the working class did not seize state power. For more than a year Solidarity and the Party-state existed side by side, in the condition which Trotsky described as 'Dual Power'. In this period large parts of the state administration broke down. But then, instead of the new people's power destroying the old state power, the still powerful military and police arms of the Party-state destroyed Solidarity as an overground mass organization.

*'In this case' because the Soviet use of that label does not *ipso facto* indicate the presence of a revolution! Soviet leaders use the term 'counter-revolution' to describe anything which they greatly dislike.

It cannot accurately be said, however, that Solidarity 'failed to take over the state', because Solidarity *never attempted* to take over the state. This remarkable self-limitation is one of the many features (its working-class religiosity is another) which makes Solidarity impossible to classify without redefining our most important terms, including the term 'revolution'. Solidarity was an attempt to make an evolutionary revolution. The specific question it posed was: can a self-organised society transform the political system of a state within the Soviet empire, by pressure from below, without violence?

One year after General Jaruzelski's violent counter-revolution the short answer to this question appeared to be 'no'. But the immediate aftermath is not the best vantage-point: the English Revolution ended with the Restoration, the French with Napoleon: only from a longer distance of time could the revolutionary scale of those events be measured. We do not yet have the necessary distance.

What we can measure, with the advantage of immediacy, are the changes wrought by Solidarity during the fifteen and a half months of its overground existence. We can test some current received opinions about the dynamics of the movement's development, and its relationship with the communist authorities, against the evidence which I have rehearsed in some detail. And I will venture a few remarks about what survives of the revolution under the Polish military variant of the Party-state.

A Revolution of the Soul

Spring 1981. 'Dolmel', the largest electrical machinery factory in Wrocław, a dirty red-brick Prussian fortress. The Solidarity chairman, Piotr Bednarz, speaks a few words of command into the telephone. Ten minutes later a chubby-faced young man in a shiny suit stumbles into the Solidarity office and seats himself awkwardly in the corner, under the photograph of Marshal Piłsudski. 'Our communist!' explains Bednarz, and the assembled company erupts in laughter. The enterprise Party Secretary joins in the laughter, but rather nervously, fingering his tie and glancing importantly at his watch. He has worked here for eleven years and known 'Piotr' for most of them. 'Why, we lived in the same hostel!' he says. Piotr, a tall, good-looking blond man in his early thirties, regards him with tolerant contempt, as schoolboys have for a bumbling but basically good-natured fellow-pupil.

The Solidarity chairman reports that precisely 4,761 of the *c.* 5,000 'Dolmel' employees are members of Solidarity. The Party Secretary reports that he has approximately 750 members, 150 fewer than in August 1980. Ninety per cent of his members are also in Solidarity. He would like to emphasize that he is all in favour of Solidarity. But also of the Party. They should both represent the workers, he says.

Perhaps they should compete in a multi-party system?

No, that is not possible, he explains, in a long discourse during which the word 'geography' keeps recurring.

'You mean, because of the Russians?'

'Yes, of course,' he mutters, blushing. Another important glance at his watch—must dash—important engagement—and out he bumbles.

Piłsudski scowls down from the wall.

Would I like to meet the new managing director? asks Piotr. (The old managing director had to go after Solidarity discovered that he had disposed of some fifty company flats to personal friends, acquaintances in the police, the Party organisation, etc. There are some 500 workers in 'Dolmel' waiting for flats. They have to wait up to ten years.) Another telephone call: 'Hi,' says Piotr, 'I'm bringing you a guest from England, OK?' Five minutes later we are all sitting in the managing director's office. The new boss is also in his thirties and, like Piotr and the Party Secretary, has spent almost all his working life in Dolmel. He speaks a technocratic language and knows exactly what he would like to do with the factory. Of the *c.* 5,000 workforce, he says, only about 1,500 are engaged in productive work. The word 'unemployment' does not pass his lips, but he talks of 'relocating' labour. He wishes to reorient his production for export: but there are so many bureaucratic hurdles, and while in theory the enterprises are already meant to be 'self-financing' (i.e. profitable) in practice the Ministry still controls foreign currency.

These practical problems of production do not, however, appear greatly to interest Piotr and his deputy, who interrupt the sermon to hand the managing director a Solidarity lapel badge. The director fingers it gingerly, nearly pricking himself on the pin. 'May I keep it?' he asks politely.

Poznań. A factory which produces production-lines. What, I ask, have been the most important changes in their lives since August? 'That,' says the Solidarity chairman, and points to a large cross on the wall. They show me photographs of the managing director speaking in front of an enormous cross, and the national colours. 'You must know our history to understand what we feel.' But what exactly has changed? Well, they say, before August they were afraid to speak their minds in the factory. Now they are not afraid. Now it is the directors who are afraid. They are reading as they have never read before: the local Solidarity news-sheets, the Solidarity Weekly, *Polityka* or *Gazeta Krakowska* when they can get hold of a copy. Then a small man with a pale face and dirty black jacket speaks up for the first time. 'You see,' he says 'it is a revolution of the soul.'

A *revolution of the soul*. I have found no better phrase than the one used by that Poznań worker in the spring of 1981 to describe what changed in the everyday lives of millions of Poles.

Important, but by no means revolutionary, practical changes were made in some factories. Apart from the nationwide achievement of free Saturdays (rescinded under martial law), there were some badly needed improvements in health and safety protection. The official accident rate actually increased because the number of accidents was being honestly recorded for the first time. Some corrupt managers were dismissed (as at Dolmel), and some blatant malpractices—for example in the allocation of holiday places—partially corrected.

Materially, however, most people were worse off at the end of this period than at the beginning. Virtually all the economic reforms remained on paper. Solidarity's best product was monuments. Just two new laws had been passed implementing the promises of the social accords. The Censorship Act of 31 July 1981 did temporarily confirm the greater *de facto* freedom of expression in the printed word which had existed since September 1981, though it did not prevent the continued gross manipulation of television and radio. The Workers' Self-Government Act of 25 September 1981 had hardly begun to change the working life of even the larger factories (where the self-governmentalists were strongest) when it was suspended by the military. Beyond the sacking of discredited officials (who often resurfaced elsewhere, in other sinecures), the institutions of central and local government were virtually unchanged.

'Nothing has changed,' said one of the young poets, 'and everything has changed.' 'It's simply that everyone feels better,' said a historian at Kraków University, 'I can't be more concrete than that. Oh yes, and when I teach the French Revolution I really feel my students understand the word "compromise" for the first time.' 'It's like before the war!' exclaimed a waiter, much too young to remember the pre-war period.

Beyond the single, monumental organisational fact of Solidarity's existence,* the most fundamental changes were all in the realm of consciousness rather than being. But the Polish workers, in contradiction to Marx, believed that ultimately consciousness (*Bewusstsein*) would determine being (*Sein*). Whatever their debt to socialist ideals, in this vital sense their priorities were Christian, not socialist. Socialism proceeds from society to the individual: people are unfulfilled, it suggests, because society is imperfect. Christianity proceeds from the individual to society: society is imperfect, it suggests, because human beings are imperfect.

Solidarity began with consciousness, and with the individual conscience. Wałęsa made this priority explicit. People should begin by 'putting their own internal affairs to rights', he declared in his first interview for the Solidarity Weekly, and they could then proceed from this individual, internal reformation to the reform of their factories, of society, of the state ... 'I don't say that everyone should be marched off to Church, but we must somehow help people to put things right inside themselves.' And talking to the Italian journalist Oriana Fallaci he paid ironic tribute to the spiritual benefits of growing up under communism:

> If you choose the example of what we Poles have in our pockets and in our shops, then ... communism has done very little for us. But if you choose the example of what is in our souls, I answer that communism has done very much for us.

*And the many smaller trades unions. In all, ninety-five unions were registered by the Warsaw Provincial Court between October 1980 and December 1981.[2]

> In fact our souls contain exactly the opposite of what they wanted. They wanted us not to believe in God, and our churches are full. They wanted us to be materialistic and incapable of sacrifices: we are anti-materialistic and capable of sacrifice. They wanted us to be afraid of the tanks, of the guns, and instead we don't fear them at all.[3]

Plainly, not all Solidarity leaders shared Wałęsa's simple Catholic commitment. But the basic moral commitment, the perception of Solidarity as a vehicle for '*moral* protest' was common to the great majority. Andrzej Gwiazda, in his open letter to Wałęsa, characterised Solidarity as a 'movement for moral revolution',[4] and the fundamentalists' central charge against the pragmatists was precisely that they were insufficiently rigorous in their application of *moral* standards to their political behaviour. Tischner characterised the transformation of consciousness wrought by Solidarity in a single poetic metaphor: 'the conscience plants forests,' he wrote, 'Solidarity is a huge forest planted by awakened consciences... Revolution is an occurrence in the realm of the spirit.'[5] To appreciate the quality of this 'revolution of the soul' one must know that for thirty years most Poles had lived a double life. They grew up with two codes of behaviour, two languages—the public and the private—two histories—the official and the unofficial. From their schooldays they learned not only to conceal in public their private opinions but also to parrot another set of opinions prescribed by the ruling ideology. In Poland, Newspeak's monopoly in the public sphere was never as complete as in other Soviet bloc countries. Apart from the independent intellectuals, the Church always spoke another language which was heard by the masses. In the 1970s a growing number of courageous individuals—known in the West as 'dissidents'—made the personal decision to live one life rather than two. They would openly say and write exactly what they thought; if the censor would not accept it then they would print it themselves; they would, in short, 'live as if they lived in a free country'. But their numbers, though growing, were still tiny. After a year of Solidarity there were ten million such 'dissidents'. In factories and news-sheets across the country people were openly saying and writing exactly what they thought in private. The workers had regained (in Alain Besançon's fine phrase) the 'private ownership of their tongues'. The word 'truth' appeared with the frequency of a punctuation-mark in the statements, speeches, graffiti and conversation of Solidarity. 'We need truth as much as we need coal',[6] Wałęsa said. In Solidarity opinion polls the demand for media which did not lie and for the teaching of Poland's 'true history' in schools came second only to the demand for freedom. Thesis 31 of the Solidarity Programme declared:

> The very language of propaganda, which damages the way we want to express thoughts and feelings, is a dangerous tool of lies. The union will seek to give back to society the Polish language, which allows people truly to understand each other.

As we have seen, the workers reacted neuralgically against any *linguistic* compromise with the regime: starting with the disputed recognition of 'the leading role of the Party' in the Gdańsk Agreement. The Congress in September 1981 broke down most of the barriers of self-censorship. Now they said exactly what they aspired to, in their own language, although they still recognised that they could not achieve it all.

The end of the double life was a profound psychological and ethical gain for countless individuals. Now at last they could speak their minds openly in the workplace as well as behind the closed doors of their homes. No longer did they need to watch their words for fear of the secret police. And now they discovered for certain that almost everyone around them actually felt much the same way about the system as they did. This was a source of tremendous relief. The poet Stanisław Barańczak compared it to coming up for air after living for years under water.[7] Being able to speak the truth in public as well as in private was part of that sense of recovered dignity—another key-word—which even the casual visitor could hardly fail to notice in the faces and bearing of the strikers (and which is captured for posterity in Andrzej Wajda's *Man of Iron*). The fact that 'we' could say what 'we' wanted in our own organisation (under the sign of the cross), and that 'they'—the managers and functionaries—would have to listen, gave the poorest employee a sense of regaining control over his own work. This sense was captured by the American Professor who found 'an entire country without alienation'.[8]

Solidarity gave people hope, hope and a sense of purpose. It gave them something to live for. The number of attempted suicides in 1981 was almost *one-third* less than in 1980.[9] According to the Episcopate group on alcoholism the consumption of pure alcohol declined by about 30 per cent in the last four months of 1980. According to official figures (which include only official sales) consumption fell from 8.4 litres of pure alcohol per head in 1980 to 6.4 litres in 1981 (the 1973 level): a dramatic effect.[10] So, in my experience, did the consumption of political jokes. People had better outlets for their energies than drinking or the composition of those brilliant, acid, powerless jokes which so often accompanied drinking.

Now of course the excitement of revolution can sweep away critical judgment, and most revolutions have begun with proclamations of high moral intent and moving outbursts of popular morality. Even the October Revolution. John Reed, in his *Ten Days That Shook the World*, vividly recalls the 'no tips here' signs on Moscow restaurant walls and the Russians' apparently insatiable appetite for knowledge and truth. 'Bliss was it in that dawn to be alive . . .' is an old refrain. Yet it is hard to think of any previous revolution in which ethical categories and moral goals have played such a large part; not only in the theory but also in the practice of the revolutionaries; not only at the outset but throughout the revolution.

Moreover, it is an indisputable fact that in sixteen months *this revolution killed nobody*. When an inflamed mob tried to lynch a policeman in Otwock (see above, pp. 177–8), Solidarity officials pleaded with them to refrain. Adam Michnik recounted his own rich experience at the receiving end of police violence to persuade the mob *not* to use violence against the police. And they refrained. The first people to be killed in the Polish revolution were workers shot by armed police in the first weeks of the 'war'. This extraordinary record of non-violence, this majestic self-restraint in the face of many provocations, distinguishes the Polish revolution from previous revolutions.

These two features, the striving for truth and non-violence on the one side, the lies and violence on the other, are intimately connected. Between the lie and violence, Solzhenitsyn writes in his 1970 Nobel Speech, 'there is the most intimate, most natural, fundamental link: violence can only be concealed by the lie, and the lie can only be maintained by violence.' And he goes on to make a bold prophecy: 'Once the lie has been dispersed, the nakedness of violence will be revealed in all its repulsiveness, and then violence, become decrepit, will come crashing down.'[11]

Poland seems to confirm the truth of the first part of Solzhenitsyn's prophecy. By the summer of 1981 the lie had been dispersed, and when it was dispersed the communist system could no longer function without the open use of force. Rarely can the credibility of a government have sunk so low, without its actual dissolution. As Kuroń remarked in an interview published in the Party youth newspaper *Sztandar Młodych* in October 1981, 'if there were to be an announcement that the government had laid a golden egg, people would say: first of all, not golden; secondly, not an egg; and thirdly, it didn't lay it but stole it.'[12] All the government could still do was to sack the paper's Editor for publishing the interview. Every Polish schoolchild saw that the emperor had no clothes. Consequently, on 13 December, the 'nakedness of violence' was 'revealed in all its repulsiveness'. The truth of the second part of Solzhenitsyn's prophecy—that 'violence, become decrepit, will come crashing down'—has yet to be confirmed.

The freedom which the Poles achieved through Solidarity (with a small and large 's') was not freedom from want. But material liberation was not their first goal. As that hand-painted banner in the bare room in Ustrzyki Dolne explained:

we don't care about life
the pig also lives
we want a life of dignity

The freedom which they did achieve, for a few months, was the freedom from fear. Yet when they spoke about freedom they meant above all—and they explained this with increasing clarity as the fear dispersed—what Poles had meant by 'freedom' for two centuries: freedom from foreign domination. 'Romantic' and 'unreasonable' as this aspiration seems to so many in the West, who happen themselves to live in independent countries, it is, in the Polish context, a strictly reasonable priority. For in the Polish experience all other freedoms—including the freedoms from want and fear—

are dependent upon, although of course they do not automatically follow from, the degree of the nation's freedom from foreign domination.

Was Solidarity, then, in content if not in form, just another in the long line of national insurrections? The answer must be 'no', not only because it is hard to conceive of a 'non-violent insurrection', but also because the leaders of this 'open conspiracy' (with one or two exceptions, like Rulewski) never imagined they could achieve what all previous insurrections had set out to achieve, full independent sovereign statehood. At most, they imagined they just might achieve a Republic which was largely Self-Governing in its internal affairs.

The insurrection comparison is none the less important, especially for a nation with such a long but selective memory. The truth is that the national uprisings of the nineteenth century were also social uprisings and they failed partly because the imperial powers managed to set one class of Poles against another (e.g. peasants against landowners in 1864). National struggle was crippled by class struggle. Now the civil crusade of Solidarity overcame some of the deepest divisions within Polish society—between town and country dwellers, between workers and intelligentsia, between the 'Two Nations' of socialists and Catholics. This overcoming was the culmination of long processes, and of the conscious efforts of many individuals. Obviously there were tensions between workers, peasants and intellectuals. If Solidarity had achieved a greater share of power these tensions would presumably have become more acute. In this, as in the moral sense, it was a backhanded advantage that they were not able to take state power.

Despite the authorities' best efforts to 'divide and rule' (deliberate efforts, as Żabiński's secret speech shows), Solidarity was not divided against itself on lines of sectional or class interest. An extensive sociological survey conducted in November and December 1981, when the political fragmentation of the movement was far advanced, revealed that basic attitudes to the state were independent of all traditional sociological determinants: sex, age, occupation, family background, education. The single, crucial divide was between supporters of Solidarity and supporters of the regime.[13] Solidarity cut across all lines of social division. That manichean dichotomy—'the power' versus 'the society'—continued to express the basic conflict. Again, it is hard to think of many examples, except in wartime, where a society has been so united for so long.

It is therefore impossible to reduce what happened in Poland to the terms of 'class struggle'. Certainly, those people whose jobs, powers and privileges were directly dependent on the continuance of Party monopolies—perhaps one to one and a half million if one includes their dependents—may be described as a client ruling class. 'As far as giving up economic privileges is concerned,' a Warsaw sociologist wryly noted in spring 1981, 'Marxists are inclined to pessimism.'[14] But the struggle against the privileged was much more than a class struggle.

One other novel aspect of this revolution deserves a mention. When Solidarity called a warning strike, the strike call was followed in the remotest corners of the country: in the tiny station buffet and the village pub as in Ursus or Huta Warszawa. This capacity for simultaneous co-ordinated action was a key to Solidarity's success. It was based on a modern telecommunications network. From the time in July 1980 when KOR activists started telephoning news of the first strikes through the automatic exchanges to foreign radio stations, which broadcast the news back to Poland, the telephone, the telex, the cassette-recorder, the duplicating-machine and the radio all played a vital role. In this sense it was a very modern revolution: telerevolution. Solidarity's operational strength was its ability to communicate rapidly nationwide. This strength was broken by the army's ability to cut those nationwide communications in one night. Thus the technology of modern communications facilitated peaceful revolution from below—but also terrorism from above.

Judgments

During the immediate aftermath, most judgments on Solidarity's development fell into three broad 'lines': (1) it was impossible from the start, or (2) Solidarity went too far (probably a majority view), or (3) Solidarity did not go far enough (a minority view). Often people told me, first, that it was impossible from the start and then, in the next breath, that Solidarity 'went too far'. However, statements (1) and (2) can no more be combined logically than statements (2) and (3). If it was 'impossible from the start', if a genuinely independent social movement could never survive inside a Soviet bloc state, then it cannot ultimately have mattered what Solidarity did or did not do. Solidarity 'went too far' by its mere existence, it had 'gone too far' already on 1 September 1980. The rest is epilogue.

Now of course there are several senses in which Solidarity was impossible. It was impossible in the Marxist-Leninist world view, that workers should feel the need to revolt against a Workers' State. It was impossible for them to be authentically represented by an organisation independent of the communist party. It was impossible for a Leninist party to share power with any such rival. But then, it was impossible that after thirty-five years of Soviet socialism the overwhelming majority of Poles should be practising Catholics; it was impossible that 75 per cent of agricultural land should still be in private hands. Not only in Poland, but all over the socialist world things are happening all the time which Marxism-Leninism has scientifically demonstrated to be impossible. Yet if Solidarity was impossible, how did it happen? If the Soviet Union 'could never tolerate' an independent workers' movement, how did it tolerate Solidarity for fifteen and a half months? The impossible happened.

This is not to say that the ideology is irrelevant. We have seen how dangerously naive it is to describe even reform communists like Rakowski as 'liberals'. A communist like Rakowski cannot be a liberal. Adherents of the 'impossibility' view are right to emphasise that the ruling class in Poland as well as the Soviet Union does not contain even a significant minority who actively wish to share power. If it did, that minority would be behaving against the grain of most historical experience, as well as against the first commandment of Leninism (all power to the party). Rakowski's vision of 'partnership' involved a Hungarian-style modification of the so-called 'Dictatorship of the Proletariat'—that is, one-party dictatorship—in the direction of 'consultative authoritarianism'. His aim was a more efficient kind of dictatorship, which, as in Hungary, relies less on physical coercion and more on satisfying consumer expectations to the obvious material advantage of the population. In this he might justifiably claim to be at least as good a Leninist as, say, his comrades Olszowski and Grabski.

Solidarity's leaders had fewer illusions about the 'liberalism' of Polish communists than many western observers. From the start they appreciated that there was a yawning gulf between the maximum which the most reform-minded men in power actively *wished* to concede and the minimum which they thought necessary for a genuinely 'Independent Self-Governing Trades Union'. They did not underrate the fact that their very existence was anathema to a ruling ideology which, though almost nobody believes in its literal ('scientific') truth, is none the less indispensable for the system. But they thought there was a slim chance that, through a mixture of massive peaceful pressure and negotiation, the communist ruling class might just be compelled to accept some long-term *modus vivendi* with Solidarity as a lesser evil, not from any 'liberal' goodwill, but from a rational perception of its own self-interest. 'The impossible', said Bronisław Geremek, 'is indispensable.'[15]

It has been the argument of this book that this was a rational hope; that on 1 September 1980 there was still a slim chance of institutionalising compromise; and that what the various actors did and said in the next fifteen and a half months is therefore not wholly irrelevant to the outcome. That the experiment would fail was, from the outset, probable; but it was not inevitable.

The second judgment, that Solidarity 'went too far', was also the 'line' of Polish and Soviet propaganda. This does not automatically mean that it is untrue, but it is an added incentive to look at the claims critically. Translated out of the Newspeak of propaganda (and such translation was discreetly accomplished by unofficial ambassadors for the military regime) the claims were three. First, by the December 1981 Radom meeting Solidarity's national leadership was actively plotting to overthrow the communist regime. Secondly, by autumn 1981 Poland had sunk into chaos and anarchy, for which Solidarity was primarily responsible. Thirdly, such an overthrow, and such anarchy, would inevitably have led to a Soviet invasion. Therefore the Polish military takeover was the lesser evil. This version has gained surprisingly wide acceptance in western foreign policy establishments. Here, for example, is the judgment of Philip Windsor, a serious and respected British international affairs analyst, in an article entitled 'What's wrong with martial law?':

> But is not martial law preferable, in some circumstances, to anarchic (rather than authoritarian) lawlessness, to the disintegration of a society, to the threat of invasion by a foreign power? ...
>
> In the case of Poland, it was clear last December that Lech Wałęsa had lost control of Solidarity, that violent crime was increasing exponentially, and even, according to some reports, that there were outbreaks of cholera because sewage workers were on strike ... What powers would a western constitutionalist have used in these circumstances?[16]

It is frankly a mystery why Poland's communist leaders are given greater credence than her democratically elected popular leaders, when there is so much documentary evidence of the former's secretive mendacity and the latter's breakneck openness. No doubt Solidarity's world public relations were as amateur as the regime's are professional. There is an old muckraker's adage that if you throw enough mud some of it will stick, especially if your victims cannot answer back—as Solidarity's leaders could not after 13 December. Soviet propaganda works on the philosophical principle of the Bellman in *The Hunting of the Snark:*

> *Just the place for a snark. I have said it thrice:*
> *What I tell you three times is true ...*

The simple, relentless, uncontradicted repetition of a single 'line' from many ostensibly diverse sources can be extremely effective.

Yet consider, for instance, one short passage from General Jaruzelski's speech on 13 December:

> Strikes, strike alerts, protest actions have become the norm. Even schoolchildren are dragged in. *Yesterday evening many public buildings were occupied.* Exhortations to a physical settling of accounts with the 'reds', with people who hold different views, are being made. *Acts of terrorism,* of threats and mob trials and also of direct coercion *abound* [my italics] ...[17]

'Yesterday evening many public buildings were occupied', 'Acts of terrorism ... abound'. Here are empirically verifiable statements.

The observer who wishes to judge the truth of the General's argument might, you would think, begin by testing these factual assertions against the known facts. And when it is found that the number of public buildings known to have been occupied on the evening of Saturday 12 December 1981 could be counted on the fingers of two hands; that there was no single public building occupied by industrial Solidarity; and that no one has yet managed to produce a single act of terrorism perpetrated inside Poland during the whole period of overground Solidarity, the interested observer might just begin to doubt the strict veracity of the General's statement.[18]

So it is with the whole wall of argument. If you step up and examine the individual bricks they crumble in your hand: they cannot bear even a cursory examination. But from afar, from London or Bonn, the wall apparently looks solid and convincing.

The claim that the Radom meeting revealed Solidarity's intentions of overthrowing the communist regime can only be sustained by arguing that the official statement of their position at the end of that meeting merely concealed their 'true' intentions, which are to be detected in the 'Radomgate' tapes. But the brilliantly executed military takeover, and Solidarity's unpreparedness for it, demonstrated *ex post facto* beyond any reasonable doubt which side was concealing its true intentions, and which was still desperately seeking a negotiated 'national agreement'.

The claim that the country was already plunged into anarchy is greatly exaggerated. By the end of November Wałęsa and his colleagues had worked so effectively as 'firemen' that the sewage workers' strike was the only major industrial dispute in progress.[19] Poland's factories were far less disrupted by strikes than they had been in October. That 'violent crime was increasing exponentially' is a 'fact' we owe solely to the Polish police and Interior Ministry. Anyone who travelled around Poland in these last weeks saw awful shortages, woefully inadequate medical care, desperation, anger and a growing awareness of impending confrontation with the authorities. But Philip Windsor's tone picture (cholera and 'anarchic lawlessness') suggests a degree of social disintegration which may have been present in Russia in 1918, or Germany in April 1945, but was not in Poland in December 1981.

Neither can we yet know whether Jaruzelski was ever actually faced with the binary choice: internal clamp-down or Soviet invasion. But if he was, it was because the Soviet leadership and his own comrades left him no other alternative, not because Solidarity left him no other alternative. Solidarity spelled out in the Radom meeting seven 'minimum conditions for a national agreement' (see above, pp. 256–7).

Three of these conditions are restatements of points in the summer 1980 social accords: no anti-union reprisals, a new Trades Union Act, limited pluralism in the mass media. The condition on economic reform is more explicitly linked to a more radical conception of workers' self-government than in point 6 of the Gdańsk Agreement. The summer accords' vague promises of public consultation on socio-economic policy are extended to direct union supervision of food distribution and a Social Council with a real share of power 'over the socio-economic policy of the state'. The demand for a far-reaching democratisation of local government—free elections to councils and the subordination of local administration to them—is nowhere mentioned in the summer accords.

Plainly, Solidarity's negotiating position 'went further' in December 1981 than in September 1980. Moreover, individual Solidarity branches, factories, pressure groups and members were canvassing desperate solutions. Thus some fundamentalist nationalists looked to free elections as a cure-all, while the Łódź self-governmentalists developed their fantasy of a nationwide 'active strike'. These must not be confused with the actual policy of the union.

To say that 'Lech Wałęsa had lost control of Solidarity' reveals a complete misunderstanding of the kind of organisation which Solidarity was. Solidarity was a democratic mass movement, not an army 'controlled' by Generals, or a Church 'controlled' by Bishops, or a Party 'controlled' by its leaders. It would be more true to say that at several points (e.g. the Warsaw Agreement) Solidarity temporarily lost control of Lech Wałęsa.

In the last two months, however, Solidarity did begin to lose control of itself. The revolution did not devour its children, but in Gdańsk the regional leadership fell apart between Gwiazda and Wałęsa factions. In other regions deep fractures had appeared, and it was only with the utmost difficulty that the National Commission could still agree a common policy. There are thus two processes which need to be explained: radicalisation and fragmentation.

When and why did this come about? Four periods can be identified. From September 1980 to March 1981 Solidarity grew with extraordinary speed and *élan*. At the end of March it was at the height of its organisational strength, and capacity to mobilise the population. Throughout this period its national leadership sought a *modus vivendi* with the Party-state on the terms of the summer social accords which the government had signed. This search was punctuated by four major confrontations: the Registration Crisis, the Narożniak Affair, the Free Saturdays dispute and Bydgoszcz. These crises showed, firstly, that many members of the communist ruling class, represented at the highest level and strengthened from Moscow, were determined not to abide by the spirit of the social accords, but rather to fight Solidarity with all the means at their disposal. This included a powerful security apparatus, which cannot be assumed to have been totally under the control of Mr Kania. Neither the Narożniak arrest nor the Bydgoszcz beatings seem to have been the considered policy of the whole Politburo. The 'Thomas-à-Becket effect' is a more likely explanation. As provocations they were failures in the short term, but in the medium term they successfully diminished the chances of compromise. The television coverage, under the control of Stefan Olszowski from December 1980, was a further permanent provocation.

Secondly, these crises showed that even among those in the Party and government who were trying to work towards a political solution, old habits died hard. The Free Saturdays dispute was not about *what* was done, but about *how* it was done. By presenting society with a *fait accompli*, as it had been accustomed to do for thirty years, the government finally won itself a far worse economic deal than it could have achieved by serious consultation. Rakowski admitted this at the time.

Solidarity's leaders (though of course not all of its members) appreciated that a Polish government with the best will in the world could not have kept all the economic promises of the summer agreements, unless it received massive economic aid from abroad. They therefore would not (and did not) keep it to the letter of those agreements. But they expected, in return, that the government would implement those points which did lie in its power (e.g. registration, access to the mass media), and keep to the spirit of the agreements. If Solidarity was not to be seriously consulted on the trades union issue of working time, what would it be consulted on?

Apart from the short-lived challenge to the security apparatus mounted by Mazowsze in the Narożniak Affair, the only respect in which Solidarity went beyond the letter of the social accords in this period was in its support for Rural Solidarity.

This period ended with the Bydgoszcz crisis, which was the most important single turning-point in the history of the movement. Solidarity was never again to reach the heights of mass mobilisation which it attained in the run-up to the general strike. The Warsaw Agreement would become the symbolic focus for deepening divisions between Solidarity activists at all levels.

From April to July 1981, Solidarity went through a period of internal heart-searching, which coincided with its regional elections. Externally, however, it held an effective industrial truce. The Party was given a three-month breathing-space in which to revitalise itself. Inside the Party there was a major revolt against the Bydgoszcz provocation, and an authentic movement to democratise it from below. But the 'horizontal' movement was defeated *before* the Extraordinary Party Congress, by a combination of internal vested interests, encoded fears and direct Soviet pressure. Despite appearances, the Party Congress was a turning-point at which the Party failed to turn.

In the third period, between the beginning of the Party Congress and the end of the Solidarity Congress, two major shifts occurred. Jaruzelski and his closest political allies shifted their attention decisively from the political to the military option—from 'appeasement' to preparations for 'war'—while Solidarity's official policy went decisively beyond the terms of the August 1980 Agreements. In August 1981 the National Commission made an explicit demand for a share of power over social and economic policy, including democratically elected local government.

I have argued that this was not, as the regime suggested, the work of any small conspiratorial group of 'Jacobins'—whether 'KOR' or 'Mazowsze' or 'the activists'—but rather a response to a complex of pressures from *below*. That is what Solidarity leaders constantly said, in the debates of the National Commission and in private conversations. The evidence is overwhelming, for anyone who cares to examine it. To sustain the alternative, conspiracy theory, one would have to argue that this was merely a form of words, a ritual invocation, like the Party's claim to act for the working class. A large part of the story of Solidarity is the story of the leadership's efforts to restrain their members when, as for example in February 1981 in Jelenia Góra and Bielsko-Biała, they wished to 'go too far' by sacking corrupt officials and reducing the privileges of the police.

In this respect, too, the Polish revolution must be contrasted with previous revolutions, in which the intellectuals had played their more traditional role of raising horizons, injecting utopian perspectives (and fantastic illusions) into the mass movement. Here, by contrast, both the 'loyal opposition' *and* the Catholic advisers *and* KOR activists like Kuroń spent most of their time attempting to puncture utopian illusions, reminding the workers who actually led the revolution of the limits of the possible. Only the fundamentalist national opposition tendency (KPN, KSN) played the more traditional role. Before August 1980 KOR may have been a Leninist 'vanguard', against Leninism. But they were not the Bolsheviks in the revolution.

Pressure from below increased partly because, as fear and the lie were dispersed, more and more people wished to articulate their true, ultimate aim: So that Poland should be Polish. Everyone carried within themselves this tension between the ideal and the possible, but after months of doing the impossible that distinction became blurred. The pressure increased also because every provocative act of official bad faith further reduced the authorities' tiny stock of credibility. Most workers failed to distinguish between the different components of 'the power' (*władza*). There was 'we' and 'they': 'They' were responsible for everything any one of 'them' did. This was, of course, the Party's totalitarian claim, but not the Polish reality.

I have argued, however, that an equally important cause of this radicalisation from below was the continued economic collapse. When, after six months of Solidarity, people had to queue longer for less, the popular reaction was not to blame Solidarity. The popular reaction was to demand more power for Solidarity. The summer agreements had promised that the government would rapidly come up with a convincing programme for leading the country out of the crisis. This it had not done. Especially in larger factories the workforces were less and less inclined to give their *nomenklatura* managers yet another chance. It is therefore easy to understand why the revived and revised idea of workers' self-government became popular in the early summer, despite the initial reserve of Solidarity's leaders. It was a popular demand before it became a National Commission demand.

In fact the economic collapse reduced both sides' room for manoeuvre. Most of Solidarity's leaders appreciated that any rational economic reform would require major price rises and unemployment. They could not therefore satisfy their members in the way that a trades union traditionally satisfies its members: by winning better wages, more jobs etc. On the contrary, the government was asking them (*had* to ask them) to sell drastic standard-of-living cuts and unemployment to their members! The National Commission was compelled to look for other kinds of gain to compensate for these losses. The popular demand for workers' self-government would help to give their members that vital sense of 'something depending on us'[20] (as Wałęsa expressed a basic purpose of Solidarity in his Open Letter to Gwiazda). It was an attempt to give new dynamism to the movement in a way which would also be economically constructive. If Solidarity was to take a share of responsibility for the economic reform, was it not reasonable that they should have a share of *power* over its implementation?

In Bujak's metaphor, Solidarity now found itself like a union of seamen on a sinking ship. Its first priority was to save the ship. This would involve great sacrifices by the crew. They demanded in return that the crew should have a say in the running of the ship. The officers would have to make material sacrifices too.

Solidarity now asked much more of the government than in August 1980; but the government was now asking more of Solidarity. At the heart of the last serious, general negotiations between the government and Solidarity was the question: on what terms would Solidarity be willing and able to sell the necessary austerity deal to society? The authorities, it was clear to all, could never win voluntary popular consent for the measures. They could only force them through at the point of a bayonet. Given the severity of the likely cuts (150 per cent price increases, up to a million temporarily unemployed) the National Commission's demands (self-government, supervision of food production and distribution, improved access to the media) were a not unreasonable basis for negotiation.

They were, however, a frontal challenge to the vital interests of the communist ruling class. They meant, in plain terms, that Comrade X in one of the Industry ministries, Comrade Y, an incompetent manager, and Comrade Z, who administered a special hospital for the security services, would lose their jobs, status, and all the perks which went with them (the access to foreign currency, the cars, the special medical care, the 'business trips' to the West). This class—predictably—put its own interests before those of the national economy. The Party which emerged from the Congress was more than ever, in Adam Michnik's striking phrase, 'a trades union for the rulers'. Now former 'appeasers' turned to the forces of repression, rather than share power. By the end of the Solidarity Congress the chances of a peaceful political solution were infinitesimal. The only real question then became: could the regime crush Solidarity without having openly to resort to help from the Red Army?

The last period, from October to December 1981, is one of success in failure for the regime and failure in success for Solidarity. Having failed to gain the support of the people for communist government, Jaruzelski successfully prepared a military takeover in near-total secrecy, behind a smoke-screen of negotiation. Solidarity failed technically and psychologically to prepare for the coup. It disastrously underestimated the regime's strength, lulled by the myth of the patriotic army and the myth of the spontaneous general strike. Moreover, its own self-discipline further deteriorated. Facing another harsh winter with not enough to eat, not enough coal to heat their flats, no shoes to keep their feet dry, no soap, no toothpaste, no washing powder, and the prospect only of worse to come, the people standing in the queues began to lose their patience and the workers their magnificent self-discipline. From the large factories there came increasingly radical demands. At moments Solidarity resembled a revolutionary army quarrelling furiously about what it would do when it got to Moscow, although in reality it was bogged down in the Pripet marshes. The Generals' autumn strategy of *reculer pour mieux sauter* worked excellently. The fragmentation and radicalisation of Solidarity facilitated both the execution of the coup, and its justification to the world.

Verbally, Solidarity supplied some of the rope with which it was hung. Few people troubled to inquire what was actually Solidarity policy, and what desperate talk. Moreover, cause and effect were confused. Many outside observers concluded, as the regime wished them to conclude, that the radicalisation and fragmentation of Solidarity in these last months was the *cause* of the military clampdown. I have argued that the reverse was the case. In this last period, Solidarity's chaotic desperation was the intended effect of the regime's deliberate strategy: to weaken and divide the revolutionary movement, to wear away its popular support, and then to crush it by force.

This account of Solidarity's development will still not find favour with those who take the third 'line': that Solidarity 'did not go far enough'. For them, the 'desperate talk', the 'active strike' fantasies of Łódź, the 'hard line' of Katowice and Szczecin, were the only realistic path for the movement. It was a fantasy to imagine that there could ever be a half-way halt, a peaceful *modus vivendi* between Party and Solidarity. They were fire and water. Either one or the other had to go. It was the self-styled 'realists' like Wałęsa and Mazowiecki who were unrealistic. Solidarity missed its chance of overthrowing the Party. It should have concentrated on winning over the police and the army: or, as was argued in Szczecin in June 1981, on emasculating the security forces while 'appeasing' the army.[21] They should have gone for the general strike, in March, and if not in March, then in the summer. They should have appealed earlier and more explicitly to the other subject peoples/workers in the rest of the Soviet Empire to rise up with them.

Reflecting the paradoxical nature of the Polish revolution, these criticisms are to be heard from the extreme left and the far right. Britain's International Socialists, for example, argue that the use of violence is 'inherent in a revolutionary perspective'. Of course, they say, the revolution might then have been crushed by a Soviet invasion,

> But blood shed in a struggle where the balance of forces is known, when the possibility of victory exists, is *less*

> *terrible* than when it is shed in the course of a definite defeat, such as that in December 1981. For a Russian invasion could have been defeated [my italics].[22]

One can only admire the *insouciant* courage with which these comrades would risk other people's lives. This, to speak with Orwell, is a kind of playing with fire by people who don't even know that fire is hot.

On any informed military assessment, the statement 'a Russian invasion could have been defeated' is plain rubbish. There were few signs of any widespread sympathy for Solidarity among the workers of any other east European country, let alone a readiness to join it in a common uprising. As for the Polish army, a crisp assessment was given by the *Polityka* columnist Daniel Passent in an article for the *Guardian* attempting to justify martial law: 'General Jaruzelski did not allow the Army to rot and used it before it became infected by Solidarity.'[23]

Of course any judgment on this point is speculative, but there is every reason to believe that Jaruzelski would have acted earlier if the forces of repression had begun to be seriously 'infected' earlier (witness the sharp reaction to the Solidarity initiative in the ordinary police), and if he failed to act, or those forces proved inadequate, then the Russians would have acted for him—whatever the human and political cost. Solidarity was right to identify this as a taboo area, where the most it could hope for in the short term was a gradual and partial limitation of police power by social pressure and the restoration of legal controls.

If Solidarity had 'gone further' in this direction it would have abandoned the whole perspective of self-limitation. The most probable outcome would have been bloody, and far more costly for both the Poles and the Soviet Union. Of course it is possible to argue that this would have been 'better' in the long term, as Poland might have become the Spanish ulcer of the Soviet Union, another Afghanistan in the centre of Europe. This would have been 'better' for the International Socialists, and some of President Reagan's right-wing foreign policy advisers—but for whom else?

Many Solidarity members, however, would argue a less extreme version of this line. Solidarity, they say, should have gone ahead with the general strike at the end of March. The workers' power was at its height, the popular mobilisation complete. There was a real chance that Solidarity could have won a decisive victory, with the government once again retreating behind a face-saving compromise and Solidarity greatly strengthened by the experience of the strike. The government would have been forced to compromise (not to abdicate); the revolt from below in the Party would have been encouraged; and the Russians might still have accepted this as the lesser evil. After the Warsaw Agreement Solidarity grew weaker, and there was no corresponding weakening of the military and security arms of the state. As Michnik subsequently observed, Solidarity became a giant with legs of steel but hands of putty; the regime was a giant with legs of putty, but hands of steel.

They would also argue that Solidarity could have 'gone much further' in preparing its ultimate deterrent—the general occupation-strike—against all possible eventualities. Michnik, in his essay 'The Polish War', smuggled out of Białołęka internment camp, recalls 'a remark by Karl Marx, to the effect that a nation or a woman cannot be forgiven that lapse in which they permit themselves to be subjugated by a scoundrel.'[24] And he, unlike the International Socialists or Reagan's advisers, has a right to say that. But such preparations would have had a different significance in March than they did in November. In March they might have increased the chances—or should I say, decreased the impossibility—of a negotiated *modus vivendi*. In November, they would have increased the quality of resistance, and therefore the scale of the 'war'.

Solidarity had *les défauts de ses qualités*. It was democratic, and because of the nature of democracy, and because this was Polish democracy, and because the nation had had no experience of democratic institutions for forty years, this diminished the unity of the movement, and thus its capacity for swift co-ordinated action. Solidarity was a profoundly moral movement, but this moral fundamentalism led some of its members to regard *any* compromise with authority as immoral and treacherous.

It can be criticised, too, for the paucity of small-scale, constructive economic initiatives in individual work-places or towns. Normally, the smallest Solidarity news-sheet was filled with declarations of high principle and discussion of the great national issues of the moment. In part, this reflected the objective restraints of a highly centralised bureaucratic economy: the doctors in the

Nowa Huta hospital, for example (see above, p. 30) knew exactly what they wanted to do to improve conditions for their patients, but they could do nothing without supplies (and foreign currency) controlled by the Ministry in Warsaw. In part, it was because the younger generation who were most active in Solidarity had little experience of taking control over their own production. They had not grown up under a system which encouraged initiative from below. It was also perhaps because the alternative, patriotic counter-culture was still dominated by the tradition of romantic idealism, rather than 'organic work'.

Yet no one can know what energies and talents for the tough, patient, thankless work of economic and social reconstruction would have been released, if the Polish people had been given a real chance to interfere in their own internal affairs. The plans for self-government were just not tried. However, when that chance was denied, many reverted, as if by a reflex action, to the old familiar superb symbolic politics of defiance. As the faint hope of a *modus vivendi* faded, so 'once again' replaces 'for once' as the milestone of our narrative, once again they sing the old hymns, once again they celebrate the old anniversaries, in the spirit of Zbigniew Herbert's 'Pan Cogito' . . .

repeat old incantations of humanity fables legends
for this is how you will attain the good which escaped you

repeat great words repeat them stubbornly
like those crossing the desert who perished in the sand

they will reward you with what they have at hand
with whips derision murder among the refuse

go for this is the only way to join the circle of cold skulls
the company of your ancestors: Gilgamesh Hector Roland
the defenders of the kingdom without limits of the city of ashes

be faithful Go[25]

Consequences

To a small minority of opposition thinkers and activists in neighbouring socialist states, the repression of Solidarity was an especially painful blow. They, unlike the majority of their compatriots, had recognised Solidarity as the best hope for a peaceful evolution of the Soviet empire which that empire had seen since the Second World War. Unlike revisionist dissidents like Medvedev in Russia and Bahro in East Germany, they no longer believed that fundamental political change could come about solely through the internal transformation of the ruling Party. In Poland, for the first time ever, a new and genuinely independent social movement had actually coexisted with the communist power. Here if anywhere was the way forward (or back?) to pluralism. President Mitterrand might proclaim grandly that we must '*sortir de Yalta*': the question which these young Hungarians and Czechs wanted answered was 'how?'. For a few months they had thought that Solidarity had found an answer. Now the Polish revolution joined the Prague Spring and the Hungarian revolution on the melancholy list of crushed European revolts against 'Yalta'.

Yet the Polish revolution was certainly the largest and the longest of these revolts. Its consequences are likely to be more far-reaching. The historian or the journalist is little better equipped than anyone else to predict what those historical consequences will be. But after one year of martial law the shape of General Jaruzelski's attempt to dismantle the achievements of the Polish revolution was fairly clear. This attempt is called, in the looking-glass language of the Soviet bloc, 'normalisation': that is, the attempt to return a European society to Soviet norms which are fundamentally alien to it. 'Normalisation' is the restoration of abnormality.

The model 'normalisation' in eastern Europe was that carried through by János Kádár in Hungary after 1956. On this model, 'normalisation' has two main stages. In the first stage all kinds of terror are used to destroy the sources of opposition to communist rule, break the back of any autonomous 'civil society' and depress aspirations in society at large. In Hungary this stage lasted about three years and cost at least 2,000 lives.[26] In the second stage the reconstructed communist Party reassumes a less directly coercive kind of rule, satisfying the depressed aspirations of society with a gradual improvement in material standards of living. Sausage compensates for the loss of freedom.

In essentials, these methods are as old as tyranny itself. Aristotle distinguishes two main ways of preserving tyranny: in the first the aim of the tyrant is to make his hostile subjects *unable* to conspire against him, in the second his more refined aim is to make his subjects *indisposed* to conspire against him.[27] 'Normalisation' starts with the first aim, but should move on to the second, since—and this is not in Aristotle!—only in the second kind of tyranny can the reality of the communist system be at all credibly reconciled with the ideology it claims to embody.

In Poland, the military regime was relatively successful in the first aim. In the course of a year it proved itself capable of dispersing the demonstrations and breaking the strikes called by Solidarity's underground leadership. The brutality of the ZOMO, military discipline in the larger factories, and the threat of unemployment—traditional weapon of the capitalist employer!—saw to that. By October 1982 the regime felt secure enough to have the Independent Self-Governing Trades Union 'Solidarity' formally dissolved by the *sejm*. The Lenin Shipyard once again came out on strike, as did tens of thousands of workers across the country, but when the shipyard workers were placed under direct military discipline (five years' imprisonment for disobeying an order) most of them returned to work. By December 1982 those of Solidarity's underground leaders who had not been arrested (notably Zbigniew Bujak in Warsaw and Bogdan Lis in Gdańsk) found themselves defamed by the regime and effectively disowned by the Primate, surrounded by a society which saw little prospect of converting its moral support into immediate political action.

Yet it must be said at once that the terror was neither as extreme nor as sustained as it had been in Hungary after the Russian invasion. By that standard, the terror of martial law was remarkably patchy and mild. The Polish Helsinki Watch Committee reported '28 proven cases' of people killed by soldiers or police during the first year of the 'war'. Many reasons can be found for this 'mildness': Jaruzelski's own hopes of making a bloodless takeover dressed up in patriotic and Bonapartist uniform (his 18 Brumaire!); the limitations imposed by the use of Polish forces; fear of further alienating western governments and creditors; fear of completely alienating the Church; and, most of all, the sheer scale of the popular movement he had to crush. It is characteristic of Polish communist politics that no policy, whether of repression or reform, is carried through consistently and comprehensively. The incompleteness of the terror, and the scale of the resistance, meant that there was still in Poland a range of opposition activity unmatched in the Soviet bloc. As a senior Hungarian Party officia. chillingly put it, Poland had not experienced the 'catharsis' which Hungary experienced in 1956. And this 'catharsis' was necessary before the regime could move on to the second state of 'normalisation'.

In this second stage Jaruzelski would need to do two things: to revive the Party and the economy. Both looked like miracles which he was unable to perform. Despite his Bonapartist rhetoric, and the hopes of some western governments, it became clear in the second half of 1982 that he was earnestly endeavouring to rebuild the strength of the Party. But the Party was still shattered, like Humpty Dumpty after his fall. Solidarity had blown a hole the size of Poland through its claim to represent the working class. Almost no one in Poland believed the alibi claim that KOR had hijacked the mass movement. Faced with such a massive popular vote of no-confidence, the Party continued to lose members as fast as it had lost confidence in itself.[28] After a year of martial law the rump Party of the apparatus still seemed incapable of resuming its 'leading role', as that was interpreted in the Soviet Union or East Germany.

There had, however, been no fundamental, structural change in the political system, which would justify giving it a new name. It was rather that the military and security forces had advanced into the front line of the politbureaucratic dictatorship, to defend the interests of the ruling class and the Soviet Union. Such a relatively more prominent role for the military and security apparatuses had been seen before in Poland, in the immediate post-war period. Indeed in a sense the regime had returned to its beginnings, when the communist Party was a tiny clique 'sitting on bayonets'. Even if this relegation of the Party proved to be of long duration, it was not easy to see how this would serve the interests of the majority of Poles, or of the West. On the contrary, a success for the Polish military could set a dangerous precedent within the Soviet empire.[29] It could strengthen the already strong hand of the military in Moscow, and enhance the attractions of militarisation to the rulers of countries like Romania and East Germany which are already highly militarised.*

*'The Soviet Union has acquired two new states,' said a martial law joke. 'Afghanistan and the state of war.'

The key to this success or failure was the economy, which was also the nub of Jaruzelski's claim to be a Cromwellian or Bonapartist General. Martial law, his ambassadors explained, was an 'umbrella', a protective carapace, under which essential economic reforms would be pushed through. When martial law was 'suspended' in December 1982 these claims had worn thin. The military had not cut through the encrusted layers of political bureaucracy. Instead, the military commissars had temporarily added another layer. 'Bayonets cannot dig coal,' Solidarity spokesmen had observed in the first weeks of martial law. In the event, coal was about the only thing which the bayonets could dig. Coal production increased by nearly 26 million tonnes in 1982, almost doubling coal exports to the West, as the miners (initially under military discipline) worked well-rewarded but compulsory Saturdays. But overall industrial production fell by a further 2 per cent compared with 1981.[30] Try as they might, official propagandists could not credibly blame this on Solidarity. In fact, by crushing Solidarity they had destroyed the political and psychological incentives for improved productivity which Solidarity would have built into any negotiated programme for economic reform. No longer did the workers have any sense of working for themselves; gone was the *élan* of the civil crusade for national regeneration; and in its place, in most factories, sullen passive resistance.

The Jaruzelski regime, moreover, had neither the material incentives to compensate for this loss, nor the resources of physical coercion to compel increased production in despite of it: neither sufficient carrots nor big enough sticks. Although they had used the first shock of the 'war' to force through food price increases of up to 300 per cent, at the end of 1982 there was still far too much money chasing far too few goods. The first visible result of a timid decentralisation was that factory managers and local political bosses used their increased powers of discretion to bribe reluctant workers with large paper wage rises—exactly as they had done in the 1970s! This had little positive effect on productivity, since there was almost nothing the workers could buy with the extra money, but sustained the appalling excess of demand over supply—an 'inflationary overhang' still estimated at zł. 500–600 billion. According to official figures, total food consumption fell by one-sixth from the desperately low level of 1981.[31]

So long as Poland's Soviet bloc allies, *or the West,* did not give Jaruzelski the means to compensate the workers for the loss of freedom, the chances of a successful 'normalisation' à la Kádár were almost nil. Looking back at the main east European crises of the last thirty years, Jacques Rupnik points to a paradoxical conclusion: on the one hand the Russians proved each time more skilful at concealing their intervention—the Red Army alone in Hungary in 1956, a collective action by the Warsaw Pact in Czechoslovakia in 1968, Polish forces in Poland in 1981—yet on the other hand the prospects of 'normalisation' have diminished in each successive case.[32] After a year of martial law in Poland the most likely short term future seemed to be an uneasy stalemate between 'the society' and 'the power'; until the next popular revolt.

That Poland could not be 'normalised'—i.e. returned to abnormality—is a lasting achievement of the Polish revolution. The suggestion that Poland in 1983 was in a *better* condition than Hungary would probably strike most western readers as absurd. Yet it is a suggestion made to me by critical intellectuals in Budapest. Of course Hungary is more prosperous, they said. Of course there is a mood of profound depression in Poland. More than a thousand Solidarity activists chose to emigrate to the West when released from internment, seeing no future for themselves in Poland. Many more retreated into 'inner emigration', refusing any active co-operation with the regime and nourishing their spiritual resistance on the unofficial publications which were still printed and read on a scale incomparably larger than before August 1980. Others sought escape in mysticism or spiritualism—the chiliasm of despair which so often follows 'failed' revolutions.

None the less, said my Hungarian friends, Poland was in a better condition than Hungary. It was in a better condition because millions of Poles, and, in particular, a whole generation of educated younger workers, had sixteen months' direct experience of democracy. Of what other communist country could that be said? It was in a better condition because for sixteen months the Poles had put an end to the lies and the double life on which every Soviet system is built. In Poland, every schoolchild knew that he or she was born with certain inalienable human rights, which were now denied. Even schoolchildren, moreover, were joining conspiratorial 'Social Resistance Circles' which disseminated information and helped the victims of martial law. In many enterprises, Solidarity's 'Clandestine Factory Commissions' continued to collect regular union dues, and paid out benefits to the sick and those sacked for participating in strikes or demonstrations. In the 'Dolmel' factory (above, p. 288), 1,600 workers on the first shift alone reportedly signed a petition for the release of Piotr Bednarz, their Solidarity Chairman. Farmers sent gifts of food to the families of interned workers; workers sent them underground publications in return. Here was not merely the traditional Polish theatre of defiance—the hymn-singing crowd round the cross of flowers in Victory Square, the Red Star above the gate of Huta Warszawa painted black in the night, the village bonfires lit on the anniversary of the Gdańsk Agreement. Here was a society which continued to *organise itself*, in independent networks of solidarity, not simply in opposition to, but in contempt of, the failed Party-state.

In Hungary, my friends explained, 'civil society' had been destroyed after 1956, and they were only just beginning, with painful slowness, to reconstruct it. But in Poland the consciousness of belonging to something called 'the society' was almost universal. This society possessed its own clearly articulated set of values, goals and symbols—they were even written down in a Programme. What had been the vision of a tiny minority of so-called 'dissidents' in December 1979 had become a *mass consciousness* by December 1981. And of course, my Hungarian friends laughingly concluded, as good Marxists we know that consciousness (*Bewusstsein*) will ultimately determine being (*Sein*).

One of the best Polish poets from the 'New Wave' of the 1970s sums up the most paradoxical result of this most paradoxical of revolutions:

> Poland, as it is today, is an occupied country—but a country of free people, who know exactly what they want, and who will not give up their struggle. It is a country in which paradoxically the only real dissidents—those who 'sit apart' (*dis sedere*) and still try to breathe under water, who behave abnormally and form a minority—are the communist rulers.[33]

11. Under Western Eyes

> Things and actions are what they are, and the consequences of them will be what they will be: why then should we desire to be deceived?
>
> Bishop Joseph Butler, *Fifteen Sermons*

Once upon a time there was Europe. Europe stretched from the Atlantic to the Urals. It included Budapest, Prague and Petersburg as well as Paris and Madrid. No account of European culture could ignore the voices of Kant from Königsberg, or Tolstoy from Yasnaya Polyana. The word 'revolution' was introduced to European discourse by Copernicus from Toruń. Before the First World War an Englishman or American of means and spirit could personally discover the whole of this heritage, passing freely, without passport, let or hindrance, from Barcelona to Kraków, or from Naples to Aberdeen.

Geographically, Poland lies at the heart of this old Europe. On Warsaw's Parade Square, beneath the Stalinist Palace of Culture, there stands a modest signpost giving the distances to other European capitals: Berlin, 518 km, London, 1,444 km, Brussels, 1,122, Moscow, 1,122. Warsaw is as close to Brussels as it is to Moscow. Historically and culturally the Poles have at least as strong a claim to belong to any European Community as the British. 'In temperament, in feeling, in mind, and even in unreason, they are western',[1] wrote the great Polish English author Joseph Conrad, and called his dissection of the Russian soul *Under Western Eyes*.

Of course, Conrad dramatically oversimplified. Poland is one of three great European nations whose histories turn on the axis East-West, and whose cultures display this constant tension. The other two are its neighbours, Germany and Russia. It would require many volumes to discuss what has been 'eastern' and what 'western' in

Poland at different times. For example, in *political* culture the egalitarian, tolerant Noble Democracy of the Renaissance places Poland somewhere to the west of France. The costumes and manners of this period, however, betray a strong influence from the East. Yet from the time of Copernicus to the time of Conrad, any definition of Europe which excluded Poland would have been dismissed as nonsense.

Since the Second World War this nonsense has been enthroned. This our continent, our common culture, has been split down the middle. Hitler began the work of destruction, bringing Soviet and American soldiers to that fateful meeting on the Elbe. Stalin, by attempting to impose a totalitarian regime on the lands he had liberated, cemented the division. First the wartime compliance of Britain and America with Stalin's ambitions, then Britain's and America's post-war resistance to them, contributed to the division of old Europe.

For a decade after 1945 the hope of one united Europe, born from the experience of two world wars, was still cherished in London as well as Warsaw, in Vienna as in Prague. Then the vision of Europe gradually faded into the reality of a west European economic community. Today, when the British say 'Europe' they mean the EEC, and think, probably with irritation, of Brussels glasshouses full of bureaucrats throwing stones. When they say 'Germany' they mean West Germany; 'Berlin', West Berlin. The world is divided into 'East' and 'West', and few pause to contemplate the absurd dispensation by which Weimar is in the 'East' but Nürnberg in the 'West', Ankara in the 'West' but Kraków in the 'East'. Those diverse branches of the European family of nations who live behind the 'Iron Curtain' are covered in a thick grey fog. Occasionally, they are remembered as poor cousins are remembered. Generally, they are forgotten as poor cousins are forgotten. Siberia begins at Checkpoint Charlie.

Now and then east Europeans break through the fog, individually, like Solzhenitsyn, or collectively, like the Hungarians in 1956 or the Czechs and Slovaks in 1968. The 'West' reacts with astonishment; with a complicated mixture of admiration and embarrassment; with indignation, when the Soviet Union pulls the fog back into place again. Then we forget.

In August 1980 the first stage of this pattern was repeated on a vast scale. The astonishment of the West knew no bounds. As television commentators tied their tongues round a mysterious Walaser, *ein gewisse Valeska, l'étonnant Valise,* this Wałęsa, western viewers tried to adjust their mental sets to accommodate Solidarity into the categories of 'East-West', 'socialism' v. 'capitalism', Left and Right.

The *range* of support for Solidarity was unique. No other movement in the world was supported by President Reagan *and* Mr Carillo, Mr Berlinguer and the Pope, Mrs Thatcher and Tony Benn, peace campaigners and NATO spokesmen, Christians and communists, conservatives, liberals and socialists. Yet this almost unanimous chorus of admiration was itself a source of deep embarrassment for many. How shaming for West German socialist peace campaigners to find themselves on the same side as President Reagan! How troublesome for an Italian Christian Democrat to support the same people as the Communists! How difficult for a Conservative to share a common platform with a trades unionist!

Much time was therefore spent in distinguishing *our* kind of support from *their* kind of support: *our* support, said the European socialist, has nothing in common with the 'hypocrisy' of Mr Reagan—*our* support, said the Reagan adviser, must not be confused with the fraudulent pretence of Mr Berlinguer. The Right, without a good word for trades unions at home, celebrated the Poles' heroic struggle against the tyranny of 'socialism'; the Left, the workers' heroic struggle for a 'true' socialism. Each side projected its own fantasies on to that far-away country about which so little was known.

I have tried to show that what happened in Poland does not fit into any of these pre-formed western moulds, and to suggest that rather than manipulating the Polish revolution until it fits into our existing categories, we might do better to adjust our categories until they fit the Polish revolution. To discuss the development of western reactions to Solidarity would require another book, since they varied not only with ideology but also very much with nationality. A German (on the Left or the Right), with a heavy legacy of guilt towards Poland, naturally reacted differently from a Frenchman (on Left or Right), conscious of the whole nineteenth-century tradition of emotional and intellectual identification with Poland, or an Englishman (on Left or Right), in whom the emotional identification of the Second World War mingled with some guilt about 'Yalta'. But I can at least point to a few significant examples of ideological embarrassment.

Embarrassment on the Left

'For the free world, Poland should be what Spain was in 1936', Barbara Toruńczyk, a Polish intellectual from the 'class of '68', wrote in January 1982. But Poland did not become Spain for the western Left. No British poet felt moved to write about Poland as Auden felt moved to write about Spain: 'I am your choice, your decision: yes, I am Spain.' While hundreds of thousands demonstrated against nuclear weapons, only hundreds—or at most a few thousand—demonstrated for Solidarity. To be sure, the possibilities of direct action were rather more limited, or at least, different and less romantic. Solidarity had no International Brigades for a latterday Orwell to join, no ambulances for a foreign poet to drive. But there were desperately-needed medical supply vans to drive, and duplicators rather than rifles to carry. As Jiří Pelikan has written:

> ... one cannot escape the strange feeling that it is a handicap for this country [Poland] to be in Europe. If such a profound revolutionary transformation had taken place under such an external threat in a nation in the Americas, Africa or Asia, the western Left would not merely have adopted resolutions of solidarity; it would have organised street demonstrations, marches, sit-ins or even strikes ...[3]

But no; instead, the outstanding British writer about Poland from the Left begins his account of *The Polish August* with the remarkable profession that 'Solidarity has been infinitely distressing to many left-wingers in the West. My hope is that this book, by explaining a little, will reduce that distress.'[4]

One cause of this distress was undoubtedly the bewildering attachment of Polish workers to that bastion of Reaction and staunch ally of the ruling bourgeoisie, the Roman Catholic Church. They ordered things better in Spain. Andrzej Wajda reports the response of the Spanish film director Buñuel on seeing Wałęsa with a rosary ... 'How can a workers' leader be religious? This is a contradiction in itself.'[5] At western 'Solidarity with Solidarity' meetings the leftist speaker deploring the role of the Church was a drearily familiar sight. With curious logic, the Church was denounced both for encouraging 'right-wing, nationalist' tendencies in Solidarity, and for pressing it (through Wałęsa's advisers) to compromise with the socialist state. The Church was also blamed for the small representation of women in the Solidarity leadership. At the same time socialist commentators endeavoured to play down or explain away the role of the Church. '... the main inspiration for Solidarity came not from the church,' Denis MacShane wrote in the *New Socialist*, 'but from the socialist lay intellectuals associated with KOR ...'[6]

The tributes paid by those 'lay Left' (*lewica laicka*) intellectuals to the Church are conveniently forgotten. In fact, the western Left spent much of its time tilting at a cardboard stereotype from half a century ago. The Polish Church, in this stereotype, was nationalist, reactionary, anti-socialist, anti-feminist, anti-Semitic. As we have seen, this stereotype has little to do with the Church of Wyszyński and Wojtyła in the 1970s, with the Pope's great speech in Auschwitz, with the ethics of open Catholicism expounded by Tischner, with the work of the younger clergy for democracy and workers' rights. It is a Polish theologian who places the concept of 'exploitation' at the centre of his social thought, and a Polish Pope who uses the Marxist concept of 'alienation' in his encyclical *Redemptor Hominis*.[7] True, the workers in the Lenin Shipyard ignored Wyszyński's appeal to return to work, but they hastened to print the Episcopate's extraordinary litany of human rights two days later (see above, pp. 65–6).

This Church which, for a decade, had spoken with growing force and clarity of God-given, inalienable human and civil rights, was, without doubt, a formative influence on the consciousness of the masses. This Church which, for centuries, had bound the Faith to the cause of national independence, in Marian mysteries that seem alien even to Catholics in more fortunate countries, this *un*changing Church was, without doubt, a source of the workers' strength, self-restraint and dignity. Wałęsa once told a group of sceptical students why he always wore the Black Madonna on his lapel. In one of his many police interrogations, he said, he had been at the end of his tether, almost crushed. In desperation he had prayed to the Black Madonna. Suddenly he had been given the strength to resist any interrogation. One can see why enlightened western socialists would be embarrassed by this simple report of the efficacy of prayer.

'Nationalism' in Solidarity was the second source of unease on the Left. What does this pejorative label mean? If it means, following George Orwell's definition in his 'Notes on Nationalism', an attitude of intolerance, a form of negative discrimination, then it is true that an intolerant 'nationalism'—speaking the language of the pre-war National Democrats—did resurface in several Solidarity regions in the last months of 1981. The tendency of this marginal nationalism was to say that, for example, a Jew or socialist is not a Pole. Such an attitude was clearly rejected by the Church. Inside Solidarity its effect was divisive, but it never found its way into the statements or policies of the National Commission (whereas the anti-Semitism of the communist Grunwald league did find its way into the official media, before and after 13 December).

If, however, 'nationalism' means love of country, and a desire to see that country free from foreign domination, then it cannot be denied that the whole of Solidarity was rabidly 'nationalist'. But what is wrong with a people's striving for national independence and full sovereign statehood? Is it not partly on the basis of national sovereignty that western peace campaigners reject the imperialist imposition of American nuclear missiles on British and West German soil? Is it not precisely this striving which the left enthusiastically supports in Africa, Asia and the Americas? How can 'nationalism' be a Good Thing there but a Bad Thing here? The problem with the Poles' patriotism would seem to be the occupying power with which it conflicts.

At the root of these double standards on the Left is the residual myth of the Russian Revolution. Of course we have come a long way from that automatic equation of 'socialism' with 'the Soviet Union' which still prevailed at the time of the Spanish Civil War. No one could write today, as Orwell wrote in 1945, 'among the intelligentsia, it hardly needs saying that the dominant form of nationalism is Communism . . .'(A Communist being 'one who looks upon the USSR as his Fatherland').[8] Yet there is still, in Ferdinand Mount's phrase, an 'asymmetry of indulgence' towards the Soviet Union as compared with other dictatorships. The historical statement 'more people were killed in the USSR during the 1930s than in Hitler's holocaust' still seems to belong for the Left in the category which Orwell called 'intolerable facts'. There is still apparently a gut feeling that somehow, in the last analysis, life is better over there. The British steelworkers' leader, Mr Bill Sirs, memorably remarked in a BBC interview at the time of the August 1980 strike: 'They [The Polish workers] are in a much better position than we are—we have dictators over us'![9] There is still, in many who would describe themselves as democratic socialists, an emotionally rooted conviction that the road to democratic socialism starts from the October Revolution. Socialism is the Russian Revolution plus the vital missing ingredients; democratic socialism is the Russian revolution plus political democracy; whatever has happened in the name of socialism, we shall start from there.

If you wish to preserve this conviction then the one thing you must not do is to go to Poland with an open mind. Seen from Poland, the continuity from Tsarist to Soviet Russia seems undeniable. Poland is the country where Soviet and Nazi security forces worked together, deporting and murdering. Here, Soviet socialism was not only imposed by force (where has it *not* been imposed by force?), but after thirty-seven years it had to be reimposed by force: by naked military and police power. With Czechoslovakia in 1968 it could at least be argued that the impulses for change came from within the communist Party, but no amount of contortion could convincingly present the Polish Party as the vanguard of the Polish revolution. Here, a Leninist Party once again proved as impossible to combine with pluralistic democracy as ice with steam. Here, in what was arguably the first authentic workers' revolution in history (for the October Revolution was not led by workers, but by the Bolsheviks in the name of the working class), a working class proclaimed for all the world to hear that the Party represented no one but the communist ruling class and the Soviet Union. The very word 'socialism' was so poisoned for the Solidarity activists by the experience of living under it, that they eliminated it altogether from their Programme. Poland showed that a centrally planned economy can perform just as well as capitalism, when it comes to creating a depression. In Poland, socialism re-produced unemployment.*

*'Rabbi, can one build socialism in one country?' 'Yes, my son, but one must live in another.'

'I am your choice, your decision: yes, I am Poland.' The Polish revolution did pose choices for western Leftists, but the choices were far more complicated than those posed by the Spanish Civil War. It is therefore not surprising that many preferred not to look too closely. Only those who, while still considering themselves 'on the Left', had already abandoned any illusions about the Russian Revolution—that is, who appreciated that a genuinely democratic socialism (which nowhere exists) has as little to do with communism (Soviet socialism) as it has with capitalism—were able to support and learn from Solidarity from the start, without embarrassment.

There were a few for whom the Polish revolution was a breaking point. In a resolution passed shortly after the imposition of martial law the PCI not only condemned the coup but also interpreted it as a signal that the 'phase of socialist development (which began with the October Revolution) has exhausted its driving force...' Italy's electors should give the PCI a mandate to seek a 'Third Road' to truly democratic communism. However, Enrico Berlinguer hastened to add that 'In saying that the historical phase opened by the October Revolution in Russia is ended, we are not at all dismissing the value of achievements realised in that phase.'[10]

Susan Sontag shocked a star-studded meeting of the New York Left by taking General Jaruzelski's demasking of communism as an occasion for self-criticism: why, she asked, had the western Left deluded itself for so long about the realities of life in eastern Europe?

> Imagine, if you will, someone who read only *Reader's Digest* between 1950 and 1970, and someone who in the same period read only *The Nation* or the *New Statesman*. Which reader would have been better informed about the realities of Communism? The answer, I think, should give us pause. Can it be that our enemies were right?[11]

Ouch! As the resulting cries and whimpers confirmed, she hit a nerve. Particularly in America, the Left is still crippled by what Jean-François Revel has labelled 'the fear of anti-Communism'. Rather than stand up and say 'Yes, I am an *anti-communist socialist*', and risk being embraced by the Right, they fled either into criticism of Solidarity, which was easier than self-criticism, or into criticism of the Right's support for Solidarity ('What about El Salvador?'). This kind of escape was easiest of all.

Embarrassment on the Right

The spectacle of the Right supporting a workers' revolution is as singular as the spectacle of the Left supporting a devout Catholic against a socialist state. Since the French revolution gave us the labels 'Left' and 'Right', one defining feature of the Right has been opposition to revolution: starting with Edmund Burke. Trades union and workers' rights are not traditionally top priorities of the Right. When the Right has supported revolutions* they have been revolutions in other countries, supported for pressing reasons of national self-interest. In 1917, Imperial Germany dispatched Lenin in a sealed train to the Finland Station because the Bolsheviks might take Russia out of the war. Lenin's German counterparts were imprisoned or murdered.

Did the Reagan administration's vocal support for Solidarity reflect the same two-faced logic? Inasmuch as that administration propped up dictatorships in Central America which brutally deny the very rights for which Solidarity was fighting, the answer must be unequivocally 'yes'. In its attitude to Central America and Central Europe the Reagan administration displayed flagrant double standards. This observation belongs in any critique of the Reagan administration's policy towards Central America. Seen from an El Salvadorian prison it must look as if Solidarity just happened to be in the right place: in the backyard of *that* nuclear superpower rather than *this* nuclear superpower.

Yet the support of Reagan's America (and not only Reagan's) for Solidarity cannot simply be reduced to the Chinese logic of superpower confrontation: Solidarity weakens the Soviet empire, therefore we support Solidarity—the enemy of my enemy is my friend.

Neither was the attitude of the American or British Right to independent trades unions in Poland necessarily incompatible with their attitude to independent trades unions in Britain or America.

At the risk of stating the obvious, we must repeat that most of

*Apart from the special case of 'revolutions of the Right' like Nazism.

the Polish workers' demands in August 1980 would make no sense in an American or British context *because they have already been achieved here,* albeit imperfectly. Solidarity was struggling in the first place for certain basic rights which citizens and trades unions in the West already enjoy. The majority of strikes in the West are for more pay. A small minority of Solidarity strikes were for more pay. At times the actions of unionists here and there were not merely different but diametrically opposed. Polish printworkers struck in order to increase the press's independence from state censorship; British printworkers struck in order to censor an independent press.[12] At times the actions of unions here and there were similar. British unionists struck in solidarity with Health Service workers in June 1982. To say that 'unions there were not like unions here' is therefore not an escape clause or even a value judgment, but a statement of fact. Actions which had the same form—e.g. a printworkers' strike—could have very different content, and it was quite consistent to support one while opposing the other. Of course it would have been inconsistent to support the right of independent trades unions to exist in Poland while opposing it in Britain or America, but the existence of independent trades unions in Britain or America was not in question.

Solidarity was struggling for certain basic values which Left and Right both professedly supported, values for which the British and American revolutions also fought: individual freedom, democratic government, the rule of law. An American administration betrays these values if it fails to support those who fight for them in Central America, not when it supports those who fight for them in Central Europe. The 'East-West' confrontation is not merely an imperial argument between two rival nuclear superpowers; it is also an argument between the American and the Russian revolutions. There is a sense in which the Polish revolution was an extension of the American revolution by other means. In this sense, President Reagan could justifiably support it on grounds of principle as well as policy.

In practice, however, the Reagan administration's response to the Polish crisis (apart from its repeated warnings against Soviet intervention) was embarrassed, confused and half-hearted in the crucial field of economic policy. The Right was embarrassed neither by Solidarity's link with the Church nor by its patriotism, but distinctly by its socialist elements. As we have seen, there were a number of socialist values which the younger generation of Poles had internalised and now turned against the state which preached them. Thus the Programme had a strong egalitarian thrust; it was unequivocally in favour of the welfare state; a majority of Solidarity members opposed the privatisation of heavy industry. The popularity of the campaign for workers' control in Polish industry was enough to give many western conservatives pause.

A larger problem for the Right was exemplified, to the point of caricature, by a few of Reagan's foreign policy advisers. They brought into office a wonderfully simple, Manichean view of the world. World politics for them was a struggle between the forces of good, represented by American democracy, and the forces of evil, embodied in Soviet communism. Soviet communism was at once a uniquely malignant ideology and merely a mask for the unchanging ambitions of Russian imperialism. This tyrannous empire could no more change its political system than the leopard its spots. It could only be forced to retreat and crumble under the pressure of superior western economies converted into superior armaments.

Solidarity did not fit into this Manichean frame. Its very existence suggested the possibility of fundamental, peaceful change from within the Soviet system: change at the periphery, it is true, but had not empires begun to change from the periphery in the past? Every day that the Soviets did not invade brought more encouragement for the opposition to American Cruise and Pershing II missiles in western Europe. Moreover, while Solidarity existed, the case for sustaining economic ties with Poland at least was embarrassingly strong.

There were therefore a few Reagan advisers who actually said, in so many words, that it would be better for America—and therefore for the 'free world'—if the Soviet Union would be forced to invade Poland. West European peace movements would be confounded. Civil war in Poland did not look too high a price to pay for accelerating the collapse of the Soviet empire—particularly if you were sitting in Washington. No doubt it was always a minority who argued the confrontation line through to this logical conclusion. But it would only be a slight exaggeration to say that the Reagan administration first produced a Polish policy after 13 December 1981.

Poland under martial law fitted much more easily into the Manichean picture. Though Soviet tanks were not actually on the streets of Warsaw, the posters proclaiming martial law were found to have been printed in the Soviet Union. Soviet political co-responsibility for the coup was really indisputable. Now the Reagan administration launched a huge television spectacular with a title taken from Solidarity's theme-song. Yet there was a subtle difference in the American version of that title. '*Żeby Polska . . .*'. was, when I first heard it in the Teatr Wielki in Warsaw in November 1980, a song about what the Poles were doing for themselves. We are retaking control of our own lives, it said, *so that* Poland *shall* be Poland. It breathed purposeful action. The American propaganda translation was 'Let Poland be Poland!' It thus became a complaint (or an order) *addressed to Moscow*. So also with the whole policy.

With relief the administration turned back to full-blooded advocacy of economic war against both Poland and the Soviet Union. Poland was now used as a stick with which to beat European governments of the centre who still clung to détente, and specifically to attack the Siberian gas pipeline deal concluded between west European contractors and the Soviet Union. The main brunt of this attack was borne by Chancellor Helmut Schmidt's social-liberal coalition government in Bonn. The Polish crisis now became a crisis of the western alliance.

Embarrassment in the Centre: Solidarity and Ostpolitik

On Sunday 13 December 1981, while the best of the Polish intelligentsia were being arrested and herded into internment camps, West and East German writers met in an unprecedented encounter in East Berlin. The declared purpose of the meeting was to talk about peace: a subject, one might think, not unaffected by the state of war declared just 60 kilometres to the east. West German television was allowed to film the whole session, and the discussion was therefore broadcast, uncensored, to most of East Germany. The West German guests were given a unique opportunity to express their disgust at what was happening in Poland. This, with a couple of exceptions, they signally failed to do.

It was left to the dissident East German writer Stefan Heym to give the lie to these ghostly proceedings. 'We are talking here about the preservation of peace,' he exclaimed, 'and completely ignoring the fact that a few kilometres away the fuse is already burning.' And again, to general (West and East) German embarrassment, 'Once before a world war began over Poland.'

On the same black Sunday the West German Chancellor, Helmut Schmidt, and the East German Party leader, Erich Honecker, concluded their three-day summit meeting with a cordial breakfast *à deux* in an East German government guest-house near East Berlin and a trip to the beautiful cathedral town of Gustrow. They were photographed jovially throwing snowballs from the balcony of the Town Hall, slapping each other on the back, and saluting—yes, saluting—each other goodbye at the railway station. In Bonn and East Berlin one was told the two leaders developed a 'special relationship'. Asked for his first reaction to the military takeover in Poland, Chancellor Schmidt said: 'Herr Honecker is as dismayed as I am, that this was necessary . . .'[13]

Though a few days later he spoke to the Bundestag in a very different tone, declaring that he stood 'entirely on the side of the Polish workers', the reaction of his government was none the less as cautious as the protests of German intellectuals were muted. They declined to join the Americans in denouncing the Soviet Union as the main author of the coup, or in blanket economic sanctions.

Over the next month West Germany was summarily tried in the world's press. Germany's criminal record—accessory to the fact of murder by Russia in three cases, mass murderer itself only forty years ago—was recalled in the columns of *Le Monde*. In the *New York Times* the defendant was found guilty of cravenness towards Moscow and disloyalty to the western alliance, from motives of base national and material self-interest.

West German publicists responded with long articles about 'how Poland was sold' by Britain and America at Yalta, and furious denunciations of the Reagan administration's double standards. For Günter Grass, American policy in Central America was the measure of Soviet evil: 'I believe . . .' (he told a West Berlin magazine) 'that Poland is entirely comparable with Nicaragua and other states in Central America, with what the United States is trying to do there and has often enough done.'[14]

Both sides cast dark and largely unfounded aspersions on the other's motives. These bitter polemics revealed once again how deep the historical resentments and misunderstandings between nations still were, in the western as well as in the eastern alliance.

To understand the West German response to Solidarity and the 'war' which crushed it, one must first understand the enormous investment which a whole generation of liberal and social democratic Germans had made in *Ostpolitik* (a term which I use to describe the version of détente initiated by the Brandt-Scheel social-liberal government with the German-Soviet treaty in 1970, and carried on by the Schmidt-Genscher government).[15] This investment was not merely economic, political and diplomatic; it was a profound intellectual and emotional investment as well.

Of course it would be naïve to ignore the material and national interests which were at stake. Trade with the East—Osthandel—was very important to West Germany's economy. By 1980 some 6.5 per cent of its exports went to Comecon countries. To put it another way, trade with eastern Europe was worth about $200 per West German head per year. Moreover, this economy needed new secure sources of energy—for instance, Siberian gas. Secondly, the interests of the 17–20 million* German hostages inside the Soviet bloc must figure large in the thinking of any West German government. The social-liberal coalition believed, with good reason, that a decade of *Ostpolitik* had brought the Germans in East and West closer together and made life in many small ways more tolerable (and more 'western') for the people of East Germany. Thirdly, West Germany had gained a much greater room for manoeuvre in international affairs. In 1969 its hands were still tied by the 'Hallstein doctrine' (according to which West Germany would not recognise any state which recognised East Germany) and by an almost day-to-day dependence on the United States for the defence of West Berlin. The four-power agreement on Berlin, and the West German treaties with the Soviet Union, Poland and East Germany, freed its hands. No one could plausibly describe West Germany in the 1980s as it used to be described in the 1960s—the 'economic giant, political dwarf'. These gains they would not lightly sacrifice.

But *Ostpolitik* was much more than the sum of these economic,

*Including the Germans in Poland, Romania and the Soviet Union.

national and state interests. The generation of Brandt and Schmidt had a dream. They saw a world where the Soviet Union was made to feel secure enough to relax its stranglehold on eastern Europe; where western economic support strengthened the hand of those east European communists who anyway wished to liberalise their regimes; where, slowly, slowly, a thaw would set in across Europe from Berlin to the Urals, and the iron and barbed-wire division of the post-war settlement would be replaced by normal frontiers between sovereign states; a world where, finally, Hitler's work might be undone.

It was a noble dream, and one which liberal German intellectuals like Heinrich Böll helped Willy Brandt to pursue against wild charges of 'treachery' from the German Right. Brandt falling to his knees before the monument to the dead of the Warsaw ghetto was a moment of moral greatness, comparable with that extraordinary letter of the Polish to the German bishops in 1965 which concluded, 'We forgive you and ask for your forgiveness'. For them, one of the original aims of détente was to facilitate gradual peaceful political change inside the Soviet bloc. One of their mottoes was '*Wandel durch Annäherung*'—change through (East and West) coming close together.

German foreign policy has rarely been inspired by more noble motives. No other western government deployed its power with such vision and consistency in the service of the European idea.

Yet the results of this policy were, as so often in human affairs, not those anticipated by its makers—and nowhere more so than in Poland. What could justly be criticised in 1981 was not the motives of *Ostpolitik* but the path taken to achieve it, not the ends but the *means* of German-led incentive détente. The Polish revolution, above all, revealed that *Ostpolitik* was based on an inadequate model of the ways in which communist regimes can (or can not) change, and the ways in which the West can influence those changes. German-led incentive détente did profoundly affect developments in Poland, but it affected them in ways which the West neither predicted nor controlled.

For a start, West German recognition of the Oder-Neisse line effectively robbed the Polish communist authorities of the bogey of West German revanchism. Few people realised the extent to which the alleged German threat had been a source of popular support for the communist authorities. Gierek had to seek his legitimacy elsewhere.

The theory of giving him and other east European leaders large western credits was that they should use them to modernise and reform their economies. It was further believed that the reform and modernisation of a socialist centrally-planned economy would automatically bring desirable political changes. A generation of more sophisticated 'technocrats' (a buzz-word of the early 1970s) would demand more free exchange of information, consultation, power sharing, decentralisation of decision-making etc., in the interests of efficiency. Finally, it was suggested that an advanced industrial society could not be repressed by the same crude means as were used, for example, in Russia.

In practice these expectations were not fulfilled. Only in Hungary and East Germany did the communist rulers to some extent use western credits to modernise and reform their economies in a rational and controlled fashion. In Romania, Ceausescu used lavish western credits for three quite different purposes: first, as a *substitute* for badly needed economic reforms, secondly, to strengthen his highly repressive neo-Stalinist regime (while repaying the West with maverick statements on foreign policy), and, thirdly, to enrich his own extended family. Like Gierek, he used western money for a neo-Stalinist kind of investment in huge prestige heavy-industrial projects (Romania's oil refineries, Gierek's Huta Katowice) wholly unsuited to earning back hard currency on world markets in the late 1970s. We have seen how the credits were used in Poland. The misuse (and plain abuse) of these funds by Poland's corrupt and incompetent communist ruling class was controlled neither internally (for in a communist system who but the Party should control it?) nor externally, by Western creditors. The warnings of independent Polish economists were ignored. Instead of encouraging gradual evolutionary change, initiated and controlled from above, western credits—misused—brought Poland to an economic crisis which was an immediate cause of the revolution from below.

Both the western contacts and the advanced western technology which came through *Annäherung* facilitated that revolution, for a time. To take but one prominent example, Janusz Onyszkiewicz, Solidarity's National Press Spokesman from April to October 1981, spent three years as a mathematics lecturer at the University of Leeds. He told me that this was a seminal period in his political education. We have seen the importance of telecommunications for Solidarity.

Yet both Solzhenitsyn and Miłosz—the Russian and the Polish Nobel Prize-winners—had warned the West that technology is not an automatic ally of democracy. They observed that the advance of technology in the twentieth century has been a critical factor enabling small groups of ruthless men to impose their will on whole populations. It is a prerequisite for a totalitarian regime. The efficiency of repression in Poland after 13 December 1981 confirmed their fears. And much of the technology for General Jaruzelski's 'terrorism from above' not only came from the West but was paid for by the West. Truncheons, tear gas and percussion grenades came to the ZOMO courtesy of companies in West Germany and Japan. So did some of their vital communications equipment. The Interior Ministry's newest computers came from Siemens.[16] German and Soviet technology were once again combined for the persecution of the Poles. Was this what Willy Brandt envisaged when he signed the Warsaw treaty with Poland?

This brings us to a central dilemma of *Ostpolitik*. The pressure of the Cold War, it was argued, had brought nothing but repression and reaction in the Soviet bloc. If the West took the pressure off communist leaders, they could be encouraged to initiate controlled evolutionary change from above. In what direction should these evolutionary changes be? Presumably in the direction of respect for human and civil rights, individual freedom, the rule of law, pluralism, democratic government. However, changes in this direction will inevitably increase the pressure from below on any kind of dictatorship. One measure of how democratic a political system is, is precisely the degree of (preferably institutionalised) pressure from below on the people in power. In this case the original strategy of *Ostpolitik* contained an inherent contradiction. Its premise was that communist rulers would make desirable changes only when they were not under pressure. But the effect of the changes which presumably the West desired would be to increase the pressure on those rulers; pressure from outside would be replaced by pressure from below; and then, if the premise was correct, those rulers presumably would feel impelled to clamp down again.

The alternative was that the changes which the West facilitated would not be of the kind which would increase the pressure from below on communist rulers: that is, would not be in the direction of democracy, pluralism, the rule of law, individual freedom, etc. This was always the communist rulers 'ideal type' of détente. Ideally they wished to use western economic support to stabilise and strengthen their regimes, while intensified ideological struggle would immunise their populations against the dangers of western infection. While the West German government talked of *'Wandel durch Annäherung'* the East German government talked of *'Friedliche Koexistenz'*—peaceful coexistence. West German leaders looked forward to a gradual overcoming of the division of Europe through a 'convergence' of the eastern and western systems. East German leaders looked forward to a temporary territorial truce between two irreconcilable systems in Europe (pending the inevitable ultimate victory of socialism). Meanwhile, the battle for socialism would continue to be prosecuted with more conventional weapons in Africa, Asia and the Americas.

Advocates of *Ostpolitik* generally failed to distinguish clearly between these two ideal types of change. 'The East Germans have achieved more areas of free speech,' they would say, and in the next breath, 'East Germany has become more sure of itself, more self-confident.' But here are two different and tendentially opposed kinds of change. The subject of the first sentence is the people of East Germany; the subject of the second is the regime. The former development tends to destabilise, the latter to stabilise (as Tocqueville commented, revolutions tend to happen when an elite loses confidence in itself). Is the aim of *Ostpolitik* to help the *peoples* of eastern Europe to more human and civil rights, or the regimes to more security? Whom is *Ostpolitik* helping to do what?

In practice, some tendencies towards the first of these ideal types of change were visible in all the main beneficiaries of *Ostpolitik* except for Romania. When the regimes loosened the lid of oppression just a little, the pent-up frustrations and aspirations of the society began to bubble over. In East Germany, for example, this was characteristically expressed by more than 100,000 people formally applying for leave to emigrate in the first year after Erich Honecker signed the Helsinki Agreement. By the end of the decade, however, the sum total of changes was much closer to the second ideal type. East Germany, like Hungary, was a more modern, efficient, militarised dictatorship, a police welfare state, which, because its leaders felt more secure, was able and willing to grant its citizens slightly more freedoms (to read, to speak, to travel), so long as they did not presume to interfere in their own internal affairs.[17]

The Poles did so presume. Poland showed most dramatically the possible consequences of the first kind of change. It revealed not only the internal contradictions of the communist system but also the internal contradictions of détente. Poland in the late 1970s had been the prize exhibit of *Ostpolitik*. It is arguable that without détente there would have been no Solidarity. Of course it was not inevitable that the increased pressure from below would assume a revolutionary shape. When you have a thaw you do not always get a flood. But Aristotle could have told us that it is highly unlikely that a society can move from dictatorship to democracy in steady, small, peaceful steps. Spain after Franco is one of very few exceptions to the rule, which is no doubt why the Spanish example was so often quoted in Poland in 1980–1. Yet the original architects of *Ostpolitik* apparently hoped that a communist politbureaucratic dictatorship would move in that direction without pressure from outside or inside. A revolution from below was not dreamed of in their philosophy. Bonn was not prepared for the Polish revolution any more than Washington was. Solidarity was an embarrassment to the social-liberal government because it posed that Gretchen question 'whom do you think you are helping to do what?' in a way which demanded an immediate political answer.

In the first months of the revolution this was not a simple either/or choice. I will argue below that there was a way in which the West might have increased the slim chances of a peaceful compromise between the authorities and the society in Poland, while helping the revolution to remain peaceful and self-limiting. But the Bonn government did not seize the opportunity to use the economic power of the West as the original architects of *Ostpolitik* envisaged. Instead, it reacted with palpable confusion, for here (in a process which would have delighted Hegel), a policy had produced its opposite: the policy of reducing tensions (*Entspannungspolitik*) had produced tensions (*Spannungen*).

After 13 December 1981 there was no longer any room for ambiguity. Yet West German liberals and social democrats still did not give a clear answer to the question 'Whom do you think you are helping to do what?' When the Schmidt government was attacked for continuing to give political and economic credit to Jaruzelski they often replied with another (rhetorical) question. Who, they asked, is really thinking about the interests of the poor suffering Polish people? It is they who will be the victims of the sanctions. The only trouble with this argument was that the poor suffering Polish people showed embarrassing signs of *supporting* President Reagan's line. Naturally it was impossible to say with certainty what the majority of the Polish people wanted. But, as Neal Ascherson observed (in the *New Socialist*):

> The evidence of Polish views since the coup on sanctions is skimpy, even contradictory. But it is highly probable that the mass of the population would strongly approve of ferocious financial sanctions against the military government, even if it is ordinary working people who suffer from them.[18]

Moreover, on the symbolic date 3 May 1982 some of the most distinguished Polish intellectuals living abroad issued an 'Appeal to the Germans' which, after briefly recalling the German-Soviet alliance in the Second World War, asked for precisely those economic sanctions which Reagan was urging on his west European allies.[19] No one who knows the history of Solidarity could imagine that the signatories of this Appeal, who included Czesław Miłosz, Leszek Kołakowski and Mirosław Chojecki, were less representative of the Polish people than the man who came to Bonn in January 1982 to plead for more credits for the military regime—one Mieczysław F. Rakowski!

Yet the doyenne of West German liberal journalists, Countess Marion Dönhoff, was moved to write of her joy that 'Bonn is the only capital, in which the Poles seek help . . .'[20] The confusion into which *Ostpolitik* had fallen could not be more clearly expressed. Not 'the Poles' were seeking help but the regime, not the society but the authorities, not Wałęsa but Rakowski.

Another liberal defender of *Ostpolitik* argued that it was, above all, a *democratic* foreign policy, because it had the support of the majority of the West German population. This may be true, but it does not make a foreign policy democratic. Hitler's foreign policy also had the support of the majority of the German population (e.g. in 1936). There is scant evidence that in 1981 the majority of the American population was opposed to Reagan's policy in Central America. Most Russians probably support Soviet policy towards eastern Europe. What makes a foreign policy democratic is its respect for the wishes of the majority *in the country affected* as well. That is what was wrong with much of Reagan's policy towards Central America. That is what has been wrong with Soviet policy towards Central Europe since 1944. This elementary principle was almost lost in the German theology of détente.

So long as this confusion persisted, what had begun as a noble and, in the fullest sense, democratic foreign policy was turned into its opposite: a policy for the support of dictatorship.

A Missed Opportunity: Western Economic Policy

Economic collapse was a primary cause of the Polish revolution and of its failure. After August 1980, continued economic collapse made it impossible for Solidarity to satisfy its members as a trades union traditionally satisfies its members, by fighting for better pay and more jobs. It further eroded the always small chance of a stable compromise between Solidarity and the authorities, and destroyed what little remained of popular confidence in those authorities. I have argued that it contributed decisively to that radicalisation from below which is characteristic of Solidarity, and at the same time to the eventual weakening of popular resistance. Because of the immediate economic straits, both sides were demanding more of each other by early summer 1981. The authorities were asking Solidarity to sell an economic regime of dire austerity to society; Solidarity demanded a political and cultural price in return.

Of course the argument about the relationship between economics and politics in the Polish revolution is complicated. Even if the economy had begun to improve it is questionable if the radicalisation and fragmentation of Solidarity could have been controlled, given the pent-up bitterness, the dispersal of the Lie and the disappearance of fear. A revolutionary mass movement develops its own momentum. Moreover, it can be argued that the lack of a political agreement was the main cause of the continued economic collapse: the political failure caused the economic failure rather than vice versa. Certainly the primacy of politics is a characteristic feature of communist regimes. The communist ruling class puts its own monopoly of power before the prosperity of its subjects, political security before economic success. In Poland a part of the *apparat* from the outset, and the Jaruzelski leadership from late summer 1981, seem to have adopted a conscious—and effective—*'politique du pire'*, waging a triumphant war of economic attrition against their own people.

Yet it is undeniable that the economy was crippled by the burden of the soaring western debt; that the downward spiral of industrial production was caused as much by the shortage of inputs from the West as by strikes and declining productivity; and that, consequently, whatever the political climate, a rapid economic recovery would only have been possible with the active co-operation of the West.

This economic dependence created the only major opportunity western governments had for actively helping the Solidarity experiment to succeed. Obviously it was an opportunity fraught with difficulty and risk. The Polish economy needed new money to the tune of $4–6 billion in 1981 (of which $3 billion was simply to refinance existing loans), with further injections of $2–4 billion per year over the next four to five years, if it was to recover sufficiently not only to feed the Poles but also to start paying back the West from a current account surplus.[21] The sums needed, say $20 billion over five years, would thus have been on a Marshall Plan scale. Polish government ministers and economic planners said they would be prepared to accept economic—but not political—conditions on these new credits. However, as we have seen in the history of Solidarity, they used a very elastic definition of the 'political'. Moreover, it was not clear whether Poland's fraternal allies were prepared to accept even those conditions which the Polish leadership might accept.

Indeed, it is arguable that the Soviet Union, East Germany and Czechoslovakia were not interested in Poland's economic recovery *while Solidarity existed*. So long as economic misery accompanied the progress of Solidarity there was little danger of the East Germans, Czechs or Lithuanians trying to imitate it. The queues, the chaos, the disease! the propagandists could exclaim—such were the inevitable consequences of revolting against the beneficent socialist state! But if Solidarity was to lead Poland back to prosperity, if the Poles were to win meat as well as freedom, then the Polish experiment would begin to be really attractive for the neighbouring peoples, and a real danger for neighbouring regimes. Thus, if the western economic initiative succeeded in turning round the Polish economy, the risk of a direct Soviet intervention might actually have increased rather than diminished.

Against these difficulties and this risk must be put the magnitude of the opportunity. In fact the difficulties and the risk are the measure of the opportunity.

A carefully co-ordinated western plan of large-scale new credits and economic aid, offered without Reaganaut propaganda but with economic strings attached, through an international economic organisation like the OECD, in autumn–winter 1980–1, would have significantly increased the always small chances of a historic compromise between Solidarity and the communist authorities in Poland. This unsung Marshall Plan would not merely have made new credits to the Polish government conditional on a full disclosure of information to the West, and on economic reforms—decentralisation, accountability of individual enterprises, controls over managerial competence, etc. It would also have explored more direct possibilities of imposing 'conditionality'. For example, it might have aimed a programme directly at supplying the wants of *private* agriculture, in cash and, more important, in kind (agricultural machinery, fuel, fertilisers, building materials, etc.). This, combined with direct food aid channelled through the Church, would have had the effect of improving supplies to the urban markets and thus reducing what had become by summer 1981 an almost unbearable pressure from below on the leaders of Solidarity, and on the regime (remember the hunger march slogan: 'A hungry nation can eat its rulers!').[22] In the short term, this aid would have softened the blow of those austerity measures which Solidarity and government economists agreed were necessary. The West could have asked the Poles to draw up lists of those intermediate goods and spare parts which were most desperately needed, and then supplied them directly.[23] (What was called, in the elegant jargon of East–West trade, 'targeting at bottlenecks'.) And so on.

Thus economic means might have been used for desirable political ends.

Of course there was no guarantee that Solidarity and the government would manage to co-operate in drawing up the lists, or use the added room for manoeuvre to work towards a *modus vivendi*. If you removed the economic factors entirely from the equation, the balance was still against success. On the other hand there was clear evidence, clearer than ever before or since in any Soviet bloc country, that in this period both the regime and the people (represented by Solidarity) wished the West to provide this aid. Solidarity leaders and government representatives came, separately, to the West and said as much. While they disagreed about the conditions, the disagreement on the basic shape of the economic reform in, say, January 1981, was not insuperable. In January 1981 Solidarity had not adopted any conception of workers' self-government, let alone the radical conception which was the spearhead of their programme nine months later. The immanent dilemma of *Ostpolitik* —whom are you helping to do what?—was temporarily suspended.

Such a Marshall Plan launched on 1 January 1981 would therefore have been a historic gamble in the spirit of détente. The phrase 'a historic gamble' comes from a fine leader in *The Times* urging precisely this course of action. But it is dated 23 September 1981. Although *The Times, Le Monde* and other major west European newspapers had argued the case for aid to Warsaw already in autumn 1980, the publicistic chorus for the historic gamble only came into full voice a year later . . . a year too late. Minerva's owl flew at dusk.

The main reasons why the West did not launch such a package are to be found not in Poland or the Soviet Union but in the West itself. They tell us not a little about our own systems. So far as governments are concerned, Poland's great misfortune was that Solidarity came at the end of a US administration. For an American initiative Solidarity came at just the wrong time. If it had come a year earlier, Carter and Brzezinski would surely have responded with a policy linking further credits to human rights. But when the Polish government came asking for $3 billion in November 1980 (and simultaneously some $5 billion from other governments) the Carter administration only had a few more weeks in office. If it had come a year later Reagan might just have had a foreign policy. As it was, the window of opportunity opened in the paralysing transition period, and by the time the Reagan administration had got over its initial posturings and confusions, if not over its ideological embarrassment, the window was already closing again.

West Germany was the obvious leader for any west European initiative, and its failure to take that lead is most difficult to explain. In part, it was no doubt a result of the unresolved contradictions outlined above. In part it was fear of the effects on East Germany. But the decisive reasons for the Schmidt government's failure to follow through the original logic of *Ostpolitik* are probably those common to all the capitalist democracies. First, every western country was in the grip of an economic recession which was already squeezing budgets hard. How could they justify giving Poland such a high priority? Furthermore, it would have to be a silent Marshall Plan, for the Soviet Union and Poland would certainly not stand for much propaganda trumpeting, least of all from West Germany. This meant there was little domestic political credit to be gained by such expenditure. Second, there was the problem of the banks.

Roughly half the Polish hard currency debt was made up of private bank loans, of which roughly half were guaranteed by western governments, and half unsecured. The banks had been encouraged by government guarantees to pitch into eastern Europe, but they themselves did not share the political motives. Indeed most bankers were at once cynical and stunningly naïve about the political systems with which they were dealing. The twentieth-century experience that, in the long-run, pluralistic democratic systems are always more efficient and competitive than totalitarian dictatorships passed them by. The argument, therefore, that the only realistic hope of getting their money back was to facilitate the introduction of a more open, pluralistic, system in Poland carried no weight with them. Instead, many of them greeted the military takeover with relief. The General would make the trains run on time. 'Who knows which political system works?' explained the head of Citibank's international division. 'The only test we care about is: can they pay their bills?'[24]

Strapping their blinkers tighter round their heads, the bankers endeavoured throughout the Polish crisis to squeeze what they could still squeeze out of Poland. While western governments did at least reschedule Poland's 1981 official debt, on exceptionally generous terms, the bankers were still arguing over their rescheduling agreement in September. True, it was an operation of staggering technical complexity, with more than four hundred banks having to co-ordinate their actions, and agree among themselves who should receive the little hard currency there was to be had. With a few exceptions, they refused to put any new money into Poland. Yet it is a sad and revealing fact that west European governments' reluctance to pour new money into Poland was conditioned largely by the justified fear that the banks would immediately take it out again. (This is what happened to some of the Soviet hard currency aid to Poland, which went directly to making principal and interest payments on the bank part of the Polish debt.)[25] In effect, then, those governments would probably have found themselves making a hard currency transfer to the banks, via a clearing-house which happened to be in Warsaw!

Yet ultimately it is perverse to blame the banks for behaving like banks. They can be blamed for incautiously stampeding into Poland in the first place, and for taking a too short-sighted view of their own financial interests, but the rationale for the Marshall Plan was political and it is the business of governments, not banks, to make economic choices for political purposes. On strictly banking criteria it did not make sense for the banks to put up large sums of new money.

In the last analysis this was a failure of political imagination in the leadership of the West. Through that frosted window of opportunity which was Poland in September 1980 they looked at the best chance for the peaceful evolution of the Soviet empire which we have seen since that empire was created. Such an evolution is the best chance for the eventual reduction of those international tensions which threaten us all with the nuclear holocaust.

The chances of the Solidarity experiment succeeding were always small. No one knew this better than the men who made it. There is no historical law which says that empires must evolve peacefully, and the post-war history of eastern Europe gives us little reason to believe that this one will. It is therefore probable that those tensions will not be reduced, and we shall, sooner or later, face a nuclear war.

Yet wherever there is a chance, however small, of diminishing that probability, we must seize it, particularly when it is created by the courage of others fighting for values which we profess.

We may risk our money. They risk their lives.

The cost of a Marshall Plan for Poland would have been of the order of $20 billion over five years. The cost of the United States' planned MX missile programme was estimated in 1981 to be of the same order of magnitude.[26] Which will have better served the interests of 'the West', not to mention Europe or the Poles: the MX missile or Solidarity?

It was, however, only after the military takeover that economic policy towards Poland became the centre of bitter controversy within the western alliance. After a year of martial law the Jaruzelski regime blamed its poor economic performance on the effects of western economic sanctions, while attributing its few successes (for example, a bumper sugar-beet crop!) to the beneficial effects of the state of war. In fact, such western economic sanctions as there were consisted essentially in the withholding of the financial privileges and *de facto* economic aid which Poland had enjoyed until 13 December 1981. The American government, for example, suspended Poland's 'most favoured nation' status. Western governments' refusal to negotiate the rescheduling of Poland's official debt in 1982 was in practice a short-term *benefit* to the Polish government which simply did not pay the interest on those loans, for more than a year.[27]

Yet it remained as true in December 1982 as it had been in September 1980 that Poland's economic recovery, and therefore political prospects, depended on the West.

The West now faced choices no less difficult, but much less promising than it had faced during the revolution. If it refused to afford further aid, then it would force the Polish people deeper into economic as well as political misery, thus probably shortening the interval before the next explosion of working-class protest. If, however, it aided the regime, then it would facilitate the process of 'normalisation'. And this in very direct ways.

For example: the most important single yardstick by which Polish workers measured their prosperity was their consumption of meat. It was meat price rises, in particular, which had sparked off working class protest in 1970, 1976 and of course, July 1980. If the

Hungarian and Czech sausage had helped Kádár and Husak to win back some grudging support from Hungarian and Czech workers, meat would be even more vital for Jaruzelski. That naïve and splendid Strike Poet in the Rzeszów Commune (see above, pp. 135–6) had touched an essential political truth when he sang:

The times are past
when they closed our mouths
with sausage.

If Jaruzelski was now to close their mouths again, he needed a great deal of sausage with which to do it. But the meat ration in 1982 was pegged at a miserable 2.5–3.5 kg a month. Moreover, it was predicted that meat production would fall by about a fifth in 1983, partly because of a poor potato harvest but also because the regime was unable to import enough fodder to sustain the animal herd.[28]

The regime was unable to import enough fodder because western exporters demanded cash on delivery. Western exporters demanded cash on delivery because western governments declined to give further agricultural export credits. If western governments gave those credits again they would, in effect, be giving Jaruzelski the sausage with which to close the workers' mouths. If the shops filled with food after a few years of the new regime this would inevitably win it some measure of grudging popular toleration. And this, in turn, would increase the attractiveness of the military variant of the politbureaucratic dictatorship to neighbouring regimes, when they got into difficulties.

In short, the West was back with that Gretchen question about *Ostpolitik*: whom do we think we are helping to do what?

Solidarity and the Peace Movement

There is a somewhat puzzling simultaneity in the post-war histories of 'East' and 'West'. The years of crisis in the East, 1956, 1968, 1980–1, have been years of crisis—or at least of startling new developments—in the West as well. The Soviet invasion of Hungary coincided with the height of the Suez crisis. 1968 saw the students on the streets in both Paris and Warsaw. Yet in both these cases the differences are obviously greater than the similarities, and any significant connections, whether causal or sympathetic, are hard to detect. In 1980 the similarity was more striking. In eastern and western Europe there arose independent mass social movements, exerting great pressure on governments and occupying the centre of the political stage. Both Solidarity and the peace movements drew their energy from the support of the young; both were exceptional in bringing together Christians and socialists on the same platform.

Yet here too the connections are hard to detect. NATO'S 'twintrack' resolution of December 1979 was not a cause of the Polish revolution, any more than the election of a Polish Pope was a cause of the peace movement. In general these two apparently parallel movements showed remarkably *little* interest in each other. Most western peace campaigners did not see their struggle against Cruise and Pershing II missiles as being linked to, let alone conditional upon, Solidarity's struggle.

A rare exception was the British-based campaign for European Nuclear Disarmament (END), which called for a nuclear-free Europe 'from Portugal to Poland'. Its chief prophet, the English social historian Dr E. P. Thompson, wrote that the West European peace movement 'cannot succeed unless we can break, somehow, across that [East-West] divide, and call forth reciprocal responses from the East.'[29] And after the military takeover in Poland he reflected: '. . . it was a tragedy that Solidarity and the Western peace movement . . . did not "recognise" each other more clearly as allies.' END called for intensive contacts between 'unofficial persons' in East and West.

However, a leading member of the international relations department attached to the National Commission in Gdańsk, Magda Wójcik, told me that she could not remember Solidarity's leadership ever having been approached by a representative of END. Indeed, there had been almost no approaches from any of the western peace movements, she said. And then she made what seemed to me a very significant remark: 'I think they were afraid of what they might find.'[30]

What they might have found, and what independent supporters of the western peace movement did find when they went to Poland, was that a great many Solidarity supporters privately thought the western peace movement was a bad thing, because it tended to weaken the West's resistance to Soviet imperialism, and, more important, that foreign and defence policy were not on Solidarity's agenda at all. Thompson subsequently described this as a missed opportunity: 'In Poland the trade union and the workplace could have offered the space [for an independent peace movement] but Solidarity never got that place on its agenda.'[31] But of course, so his argument goes, Solidarity's leaders had much more urgent concerns; 'Solidarity was preoccupied, twenty four hours a day, with its work as a union'; once they had established the union, then they could have moved on to the peace question.

This nicely blurs an essential point. It is not true that Solidarity never got disarmament on to its agenda simply because it had more important priorities. The truth is that at the outset it *deliberately kept the whole area of defence and foreign policy off the agenda*, because it saw this as a precondition for any peaceful compromise with the communist regime. The lesson Solidarity had learned from Hungarian and Czech experience was precisely that it had no chance of success if it threatened what the Soviet leadership perceived as its vital strategic interests. Its resounding silence on these issues was deliberate, necessary and central.

It is, however, true that the verbal taboo was broken by Bogdan Lis, Jan Rulewski and the economist Stefan Kurowski, in speeches to the Solidarity Congress. Lis went so far as to say: 'It is not a case here of criticising one of the blocs. No. We shall speak up against armaments in East and West.'[32] These speeches were symptomatic of two developments. They were part of that fundamentalism which crashed through the barriers of self-censorship at the Congress, and they were part of that complex response to the economic collapse which ineluctably pushed back the ratchet of self-limitation. Lis, Kurowski, and Rulewski all argued not from the danger of nuclear war or the arms race but from the needs of Polish industry and the Polish consumer. In our state of economic collapse, they said, when many people do not have enough to eat, it is nonsense that so much money, and so many scarce raw materials (e.g. coal) should be channelled into the production of tanks (Lis's example) and perhaps (Lis hinted) to the Soviet Union. It was in this context, and only in this context, that the suggestion of a cut in armaments expenditure was incorporated into the Solidarity Programme. Otherwise, Solidarity's elected national leadership observed their original self-denying ordinance on defence and foreign policy to the bitter end. Pragmatically, they reckoned that, if they were to stand any chance of finding a peaceful *modus vivendi* with the communist regime, a peace movement was what they could not be.

At first, they recognised as western 'allies' almost anyone who declared themselves as 'allies'. Later, they became more discriminating about their western supporters. They did not particularly recognise the western peace movement as an ally because the western peace movement did not particularly distinguish itself as an ally, by vocal or practical support where it mattered. They were more inclined to recognise in the initials NATO an ally, because the voice of NATO was actually heard loud and clear, for example in December 1980, warning the Soviet Union against armed intervention. If 300,000 people had marched through the streets of Bonn to warn the Soviets against intervention, as they did in October 1981 to protest against NATO's new Pershing II and Cruise missiles, then Solidarity members might have begun to think seriously about their nearest western counterparts. This was not because of some consuming Polish national egotism, but because the real opportunities for explicit demonstrations of support between these two movements were all on the western side.

It was plausibly argued that one factor on the Soviet balance sheet against overt military intervention in Poland was the damage that this might do to the popularity of the peace movement in western Europe, which Moscow was obviously eager to encourage. How much larger would that factor have been if the western peace movement had linked its cause explicitly to the fortunes of Solidarity?

It was also argued, (for example by E. P. Thompson in Britain and Bernt Engelmann in West Germany)[33] that the peace movement missed an opportunity to help the Solidarity experiment by reviving the Rapacki plan for a nuclear-free zone in Central Europe.

In the event, the western peace movement made no such linkages. Before the US government had committed itself even to a lopsided 'Zero Option' for theatre nuclear missiles, Poland was plunged into a 'state of war'. The second largest army in the Warsaw Pact was deployed to crush a democratic, self-organised social movement which did everything in its power *not* to threaten Soviet strategic interests, and did not even speak about nuclear disarmament. The response of the peace movement (particularly in

West Germany) to General Jaruzelski's declaration of war was extraordinarily muted. Only a few of its leaders acknowledged publicly and unambiguously that this was not only a defeat for freedom but also a defeat for peace. Even now, the masses of the peace movement did not take to the streets for Solidarity.

They, too, contributed to the Poles' sense of being once again let down by the West. When I met the historian Bohdan Cywiński in Paris (traditional capital of Poland's 'spiritual government' of intellectuals in involuntary exile) in 1982, I reminded him that the last time we had met, in Warsaw in August 1980, he had compared the situation in Poland to the beginning of the 1905 revolution. 'Ah yes,' he replied, 'and now perhaps we are waiting for 1914?' That freedom which the Poles were unable to win for themselves through revolution they had then won through the First World War. And he went on to remind me, with the same slow passion, that there was a long tradition of Poland's freedom *conflicting* with Europe's peace. How often before—in the 1790s, the 1830s, the 1860s—had the Polish nation been crucified so that her neighbours could sleep more easily in their beds!

Yet of course he did not hope for war. Only in the darkness of Poland under martial law did a few people nourish the apocalyptic illusion of national liberation through a Third World War. No rational person could imagine that a free Poland would arise from the ashes of nuclear confrontation, as a free Poland had arisen from the ashes of the First World War. But he could imagine that those western peace campaigners who professed an attachment to the idea of Europe from Portugal to Poland, and of 'dialogue' between social movements in East and West, might listen to what the Poles had to say about the relationship between freedom and peace.

'There is nothing more important than peace,' Heinrich Albertz, one of the grand old men of the West German peace movement, reiterated when pressed about his attitude to Poland. This sentence commanded widespread assent among young peace activists in the free countries of western Europe. If it came to the choice, they said, we would rather live under Soviet domination than risk a nuclear war. If you talked to their contemporaries who actually *lived* under Soviet domination, however, you were likely to receive a different opinion. It was a group of Polish schoolchildren who chose as the motto of their unofficial journal the words 'dangerous freedom is dearer to me than safe bondage'.[34] When the Poles came to their workplaces at the end of March 1981, armed only with sleeping-bags and Thermos flasks, to prepare for the general strike against a barrage of intimidation, they were expressing that priority. We will not ourselves use violence, they said, but we are prepared to risk violence being used against us, in order to win more freedom.

This is, of course, a question of personal choice. Yet there is also a cogent political argument for the latter priority. The premise of this argument is that communist governments are not inherently less inclined to make war than capitalist ones. In the period 1980–2 the view was widespread in western Europe that the United States was a greater danger to world peace than the Soviet Union. The east European peoples who had themselves felt the cutting edge of the Soviet Union's long 'struggle for peace'*—the Poles, the Latvians and Estonians, the Lithuanians, the Ukrainians, the Hungarians, the Czechs and the Slovaks—were less easily convinced. They considered that the Soviet government needed restraining by a pacific public opinion quite as much as the American government did. The Czech intellectual who writes under the pseudonym Václav Racek put the point quite bluntly, in an open letter to E. P. Thompson. 'Without the existence of human rights in the East there is no possibility of disarmament in those countries . . . liberty is a necessary precondition for peace.'[35]

Indeed, the thinkers of END half-recognised this themselves, when they made their success dependent on the response from peoples in the East. But before those peoples could begin to impose their will for disarmament on their governments they had first to win the power to impose their wills at all. The unofficial peace groups which sprang up in East Germany and Hungary in this period were brave and admirable initiatives, but the defence policies of the East German and Hungarian regimes were not influenced by them in any significant way. Solidarity was the first self-organised social movement in the Soviet bloc to win itself the power to impose its will on *any* area of government policy. If it had survived, then perhaps after a few years it might have begun very gradually to exert a democratic influence over some aspects of

*'Rabbi, will there be a Third World War?' 'No, my son, but the struggle for peace will one day become so fierce that no house will be left standing.'

foreign and defence policy as well. Then, perhaps, in one or two decades, it might even have been possible to talk accurately about a 'peace movement' in eastern Europe in the sense that one could talk about a 'peace movement' in western Europe. One could therefore argue that in 1981 the western peace movement's pursuit of peace was not inimical to but dependent on the Poles' pursuit of freedom.

Solidarity was a supremely peaceful movement; but it was not a peace movement. Solidarity refused that binary choice, 'red or dead', to which the argument for unilateral disarmament is too often reduced. 'Red or dead' was precisely the choice with which their communist rulers had blackmailed them for thirty-five years. Under sly code-phrases like *'raison d'état'* the Party had in effect threatened: if you do not accept our dictatorship, the Red Army will invade again. By 1982 communist ideology in Poland had been reduced to this single argument. Solidarity refused to accept that these were the only possibilities. It sought a third way between communism and war. It was defeated by a communist war.

Hope

During this war, the grey blanket of fog was slowly pulled back over Poland, obscuring from western eyes the landscape which for sixteen months had been so brightly illuminated. Peering into the darkness of the next few years it was difficult to find many points of light, for the Poles, for Europe, or for 'the West'. Yet it would be perverse and wrong to end a book about Solidarity on this note of gloom. For Solidarity was the most infectiously hopeful movement in the history of contemporary Europe, and its long-term legacy is one of hope.

While the fog was dispersed we were privileged to watch the Poles fighting, with extraordinary courage, dignity and self-restraint, for values which most of us can hardly fail to recognise as our own—individual freedom, democratic government, the rule of law, free speech—values born from the common culture of old Europe. At a time when many young people in the West seemed to doubt the primacy of these values, in the face of economic recession and the threat of nuclear war, young Polish workers, who had lived all their lives under communism, were daubing on a crane in the Lenin Shipyard the words 'Man is born and lives free'. We knew, perhaps, that in all these east European countries, yes, also in Russia, a few exceptional individuals were fighting to keep alive these values, with a constancy and courage rarely matched in the West. But here, suddenly, was a whole nation doing so, though half a million troops massed on Poland's frontiers to silence them. As only a sick man knows the full value of health, so it took an unfree people to remind us of the real value of freedom.

They did not, however, merely reassert old values. Solidarity was not just what Poland was for G. K. Chesterton:[36] the bulwark of Christian civilisation against the diabolical materialism of the East. As we have seen, young Poles measured their rulers' conduct both against traditional, European and Christian standards, and against some of the socialist values which those rulers had preached. They found the regime wanting by the standards of equality and full employment (which means more than everyone having a nominal workplace) as well as by the standards of free speech, freedom of worship or political pluralism. Moreover, from the common experience of suffering under a totalitarian regime Polish Christians and democratic socialists had found their way to a common rallying ground in the defence of fundamental human and civil rights, although (unlike in Central America) they never lost sight of their fundamental disagreement about the nature of man and society.

Anyone who troubles to read Solidarity's Programme, or some of the speeches I have quoted in this narrative, will see that the Poles in fact produced a quite original mixture of ideas drawn from diverse traditions. In politics, they clove to the central principles of liberal democracy, but they combined this with proposals for a kind of radical devolution, social control and local self-government which did not exist in the West. Hannah Arendt has pointed out that this vision of units of small-scale self-government, combined by federation, seems to have emerged spontaneously in revolution after revolution.[37] For culture and education, their ideals could best be characterised as conservative-restorationist. In economics, they wished to combine the market, self-government and planning.

Obviously the one-year-old Solidarity did not hatch a full-fledged plan for a Polish 'third way'. Particularly in economics they were only beginning to grope towards new solutions and their ideas on workers' self-government would probably have changed beyond recognition with a few years' trial and error. But for all its internal inconsistencies and incompleteness, their Programme will stand comparison with any produced in western or eastern Europe in the same period; it contains some ideas which are new; and, above all, it demonstrates the possibility of quite new combinations of ideas—conservative, liberal and socialist.

By these ideas, by the mere fact of its existence, Solidarity embodied what Hannah Arendt identifies as the original grace of revolution: the human capacity for beginning new things. What science of History, what determinist laws, could have predicted Solidarity? By all those laws it was impossible: a workers' revolution under the sign of the cross against a 'Workers' State'! The course of the Polish revolution, furthermore, was the result of particular decisions by individual human beings. It was in itself, whatever its results, a glorious manifestation of free will.

Can we learn anything from it? Or will the experience simply not translate? An underground Solidarity publication echoes this doubt, quoting the sharp remark of Vladimir Bukovsky on arriving in the West: 'I do not come from the leftist camp or the rightist camp—I come from a concentration camp.' Yet the point is precisely to learn from other people's experience, however remote, without having to go through it ourselves.[38] And perhaps some of the Poles' concerns and aspirations are not so remote after all.

In the West, too, more and more people are seeking intellectual ways beyond the post-war stereotypes of Soviet socialism and American capitalism, and beyond the existing party-political moulds. In the West, too, more and more people are seeking political ways beyond the division of Europe, and towards that 'Europe of peoples' which Churchill spoke of in 1945. In the West, too, the sense of national identity—as culturally beneficial as it can be politically dangerous—is not growing weaker.

At the very least, the Polish experience should put our own in perspective. One particular distorted perspective was exemplified by the Editor of the influential West German weekly, *Stern*, in a leading article justifying martial law in Poland. The article was entitled, in a novel variation of Pontius Pilate's famous quip, 'Freedom—what is that?' 'We citizens of the Federal Republic are free people,' Mr Henri Nannen concluded. *'Are our 1.7 million unemployed also?* Freedom—what is that?'[39] (my italics). However economically circumscribed the freedom of the unemployed is, there is *no* sense in which an employed Polish worker was *more free* in January 1982 than an unemployed West German worker. Of course there is no perfect freedom on earth; of course it is difficult to define freedom in the abstract; and yet I will not hesitate to offer and defend as a working definition: 'Freedom is what a West German worker, employed or unemployed, did, and what a Polish worker, employed or unemployed, did not have in January 1982.' No one who has really understood the Polish revolution will so confuse our unperfect freedom with their unfreedom.

Similarly, no one who has understood the history of Solidarity could suppose for one moment that the American role in western Europe is politically, socially, economically or culturally comparable with Soviet domination over eastern Europe. The political problem of overcoming the division of Europe is the problem of loosening that Soviet stranglehold. The question for a movement of peoples in western Europe is not, 'How do we loosen the grip of our American "Big Brother"?' but, 'How can we help the east European peoples to loosen the grip of the Soviet "Big Brother"?' It is arguable that one of the ways to do this is to put democratic pressure on NATO to reduce the military pressure on the Soviet Union. But that is a point which has to be argued, in particular against the opposite conviction of a great many east Europeans, who do, after all, have rather more direct experience of Soviet imperialism than us.

For western governments, one obvious lesson of Solidarity would seem to be that political change in the Soviet bloc is as likely to be spasmodic, 'revolutionary' and forced from below, as gradual, evolutionary and controlled from above. In the past these spasms have occurred roughly every twelve years: 1956, 1968 and '70, 1980. But with the whole bloc in such economic straits (due to the political straitjacket) it is unlikely to be another twelve years before the next revolutionary upheaval. Western nations should therefore prepare themselves to support the next one better than they did Solidarity. The experience of the last decade suggests that while the West's economic power cannot be used effectively as a lever or as a stick, it can sometimes be used *to facilitate* desirable economic and political reforms which an east European regime wishes, or is compelled by pressure from below, to introduce.

Obviously the place and time of the next upheaval is hard to predict. But one key to predicting the unpredictable is to listen to the voices from below as well as the voices from above in eastern Europe. If western policy-makers had listened to Kuroń and Michnik as they listened to Gierek and Rakowski in 1979, they would have had a better idea of what was likely to happen in Poland. Solidarity was not a projection of Rakowski's notions of reform communism. Solidarity was the extension of the democratic opposition's vision of a society organising itself to wrench ever greater areas of freedom from the failing grasp of the Party-state. Moreover, such dialogue should not be too disagreeable to western policy-makers, since the values of the opposition are so much closer to our own. It is not the Rakowskis and Kádárs who are the true liberals in eastern Europe.

As for the Poles, one thing at least is certain: they will not forget. Though Solidarity's cells fade away even in the industrial strongholds, though the Solidarity badges, the photos and the tapes are pushed to the back of the bottommost drawer, the dramas, the ideals and the political methods of the Polish revolution will live on, in this most tenacious of national memories, as myth—and as precedent. This simple statement 'They will not forget' is a statement of the first political importance. As Milan Kundera writes, out of the bitter experience of Czechoslovakia's 'normalisation', in the Soviet world 'The struggle of man against power is the struggle of memory against forgetting.'

They will not forget, as the world will forget, and the Soviet masters of forgetting want us to forget. And just because they will not forget, there will certainly come a day, sooner or later, when we, and the masters of forgetting, will again be reminded that the Poles are still waiting, impatiently, for freedom. As the call of the bugle sounds every hour from the tower of St Mary's Cathedral across the great square of Kraków, so their call will sound once more, across the world.

Postscript to the Third Edition

Marshal Kulikov marched in, wearing his full Soviet marshal's uniform. He was greeted by the frail, upright figure of General Jaruzelski, in a civilian suit, but also by former Solidarity leaders such as Zbigniew Bujak and American cold warriors such as Richard Pipes. For this was sixteen years on, November 1997, and we had gathered in an austere holiday camp at Jachranka, near Warsaw, to discuss the Polish crisis of 1980–1.[1]

There were amazing confrontations across the table. Zbigniew Brzezinski, President Carter's National Security Adviser in 1980, told Marshal Kulikov that if the Soviet Union had invaded the West, he, Marshal Kulikov, would have been killed by the Americans within three hours. (I watched Kulikov fiddle irritably with his earphones, as if he couldn't believe what he was hearing from the interpreter.) Bujak asked the Marshal, 'Didn't you want to get to know us?' Kulikov replied that he regretted not getting to know the Solidarity leaders but 'I worked within a certain framework' and 'I would have been ticked off.' The old Russian soldier's face turned a deeper shade of crimson when Tadeusz Mazowiecki exclaimed that the Soviet Union had collapsed 'like a worn-out carpet'.

Jan Nowak, a hero of the non-communist Polish resistance during the Second World War, accused General Jaruzelski of craven subservience in his relations with Brezhnev. Visibly trembling with emotion, Jaruzelski replied: 'I would have talked on my knees, I would have kissed his feet, if it would have served Poland.' It was like watching a real-life encounter between de Gaulle and Petain. But the main subject of the two days was, as Mazowiecki lightly put it, 'whether we were right to be afraid of that Marshal Kulikov or not'.

Here, a dramatic argument developed between Kulikov and Jaruzelski. Kulikov flatly denied that there had been any threat of Soviet intervention: 'With all my responsibility as a soldier I declare that there was no plan, no documents were prepared for an intervention.' A diagram found in the East German archives, which shows a military plan for East German forces to cross the Polish frontier, was just a falsification. And he brandished a red notebook. This, he said, was his personal adjutant's record of his stay in Poland in December 1981, and it would bear out his claim. He was supported by his then Chief of Staff, General Gribkov, another veteran Soviet warhorse, who explained that one must distinguish between 'plans' and 'sketches of plans'. Anyway, he thundered, these 'sketches of plans' were only prepared in case of NATO interference in Poland. For a moment all the Poles round the table, despite all their unbridgeable differences of biography, were joined in ironical recognition of good, old-fashioned, ham-fisted Soviet lying: Jaruzelski smiling along with Nowak and Brzezinski. But then, having completely contradicted Jaruzelski's version of events, Kulikov and Gribkov went on to praise him fulsomely as a fine leader and a Polish patriot—to poor Jaruzelski's evident discomfort, and the wry amusement of others round the table.

When the session was over, I saw Jaruzelski approach Kulikov in a state of great agitation. According to someone who was nearer to them, Jaruzelski said, in Russian: 'You know what you told me then. How could you let them do this to me, in front of the Americans?' Kulikov looked embarrassed. Then the bulky marshal in full uniform leaned forward, embraced the Pole and kissed him on the cheek. They shook hands, and the former Polish leader visibly calmed down. It was a pathetic, half-comic moment, which somehow encapsulated Jaruzelski's personal tragedy. With friends like that, what need of enemies?

Wojciech Wladyslawovich and the lesser evil

Would the Russians have invaded? We now have extensive documentation from some of the most secret archives of the Soviet bloc. Yet we still cannot say with final clarity—and never will. For part of the historical truth is that Soviet leaders themselves did not know exactly what they would do if their Polish allies failed to 'restore order' on their own. The Russian records for 1956 and 1968 show a similar picture of confusion and vacillation in response to the Hungarian and Czechoslovak crises. Soviet leaders did not know what they were going to do until they did it. None the less, these new sources enable us to say a lot more than we could at the time.

The most general conclusion was well summed up at the Jachranka Conference by Georgii Shakhnazarov, one of Gorbachev's key aides on relations with Eastern Europe, an area in which he was already working in 1980/81. On the question whether there was a serious possibility that the Soviets would invade, he said simply, 'We didn't want to, but we might have.'

More specifically, it was in early December 1980 that the Soviet Union came closest to ordering a Warsaw Pact intervention. East German and Czech records indicate actual plans (by no means just 'sketches of plans') for Warsaw Pact forces to cross the Polish border at zero hours on 8 December 1980, ostensibly as part of the Warsaw Pact 'Soyuz' ('Alliance') manoeuvres. The then Polish Party leader, Stanisław Kania, the most credible witness from the communist side at the Jachranka Conference and author of the most useful of all the Polish communist leaders' memoirs, describes the Warsaw Pact summit in Moscow on 5 December as 'Poland on trial'. That evening, he had a private meeting with the Soviet leader. According to Kania, Brezhnev summed up with the words: 'All right, we won't go in. But if there are complications, we will go in. But without you, we won't go in.'[2]

Why did they draw back from the brink? Soviet records refer to their fear of 'a second Afghanistan'. According to Brzezinski, President Jimmy Carter sent a message through the hot line to Brezhnev on 3 December, warning of the grave consequences that would follow from intervention: receipt confirmed at 4.21 p.m. Brzezinski believes this threat was particularly credible to the Russians because they knew the Carter administration had organised support for the armed resistance in Afghanistan. Washington also orchestrated a chorus of warnings from other world leaders, ranging from the Pope through Helmut Schmidt to Rajiv Gandhi.[3] Kania claims that he also warned Brezhnev in apocalyptic terms of the consequences of an invasion: the Poles would rise up, young men would throw Molotov cocktails at Russian tanks, the good name of socialism would be destroyed and the Americans would be triumphant everywhere. Doubtless all these warnings had some effect. But the other side of the story, the side that Kania is more reluctant to tell, is that he and his comrades gave assurances that they would themselves vanquish the class enemy.

The internal solution using Polish military and police forces, known in Polish as the 'state of war' and in English as martial law, had been discussed as an option by the Polish authorities during the August 1980 strikes. Following the climacteric of December 1980, attention shifted from invasion to martial law, although the military contingency plan for Warsaw Pact intervention remained in place, and was refined in the first half of 1981. In his memoirs, Jaruzelski tells a story of constantly escalating Soviet pressure on him to take the path of domestic repression; Kania speaks of peaks and troughs. Of the reality of pressure there can be no doubt.

Planning for the implementation of martial law was elaborated throughout 1981, under the supervision of the National Defence Committee, known by its Polish acronym as KOK. The original codename for the operation was 'Spring'. The CIA knew of these preparations because they had a spy close to Jaruzelski, Colonel Ryszard Kukliński. He has subsequently given his own account, and a few of his top-secret telegrams, signed 'Jack Strong', have been declassified. 'Jack Strong' was one of the sources that warned Washington of the invasion threat in early December 1980.

On 15 September 1981, 'Jack Strong' reported a top-secret meeting of the National Defence Committee (KOK), chaired by Jaruzelski, at which detailed plans for the imposition of martial law were discussed. We now also have the minutes of that meeting, which took place on 13 September—that is, after the first round of the Solidarity congress which had launched its impolitic 'Message to the Working People of Eastern Europe'. According to the minutes, Jaruzelski stressed the importance of finding an occasion to introduce martial law 'which in no circumstances will be assessed as a provocation from the government side but rather in sufficient measure will make clear to society exactly this necessity'. This was not a final decision to impose martial law, but the record does support the argument I made in Chapter 8 (largely from circumstantial evidence) that, from some time in the early autumn, the people around Jaruzelski were both actively preparing for martial law and looking for a suitable political pretext to introduce it.

A nice sample of the kind of heavy breathing Polish leaders heard from Moscow is to be found in the Russian transcript of a telephone conversation between Brezhnev and Kania on 15 September 1981 (the same day that 'Jack Strong' sent his secret telegram to Washington). After waxing indignant at what he called Solidarity's 'Appeal to the Peoples of Eastern Europe,' and complaining that 'raging anti-Sovietism has engulfed Poland,' Brezhnev went on.

> I believe it is important to emphasise once again that, in today's complicated world situation, the course of events in Poland is forcing the socialist commonwealth to confront the even thornier question of how to maintain security in the centre of Europe. If Poland is ruled by Solidarity, who will guarantee the inviolability of the commonwealth's vital lines of communication that pass through the P[olish] P[eople's] R[epublic], including strategic lines of communication? How could we, the participants in the Warsaw Pact, ensure the preservation of the results of World War II, which were codified in well-known political and legal documents?
>
> I want to emphasise once again, Stanisław, that the fate of socialism in Poland and the outcome of the political struggle in your country profoundly affect all the fraternal countries.[4]

Kania seems to have twisted and turned, but not to have been ready to do what was called for. Jaruzelski, who replaced him as Party leader on 18 October, evidently was. Kukliński argues that the decision to introduce martial law was probably taken by the end of October, although we do not have a document where that is explicitly stated.[5]

There is no doubt that Soviet pressure on Jaruzelski continued to be intense. Doubtless he convinced himself that introducing martial law was the least bad thing, not just for himself and his colleagues but also for his country, taking into account all the circumstances, domestic and international, as he saw them at the time. (During the Jachranka Conference, Jaruzelski kept stressing the need to remember what he called 'the realities of that time', but those 'realities' were internal and subjective as much as external and objective.) This is not at all the same thing as saying that, faced with a direct choice between a Soviet invasion and doing the job with his own Polish forces, he 'chose the lesser evil.'

In fact, the new evidence on this point tells a very different story. It shows that, by December 1981, Soviet leaders were determined not to send in their own troops. According to the minutes of the Soviet Politburo meeting on 10 December, Yuri Andropov, then head of the KGB and soon to be Brezhnev's successor, said, 'We do not intend to introduce troops into Poland. That is the proper position, and we must adhere to it until the end.' And the veteran Foreign Minister, Andrei Gromyko, added: 'We must somehow try to dispel the notions that

Jaruzelski and other leaders in Poland have about the introduction of [Soviet] troops. There cannot be any introduction of troops into Poland.'[6]

So what were these 'notions that Jaruzelski and other leaders in Poland have . . .'? In 1992, General Gribkov created a small stir with an article claiming that Jaruzelski, far from resisting Soviet intervention, had actually been pleading for Soviet military assistance in December 1981, since he feared that his own forces would be incapable of defeating Solidarity on their own. As we saw at Jachranka, Gribkov is not the most reliable witness. But the original Soviet Politburo record is another matter. Then there is the red notebook brandished by Marshal Kulikov. Immediately afterwards, Mark Kramer, an outstanding Harvard historian of Soviet–East European relations, approached the keeper of the notebook, Kulikov's personal adjutant, Lieutenant-General Viktor Anoshkin. In the end, Kramer was able to copy and transcribe much of the extraordinary material it contains.[7]

It tells, in note form, a riveting story of the introduction of martial law as seen by the Soviet military delegation to Warsaw, headed by Marshal Kulikov. On 11 December, it records that Jaruzelski had sent a message to Moscow via the Soviet Ambassador in Warsaw with four questions, of which the third was 'Can we count on assistance of a military sort from the USSR?' Anoshkin then notes the answer from the Soviet Central Committee secretary responsible for relations with East European parties, Konstantin Rusakov: 'No troops will be sent.' In the margin is written 'This is terrible news for us!! A year and a half of chattering about the sending of troops went on—now everything has disappeared. What is Jaruzelski's position now?!' According to Anoshkin, this was his summary of Jaruzelski's response to Rusakov's blunt message that 'no troops will be sent'.

The Anoshkin notebook has to be treated critically, like every other historical source—and, especially, Soviet sources. However, it is consistent with other evidence. It does not, self-evidently, indicate that Jaruzelski wanted the Russians to invade. It does suggest that, fearful of popular reaction to the imposition of martial law, he was looking for a guarantee of Russian military support if things went wrong—a guarantee which the Russian leadership plainly refused to give. Now this is a very long way indeed from a straight choice of the 'lesser evil' between the Russians doing it and the Poles doing it themselves.

It is also consistent with what we know of Jaruzelski. Yes, he was (and is) a Polish patriot; but then, Pétain was a French patriot and Quisling a Norwegian one. He can claim a place of honour in Polish history for the way he initiated and then presided over the transition to democracy in 1989 to 1991. He was intelligent and cultured, speaking excellent Polish (in stark contrast to most Polish communist leaders, and to his successor as President, Lech Wałęsa). However, he was also a weak man; at some level even a broken man. Broken, I would speculate, especially in his relationship to Russia, by the traumatic experience of exile to the Soviet Union after 1939, where he saw his emaciated father die shortly after being released from a Soviet camp. He always attempted to do the best he could within his given framework, but never—except, perhaps, in 1989—had the imagination and courage to reach beyond it. Someone who attended the same Jesuit secondary school in the 1930s recalls that young Wojciech was always the first to put up his hand when teacher asked a question: the goody-goody. Then he was the model pupil of the Soviets, and one is bound to wonder what a young Pole of highly suspect social background, son of a Piłsudskiite landowner, had to do to gain his masters' trust in the Stalinist 1940s. Then he became a model general of the Warsaw Pact. In 1980–1 he never managed, never dared, to reach beyond the given framework.

That's a lot to ask of anyone, of course. But the new evidence does return us to the question: what if he had acted differently? At Jachranka, Jan Nowak asked specifically: what if Jaruzelski had behaved in 1981 like Gomułka in 1956, trying to lead the domestic reforms and refusing to be intimidated by Soviet pressure? Jaruzelski himself gave a thoughtful answer. The historical situations were quite different, he said. In 1956, Polish society had still been ready to support a reform communist leader. In 1980, Polish society was anti-socialist, there was (he claimed) something close to anarchy, and in Moscow you had late Brezhnev not early Khrushchev. But the key difference he did not mention was that in 1956 the Russians were prepared to invade, as they did in Hungary, while, as we can now see, in 1981 they were determined not to if they could possibly avoid it.

So the big question remains: what if Jaruzelski had recognised that chance, defied Soviet pressure and sought a real compromise with Solidarity in 1981? Then, you might retort, the Soviets would have found someone else to do the dirty work for them. But that would not have been so easy. There were not many—if any—other people left who had the position within what remained of the Party, as well as in the military and police power structures, and the residual authority in the country at large, to impose martial law.

Could the Soviets ever have accepted such a real power-sharing compromise with Solidarity? There is, in the record of the Soviet Politburo meeting on 10 December 1981, an astounding sentence. After his categorical statement that the Soviet Union should not go into Poland, Andropov remarks: 'I don't know how things will turn out in Poland, but even if Poland falls under the control of Solidarity, that's the way it will be.' (Another translation gives his conclusion as 'so be it')[8] He goes on to explain why: 'If the capitalist countries pounce on the Soviet Union, and you know they have already reached agreement on a variety of economic and political sanctions, that will be very burdensome for us. We must be concerned above all with our own country and about strengthening the Soviet Union.'

Thus the new evidence actually reinforces the argument I advanced in this book: that there was a chance, albeit a slim one, of a different outcome. Even within the severe, objective constraints of the autumn of 1981, Jaruzelski might have acted otherwise. Andropov's remark suggests that his acting otherwise might just possibly have meant that some of what happened all over Central Europe in 1989 could have happened in Poland already in 1981—although one must stress again that to say Soviet leaders did not want to intervene is not to say that they would not have in the end. To have acted differently, Jaruzelski would have had to be a different person. But the historical facts do not allow him to pass the buck to History, with a capital H, or 'the realities of that time', or credibly to maintain that the only alternative was a Soviet invasion. Individuals make history and a tragic burden of personal historical responsibility for what happened on 13 December 1981 rests on the shoulders of the man whom the Russians called Wojciech Wladyslawovich.

By the same token, he can take personal credit for his part in the peaceful changes that began in Poland seven years later. Jaruzelski himself would argue that the crackdown was a painful precondition for the opening of 1989, but that is to substitute a retrospective account of 'historical necessity' for a historical reality that was (and is) always filled with contingency and individual choice. It may even be that he personally saw the opening of 1989 as a way to redeem himself for the tragic closure of 1981. Neither was inevitable. Both depended on him. Readers must make their own judgment on whether the credit outweighs the blame.

Workers and Intellectuals

While the main ongoing controversy about the history of Solidarity has concerned the Soviets and martial law, in the Western scholarly literature there has been another debate. This was prompted by revisionist accounts of Solidarity published in the early 1990s by Roman Laba and Lawrence Goodwyn.[9] Laba, whose work was the considered product of some important original research, and Goodwyn, whose book tried to make up in academic bluster for what it conspicuously lacked in real knowledge, argued that an 'élite thesis' dominated both Polish and Western accounts of Solidarity—including this book. The 'élite thesis' allegedly claimed that it was the opposition intellectuals, especially those in KOR, who had given the workers the idea of demanding free trade unions, and generally were responsible for Solidarity.

The revisionists now asserted, by contrast, that the free trades union Solidarity was the product of what Goodwyn portentously called the 'long-hidden history of what needs to be understood as the self-activity of the Polish working class'. In plain English, the workers thought of it themselves. More empirically, Laba showed that workers on the Baltic coast had already been demanding free trades unions in a number of strikes in 1970 and 1971. Other scholars weighed in to the debate, and the interested reader will find guidance to it in the accompanying footnote and new Bibliography.[10] Here, I want only to summarise a few main points that relate specifically to the interpretation given in this book.

As usual, revisionists caricature. In my Introduction, a whole section (pp. 11–15) is devoted to the workers' own political learning process, and I stress there that 'December 1970 is the single most important date in the prehistory of Solidarity.' It is true that I go on to place great emphasis on the role of opposition intellectuals, and especially that of KOR, in forging ties both with the Church and the workers (pp. 19–31). At one point I even say that 'before August 1980 KOR worked very much as Lenin recommended (in *What is to be Done?*) the conspiratorial communist party should work, raising the political consciousness of the proletariat in key industrial centres'. This is a conceit that I would not repeat if I wrote the book today. But the main concept I use to characterise the relationship between workers and intellectuals is 'alliance'. In the light of all the subsequent research, this still seems to me the right term.

What distinguished Poland from all the other states in Eastern

Europe, and what made Solidarity possible, was precisely the alliance between these two social groups. This is demonstrably the case in the most important place for the prehistory of Solidarity: Gdańsk. The Committee for Free Trades Unions on the Coast was the meeting-point of intellectual opposition and disaffected workers. Here, workers like Wałęsa and Bogdan Lis joined with people like Andrzej Gwiazda, an engineer described in Solidarity's 1981 *Who's Who* as 'from an intelligentsia family', and the crucially important figure of Bogdan Borusewicz, a KOR member and history graduate from the Catholic University of Lublin. This Committee was, in turn, of the first importance in the strike at the Lenin Shipyard. All three members of the Executive of the Presidium of the Inter-Factory Strike Committee (MKZ) had belonged to it (Wałęsa, Lis, Kołodziej), as had another four of the remaining fifteen members of the Presidium.

However, the argument should be refined in two ways. Firstly, if one looks closely at those involved, you sometimes find that they don't easily fit the relentless dichotomy of 'intellectuals' versus 'workers'. Take Krzysztof Wyszkowski, for example, the man who may have suggested for the shipyard strike bulletin—and hence perhaps the whole movement—the name 'Solidarity'. He was a carpenter who spent his spare time preparing for *samizdat* publication the works of the twentieth-century classic Polish writer Witold Gombrowicz. 'Worker' or 'intellectual'? In fact, many Solidarity activists were of the intermediate kind whom Warsaw intellectuals condescendingly called a *pół-inteligent*, meaning, roughly, a 'half-intellectual', or someone half-belonging to the intelligentsia. Many had the kind of higher technical education much favoured and expanded by the communists, yet themselves identified with the traditional, patriotic values of the classical intelligentsia. They were vital semi-conductors between the two large social groups.

Secondly, it none the less remains true that in the August strikes it was the workers, above all, who would not compromise on the demand for free trades unions. This is a point on which all the intellectual advisers present in the shipyard agree, and it should have been stressed more clearly in this book. Leaders of KOR such as Jacek Kuroń and Adam Michnik, painfully aware of the limits of Soviet tolerance, thought free trades unions were impossible. Adam Michnik humorously recalls that he was supposed to go to Gdańsk to convince the workers that this was a wild idea:

> Since I was known and rather liked there, perhaps I might have convinced them. Fortunately, I was arrested. I couldn't go to Gdańsk and convince them and so Solidarity was created.[11]

The pithiest summary of KOR's relationship to the Gdańsk workers who created Solidarity came from Lech Wałęsa, in a discussion published in the Gdańsk weekly *Czas* in December 1980:

> The whole point is that KOR taught us this job. Now the pupils have surpassed their teachers.[12]

Yet it was Wałęsa who insisted that the workers still had need of intellectual advisers. It was he who told Bronisław Geremek and Tadeusz Mazowiecki they must stay in the shipyard and form a group of 'experts'. (In Szczecin, where there were no intellectual advisers, the resulting agreement was a weaker document, although Szczecin had been more important than Gdańsk in 1970.) Geremek gives a revealing illustration of their relationship, from the strike negotiations. Since 'free trades unions' sounded too aggressive, he recalls, the advisers hit upon the pleonastic 'independent, self-governing, trades unions', reckoning that they could sacrifice the word 'independent' in negotiations but keep the 'self-governing' (a Machiavellian ploy not uncharacteristic of Geremek himself). Sure enough, the government side-questioned the pleonasm. But Wałęsa would not budge. It was only one word, he said, it sounded so nice, and since the unions were to be independent why not let them be called 'independent'? After a moment of silence, applause flowed in from the hall. And so Solidarity was born with that insistent, resounding pleonasm: independent, self-governing.[13]

In fact, the whole history of Solidarity, from August 1980 right through until the summer of 1990, was shaped by this interaction between workers and intellectuals in general, and Wałęsa and his advisers in particular. Solidarity meant, among other things, the solidarity of these classes and individuals. When Solidarity broke up in 1990, it was also a split between workers and intellectuals in general, and those individuals in particular. Solidarity lived by their alliance, and died with it.

Repressed, then Reborn: Solidarity, 1982–1989

Historical judgments are not only changed by the emergence of new evidence. They are changed also by the mere passage of time, and the new perspectives that later developments bring. At almost every date from 13 December 1981 to the summer of 1988 one could hear the judgment firmly expressed, not just by functionaries of the Polish United Workers' Party but by intellectual and political authorities in the West, that Solidarity was finished, a thing of the past. It would never rise again. To be fair, in the darkest times even Solidarity activists themselves often doubted whether Solidarity would ever return to play an active, public, officially accepted part in Poland's political life. No one, but no one, anticipated the speed and scale of Solidarity's triumphant return in the year of wonders, 1989.

With hindsight one may say that the seven long years of struggle by Solidarity's leaders, underground activists and supporters, 'paid off'. But for at least half that period there seemed to be scant chance that it would. To appreciate the real quality of that struggle you have to put yourself back into the psychological position of the early 1980s, with the ZOMO riot police ruling the streets, long prison sentences, and no change at all coming from the succession of sick old men in the Kremlin. I mention in this book that young people referred to the martial law period simply as 'the war'. While there was clearly no comparison with the horrors of wartime occupation, it would be equally wrong to suggest that Poland in these years was a country at peace, in the sense that, say, Britain or France were at peace.

According to the Polish Helsinki Committee, in the period from 13 December 1981 to March 1985, at least seventy-eight people lost their lives as a result of the use of force by members of the police and security services.[14] The most notorious of these incidents was the kidnapping and murder of Father Jerzy Popiełuszko in 1984. Thousands more were interned, imprisoned, beaten or harassed. Solidarity activists spent as much as five years in hiding, wearing disguises and carrying false papers, with special receivers tuned to the police wavelengths. Many more led secret second lives, printing *samizdat* books and journals on hidden offset machines. Occasionally the television or radio news would be interrupted by a short broadcast from a Solidarity pirate transmitter. It was the latest and not the least colourful chapter in that thick volume entitled 'Polish resistance'.

Another book would be needed to chart and analyse the history of Solidarity in these seven years. A few milestones are indicated in the updated Chronology to this edition. The period may very roughly be divided into two halves. In the first half, from 1982 to 1985, Solidarity's leaders, and those who identified with the movement, fought an essentially defensive action. While there were innumerable debates about strategy and tactics, the shared minimal objectives were to keep something called Solidarity alive, to protect the remaining areas of freedom and self-organisation, in the underground press, in culture, in academic life, under Church auspices, to some extent even in the workplace, and generally to frustrate the regime's strategy of Polono-Kádárite 'normalisation'.

In this period Solidarity had what might be termed negative successes. Despite intensive efforts at cajolement by the regime, including the usual material incentives, the majority of the workers did not join the new, official trades unions (OPZZ). Most intellectuals, academics and artists also refused to collaborate. Solidarity appealed to people to boycott local and national elections, and between one quarter and one half of the electorate did so—although how many in response to Solidarity's appeals and how many from sheer indifference is an open question. Although Western governments gradually lifted economic sanctions, they did not give the Jaruzelski regime the full recognition, let alone the economic help, that it desired. Indeed, from 1984 onwards it became the custom for Western official visitors demonstratively to meet with leading Solidarity advisers, and to make such gestures as visiting the grave of Father Popiełuszko. At the same time, the basic structures of Solidarity in enterprises and regions were getting weaker rather than stronger. While there was still the semblance of a national leadership, with a rather uneasy co-operation between Wałęsa and the underground Temporary Co-ordination Commission (TKK), Solidarity had been destroyed as a nationwide organisation.

From the regime's point of view, the greatest failure of this period was the lack of a significant economic recovery. The theory had been that radical economic reform would be pushed through by a strong military government, under the protective carapace of martial law. This had not happened. People were not motivated to work. The West would do little to help, so long as the authorities did not talk to Solidarity. So, although there had been—on paper at least—a modest recovery of industrial production, national income remained below the

1979 level. There was certainly not enough food in the shops to shut people's mouths, as Husak had succeeded in doing in Czechoslovakia, and Kádár in Hungary. In a sense this was a 'success' for Solidarity. But Solidarity's leaders and advisers were well aware that it was a profoundly ambiguous 'success'. For, as a Solidarity report entitled *Poland Five Years after August*[15] amply documented, the whole country was in a deepening crisis, whether measured by foreign debt, capital investment, real wages, pollution levels or standards of health care. The first priority was—had to be—to combat this crisis together.

Although, in retrospect, the appointment of Mikhail Gorbachev as Soviet Party leader in March 1985 was an external turning-point for Poland, as for all other East European countries, this was not immediately apparent. The first statements on Eastern Europe coming from Gorbachev, and from other official Soviet sources, stressed continuity rather than change. There was no precipitate or explicit renunciation of the Brezhnev Doctrine. And in Poland itself, the spring trial and imprisonment of three prominent Solidarity leaders, Frasyniuk, Lis and Michnik, hardly augured well for dialogue.

The internal turn really began a year later, with the amnesty of September 1986, which brought the release of virtually all political prisoners, and allowed other activists to come out from hiding. In the next year, Solidarity consolidated its national leadership. Wałęsa formed a 'Temporary Council' of the Independent Self-Governing Trades Union 'Solidarity', and then, after some fraught discussions, merged this with the underground Temporary Co-ordination Commission (TKK) to form a National Executive Commission (KKW). This was all, of course, still strictly illegal. But Wałęsa, though sometimes hauled in for police 'conversations', was not arrested. At the same time, meetings of official Western visitors with senior Solidarity advisers became almost routine. As the journalist turned communist politician Mieczysław F. Rakowski acknowledged in a leaked 'secret memorandum' written in October 1987, 'in practice we have recognised the opposition as a lasting element on the country's political map'.[16]

At first glance the establishment of a Consultative Council of intellectuals reporting to Jaruzelski (who was now formally head of state) might seem to be a parallel development, reflecting a deliberate opening of the regime. The reality was rather more complicated. In fact, from the very outset the Jaruzelski regime had pursued a Kádárite 'politics of inclusion'. But the real point about the politics of inclusion was whom they excluded. The government spokesman Jerzy Urban, a figure whom most Poles loved to hate, never tired of repeating that Lech Wałęsa and Solidarity would never again be a partner for the authorities. By 1987 the regime was prepared to work with the Church, with other independent groupings, with almost everyone except Solidarity. To be sure, the fronts were no longer quite as hard as they appeared. In July 1987, for example, Józef Czyrek, then a Central Committee secretary, met with representatives of the Clubs of the Catholic Intelligentsia, who had very close ties to Solidarity. They demanded the return of 'trade union pluralism'. The line between 'the politics of inclusion' and the renewal of dialogue with Solidarity began to be blurred.

Meanwhile, the authorities sought public approval for a 'second stage' of economic reform, requiring acute but supposedly transitional austerity, through the instrument of a referendum—the first in Poland since 1946. Although the questions were carefully tilted so as to encourage the answer 'yes', and although some two thirds of those who actually turned out did in fact vote 'yes', the authorities had defined 'success' as approval from more than 50 per cent of *all eligible voters.* They thus plucked failure out of what might otherwise have been success. In any case, they did not get the direct popular mandate for the austerity measures and reforms which Solidarity economists also considered to be indispensable. At this point, Solidarity advisers came up with the notion of an 'anti-crisis pact' between Solidarity and the authorities.[17] Regime advisers, by contrast, talked of a 'round table', including everyone except Solidarity. The positions were nothing like so far apart as they had been in December 1981; yet they were still irreconcilable.

The decisive breakthrough came in 1988, and it came, as it had in 1980, from the workers. In response to price increases, the country's large enterprises—Solidarity's traditional strongholds—once again came out on strike, first in the spring, then in a still larger strike wave in the historic month of August. The strikers chanted '*Nie ma wolności bez Solidarności!*'—'There's no liberty without Solidarity!' As I saw for myself inside a Lenin Shipyard surrounded by riot police, many of the strike leaders were the same as in 1980, but the rank and file were young workers who had been children in 1980. A new Solidarity generation. For all the prior, informal élite negotiations, the force of economic failure, the growing flexibility of some on the regime side, and the increasing permissiveness of Gorbachev, the fact remains that it was, once again, the workers who actually brought the authorities to the table.

On 31 August 1988, the eighth anniversary of the Gdańsk Agreement, General Czesław Kiszczak, the Interior Minister, formally received Lech Wałęsa to discuss the situation. The proposal they discussed was that of a 'round table'—but a round table including Solidarity. In form, Solidarity thus accepted an idea that had come from the regime side. In content, this was a great victory for Solidarity. After his meeting with General Kiszczak, Wałęsa appealed for an end to the strikes, saying that he would ensure the re-legalisation of Solidarity, without which there could be no liberty.

And so he did, although the path to the formal re-registration of the Independent Self-Governing Trades Union 'Solidarity' on 17 April 1989 was anything but straight or easy. I have told the story of Poland's part in the year of wonders, 1989, in my book *We the People*. It is the story of the tortuous negotiations leading up to Eastern Europe's first Round Table, from February to April, of Solidarity's electoral triumph on 4 June and the developments that led straight from that to the appointment of Tadeusz Mazowiecki as Eastern Europe's first non-communist Prime Minister for more than forty years.

'I come,' Mazowiecki declared, when presenting his new coalition government to parliament, 'as a man of Solidarity, faithful to the heritage of August . . .' There is no doubt at all that the heritage of August 1980, reaffirmed in the strike of August 1988, was one of the things that brought him there. Of course the profound economic crisis, the attitude and example of the West, and Gorbachev's 'Sinatra Doctrine' ('You do it your way') were also primary causes. Of course communism ended in other East European countries within a very short space of time. But Poland was first: in the year, as it had been in the decade.

United in defeat, divided in victory

Solidarity in the autumn of 1989 was a very different thing from Solidarity in autumn 1980. As a trade union it was, although legal again, relatively weak, with scarcely 2 million members. In place of the familiar political scene with its three great armies—Solidarity, Church and the Authorities—there was a quite new political landscape, in which the major players were the Government, the Parliament, the Presidency and, as a wild card, Lech Wałesa. Many of the movement's outstanding figures now held high positions, not only Mazowiecki as Prime Minister, but Kuroń as Labour Minister, Geremek as head of the Solidarity parliamentary group (formally the Citizens' Parliamentary Club), Michnik as an MP and editor of the Solidarity daily, *Gazeta Wyborcza*. Beyond this, the heritage of Solidarity could be claimed by the movement of regional and local Citizens' Committees, initially set up to fight the June elections. More broadly still, Solidarity survived as a set of memories, symbols, values, an ethos and a tradition, although there were, as there had always been, major differences in the interpretation of that ethos and tradition.

In the first six months of the Mazowiecki government, the heritage of Solidarity proved a considerable asset. Despite, or perhaps because of, having fought each other so long and hard, former communist rulers and new opposition ones worked together in Poland better than almost anywhere else. At the top, there was a remarkable display of political maturity and tolerance. General Kiszczak served courteously and—so far as one could judge—loyally in the government of his former prisoner, Tadeusz Mazowiecki. President Jaruzelski was a model of self-restraint. This curious grand coalition proved initially to be remarkably strong and popular as well. In response to the economic woes that had grown still more acute over the decade of political struggle, it had to take even more radical and painful economic measures than would have been needed in 1980. In the first month of anti-inflationary shock therapy, known by the name of the Finance Minister as the 'Balcerowicz Plan', average real incomes fell by nearly one third. Yet miraculously, the working people of Poland did not at once rise up against these harsh measures. For to rise up against a government so clearly born of Solidarity would be to rise against themselves.

This extraordinary unity did not, however, long survive the demise of the common enemy. Once it was clear that communism was really finished all over Eastern Europe, once Czechoslovakia had Václav Havel as President and entirely free elections were being held in all neighbouring countries, then Poland's rigged coalition—the product of the Round Table agreements—seemed increasingly a relic of the past rather than a model for the future. Discontent grew across the country, not only at the economic hardship, but also at the slowness of political change, at the survival of Jaruzelski and other prominent communists in high positions, and, lower down, at members of the *nomenklatura* exploiting the unclear legal conditions of privatisation to take over as capitalists the enterprises they had formerly commanded as communists. Accumulated stresses, conflicts and divisions between activists from the Solidarity movement, some dating back well before 1980, some originating in the history narrated in this book, others coming from the years of underground struggle, others again emerging only from the changed positions of the most recent past: all found expression in fierce arguments conducted through the media and in the Civic Committees.

Yet what decisively transformed this confused political scene was the impact of one man: Lech Wałęsa. In the spring of 1990 Wałęsa declared that the changes were going too slowly. There was a danger of a 'new monopoly' [that is, of power], and a need for 'acceleration'. He launched what he himself called a political 'war at the top', with all his rhetorical skill and charm. The Second National Congress of the Independent Self-Governing Trades Union 'Solidarity', held in late April in the same hall in Gdańsk where the first congress had met in 1981, was, of course, a celebration of the movement's triumph and a discussion of the union's future. Yet it was no longer a central and decisive event of Polish politics. Instead, it seemed almost a passing episode in Wałęsa's campaign to break the mould which he himself had done so much to create less than a year before. Wałęsa was re-elected as Chairman, by a majority of 77.5 per cent (compared with 55 per cent in 1981), but used the occasion to attack his former intellectual advisers, now in power in Warsaw, and to affirm his candidacy for the Presidency of what was now called simply the Republic of Poland.

There were two sides to Wałęsa's campaign. With his matchless nose for popular feelings, he was articulating genuine and growing discontents. But he was also expressing his own very personal discontent at finding himself without an appropriate position. Indeed, in those first six months there had been moments when he did seem marginalised, up there in Gdańsk, while all the action, and all the important foreign visitors, were down in Warsaw with his former advisers, with Mazowiecki, Geremek, Kuroń, Michnik, and the rest. His resentment also spoke of the tensions between workers and intellectuals. 'Must the President really speak fluent French in order to improve the lot of the working class?' he rhetorically asked at the Solidarity congress. And in a ghost-written instant memoir of the years 1985 to 1990, he fumed at the 'gentlemen from the capital (drinking coffee with cream)':

> After the interviews of Messrs Michnik and Geremek—full of venom and unfulfilled political ambitions—it was somehow forgotten that I am a Nobel Peace Prize winner and this great honour is after all not given just for a pretty face. In the accounts of many [foreign] journalists, I once again became only an electrician—a limited *robol* [a contemptuous term for a worker] with ambitions to lead a 40 million strong nation in the heart of Europe.[18]

The trouble was that Wałesa seemed at times unable to distinguish clearly between what Poland needed and what he personally needed. 'Poland is waiting for your criticisms!' he cried, when rudely summoning the venerable Catholic editor Jerzy Turowicz to the podium, at the beginning of a stormy meeting of the central Citizens Committee in June 1990. But Poland was not waiting for Mr Turowicz's criticisms. Indeed, most of Poland probably did not know that Mr Turowicz had made any criticisms. For 'Poland' read 'Wałesa'.

As will be clear to any reader of this book, even in 1980–1 the young Wałesa had a high-handed, authoritarian style, and a rather ambivalent attitude to democracy. World fame and the Nobel Prize greatly strengthened these inclinations. Václav Havel may have adopted a slightly more upright posture and steely glance when he became President of Czechoslovakia, but Wałesa . . . not just his manner but his whole physical person was transformed. From being the skinny shipyard wag he became a portly king, a stately marshal. So long as Solidarity was fighting a (peaceful) war against communist dictatorship this was all to the good. In war, you need a strong leader, and Wałesa's contribution to keeping Solidarity alive and relatively united throughout the seven lean years was unique. But where would he fit into a peacetime democracy?

In 1981, his critics said Wałesa behaved like a dictator inside Solidarity. In 1990, his critics—now including the intellectual advisers who had been his closest supporters—said that he might behave like a dictator, not just in Solidarity, as its Chairman, but in Poland, as its President. There were, indeed, worrying symptoms, such as his habit of talking about himself in the third person, as 'Wałesa'. Wałesa could not accept this, he would say, Wałesa will not do that. But he said many different, often contradictory things, and seemed genuinely unsure of the direction in which he wanted to go. In the event, the result of his campaign was not to create a new authoritarian system around himself, but to accelerate the process of political pluralisation among the heirs of Solidarity. Looking back, in a conversation I had with him in spring 1999, Wałesa argued that this division was inevitable, necessary and healthy. If Poland was to have pluralism and democracy, then it needed competing parties. And he used a characteristically vivid simile:

> During a war, the rabbi and the bishop walk side by side—there is no difference between the two. But when they arrive at Freedom Station, the rabbi rallies his own people around him—because he knows them better and trusts them more—and the bishop rallies his.[19]

Yet for everyone involved, this was a painful process. In all the post-communist countries of the former Eastern Europe, people had difficulty adapting to the kind of regular and regulated political conflict that is the daily bread of democratic pluralism. They had all been used to a certain basic sense of social unity against the common enemy: against Them, *Oni*. But nowhere was this social unity so real as in Poland, and nowhere had it found such a strong, sustained political expression as it did in Solidarity. For thousands of individual men and women, Solidarity was a part of their identity, of their emotional life. Everyone found it difficult to exchange the high-flown, moralistic, anti-political vocabulary of social unity for a more normal, Party-political language. There was no mistaking the genuine pain, sorrow, and often bitterness felt at the parting of ways with former comrades. But part they did, forming or joining different parties.

The final act in the break-up of Solidarity was the presidential campaign of the autumn of 1990, which saw Tadeusz Mazowiecki standing for president against Lech Wałesa: the Warsaw intellectual against the Gdańsk worker. Most, though not all, of the former intellectual advisers and activists of Solidarity supported Mazowiecki. Wałesa won.

From 1982 until 1989, the leading underground weekly, *Tygodnik Mazowsze*, carried on its masthead the following words: 'Solidarity will not be divided or destroyed—Lech Wałesa.' Indeed, General Jaruzelski did not succeed in dividing or destroying Solidarity. Lech Wałesa did. What he, more than anyone, had kept together, he, more than anyone, deliberately pulled apart.

More generally, liberation and democracy succeeded where dictatorship and repression failed. *Nie ma wolności bez Solidarności* proclaimed the masthead of *Gazeta Wyborcza*, echoing the strikers of 1988—'There's no liberty without Solidarity.' When Wałesa asked them to remove the word 'Solidarity' (printed, of course, in the characteristic jumbly red lettering), someone suggested that they should leave a truncated motto: 'There's no liberty . . .' But a more accurate revised version would perhaps have read: 'There's no Solidarity in liberty.' That might apply not only to Solidarity with a large S, and not only to Poland.

What's in a name? 'Solidarity' in the 1990s

To tell the story of Polish politics in the 1990s would go well beyond the bounds of this Postscript. But some mention must be made of what happened to the heirs of Solidarity. One thing that distinguished Poland from other post-communist countries was the proportion of its new political élite that had previously been engaged in anti-communist opposition. Wałęsa was for five years a high-handed, erratic President, with some fairly shady associates, but the fears of his former advisers proved unfounded and he consistently supported the building of a free-market economy. Meanwhile, former Solidarity activists could be found in most parties, except on the post-communist left. In the first few years, these parties, and their membership, changed with bewildering speed.

There remained, however, a trades union with the familiar name, NSZZ Solidarność. At its Third National Congress in February 1991, a little-known 41-year-old cybernetician from Silesia called Marian Krzaklewski was elected Chairman, in succession to Wałęsa. The rump organisation decided to fight in the party-political arena, as well as operating as a trades union in the workplace. Its political profile was now clearly that of the nationalist, Catholic, populist right. Whereas the post-Solidarity liberal intelligentsia very largely supported the free-market reforms initiated by Mazowiecki's Finance Minister, Leszek Balcerowicz, the new Solidarity opposed many of them, in the name of the working class. People of other persuasions, some of whom had given a decade of their life to working for Solidarity, now spoke of 'the first Solidarity', to distinguish it from the current version.

As a competitor in parliamentary politics, Solidarity at first did quite badly. It won only 5.1 per cent of the vote in the October 1991 election. To demonstrate that it was still a force, Krzaklewski orchestrated a parliamentary vote to depose a coalition government led by Hanna Suchocka, a Prime Minister from the main party of the post-Solidarity intelligentsia, and committed to further free-market reforms. Far from benefitting Solidarity and the right in the subsequent, early election of September 1993, this resulted in a disaster for the fragmented right, just 4.6 per cent for Solidarity itself, and a triumph for the post-communist Alliance of the Democratic Left. In effect, Solidarity brought the post-communists back to power. Fortunately, the post-communists were determined to prove that they could be even better democrats than the post-Solidarity side, so the main strategic directions of government policy remained unchanged: towards the integration of Poland into the West and towards the completion of a Western-style market economy.

Two years later, in the November 1995 presidential election, the post-Solidarity groups were still divided. Jacek Kuroń stood as a candidate against both Lech Wałęsa and the post-communist Aleksander Kwaśniewski. When it came to a run-off between Wałęsa and Kwaśniewski, the post-Solidarity forces, and the Church, rallied at the last minute behind Wałęsa. But it was too late. The former government spokesman Jerzy Urban, now publisher of a highly scurrilous and commercially successful weekly called *Nie* (*No*), published a selection of all the horrible things Wałęsa's old-new allies had said about him since 1990, sarcastically entitled 'Wałęsa's a monster, so vote for him.' Kwaśniewski won.[20]

Shockingly, six years after the end of communism, both the Prime Minister and the President were post-communists. The post-Solidarity side clearly had to do something in response. What might crudely be characterised as the post-Solidarity liberal intelligentsia pulled together in a party now called the Freedom Union, its leading figures including Mazowiecki, Geremek and the architect of Poland's post-1990 'shock therapy', Leszek Balcerowicz. Meanwhile, Krzaklewski assembled around his Solidarity a rainbow coalition of parties on the anti-communist right, and called it Solidarity Electoral Action. Adopting the modern electioneering techniques which the post-communists had been the first to master, Solidarity Electoral Action won a third of the vote in the parliamentary election of September 1997, while the Freedom Union gained a very respectable 13.4 per cent. Together, the two main post-Solidarity groupings formed a new government, with Jerzy Buzek, a close associate of Krzaklewski's, as Prime Minister, and Bronisław Geremek as Foreign Minister. Again, the main strategic lines of policy changed much less than the rhetoric.

The Polish secret in the 1990s was: great discontinuity of parties and governments, great continuity of policies. Partly because there was in fact so little fundamental disagreement about policy, the biggest single divide in Polish politics in 1999 remained that between post-communist and post-Solidarity. But a post-Solidarity government was working in quite successful 'cohabitation' with a post-communist president. Polish democracy had come of age.

What about the workers who started it?

In the spring of 1999 I went back to Gdańsk, with a BBC television crew, to see what had happened to the workers who started it all.[21] I found the Lenin Shipyard, now just called the Gdańsk Shipyard, looking more like a museum of industrial archaeology than a working shipyard: chest-high weeds, rusting warehouses, antiquated equipment. Where nearly 17,000 people had worked in 1980, there were now scarcely 2,000, building only one or two ships a year.

We witnessed a dramatic confrontation between Lech Wałęsa and the shipyard workers, in the very room where the August 1980 negotiations had taken place. They angrily asked: What had he done for the shipyard as President? When was the last time he came here? Why were the shares they had been given in the yard now worth less than the paper they were printed on? And they complained that the workers were the losers, as usual. Referring to a famous remark of Wałęsa's, Kazimierz Kłosiński exclaimed: 'You said that you would leave the communists standing in nothing but their socks, but in fact you left us without even our socks on.' 'I suppose you think you'd be a better President?' replied Wałęsa. 'Yes, of course,' said Kłosiński.

We tracked down Anna Walentynowicz, the crane driver with whom it all began. Now a stout, elderly woman with a penetrating voice, she was even more extreme in her criticism. She told me she was now convinced that Wałęsa had all along been an agent of the secret police. (In the early 1990s, Wałęsa was accused by a right-wing interior minister with access to the secret police files of having been an informer, with the code-name 'Bolek'. He vehemently denied having been a regular informer, but in the meeting with the shipyard workers he acknowledged that, as a very young man, under interrogation in the 1970s, he 'signed something'. 'In those days,' he said, 'everyone they locked up was signing things . . .') Together with Andrzej Gwiazda, Walentynowicz had become an activist of the Catholic, nationalist right. She ranted against former Solidarity advisers such as Geremek and Michnik, said the communists were still running the economy and the entire parliament was in the pay of George Soros. 'The people were cheated and, contrary to appearances, Solidarity was used to destroy the nation, to plunge it into poverty, to create conditions that are even worse than under communism.'

Walentynowicz is an extreme case, almost a pathological one. And the shipyard, too, is a special case. In the early 1990s it fell victim to a combination of bad management and a reluctance on the part of Solidarity to take the necessary cuts. Here, of all places, who would dare tell Solidarity what to do?) So long as Wałęsa was president, it was not allowed to go bankrupt. (He even privately helped to arrange new bank loans, so the workers' complaints were scarcely justified. But in 1996, after he ceased to be President, it was finally declared bankrupt, provoking a brief eruption of protest from the workers. Yet other Polish shipyards had done better, with superior management and more co-operative unions, and the Gdańsk shipyard was then bought by the flourishing Gdynia yards. They proposed to sell off a large part of the site for development: shops, offices, apartments for Polish yuppies. Perhaps it would be called 'Gdańsk Docklands'? However, shipbuilding would continue on a consolidated, smaller site.

We also met former shipyard workers who had done well in the new freedom. There was Maciej Lewandowski, for example, who took a chance in 1989 and set up a small sawmill with a few colleagues. Initially, they operated the machines with their own hands. Now he employed fifty-six people. He had a nice house, with a small sauna, and a holiday apartment in Spain. His daughter went to a private school. He told me that, for him, the shock of going to the West was finding that things there were not much brighter and smarter than in Poland today: 'the shock was that there was no shock'. There were others like him. Furthermore, unemployment in Gdańsk was low, and most of the workers laid off from the yard had found other jobs, mainly in the booming private sector.

None the less, the general tenor of what the Gdańsk workers wanted to tell me in 1999 was gloomy and disillusioned, whether they were employed in the yards or in new private firms. The workers were still at the bottom of the pile, they complained. They had paid a heavy price for the transformation from a planned to a market economy. Yes, they had freedom: but what good was that if you had no money to buy the shiny goods in the shops? And what use was a passport if you could not afford to travel? They had imagined capitalism to be very different. They deeply resented the fact that former communists had not only gone unpunished but also made private fortunes in the transition—and a political comeback as well. They also missed the everyday solidarity of life under oppression. In the new freedom, they said, it was each man for himself—and the devil take the hindmost. There was more stress and less security.

Yes, they no longer needed to be afraid of the secret police—and that was a huge gain. But now they were afraid of their employers, who might sack them if they spoke out of turn. There was precious little solidarity between individual employees. In private firms there would, typically, be no trades unions at all. Solidarity keep out! One private employer, the owner of a small printing firm, told me he would sack anyone who tried to form a union in his business. Yet he was himself a former worker at the Lenin Shipyard.

Rationally, one can say that all of this is 'the cost of transition', and hope that in another ten years these workers, too, will reap the benefits. After all, West German workers were still quite hard up in 1955. Economic miracles take time to filter down. But for now, the irony is painful. Workers started the great changes, yet they have paid the highest price. Solidarity was originally a trades union, yet the result of its triumph is that Gdańsk workers are employed by their former workmates, now turned capitalist, in private firms with no trades unions at all.

Icebreaker

The Polish revolution of 1980–1 was, in its methods though not in its outcome, the first velvet revolution. Solidarity was a pioneering Polish form of massive social self-organisation, with the general objective of achieving, by means of peaceful pressure and negotiation, the end of communism. In this, it ultimately succeeded. Some of the larger claims made for Solidarity, with a touch of old Polish messianism, must be discounted. It did not offer a model of a new politics *tout court*. It was not the primary cause of Gorbachev's reforms. None the less, the impact of the Polish events on Soviet policymakers and intellectuals was considerable. And major elements of the new politics developed by Solidarity in Poland—the forms of peaceful protest and civic resistance, the élite negotiations symbolised by the Round Table—were subsequently to be seen across Central Europe in 1989. Poland was the icebreaker for the end of the Cold War.

The return of Solidarity envisaged in my conclusion, written still under the shadow of martial law, occurred more triumphantly, completely and peacefully than anyone would have predicted at that time. As I was well aware when I wrote the last sentence of this book, the call of the bugle that sounds the hour from St Mary's Church in Kraków is always cut short, to commemorate the death of a bugler from a Tartar arrow in 1241. For two hundred years, since the Partitions of the late eighteenth century, Polish bids for freedom had been foiled by outsiders. In 1983, I anticipated both that there would be another bid for freedom and that it would again be foiled. But it was not. For all the discontents that I found when I returned to Gdańsk, Poland today is a flourishing capitalist democracy. And, incredibly, there are no major external threats to Polish freedom.

If one had said to anyone in 1979 that in twenty years Poland would be a member of NATO, they would have consigned you to a lunatic asylum. Well, Poland became a member of NATO in March 1999. It is negotiating to join the European Union. Of the two powers that several times devoured it in the past, Russia is weak and divided, while Germany, though strong and united, is a stable liberal democracy. So it really seems that the forty-year-old cycle of popular protests against communist power and the two-hundred-year-old cycle of national uprisings against foreign domination might just have ended together. The new Poland still has great problems, but they are different problems: the problems of a free country confronting the legacy of those forty, and, in a deeper sense, of those two hundred years.

The Polish revolution was the first great contraction in the birth of this new Europe. If the European order that we called in shorthand 'Yalta' began in Poland, there is a real sense in which the end of 'Yalta' also began in Poland. With hindsight, one might say that this book describes the beginning of the end.

T.G.A., OXFORD/STANFORD, AUGUST 1999

Chronology

966		Baptism of Mieszko I in the Latin rite
1569–1795		POLISH–LITHUANIAN 'REPUBLIC' (Elective Monarchy)
1772		First Partition
1791	3 May	Liberal Constitution
1793		Second Partition
1794		Kościuszko's National Uprising
1795		Third Partition
1830–1		November Uprising
1863–4		January Uprising
1905		Revolution in Russian Poland
1918	11 November	Józef Piłsudski assumes power in Warsaw
1918–39		SECOND REPUBLIC (Independent Poland)
1939	23 August	Nazi–Soviet Union Non-Aggression Pact
	1 September	Germany invades Poland
	17 September	Soviet Union invades Poland, leading to Fourth Partition
1940		Murder of Polish officers in Katyn
1943	April	Warsaw Ghetto Uprising
1944	August–October	Warsaw Uprising
1944–45		Liberation and Occupation of Polish lands by Soviet and Polish armies. Installation of Provisional Government following the
1945	February	Yalta Agreement.

Chronology

1945–7		Civil war
1948		Formation of Polish United Workers' Party (PZPR)
c. 1949–55		Period of full Stalinism
1956	June	Poznań Workers' Uprising
	October	The 'Polish October'; Władyslaw Gomułka reappointed Party leader
		Soviet invasion of Hungary
1966		Celebrations of the Polish Millennium
1968	March	Violent repression of student protests. Anti-Semitic campaign and purge.
	August	Warsaw Pact forces invade Czechoslovakia
1970	December	Workers' protests precipitated by food price rises. Bloodshed on the Baltic coast (Gdańsk,
–1971	February	Gdynia, Szczecin). Edward Gierek replaces Gomułka as Party leader.
1976	June	Workers' protests precipitated by food price rises. Violence in Radom and Ursus.
	September	Formation of KOR (Workers' Defence Committee)
1978	October	Cardinal Karol Wojtyła, Archbishop of Kraków, elected Pope John Paul II
1979	June	Pope's visit to Poland
1980	February	Party Congress. Edward Babiuch replaces Piotr Jaroszewicz as Prime Minister
	July	Workers' protests precipitated by food price rises. No violence
	14 August	Beginning of strike at Lenin Shipyard in Gdańsk
	30 August	Signature of SZCZECIN and
	31 August	GDAŃSK agreements
	3 September	Signature of Jastrzębie Agreement

	6 September	**Stanisław Kania replaces Gierek as Party leader**
	7 September	**Lech Wałęsa received by Cardinal Wyszyński**
	17 September	**Representatives of thirty-five independent trades union founding committees agree to apply jointly for legal registration as the nationwide Independent Self-Governing Trades Union 'SOLIDARITY'**
	22 September	**First meeting of Solidarity's National Co-ordinating Commission (KKP) in Gdańsk**
	3 October	**Nationwide one-hour 'warning strike'**
	24 October	**Changes made by Warsaw Provincial Court to Solidarity statutes begin REGISTRATION CRISIS**
	10 November	**Supreme Court registers Solidarity**
	11 November	**Pre-War Independence Day unofficially celebrated**
	14 November	**First meeting of Lech Wałęsa and Stanisław Kania**
	20–28 November	**'NAROŻNIAK AFFAIR'**
	5 December	**Warsaw Pact summit in Moscow**
	8 December	**NATO says Warsaw pact forces fully mobilised on Poland's frontiers**
	16 December	**Inauguration of martyr's memorial in Gdańsk**
1981	**2 January**	**Peasants' occupation-strike begins in Rzeszów**
		FREE SATURDAYS DISPUTE
	10 January	**First disputed Saturday**
	15 January	**Lech Wałęsa meets Pope John Paul II in Rome**
	24 January	**Majority of workers take free Saturday**

28 January– 6 February	Strikes in many areas. General strike in Bielsko-Biała Province
9 February	General strike in Jelenia Góra Province
10 February	General Wojciech Jaruzelski becomes Prime Minister at Eighth Plenum of Central Committee
17 February	Recognition of Independent Students' Union
18 February	RZESZÓW AGREEMENT ends peasants' occupation-strike
4 March	Polish and Soviet Party leaders sign joint communiqué in Moscow after Soviet Party Congress
8–9 March	Private farmers' Congress in Poznań
19 March	Beating of three Solidarity activists begins BYDGOSZCZ CRISIS
27 March	Nationwide four-hour 'warning strike'
31 March	'Warsaw Agreement': suspension of prepared nationwide general strike
15 April	Party 'horizontal movement' activists meet in Toruń
12 May	Supreme Court registers RURAL SOLIDARITY
28 May	Death of Cardinal Wyszyński
9–10 June	Eleventh Plenum of Central Committee to discuss Letter from Soviet Central Committee
28 June	Poznań ceremonies on anniversary of 1956 uprising
7 July	Bishop Józef Glemp named as new Primate
14–18 July	EXTRAORDINARY PARTY CONGRESS
24–26 July	Solidarity's JULY DEBATES
31 July	*Sejm* passes Censorship Act

3–6 August	Breakdown of national negotiations between Solidarity and government. Protest motorcade blocks Warsaw city centre.
12 August	Solidarity's 'Appeal to Union members and the whole society'
5–10 September	First 'round' of SOLIDARITY CONGRESS in Gdańsk
25 September	*Sejm* passes compromise Act on Workers' Self-Government
27 September–7 October	Second 'round' of SOLIDARITY CONGRESS
18 October	General Jaruzelski replaces Stanisław Kania as Party leader
25 October	Military operational groups ordered into the countryside
4 November	Meeting of General Jaruzelski, Archbishop Glemp and Lech Wałęsa
23 November	Government announces that military operational groups will be sent into the cities
28 November	Sixth Plenum of Central Committee concludes with demand for Extraordinary Powers Bill
1 December	Warsaw Pact Defence Ministers meet in Moscow
2 December	Riot police end occupation of Warsaw Fire Officers' Academy
3 December	RADOM MEETING of Solidarity's Presidium and regional chairmen
11–12 December	Solidarity's National Commission meets in Gdańsk
13 December	General Jaruzelski declares 'STATE OF WAR'. Solidarity leaders and activists 'interned'
27 December	Last major occupation-strike ended in 'Piast' mine

Chronology

1982	22 April	Formation of Solidarity's underground Temporary Co-ordinating Commission (TKK)
	1 & 3 May	Demonstrations in response to calls from Solidarity underground
	31 August	Major demonstrations on anniversary of Gdańsk Agreement
	October	New law on trades unions legally dissolves Independent Self-Governing Trades Union 'SOLIDARITY'. Protests. Strike at Lenin Shipyard ended by militarisation
	December	Martial law 'suspended' from end of year
1983	16–23 June	Pope's second visit
	22 July	Martial law 'lifted'
	5 October	Lech Wałęsa awarded Nobel Peace Prize
1984	20 June	Solidarity-led boycott of local government elections
	19 October	Father Jerzy Popiełuszko abducted and murdered by functionaries of the secret police (SB)
1985	11 March	GORBACHEV becomes General Secretary of the Communist Party of the Soviet Union
	May–June	Gdańsk trial of Solidarity leaders, Władysław Frasyniuk, Bogdan Lis, Adam Michnik
	18 October	Solidarity-led boycott of elections to *Sejm*. Authorities claim 78.8 per cent turn-out, Solidarity claims 66 per cent
	6 November	General Jaruzelski becomes Chairman of the Council of State. New Prime Minister is Zbigniew Messner
1986	11 September	AMNESTY includes virtually all political prisoners

	29 September	Lech Wałęsa forms Temporary Council of Independent Self-Governing Trades Union 'Solidarity'
	6 December	Wojciech Jaruzelski forms Consultative Council
1987	8–14 June	Pope's third visit
	11 July	Central Committee Secretary Józef Czyrek meets with representatives of Clubs of Catholic Intelligentsia
	25 November	Lech Wałęsa combines Solidarity's Temporary Council and Temporary Co-ordinating Commission (TKK) to form new National Executive Commission (KKW)
	30 November	Referendum on 'second stage of economic reform'. Authorities narrowly miss absolute majority of registered voters
1988	April–May	Strikes including major Solidarity strongholds such as Lenin Shipyard
	August	Second, larger wave of strikes, ended after
	31 August	Meeting between Lech Wałęsa and General Kiszczak, and first formal discussion of Round Table talks with Solidarity
	27 September	Mieczysław F. Rakowski becomes Prime Minister
	30 November	Television debate between Lech Wałęsa and leader of the official trades unions (OPZZ), Alfred Miodowicz
	18 December	Wałęsa establishes Citizens' Committee
1989	16–18 January	Tenth Plenum of Central Committee concludes with agreement in principle to relegalisation of Solidarity

	6 February–5 April	ROUND TABLE talks
	17 April	Legal (re)registration of Independent Self-Governing Trades Union 'Solidarity'
	4 June	ELECTIONS give Solidarity candidates 35 per cent of seats in *Sejm* (the maximum agreed at the Round Table) and 99 out of 100 seats in the new upper house, the Senate
	24 August	Veteran solidarity adviser TADEUSZ MAZOWIECKI appointed Prime Minister
	12 September	Mazowiecki announces successful formation of 'grand coalition' government with minority of communist ministers
	December	Parliament passes package of laws for the so-called 'Balcerowicz plan' of economic transformation, changes name of state back to Republic of Poland and restores crown to eagle
1990	1 January	Introduction of first stage of 'Balcerowicz plan'. No wave of strikes
	27 January	Lenin Shipyard in Gdańsk is given back its pre-war name, Gdańsk Shipyard
	19–25 April	Solidarity's Second National Congress
	24 June	Break-up of Citizens Committee Tadeusz Mazowiecki resigns as Prime Minister in order to fight presidential election against Lech Wałęsa.
	9 December	Lech Wałęsa elected President of the Republic of Poland
1991	23–24 February	Marian Krzaklewski elected Chairman of Solidarity at its Third National Congress

	27 October	First fully free parliamentary elections. Rump 'Solidarity' gains only 5.1 per cent of vote
1993	19 September	Post-communist Alliance of the Democratic Left wins parliamentary elections and forms government
1995	17 November	In presidential elections, post-communist Aleksander Kwaśniewski defeats Lech Wałęsa and becomes second President of the Republic of Poland
1996	6 August	Gdańsk Shipyard declared bankrupt. Employees protest
1997	21 September	Parliamentary elections result in formation of a post-Solidarity coalition government composed of Solidarity Electoral Action and the Freedom Union. Jerzy Buzek is Prime Minister, Bronisław Geremek becomes Foreign Minister
1999	12 March	Poland joins NATO

Abbreviations

AK	*Armia Krajowa*: Home Army
AS	*Agencja Solidarność*: Solidarity (news) Agency
BIPS	*Biuro Informacji Prasowej KKP NSZZ 'Solidarność'*: Press Information Bureau of Solidarity
CRZZ	*Centralna Rada Związków Zawodowych*: Central Council of Trades Unions
DiP	*Doświadczenie i Przysztość*: Experience and the Future (Discussion group)
KIK	*Kluby Inteligencji Katolickiej*: Clubs of the Catholic Intelligentsia
KK	*Komisja Krajowa*: National Commission (of Solidarity: from 7 October 1981)
KKP	*Krajowa Komisja Porozumiewawcza*: National Co-ordinating Commission (of Solidarity: subsequently KK)
KOR	*Komitet Obrony Robotników*: Workers' Defence Committee (subsequently KSS—'KOR')
KPN	*Konfederacja Polski Niepodlegtej*: Confederation for an Independent Poland

KSN	*Klub Służby Niepodległości*: Club for the Service of Independence
KSR	*Konferencja Samorządu Robotniczego*: Conference of Workers' Self-Government
KSS—'KOR'	*Komitet Samoobrony Społecznej—'KOR'*: Social Self-Defence Committee—'KOR'
KZ	*Komisja Zakładowa*: Factory Commission (of Solidarity)
MKR	*Międzyzakładowa Komisja Robotnicza*: Interfactory Workers' Commission (regional level of Solidarity)
MKS	*Międzyzakladowy Komitet Strajkowy*:Interfactory Strike Committee
MKZ	*Międzyzakladowy Komitet Założycielski*: Interfactory Founding Committee (regional level of Solidarity)
MO	*Milicja Obywatelska*: Civil Militia (ordinary police)
NSZZ	*Niezależny Samorzadny Związek Zawodowy*: Independent Self-Governing Trades Union
NZS	*Niezależny Związek Studentów*: Independent Students' Union
OBOP	*Ośrodek Badania Opinii Publicznej*: Public Opinion Research Centre (of Polsh Radio and TV)
OBS	*Ośrodek Badania Opinii Publicznej*: Public Opinion Research Centre (of Polish Radio and TV)
OBS	*Ośrodek Badań Społecznych NSZZ 'Solidarność'*: Solidarity Centre for Social Research (Mazowsze)
OPSZ	*Ośrodek Prac Społeczno-Zawodowych*: Centre for Socio-Professional Studies (of Solidarity)

PAP	*Polska Agencja Prasowa*: Polish Press Agency
PPN	*Polskie Porozumienie Niepodległościowie*: Polish League for Independence
PPS	*Polska Partia Socjalistyczna*: Polish Socialist Party (1892–1948)
PRL	*Polska Rzeczpospolita Ludowa*: Polish People's Republic
PZPR	*Polska Zjednoczona Partia Robotnicza*: Polish United Workers' Party (1948–?; 'the Party')
RMP	*Ruch Młodej Polski*: Young Poland Movement
ROPCiO	*Ruch Obrony Praw Człowieka i Obywatela*: Movement for the Defence of Human and Civil Rights
SB	*Służba Bezpieczeństwa*: Security Service (secret police, popularly known by pre-1956 acronym UB)
SD	*Stronnictwo Demokratyczne*: Democratic Party
TKN	*Towarzystwo Kursów Naukowych*: Society of Academic Courses (the 'flying university')
TS	*Tygodnik Solidarność*: Solidarity Weekly
WOG	*Wielkie Organizacje Gospodarcze*: Great Economic Organisations
WOP	*Wojsko Ochrony Pogranicza*: Frontier troops
WOW	*Wojsko Ochrony Wewnętrznej*: Internal Defence Forces
WRON	*Wojskowa Rada Ocalenia Narodowego*: Military Council of National Salvation

WRZZ	*Wojewódzka Rada Związków Zawodowych*: Provincial Council of Trades Unions
WSW	*Wojskowa Służba Wewnętrzna*: Army Security Service
ZLP	*Związek Literatów Polskich*: Polish Writers' Union
ZMP	*Związek Młodzieży Polskiej*: Union of Polish Youth (1948–56)
ZOMO	*Zmotoryzowane Oddziały Milicji Obywatelskiej*: Motorised Units of Civil Militia (riot police)
ZSL	Zjednoczone Stronnictwo Ludowe: United Peasant Party (1949–?)

Notes

Full details of works cited are to be found in the Bibliography. Wherever possible I have cited reliable English translations. The following abbreviations are used in the source notes:

AS: Solidarity (news) Agency Bulletin
ICPA Bulletin: Information Centre for Polish Affairs, *Uncensored Poland News Bulletin*
Labour Focus: Labour Focus on Eastern Europe
RFE: Radio Free Europe, Research Department
TS: Solidarity Weekly

Introduction

1 Polonsky, p. 250
2 Polonsky, p. 255.
3 Ciechanowski (1980), pp. 293–5.
4 cf. Ascherson, p. 53, and review by Leszek Kołakowski in *The New Republic* (Washington), 14 April 1982, pp. 24 ff.
5 cf. his *The Alternative in Eastern Europe* (NLB, London, 1978).
6 On the basic structures of the regime see also Marek Tarniewski in *Survey*, vol. 25, no. 1, pp. 118 ff.
7 cf. Chęciński, passim.
8 On *nomenklatura* see the chapter by Aleksander Smolar in Brumberg (ed.). The 1972 *nomenklatura* list is reprinted in MacShane, pp. 163 ff, and Brumberg (ed.), pp. 165 ff. See also 'Controversy over Nomenklatura in Poland' by Takayuki Ito in *Journal of East and West Studies*, vol. XI, no. 1, 1982, pp. 49–95 (I am grateful to Aleksander Smolar for this reference). The classic justification of the use of the word 'class' is still Milovan Djilas, *The New Class* (Thames & Hudson, London, 1957).

9 Milosz (1980), p. 105.
10 Pełczyński, p. 306; Karpiński, p. 26; Chęciński, pp. 55–7.
11 Pełczyński, p. 363; Lewis, pp. 234–6.
12 See Martin Malia's illuminating 'Poland: 'The Winter War' in *The New York Review of Books*, 18 March 1982.
13 On the 'Polish October' see the useful review article by George Sakwa in *The Polish Review*, pp. 354 ff.; Ascherson, pp. 66–79; and, for some vivid description, Flora Lewis, *The Polish Volcano*.
14 Włodzimierz Brus in Brumberg (ed.), p. 30.
15 For December 1970 see Pełczyński, pp. 403–6; chapters 1–3 in Blazynski; Pełczyński, 'The Downfall of Gomulka' in A. Bromke and J. W. Strong (eds), *Gierek's Poland* (Praeger, New York, 1973).
16 cf. Potel, *Mémoire*, passim. For Wałęsa, *The Book*, especially the excellent introduction by Neal Ascherson and the chapter by Maria Janion.
17 Quoted in Blazynski, p. 45.
18 cf. for example, the biting attack by Szczypiorski (1982). The best accounts of the political economy are those by Brus in Brumberg (ed.) and, with a wealth of detail, in Alec Nove and others (eds), *The East European Economies in the 1970's* (Butterworth, London, 1982), pp. 91–138; but see also Domenica Mario Nuti, 'The Polish Crisis: Economic Factors and Constraints' in *The Socialist Register*, 1981, pp. 104–43; and Portes (1981).
19 A point made by Brus in Brumberg (ed.), p. 28.
20 Figures from Brus in Nove (ed.), pp. 92 and 95.
21 Szczypiorski, p. 95.
22 Brus in Brumbrg (ed.), pp. 38–9. For an interesting comparison with Hungary see George Schöpflin, 'The Politics of Agriculture in Eastern Europe' in S. White and others (eds), *Communist Political Systems* (Macmillan, London, 1982). See also my articles in *The Times*, 23 and 24 February 1981.
23 Blazynski, pp. 257–61; Pełczyński, p. 435.
24 cf. Raina (1978), pp. 210–18 and passim.
25 For the original membership cf *Der Spiegel*, no. 49, 1976, pp. 173–4; Zagajewski, pp. 159–60; and now, authoritatively, Jan Józef Lipski, *Komitet Obrony Robotników: KOR* (Aneks, London, 1983).
26 See particularly the two special numbers of *Survey*, vol. 24, no. 4 and vol. 25, no. 1; *Index on Censorship*, vol. 8, no. 6, Nov–Dec 1979; and the works by Raina (1978) and (1981).

27 Zagajewski, p. 164.
28 Pełczyński, p. 438.
29 cf. Andrzej Micewski, *Katholische Gruppierungen in Polen, PAX und ZNAK 1945–1976* (Kaiser, München, 1978) and Michnik's *Kościól, Lewica, Dialog*. I am grateful to Professor Leopold Tyrmand for a fascinating conversation on this subject.
30 Blazynski, p. 275.
31 Raina (1981), pp. 410–16.
32 First published in *Kultura* (Paris), June 1971, and in English in *Survey*, summer 1971.
33 Raina (1981), pp. 370–4. On *Robotnik* see also *TS*, no. 2, p. 14.
34 Potel, *Summer*, pp. 25 ff.
35 Raina (1981), p. 375.
36 Pełczyński, p. 450.
37 See especially, Alex Pravda, 'Poland 1980: From "Premature Consumerism" to Labour Solidarity', in *Soviet Studies*, vol. XXXIV, no. 2, April 1982, pp. 167–99, and Stefan Nowak, Values and Attitudes of the Polish People', in *Scientific American*, vol. 25, no. 1, pp. 53–7. On inequality see also a famous article from TS, 16 October 1981, reprinted in Brumberg (ed.), pp. 172–9.
38 See Alexander Tomsky, 'John Paul II in Poland', in *Religion in Communist Lands*, vol. 7, no. 3, autumn 1979; Radio Free Europe Research, *The Pope in Poland*; superb reports by Neal Ascherson and Peter Hebblethwaite in the *Spectator*, 9 and 16 June 1979.
39 Tomsky, p. 165.
40 Quoted by Hebblethwaite, Tomsky, ibid.
41 Potel, *Mémoire*, pp. 156–9.
42 ibid., *The Book*, pp. 41–2.
43 Kuczyński, pp. 150–4.
44 For Lublin see Singer, pp. 213–17 and RFE Chronology no. 1.

1 Inside the Lenin Shipyard

For this chapter I have collated my own notes and recollections with the extensive accounts in *Biuletyn Informacyjny* (KOR), no. 6, 1980; *punkt*; Giełżyński and Stefański; Toruńczyk (ed.); TS, nos 21 and 22; Gatter-Klenk; *The Book*; RFE, *Strikes*; Ascherson, pp. 145–68; Potel, *Summer*; Raina (1981), pp. 461 ff.; and the important reminiscences by Lech Bądkowski in *Zapis*, no. 17 (London, 1981), pp. 68–99;

Jadwiga Staniszkis, 'The Evolution of Forms of Working-Class Protest in Poland: Sociological Reflections on the Gdańsk-Szczecin Case, August 1980', in *Soviet Studies*, vol. XXXIII, no. 2, April 1981, pp. 204–31; Tadeusz Kowalik in *Zeszyty Literackie*, no. 2 (Paris, 1983). The Strike Information Bulletins (*Solidarność*) are translated in full in *Labour Focus*, vol. 4, nos 1–3. Bolesław Sulik generously made available tape-recorded interviews collected for the Granada TV drama-documentary 'Strike!', and gave me the benefit of his invaluable researches. I have unfortunately not been able to use Dr Anthony Kemp-Welch's *The Birth of Solidarity* (Macmillan, London, 1983) which should provide an authoritative account of the shipyard negotiations, but I am very grateful to Dr Kemp-Welch for checking the direct quotations in my text and commenting on an earlier draft of this chapter. A superb film was made of the negotiations at the time, *Robotnicy '80* (Workers '80), extracts from which can also be seen in Andrzej Wajda's magnificent faction *Man of Iron*. There are eloquent still photographs in Puls Publications' *Gdańsk 1980—pictures from a strike.*

1 Potel, *Summer*, pp. 32–3.
2 See the interviews in *Solidarność*, no. 11; *Labour Focus*, vol. 4, nos. 1–3, pp. 30–1.
3 To illustrate the difficulties of precise reconstruction, compare the versions of this speech given in *Labour Focus*, vol. 4, nos. 1–3, pp. 30–1; *punkt*, p. 10; Ascherson, p. 147; Potel, *Summer*, p. 45; Gielżyński and Stefański, p. 26.
4 Gatter-Klenk, p. 9.
5 Recorded on a tape made at the time—Granada TV archive.
6 Dobbs, p. 90.
7 ibid.,p. 91.
8 *The Book*, pp. 195–6.
9 Original in the author's possession.
10 Polish text in *Protokoły*; English in Raina (1981), pp. 486–8.
11 *The Book*, pp. 129–30.
12 cf. Gielżyński and Stefański, p. 61.
13 *punkt*, p. 17, has 263, *Solidarność*, no. 12, has 253.
14 The most reliable account of this meeting seems to be that by two *Polityka* journalists, Gielżyński and Stefański, pp. 66–7, which I have followed here.

15 Milewicz in Toruńczyk (ed.), p. 64.
16 ibid., p. 65.
17 ibid., pp. 69–70.
18 For Szczecin see the excellent account by Oliver MacDonald in *Labour Focus*, vol. 4, nos 1–3, pp. 16 ff.
19 TS, 22, p. 4.
20 Reported by Waldemar Kuczyński.
21 cf. Bądkowski in *Zapis*, no. 17, p. 80; Kołodziejski in *The Book*, pp. 146–7.
22 'Gdański "Starzyk"' in *Przestańcie stale nas przepraszać* (duplicated, Gdańsk, August 1980)—a splendid collection of the strikers' verses—p. 10.
23 Quoted in Raina (1981), p. 524.
24 *Nowe Drogi*, no. 10–11, October–November 1980, p. 46 (I am grateful to Tony Kemp-Welch for this reference).
25 cf. *Labour Focus*, vol. 4, nos 1–3, p. 18.
26 In *Soviet Studies*, vol. XXXIII, no. 2, April 1981, p. 213.
27 cf. *Polityka*, 3 January 1981, p. 2.
28 Compare and contrast the accounts by Staniszkis and Kowalik, loc. cit. I am indebted to Dr Kowalik for further explication and detail on this point.
29 cf. *Labour Focus*, vol. 4, nos 1–3, p. 25.
30 ibid., p. 22.
31 cf. the account by Ewa Milewicz in Toruńczyk (ed.), pp. 78–81.
32 There is, for obvious reasons, no reliable account of the Gwiazda-Jagielski meeting, but the fact that it took place is confirmed by several participants (and on the Granada tapes).
33 cf. *punkt*, p. 43.
34 ibid., p. 44.

2 *A New Social Contract?*

1 Full texts in Polish in *Protokoły*. English translations in Ruane, pp. 296 ff. Ascherson, pp. 280 ff., Brumberg (ed.), pp. 314 ff., etc.
2 cf. article by Mario Nuti in *The Socialist Register*, 1981, pp. 104–43.
3 Quoted in *Dissent*, winter 1981, p. 32.
4 ibid., p. 34.
5 *Labour Focus*, vol. 4, nos 1–3, p. 47.
6 *Labour Focus*, vol. 4, nos 4–6, p. 10

7 Lenin, p. 99 and *The Book*, p. 147.
8 Poll by Polish Radio and TV's Public Opinion Research Centre (OBOP), quoted by J. Kurczewski in *Kultura* (Warsaw), 1 March 1981, p. 9. English in *Polish Perspectives*, vol. XXIV, no. 6–7, p. 24.
9 BBC Monitoring Service translation quoted by Ruane, p. 54.
10 ibid., pp. 56–60.
11 Interview, 4 November 1980.
12 cf. *The Times*, 27 November 1980 and information from ICPA.
13 *Der Spiegel*, 15 September 1980, pp. 148–50.
14 Excellently reported by Bernard Guetta in *Le Monde*, 28–30 November 1980.
15 *Biuletyn Informacyjny*, no. 6, 1980. English translation in *Dissent*, winter 1981, pp. 34 ff.
16 BBC Monitoring Service translation quoted by Ruane, p. 94.
17 Mlynář, pp. 238–9.
18 Ruane, pp. 97–8.
19 Abraham Brumberg in the *TLS*, 11 June 1982.
20 cf. Chęciński, chapter 15, passim.
21 Quoted in *Wektory*, no. 1 (1), August 1981, pp. 49–50, and *Aneks*, no. 27, 1982, p. 128.
22 Ruane, p. 103.
23 *Polish Perspectives*, vol. XXIV, no. 6–7, p. 23.
24 Figures from Mario Nuti in *The Socialist Register*, 1981, p. 106, Portes, pp. 18–20, and interview with Professor Zdzislaw Grochowski, Deputy Agriculture Minister, Warsaw, 2 February 1981.
25 Kuczyński, p. 157.
26 *L'Alternative*, Dossier, p. 61; *Życie Warszawy*, 8 April 1981, gives zł. 2,000–2,800 monthly.
27 Komisja do spraw Reformy Gospodarczej, *Podstawowe Założenia Reformy Gospodarczej* projekt (Warsaw, January 1981), paragraph 79 (c).
28 Interview with Professor Jan Kielanowski, Warsaw, 2 November 1980.

3 Inside the Rzeszów Commune

1 RFE, Chronology 2, pp. 99 and 105.
2 Polish texts in TS, no. 1, p. 14, and AS, no. 4, pp. 201 ff. A slightly unreliable English translation in RFE, Chronology 3, pp. 101 ff.

4 The Ides of March

1 *The Times*, 10 January 1981.
2 *Polityka*, 17 January 1981.
3 Some 600 pages of such instructions were smuggled out of Poland by a disillusioned censor in 1977 and published by Aneks as *Czarna Ksiega Cenzury PRL* (to be published in English by Random House). These quotations are from *Survey*, vol. 24, no. 4, p. 174.
4 *Polityka*, 26 September 1981.
5 All quotations from AS, no. 1, pp. x–xiv.
6 Quoted in the translation by the ICPA.
7 For Jaruzelski see RFE Background Report no. 72, 13 March 1981, by Ewa Celt; *Le Monde*, 11 February and 15 December 1981; *Financial Times*, 11 February 1981; Johnson and others, pp. 47–8.
8 Quoted by J. Kurczewski in *Polish Perspectives*, vol. XXIV, no. 6–7, 1981, p. 23.
9 *Le Monde*, 21 March 1981.
10 For more details see RFE Background Report no. 59, 2 March 1981, by Anna Sabbat.
11 Ruane, pp. 127 ff.
12 In *Prologue to Gdańsk*, p. ix.
13 AS, no. 7, p. 407.
14 TS, no. 1, p. 3. German translation in *Der Spiegel*, no. 15, 1981, pp. 162 ff.
15 ICPA Bulletin no. 5, 1981, pp. 11–12.
16 cf. AS, no. 9, pp. 205 ff.
17 Quoted by Bernard Guetta in *Le Monde*, 27 March 1981.
18 Wiesława Grochola in TS, no. 1, p. 7.
19 Quoted in Ruane, p. 139.
20 Quoted in ICPA Bulletin no. 5, 1981, p. 4.
21 AS, no. 8, pp. 001 ff.
22 AS, no. 11, p. 401. Jurczyk repeated the gist of this account when answering a question at the Solidarity Congress, cf. AS, no. 41, p. 311. But see also Geremek's response in *Jednośc*, 176 April 1981.
23 AS, no. 10, pp. 001 ff.
24 Jolanta Strzelecka in TS, no. 3, p. 13.
25 *The Book*, pp. 190–1.

26 TS, no. 2, p. 1.
27 ibid., p. 3.
28 TS, no. 4, p. 5.
29 Zeszyty OPSZ, no. 1, p. 167.
30 TS, no. 2, p. 1.

5 Democratic Communism?

1 Interview, Warsaw, 13 January 1981.
2 Interview, Kraków, 29 April 1981.
3 TS, no. 7, p. 2.
4 Ruane, p. 154.
5 Quoted in *Der Tagesspiegel*, 10 April 1981.
6 Figures from Dr George Kolankiewicz; see also Jadwiga Staniszkis in *Soviet Studies*, vol. XXXIII, no. 2, April 1981, p. 228.
7 Kolankiewicz in Woodall (ed.), pp. 64 ff.; *Labour Focus*, vol. 4, nos 4–6, pp. 50–2.
8 Ruane, p. 177.
9 Kolankiewicz in Woodall (ed.), p. 68; Ruane, p. 2; Christopher Bobiński, in *Financial Times*, 16 April 1981.
10 *Kultura*, 21 June 1981, p. 2.
11 Kolankiewicz in *The Times*, 13 July 1981.
12 *Trybuna Ludu*, 26 June 1981.
13 Iwanow interview in the Nowa Press Service Bulletin no. 5, 31 May 1981, p. 5. Election procedures: 'Przy nadzieji demokracji' in *Prawo i Życie*, 28 June 1981. I am grateful to Dr George Kolankiewicz for the latter reference.
14 The *Observer*, 24 June 1981.
15 cf. TS, no. 10, p. 1.
16 Anna Strońska in *Polityka*, 5 December 1981; RFE Background Report no. 213, 13 October 1982, by Anna Sabbat-Swidlicka.
17 cf. *The Times*, 11 June 1981, p. 6; Ruane, pp. 180–1.
18 Ruane, p. 194.
19 Mark Frankland in the *Observer*, 21 July 1981.
20 ibid.
21 Iwanow in Nowa Press Service Bulletin no. 5, 31 May 1981, p. 6.
22 cf. AS, no. 21, p. 502.
23 Ruane, p. 211.

6 What Partnership?

1 Supplement to TS no. 19: 'O sytuacji w kraju i Związku' (texts of the July Debates), p. 2.
2 Michnik in *Der Spiegel*, no. 33, 1981, p. 84.
3 Mario Nuti in *The Socialist Register*, 1981, p. 127.
4 ibid.
5 cf. *Le Monde*, 6 August 1981, p. 5 and TS, no. 3, p. 14.
6 cf. my article in *The Times*, 12 August 1981, p. 8. Individual cases taken from numerous Solidarity bulletins. I am very grateful to Mr Christof Hyla for sending me a constant flow of these.
7 Nuti, op. cit., p. 120.
8 A remarkable example of special supplies to the army was actually filmed by a BBC 'Panorama' team in December 1981.
9 But cf. *The Times*, 20 November 1981, p. 9: 'Mr Anton Rajkiewicz, the Minister of Labour, said that strikes had cost the country 10,500,000 hours in lost production this year'; i.e. less than one *hour* per worker.
10 Nuti, op. cit. p. 131.
11 Supplement to TS no. 19 (see n. 1 above), p. 12.
12 OBS survey quoted in *Labour Focus*, vol. 5 nos 2–4, p. 25.
13 Interview with Jerzy Milewski, London, 19 August 1982, RFE Background Report no. 211, 24 July 1981, by Cam Hudson.
14 AS, no. 21, p. 312.
15 *Robotnik*, no. 79, translated in *Labour Focus*, vol. 5, nos 1–2, p. 18.
16 ibid. p. 16.
17 Network 'Position on Social and Economic Reform of the Country' in special no. of *Solidarność* (Gdańsk), 5 September 1981, pp. 18 ff. The draft was already presented to a Network conference in early June, cf. AS, no. 19, pp. 204–5.
18 *Robotnik*, no. 79, translated in *Labour Focus*, vol. 5, nos 1–2, p. 16.
19 Supplement to TS, no. 19 (see n. 1 above), p. 7.
20 Interesting remarks on Solidarity's 'political moralism' in Staniszkis, pp. 137 ff. On Gdańsk regional elections see RFE Background Report no. 251, 3 Sepbember 1981, by Anna Gaworzewska.
21 Supplement to TS, no 19 (see n. 1 above), p. 8.
22 ibid., pp. 2–3.
23 Nuti, op. cit., p. 13.

24 cf. RFE Chronology 4, pp. 187 ff., for the full text in English translation.
25 ICPA Bulletin no. 12, 1981, pp. 9–10.
26 TS, no. 20, p. 3; AS, no. 27, pp. 001 ff.; *Polityka*, 15 August 1981, pp. 1 and 6; *Trybuna Ludu*, 5 and 8–9 August 1981; ICPA Bulletin no. 12, 1981, passim.
27 TS, no. 20, p. 3; AS, no 28, pp. 001 ff.; *Polityka*, 15 August 1981, p. 6; *Trybuna Ludu*, 8–9 August 1981; ICPA Bulletin no. 12, 1981, passim.
28 All Fallaci interview quotations from *The Times*, 22 and 23 February 1982.
29 On Rakowski see Biography in RFE, Situation Report no. 4, 13 March 1981, pp. 18 ff.; interview in *Marxism Today*, October 1981, pp. 9 ff.; a brilliant and cruel sketch by Leopold Tyrmand in *Kultura* (Paris), no. 12/411, December 1981, pp. 93–109; and numerous interviews in the western press.
30 Quotations from the translations in *Der Spiegel*, no. 7, 1982, p. 116.
31 Rakowski, op. cit.
32 TS, no. 20, p. 3.
33 TS, no. 21, p. 1.
34 AS, no, 32, p. 401, quoting *Wiadomości Dnia*, no. 174.
35 *Tygodnik Powszechny*, no. 25, 1981, p. 5.
36 ICPA Bulletin no. 12, 1981, p. 18; *Tygodnik Powszechny*, 23 August 1981, p. 1.
37 Ruane, p. 228.

7 Noble Democracy

1 TS, no. 24, p. 3.
2 ibid., p. 5.
3 BIPS, wydanie zjazdowe, no. 10 (315), 27 September 1981.
4 BIPS, wydanie zjazdowe, no. 11 (316), 27 September 1981.
5 cf. the account by J.-Y. Touvais in *L'Alternative*, Dossier, pp. 158 ff.
6 AS, no. 36, p. 602.
7 AS, no. 36, pp, 402–7; *Le Monde*, 10 September 1981.
8 Bernard Guetta in *Le Monde*, 26 September 1981.
9 AS, no. 41, p. 106.

10 AS, no. 40, pp. 301 ff.
11 cf. the map in AS, no. 38.
12 *Glos Wolny*, nos 21 and 22, quoted in *L'Alternative*, Dossier, p. 161.
13. AS, no. 38, pp. 32–3; TS, no. 26, pp. 5–6; for Rozpłochowski, TS, no. 28, p. 8.
14 AS, no. 41, p. 306.
15 ibid., pp. 309 ff.; TS, no. 28, p. 8.
16 AS, no. 42, p. 107.
17 RFE, Background Report no. 291, 19 October 1981, p. 6.
18 cf. *L'Alternative*, Dossier, p. 161.
19 Davies, p. 75.
20 BIPS, wydanie zjazdowe, no. 11 (316), 27 September 1981.
21 Supplement to TS, no. 3.
22 For reasons of space I have unfortunately been unable to print the Programme in full. I have used the translation by ICPA, Bulletin no. 16, 1981. Other translations in *Labour Focus*, vol. 5, nos 1–2; RFE, Chronology 4, pp. 97–153.
23 Interview, 19 August 1982, cf. also Geremek in TS, no. 27.
24 AS, no. 40, pp. 301 ff.
25 Nowak, op. cit., p. 29.
26 AS, no. 36, p. 202.
27 Tischner, p. 147.
28 ibid., pp. 73–81.
29 cf. *Encounter*, October 1978, pp. 46–7.
30 AS, no. 41, p. 201.
31 In *Labour Focus*, vol. 5, nos 1–2, p. 22.
32 AS, no. 43, p. 305.
33 AS, no. 42, p. 206.

8 Confrontation

1 AS, no. 44, p. 205, cf. also *Congress Post* (BIPS Foreign Dept.), 4 October 1981, p. 4.
2 *The Times*, 22 February 1982, p. 8.
3 *Der Spiegel*, no. 53, 1981, p. 68.
4 International Institute for Strategic Studies (IISS), *The Military Balance 1982–1983* (London, 1982), pp. 22–3; Michael Chęciński in *Osteuropa Archiv*, 5/82, pp. 382–5; Johnson and others, esp.

pp. 30–1 and 50–3. Johnson and others say the WOW was under the Defence Ministry, Chęciński that it was subordinated to the Interior Ministry. Plainly there is an inner history of relations between the army and security apparatuses which is still to be revealed.

5 *Labour Focus*, vol. 5, nos. 1–2, p. 16.
6 AS, no. 7, p. 407.
7 ICPA Bulletin no. 8, 1982, p. 20.
8 Christopher Bobiński in the *Observer*, 17 January 1982.
9 *Życie Warszawy*, 7 November 1981.
10 *Le Monde*, 1 December 1981.
11 Ruane, pp. 270–2.
12 AS, no. 58, p. 301.
13 *The Times*, 22 February 1982.
14 AS, no. 58, p. 201.
15 AS, no. 46, pp. 102–3.
16 Interview with J. Milewski, London, 19 August 1982; AS, no. 45, p. 205, and no. 46, p. 208.
17 AS, no. 50, p. 401; Touraine, p. 244.
18 cf. *L'Alternative*, Dossier, pp. 198–202.
19 John Darnton in the *New York Times*, 22 October 1981; Neal Ascherson in the *Observer*, 22 November 1981.
20 cf. Bernard Guetta in *Le Monde*, 5 November 1981 and TS, no. 33, p. 3.
21 AS, no. 46, pp. 103 ff.; TS, no. 33, p. 3.
22 AS, no. 50, p. 401.
23 Bernard Guetta in *Le Monde*, 13 November 1981.
24 *Głos Wolny*, no. 4.
25 KSN, 'Do Narodu Polskiego', in *Śpiewniczek Pieśni Patriotycznej* (Warsaw, 1981).
26 TS, no. 36, pp. 3–4.
27 cf. *Robotnik*, no. 77.
28 Zbigniew Kowalewski, reprinted in *Labour Focus*, vol. 5, nos 1–2, pp. 25 ff.
29 *Der Spiegel*, no. 45, 1981, p. 148.
30 cf. his article in *Le Monde*, 7 January 1982.
31 AS, no. 46, p. 108.
32 cf. the account by Daniel Passent (an observer not over-sympathetic to Solidarity) in *Polityka*, 29 November 1981 and AS, no. 53.

33 The Declaration is printed as *Robotnik*, no. 80 and translated in ICPA Bulletin no. 18, 1981.
34 ICPA Bulletin no. 18, 1981, pp. 12–14.
35 Interview in January 1982 with Ewa Milewicz, ICPA Bulletin no. 3, 1982, pp. 38 ff.
36 Quoted in *Słowo Powszechne*, 12 December 1981.
37 *Labour Focus*, vol. 5, nos 1–2, pp. 25 ff.
38 This paragraph closely follows the eyewitness account of Bernard Guetta published in *Le Monde*, 16 December 1982, supplemented with details from Kowalewski.

9 'War'

1 English text in ICPA Bulletin no. 20, 1981, pp. 8 ff.
2 Document from ICPA.
3 Photocopy in the author's possession.
4 'Relacja z Huty Katowice', by a 28-year-old technician, in ICPA Polish language Bulletin no. 3, 1982, pp. 13–15.
5 *Labour Focus*, vol. 5, nos 1–2, pp. 31–2; *Sunday Times*, 27 December 1981.
6 Personal information.
7 English text in ICPA Bulletin no. 20, 1981, pp. 21 ff.
8 *Sunday Times*, 28 March 1982, p. 5.
9 ICPA Bulletin no. 2, 1982, pp. 35–6.

10 What Revolution?

1 *The Book*, p. 147.
2 RFE Chronology 4, p. 89.
3 TS, no. 2, p. 15.
4 AS, no. 11, p. 205.
5 Tischner, pp. 86–7, 125.
6 TS, no. 22, p. 1.
7 cf. *Kontinent*, no. 23, pp. 3–8.
8 American professor quoted by Miłosz in *Le Monde*, 2 March 1982.
9 *Rocznik Statystyczny*, 1982, p. 47; 1980: 4, 693; 1981: 3, 155.
10 Episcopate source to the author in January 1981. Official figures from *Problemy Alkoholizmu*, no. 2, February 1983, p. 17.
11 Solzhenitsyn, p. 27.

12 *Sztandar Młodych*, 10–11 October 1981; English translation in RFE Background Report no. 307, 9 November 1981, by Nika Krzeczunowicz.
13 *Krytyka*, no. 13–14, pp. 33–52.
14 Jacek Kurczewski in *Polish Perspectives*, vol. XXIV, no. 6–7, 1981, p. 26.
15 *Le Monde*, 17 December 1980.
16 *The Democrat*, 28 October 1982, p. 28.
17 Translation in ICPA Bulletin no. 20, 1981, p. 8.
18 Unless there were numerous occupations that were reported in neither the official nor the unofficial media.
19 cf. AS, no. 57; official daily press; BBC and RFE monitoring of Polish Radio and TV.
20 AS, no. 11, p. 205.
21 I am very grateful to Anders Åslund for this first hand information.
22 *International Socialism*, no. 15, p. 100.
23 The *Guardian*, 1 November 1982, p. 7.
24 Translation in ICPA Bulletin no. 9, 1982, p. 21.
25 The conclusion of Zbigniew Herbert's poem 'Mr Cogito's Envoi'.
26 I am grateful to George Schopflin for this estimate.
27 Aristotle, pp. 224–31.
28 cf. *Trybuna Ludu*, 11 February 1983, 'Dokumentacja'.
29 cf. Michel Tatu in *Le Monde*, 3 November 1981; C. Castoriadis, Devant la Guerre (Fayard, Paris, 1981); on East Germany, my *Und willst du nicht mein Bruder sein . . . Die DDR Heute* (Rowohlt, Hamburg, 1981), chapter 6.
30 *The Times*, 20 January 1983.
31 ibid, and the *Observer*, 23 January 1983.
32 Jacques Rupnik, 'The military and "normalisation" in Poland', unpublished paper for an Open University Conference, September 1982.
33 Quoted in *Kontinent*, no. 23, p. 8.

11 Under Western Eyes

1 'A Note on the Polish Problem' (1916) in *Notes on Life and Letters* (Dent, London, 1921), p. 181.
2 In Li (ed.), p. 404.

3 *Le Monde*, 3 November 1981.
4 Ascherson, p. 10.
5 *The Book*, p. 184.
6 *New Socialist*, September–October 1981, pp. 46 ff.
7 cf. Jósef Tischner, 'Drogami ludzkich spraw' in *Tygodnik Powszechny*, 22 April 1979.
8 George Orwell, 'Notes on Nationalism' in *Collected Essays, Journalism and Letters* (Penguin, London, 1970), vol. 3, p. 414 and passim.
9 Quoted by Christopher Booker in the *Daily Telegraph*, 3 October 1981.
10 Berlinguer, pp. 16 and 36.
11 Quoted by Christopher Hitchens in the *Observer*, 20 June 1982, p. 27.
12 cf. Paul Johnson in the *Spectator*, 14 August and 30 October 1982.
13 Quoted by Wolf Biermann in Böll and others, p. 43. The quotation is confirmed by a Federal Press Office (BPA) report.
14 *tip* (West Berlin), no. 1, 1982, p. 16.
15 See Böll and others; Stent; Griffith; passim.
16 John van Meer, 'Banks, Tanks and Freedom' in *Commentary*, vol. 74, no. 6, December 1982, p. 24.
17 cf. my *Und willst du nicht mein Bruder sein ... Die DDR Heute* (Rowohlt, Hamburg, 1981), passim.
18 *New Socialist*, March–April 1982, p. 53.
19 Printed in German in *Die Welt*, 28 April 1982. Polish text in *Kontakt*, nos 5 and 6, September–October 1982, p. 74.
20 In Böll and others, p. 68.
21 Estimates based on Portes, pp. 40–1; interviews with Polish economists; Anthony H. Cordesman, 'Poland and Western Defense: A Priceless Window of Opportunity', in *Armed Forces Journal International*, November 1981.
22 cf. Richard Davies, 'The United States and Poland 1980–82' in the *Washington Quarterly*, spring 1982, especially p. 147.
23 Richard Portes, letter to *The Times*, 24 September 1981.
24 John van Meer in *Commentary*, December 1982, p. 17.
25 Richard Portes, letter to *The Times*, 24 September 1981.
26 Information from the International Institute of Strategic Studies.
27 *The Times*, 2 March 1983.

28 Jacek Rostowski, 'The Best Way to Help Poland', in *The Times*, 24 January 1983.
29 *Zero Option* (Merlin Press, London, 1982), p. 112.
30 Interview, London, 19 August 1982.
31 Interview with Oliver MacDonald in *Labour Focus*, vol. 5, nos 5–6, p. 10
32 AS, no. 41, p. 304
33 Thompson, p. 136 and passim; Engelmann in Böll and others (eds), pp. 80–2.
34 *Uczeń Polski* (The Polish Pupil), an unofficial publication founded by a group of secondary-school pupils in Gdańsk in June 1979.
35 *New Statesman*, 17–24 December 1982, pp. 14–15.
36 And for the Literary Editor of the *Spectator*: see A. N. Wilson, 'Peccavi', in the *Spectator*, 1 January 1983.
37 Arendt, chapter 6.
38 Quoted in *Labour Focus*, vol. 5, nos 5–6, p. 23.
39 *Stern*, 21 January 1982.

Postscript to the Third Edition

1 The conference was organised by the Cold War International History Project, based at the Woodrow Wilson Center in Washington, DC, the National Security Archive, an independent institution also based in Washington, and the Institute of Political Studies in Warsaw. It was their extraordinary achievement to bring all these witnesses together. The following two sections in the text are based on my own extensive notes from the Jachranka Conference; the photocopied document book prepared by the conference organisers, a revised version of which is to be published by Central European University Press; Cold War International History Project, *Bulletin*, Issue 11; Kramer, 'Soviet Deliberations'; Mastny, 'Soviet Non-Invasion'; and the Jaruzelski, Kiszczak and Kania memoirs, as well as *Wejdą, nie wejdą*, listed in the new Bibliography. Where no precise reference is given, the source is my notes or the unpaginated and unpublished document book.
2 Kanie quoted this at the conference, as he does in Kania, *Zatrzymać Konfrontację*, p. 91.

3 Brzezinski made these points at the conference and in conversation with the author. See also Brzezinski, *Power and Principle*, and Brzezinski, 'White House Diary'.
4 In Kramer, 'Soviet Deliberations', pp. 144–5.
5 See Kukliński, 'Wojna z narodem'.
6 See Kramer, 'Soviet Deliberations', pp. 165–6.
7 The transcript, and Kramer's analysis of it, can be found in Cold War International History Project, *Bulletin*, Issue 11.
8 See Kramer, 'Soviet Deliberations', p. 165. The alternative translation 'so be it' is given in Mastny, 'Soviet Non-Invasion', p. 29.
9 See Laba, *Roots of Solidarity*, and Goodwyn, *Breaking the Barrier*.
10 Significant contributions include Bernhard, 'Reinterpreting Solidarity', Garton Ash, 'Poland after Solidarity', Karabel, 'Polish Intellectuals', Ost, *Solidarity*. Important original testimony in Geremek, 'Eksperci', Kowalik, 'Experts', 'Solidarity and KOR', and 'Voices from Poland'.
11 Quoted in Ost, *Solidarity*, p. 77. See also Zuzowski, *Political Dissent*, p. 179.
12 This in 'Solidarity and KOR', p. 14.
13 See Geremek, 'Eksperci', p. 63.
14 See *Human Rights in Poland*.
15 That is, *Polska 5 lat po sierpniu*.
16 The sixty-page typescript was entitled 'Reflections on some aspects of the political and economic situation in the Polish People's Republic in the second half of the nineteen eighties', signed and dated, 'Warsaw, 8.6–10.10.1987'. Rakowski privately confirmed that it was genuine.
17 This is according to Bronisław Geremek, 'Warszawska wiosna?', *Tygodnik Powszechny*, 23 April 1989. Geremek publicly launched the idea in the February 1988 issue of an official monthly, *Konfrontacje*.
18 Wałęsa, *Droga do Wolności*, as translated and quoted in Garton Ash, 'Poland after Solidarity'.
19 Interview, 11 March 1999, for the BBC TV series 'Freedom's Battle', see note 21 below.
20 For a description and analysis of this election, see my *History of the Present*.
21 This was for a three-part BBC TV documentary series, entitled *Freedom's Battle*, on the great changes in Central Europe over the

twenty years since 1979. All quotations in the following section are from transcripts of the interviews recorded for the programme.

Bibliography

L'Alternative. Numéro Special, *Pologne. Dossier de Solidarité*, Paris, 1982.

ARENDT, HANNAH. *On Revolution*, Penguin, London, 1973.

ARISTOTLE. *The Politics*, Penguin, London, 1962.

ASCHERSON, NEAL. *The Polish August: The Self-Limiting Revolution*, Allen Lane, London, 1981.

BERLINGUER, ENRICO. *After Poland*, Spokesman, Nottingham, 1982.

BLAZYNSKI, GEORGE. *Flashpoint Poland*, Pergamon Policy Studies, Oxford, 1979.

BÖLL, HEINRICH, and others (ed.). *Verantwortlich für Polen?*, RoRoRo Aktuell, Hamburg, 1982.

The Book of Lech Wałęsa, Allen Lane, London, 1982.

BRUMBERG, ABRAHAM (ed). *Poland: Genesis of a Revolution*, Random House, New York, 1983.

BRUS, WŁODZIMIERZ, and others. *Polen—Symptome und Ursachen der Krise*, VSA-Verlag, Hamburg, 1981.

CHECIŃSKI, MICHAEL. *Poland: Communism, Nationalism, Anti-Semitism* Karz-Cohl, New York, 1982.

CIECHANOWSKI, J. M. Chapters 10 and 11 in *The History of Poland Since 1863* (ed. R. F. Leslie), CUP, Cambridge, 1980.

DAVIES, NORMAN. *God's Playground. A History of Poland*, vols I and II, Clarendon Press, Oxford, 1981.

DOBBS, MICHAEL, and others. *Poland, Solidarity, Wałęsa*, Pergamon Press, Oxford, 1981.

DROSS, ARMIN TH. *Polen. Freie Gewerkschaften im Kommunismus?*, RoRoRo Aktuell, Hamburg, 1980.

GATTER-KLENK, JULE. *Vielleicht auf Knien, aber Vorwärts! Gespräche mit Lech Wałęsa*, Athenäum, Königstein Ts., 1981.

Gdańsk 1980—pictures from a strike, Puls Publications, London, 1981.

GIEŁŻYŃSKI, WOJCIECH and STEFAŃSKI, LECH. *Gdańsk. Sierpień '80*, KiW, Warsaw, 1981.

GRIFFITH, WILLIAM E. *The Ostpolitik of the Federal Republic of Germany*, MIT Press, Cambridge, Mass., 1978.

HERBERT, ZBIGNIEW. *Selected Poems*, OUP, Oxford, 1977.

International Socialism no. 15—'Solidarność From Gdańsk to Military Repression', by Kara Weber and Colin Barker.

JOHNSON, R. W. and others. *East European Military Establishments: The Warsaw Pact Northern Tier*, Rand Corporation Study, Crane Russak, New York, 1982.

KARPIŃSKI, JAKUB. *Countdown. The Polish Upheavals of 1956, 1968, 1970, 1976, 1980 . . .*, Karl-Cohl, New York, 1982.

KONWICKI, TADEUSZ. *The Polish Complex*, Farrar, Strauss, New York, 1982.

KUCZYŃSKI, WALDEMAR. *Po Wielkim Skoku*, Warsaw, 1981.

LANE, DAVID and KOLANKIEWICZ, GEORGE. *Social Groups in Polish Society*, Macmillan, London, 1973.

LENIN, V. I. *What is to be Done?* Foreign Languages Press, Peking, 1975.

LESLIE, R. F. (ed.). *The History of Poland Since 1863*, CUP, Cambridge, 1980.

LEWIS FLORA. *The Polish Volcano. A Case History of Hope*, Secker & Warburg, London, 1959.

LI, PIERRE (ed.). *Quand Les Journalistes polonais Parlaient*, Mégrelis, Paris, 1982.

MACSHANE, DENIS. *Solidarity. Poland's Independent Trade Union*, Spokesman, Nottingham, 1981.

MICHNIK, ADAM. *Kościót, Lewica, Dialog*, Instytut Literacki, Paris, 1977 (French: *L'Églisse et la Gauche*, Seuil, Paris, 1979).

MIŁOSZ, CZESŁAW. *The Captive Mind*, Penguin, London, 1980.

———*Native Realm, Sidgwick & Jackson/Carcanet, London, 1981.*

MILYNÁR ZDENĚK. *Night Frost in Prague*, C. Hurst & Co., London, 1980.

MYANT, MARTIN. *Poland: A Crisis for Socialism*, Lawrence & Wishart, London, 1982.

OFFREDO, JEAN. *Lech Wałęsa ou L'Eté polonais*, Cana, Paris, 1981.

PEŁCZYŃSKI, ZBIGNIEW. Chapters 12–17 in *The History of Poland Since 1863*, ed. R. F. Leslie, CUP, Cambridge, 1980.

POLONSKY, ANTONY (ed.). *The Great Powers and the Polish Question* L. S. E./Orbis, London, 1976.

POMIAN, GRAŻYNA (ed.). *Polska 'Solidarność'*, Instytut Literacki, Paris, 1982.

POMIAN, KRZYSZTOF. *Pologne: Défi à L'Impossible?*, Editions Ouvrières, Paris, 1982.

PORTES, RICHARD.. *The Polish Crisis: Western Economic Policy Options*, Royal Institute of International Affairs, London, 1981.

POTEL, JEAN-YVES. *Gdańsk La Mémoire Ouvrière 1970–1980*, Maspero, Paris, 1982.

——— *The Summer Before the Frost*, Pluto Press, London, 1982.

Prologue to Gdańsk, A Report on Human Rights by the Polish Helsinki Watch Committee, English edition, London, 1981.

Prokoły Porozumień Gdańsk, Szczecin, Jastrzębie. Statut NSZZ 'Solidarność', KAW, Warsaw, 1980.

Punkt, no. 12, 1980. *Almanach Gdańskich Środowisk Twórczych.*

RADIO FREE EUROPE RESEARCH. *Poland: A Chronology of Events*, nos 1–4, July 1980—December 1981.

——— *The Pope in Poland*, Munich, 1979.

——— *August 1980. The Strikes in Poland*, Munich, 1980.

RAINA, PETER. *Political Opposition in Poland 1954–1977*. Poets & Painters Press, London, 1978.

——— *Independent Social M‿.ements in Poland*, L.S.E./Orbis, Lonson, 1981.

RAKOWSKI, MIECZYSŁAW F. *Partnerstwo*, KiW, Warsaw, 1981.

RUANE, KEVIN. *The Polish Challenge*, BBC Publications, London, 1982.

SINGER, DANIEL. *The Road to Gdańsk*, Monthly Review Press, New York and London, 1981.

SOLZHENITSYN, ALEXANDER. *'One Word of Truth . . .'*, Bodley Head, London, 1972.

STANISZKIS, JADWIGA. *Pologne: La Revolution autolimitée*, PUF, Paris, 1982.

STANKIEWICZ, W. J. (ed.). *The Tradition of Polish Ideals*, Orbis, London, 1981.

STENT, ANGELA. *From Embargo to Ostpolitik*, CUP, Cambridge, 1981.

SZCZYPIORSKI, ANDRZEJ. *The Polish Ordeal: The View from Within*, Croom Helm, London, 1982.

TAYLOR, JOHN. *Five Months with Solidarity*, Wildwood House, London, 1981.

TISCHNER, JÓSEF. *Ethik der Solidarität*, Styria, Vienna, 1982.

TORUŃCZYK, BARBARA (ed.). *Gdańsk 1980, oczyma świadków*, Polonia Book Fund, London, 1980.

TOURAINE, ALAIN and others. *Solidarité. Analyse d'un Mouvement social. Pologne 1980–1982*, Fayard, Paris, 1982.

VALE, MICHAEL (ed.). *Poland. The State of the Republic*, Reports by the Experience and Future Group (DiP), Pluto Press, London, 1981.

Who's Who, What's What in Solidarność. Leksykon Związkowy, BIPS, Gdańsk, September 1981.

WOODALL, JEAN (ed.). *Policy and Politics in Contemporary Poland, Reform, Failure, Crisis*, Pinter, London, 1982.

ZAGAJEWSKI, ADAM. *Polen. Staat im Schatten der Sowjetunion*, Rowohlt, Hamburg, 1981.

Zeszyty OPSZ, no. 1, Papers of the Solidarity Centre for Socio-Professional Studies, IWZZ, Warsaw, 1981.

Supplementary Bibliography

This supplementary bibliography lists publications important for the history of Solidarity that have appeared since 1983, plus a couple that I omitted at that time.

ANDREWS, NICHOLAS. *Poland 1980–81: Solidarity versus the Party*, National Defense University Press, Washington, DC, 1985.

BARKER, COLIN. *Festival of the Oppressed: Solidarity, Reform, and Revolution in Poland, 1980–81*, Bookmarks, London, 1986.

BERNHARD, MICHAEL. *The Origins of Democratization in Poland*, Columbia University Press, New York, 1993.

———'Reinterpreting Solidarity', *Studies in Comparative Communism*, xxiv: 3 (September 1991), pp. 313–30.

———'The Strikes of June 1976 in Poland', *East European Politics and Societies*, i:3 (Fall 1987), pp. 363–92.

BERNSTEIN, CARL, and POLITI, MARCO. *His Holiness*, Doubleday, New York, 1996.

BRZEZINSKI, ZBIGNIEW. *Power and Principle: Memoirs of the National Security Adviser, 1977–1981*, Farrar, Straus & Giroux, New York, 1985.

———'White House Diary, 1980', *Orbis*, Winter 1988, pp. 33–48.

BUJAK, ZBIGNIEW with ROLICKI, JANUSZ. *Przepraszam za Solidarność*, BGW, Warsaw, 1991.

CLARK, JOHN and WILDAVSKY, AARON, *The Moral Collapse of Communism: Poland as a Cationary Tale*, Institute for Contemporary Studies, San Francisco, 1990.

Cold War International History Project, *Bulletin*, Issue 11.

DRZYCIMSKI, ANDRZEJ and SKUTNIK, TADEUSZ (eds.). *Zapis rokowań gdańskich*, Editions Spotkania, Paris, 1986.

CYWIŃSKI, BOHDAN. *L'expérience polonaise*, Éditions Universitaires, Fribourg, 1985.

GARLICKI, ANDRZEJ. *Z tajnych archiwów*, BGW, Warsaw, 1993.

GARTON ASH, TIMOTHY. *History of the Present: Essays, Sketches and Despatches from Europe in the 1990s*, Penguin, London, 1999.

———'Poland after Solidarity', *New York Review of Books*, 13 June 1991.

———*The Uses of Adversity: Essays on the Fate of Central Europe*, New edition, Penguin, London, 1999.

———*We the People: The Revolution of 1989 Witnessed in Warsaw, Budapest, Berlin and Prague*, New edition, Penguin, London, 1999.

GEREMEK, BRONISŁAW. 'Eksperci w Gdańsku', *Widnokrąg*, Summer–Autumn 1986.

GIEREK, EDWARD with ROLICKI, JANUSZ. *Replika*, BGW, Warsaw, 1990.

GIEREK, EDWARD. *Smakżycia*, BGW, Warsaw, 1993.

GOODWYN, LAWRENCE. *Breaking the Barrier: The Rise of Solidarity in Poland*, OUP, Oxford, 1991.

HOLZER, JERZY. *Solidarność 1980–1981. Geneza i historia*, Instytut Literacki, Paris, 1984.

Human Rights in Poland since December 1981. A Report by the Polish Helsinki Committee for the Human Rights Experts Meeting in Ottawa, May 1985, US Helsinki Watch, New York, 1985.

JAKUBOWICZ, SZYMON. *Bitwa o samorząd 1980–1981*, Aneks, London, 1988.

JARUZELSKI, WOJCIECH. *Stan wojenny: Dlaczego*, BGW, Warsaw, 1992.

JASTRĘBSKI, ANDRZEJ (ed.). *Dokumenty Komitetu Obrony Robotników i Komitet Samoobrony Spolecznej 'KOR'*, PWN-Aneks, Warsaw-London, 1994.

KANIA, STANISŁAW with URBAŃCZYK, ANDRZEJ. *Zatrzymać konfrontacje*, BGW, Warsaw, 1992.

KARABEL, JEROME. 'Polish Intellectuals and the Origins of Solidarity: The Making of an Oppositional Alliance', *Communist and Postcommunist Studies*, 26:1, March 1993, pp. 25–46.

KEMP-WELCH, ANTHONY (ed.). *The Birth of Solidarity*, Macmillan, London, 1991 (Second edition).

KENNEDY, MICHAEL D. *Professionals, Power, and Solidarity in Poland: A critical sociology of Soviet-type society*, CUP, Cambridge, 1991.

KISZCZAK, CZESŁAW with BEREŚ , WITOLD and SKOCZYŁAS, JERZY. *Generał Kiszczak mówi . . . prawie wszystko*, BGW, Warsaw, 1991.

KOLANKIEWICZ, GEORGE and LEWIS, PAUL G. *Poland: Politics, Economics, and Society*, Pinter, London, 1988.

KOWALEWSKI, ZBIGNIEW. '"Solidarnośé" i walka o samorząd załogi', Łódź, 1981 (no publisher).

KOWALIK, TADEUSZ, 'Experts and the Working Group', in Anthony Kemp-Welch (ed.), *The Birth of Solidarity*, Macmillan, London, 1991.

KOWLASKI, SERGIUSZ. *Krytyka solidarnościowego rozumu*, PEN, Warsaw, 1990.

KRAMER, MARK. 'Soviet Deliberations During the Polish Crisis, 1980–1981', *Cold War International History Project, Special Working Paper No. 1*, Washington, DC, 1999.

KUBIK, JAN. *The Power of Symbols Against the Symbols of Power*, The University of Pennsylvania Press, University Park, 1994.

KUKLIŃSKI, RYSZARD. 'Wojna z narodem widziana od środku' (interview), *Kultura*, April (4) 1987, pp. 3–57.

KURCZEWSKI, JACEK. *The Resurrection of Rights in Poland*, OUP, Oxford, 1993.

KUROŃ, JACEK. *Wiara i wina. Od i do komunizmu*, London, 1989.

KURSKI, JAROSŁAW. *Wódz*, Pomost, Warsaw, 1990.

LABA, ROMAN. *The Roots of Solidarity: A Political Sociology of Poland's Working-Class Democratization*, Princeton University Press, Princeton, NJ, 1991.

LEPAK, KEITH JOHN. *Prelude to Solidarity. Poland and the Politics of the Gierek Regime*, Columbia University Press, New York, 1988.

LEWANDOWSKI, JANUSZ and SZOMBERG, JAN. *Samorząd w dobie 'Solidarności'*, Odnowa, London, 1985.

LIPSKI, JAN JÓZEF. *KOR: A History of the Workers' Defense Committee in Poland, 1976–1981*, University of California Press, Berkeley, 1985.

LITYŃSKI, JAN. *Solidarność: znaki zapytania, próby odpowiedzi*, Słowo, Warsaw, 1985.

ŁOPIŃSKI, MACIEJ, MOSKIT, MARCIN, WILK, MARIUSZ. *Konspira: Solidarity Underground*, University of California Press, Berkeley, 1990.

MASON, DAVID. *Public Opinion and Political Change in Poland, 1980–1982*, CUP, Cambridge, 1985.

——— 'Solidarity as a New Social Movement', *Political Science Quarterly*, ci:1 (Spring 1989), pp. 41–58.

MASTNY, VOJTECH. 'The Soviet Non-Invasion of Poland in 1980/81 and the End of the Cold War', *Cold War International History Project, Working Paper No. 23*, Washington, DC, 1998.

MAZOWIECKI, TADEUSZ. *Internowanie*, London, 1983.

MICHNIK, ADAM. *Czego chcemy i co możemy. 'Soldarność' i historia*, Wydawnictwo Komitetu Kultury Niezależnej, Warsaw, 1985.

——— *Między panem a plebanem*, Kraków, 1995.

MODZELEWSKI, KAROL. *Dokąd od komunizmu*, Warszawa, 1993.

NAWROCKI, GRZEGORZ. *Polak z Polakiem*, Warszawa, 1990.

OST, DAVID. *Solidarity and the Politics of Anti-Politics*, Temple University Press, Philadelphia, 1990.

PASIERB, BRONISŁAW (ed.). *Władza wobec 'Solidarności. Sierpień 1980–Grudzień 1981. Podstawowe dokumenty*, Wydawnietwo Uniwersytetu Wroclawskiego, Wroclaw, 1993.

PAWŁOW, WITALIJ. *Byłem rezydentem KGB w Polsce*. BGW, Warsaw, 1994.

PERNAL, MAREK. *Kalendarium Solidarności 1980–1989*, Warszawa, 1990.

——— and SKÓRZYŃSKI, JAN. *Kalendarium. Solidarnśc 1980–1989*, Versus, Warsaw, 1990.

PERSKY, STAN. *At the Lenin Shipyard*, New Star Books, Vancouver, 1981.

PERSKY, STAN and FLAM, HENRY (eds.). *The Solidarity Sourcebook*, New Star Books, Vancouver, 1982.

Polska 5 Lat po Sierpniu, Aneks, London, 1986.

POTEL, JEAN-YVES. *The Promise of Solidarity: Inside the Workers' Struggle, 1980–1982*, trans. Phil Markham, Praeger, New York, 1982.

RACHWALD, ARTHUR R. *In Search of Poland: The Superpowers' Response to Solidarity, 1980–1989*, Hoover Institution Press, Stanford, CA, 1990.

RAKOWSKI, MIECZYSŁAW F. *Jak to się stało*, Warszawa, 1991.

RENSENBRINK, JOHN. *Poland Challenges a Divided World*, Louisiana State University Press, Baton Rouge, LA, 1988.

Rok 1989. Bronisław Geremek Opowiada. Jacek Zakowski Pyta, Plejada, Warsaw, 1990.

SANFORD, GEORGE (trans. and ed.). *The Solidarity Congress, 1981*, Macmillan, London, 1990.

SKÓRZYŃSKI, JAN. *18 dni Sierpnia: Solidarność*, Omnia, Warsaw, 1990.

'Solidarity and KOR: An Interview with Gdańsk Leaders', *Labour Focus on Eastern Europe*, iv:4–6 (Winter–Spring 1981). No page numbers.

SPISKI, PIOTR (ed.). *Od trzynastego do trzynastego*, Polonia, London, 1983.

STANISZKIS, JADWIGA. *Poland's Self-Limiting Revolution*, Princeton, 1984.

——— *The Dynamics of the Breakthrough in Eastern Europe: The Polish Experience*, Berkeley, 1991.

SZEJNET, MAŁGORZATA and ZALEWSKI, TOMASZ. *Szezecin: grudzień, sierpień, grudzień*, Aneks, London, 1986.

SZULC, TAD. *Pope John Paul II*, Scribner, New York, 1995.

Tajne dokumenty. Państwo-Kościół 1980-1989, Aneks, London, 1993.

TISCHNER, JOZEF. *The Spirit of Solidarity*, San Francisco, 1984.

'Voices from Poland', *Social Text*, Spring 1982, pp. 5–21.

WAŁĘSA, LECH. *A Way of Hope*, Henry Holt, New York, 1987.
——— *Droga do Wolności: 1985–1990 Decydujące Lata*, Spotkania, Warsaw, 1991.
Wejdą, nie wejdą. Polska 1980–1982; wewnętrzny kryzys, międzynarodowe uwarunkowanie, London, 1999.
WESCHLER, LAWRENCE. *The Passion of Poland: From Solidarity through the State of War*, Pantheon, New York, 1984.
WEYDENTHAL, JAN B. DE, PORTER, BRUCE D., DEVLIN, KEVIN. *The Polish Drama: 1980–1982*, Lexington Books, Lexington, Mass., 1983.
WIEVORKA, MICHEL. *Les Juifs, la Pologne, et Solidarność*, Denoël, Paris, 1984.
WŁODEK, ZBIGNIEW (ed.). *Tajne dokumenty Biura Politycznego: PZPR a 'Solidarność' 1980–1981*, Aneks, London, 1992.
ZUZOWSKI, ROBERT. *Political Dissent and Opposition in Poland: The Workers' Defense Committee 'KOR'*, Praeger, Westport, Conn., 1992.
ZWOŹNIAK, ZDZISŁAW. *Jak sié rodzila Solìdarność Region Śląsko-Dabrowski 1980-81*, Pomost, Warsaw, 1980.

INDEX

A

B

F

G

K

L

Q

R

S

Y

Z